Women for Peace

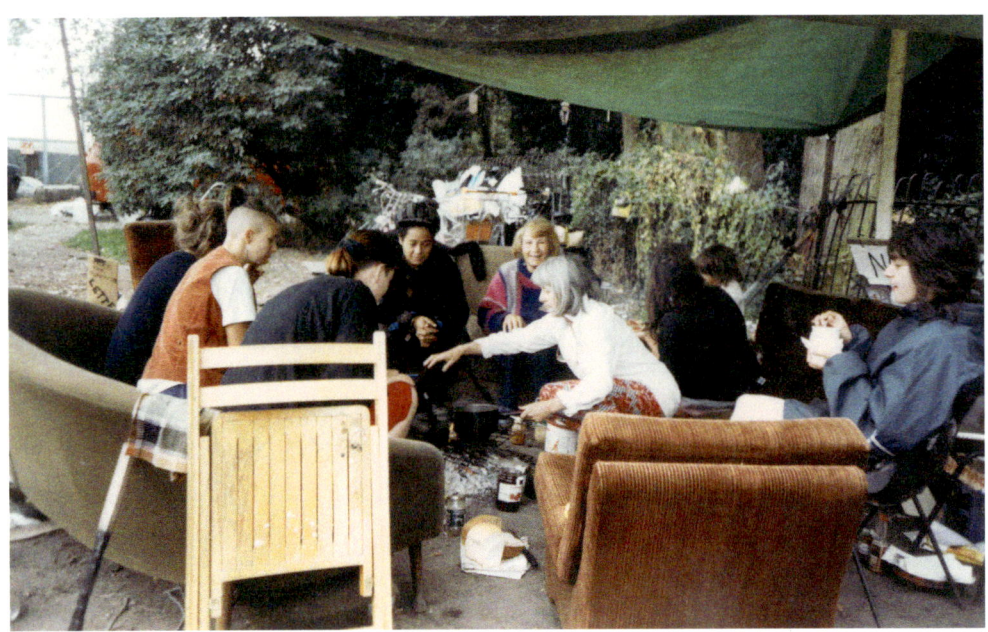

Above: A group of Greenham women at Blue Gate. Thalia Campbell (centre, in the white shirt) remembers this as how the camp typically appeared, with a campfire at the heart and an array of donated furniture. When there were evictions at Blue Gate, belongings were piled into shopping trolleys and prams, and the women could run in three different directions, as three roads converge on the Common at this point.

Women for Peace

Banners from Greenham Common

Charlotte Dew

Four Corners Irregulars
Nº 8

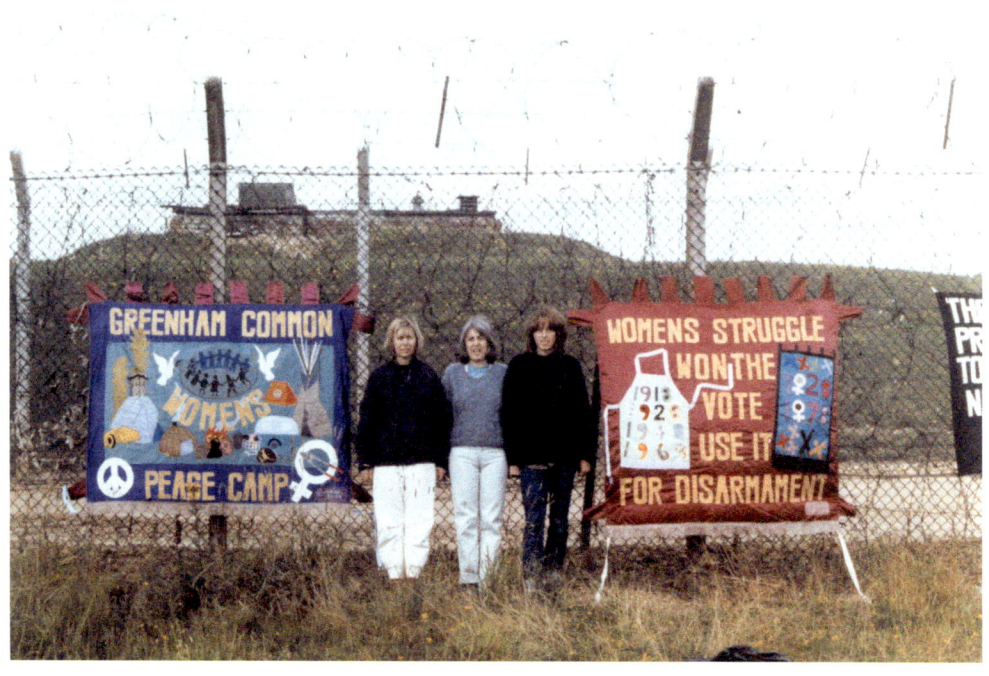

Above, from left to right: Mary Coughlin, Thalia Campbell, Lucy Campbell at Greenham Common, standing between their banners, late 1980s.

Next pages: *Women For Peace* banner, unknown artist.

Contents

Introduction 9

Banners at Greenham
   The Greenham Protests 15
   The First Greenham Banners 24
   The History of the Banner and its Influence at Greenham 32
   How Were the Greenham Banners Used? 38

Themes
   Peace and Anti-Nuclear Banner Designs 57
   Anti-Cruise Banners 64
   Fear for Future Generations 68
   Banners against Male Dominance and Aggression 86
   Embrace the Base 98
   International Banner Designs 108
   Greenham Women's Peace Camp Banner Designs 119
   Other Marches and Protest Sites 134
   Banners Representing Groups and Organisations 148

Experience
   Making 178
   Creativity at the Camp 186
   Artist Banner Makers 198
   At Greenham Common: Ginette Leach 206
   At Greenham Common: Juliet Nelson 212
   Greenham Banners Beyond the Campaign 216

Author's Note 219
Acknowledgements 219
Bibliography 220
Notes 221

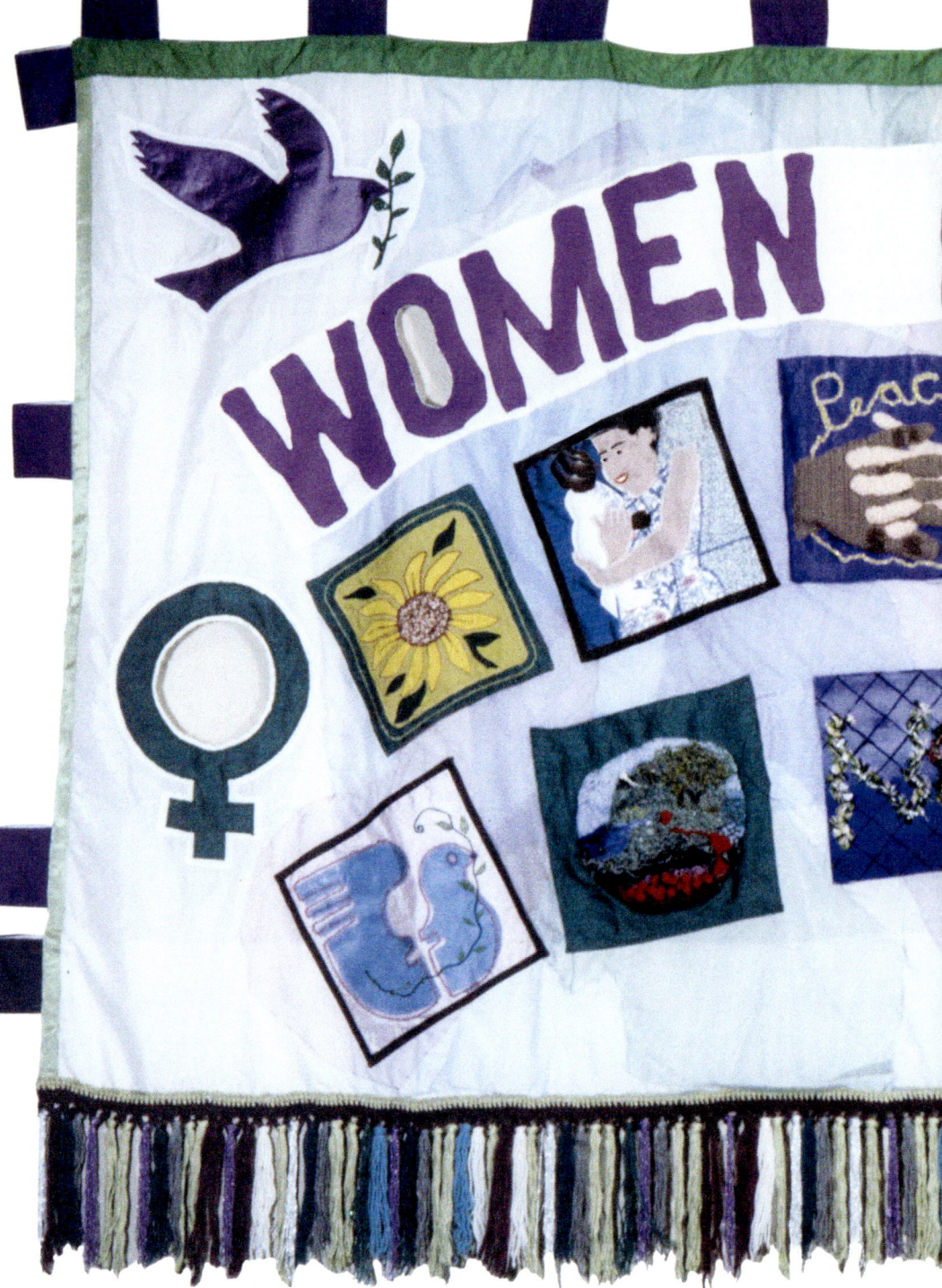

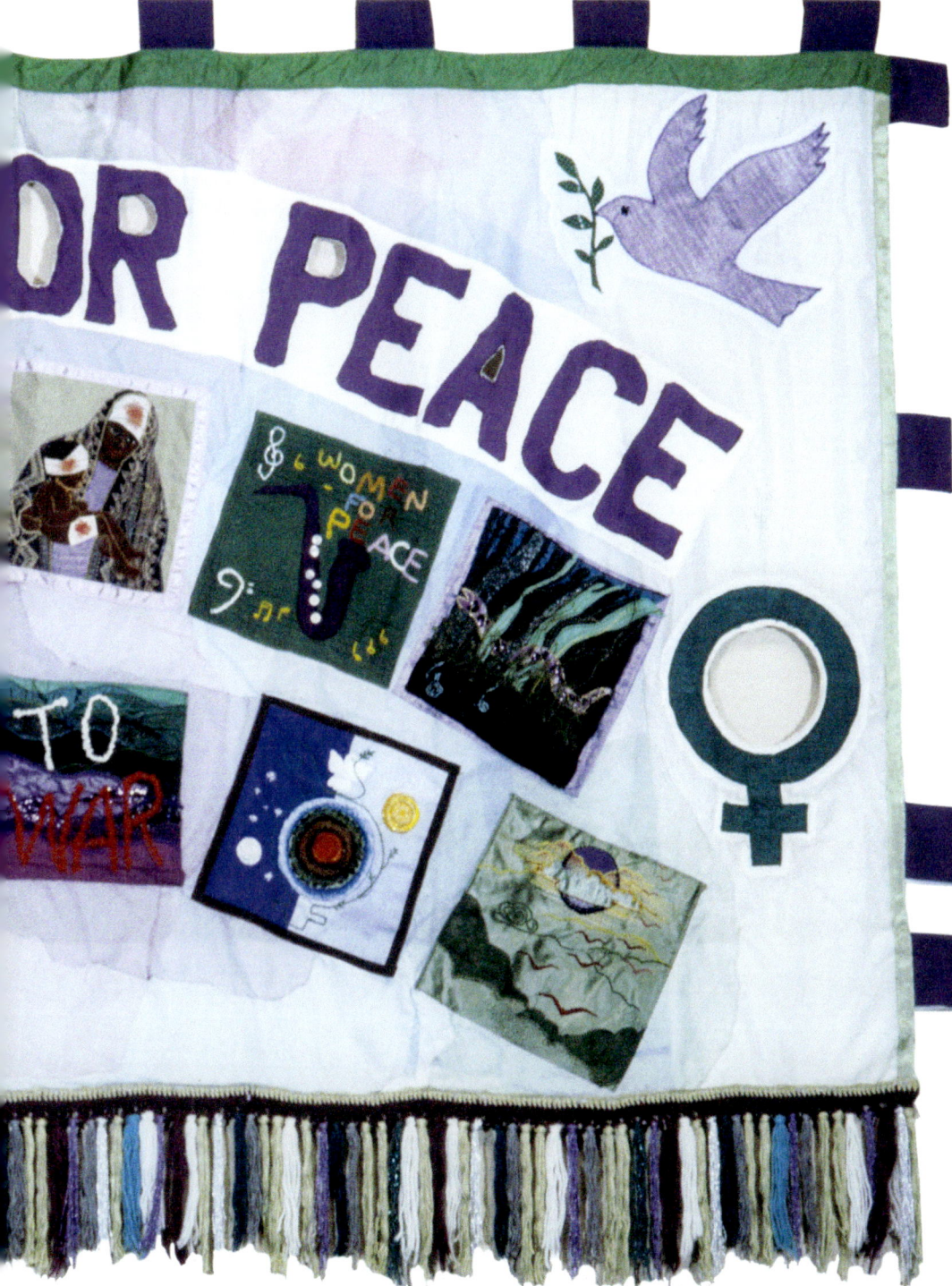

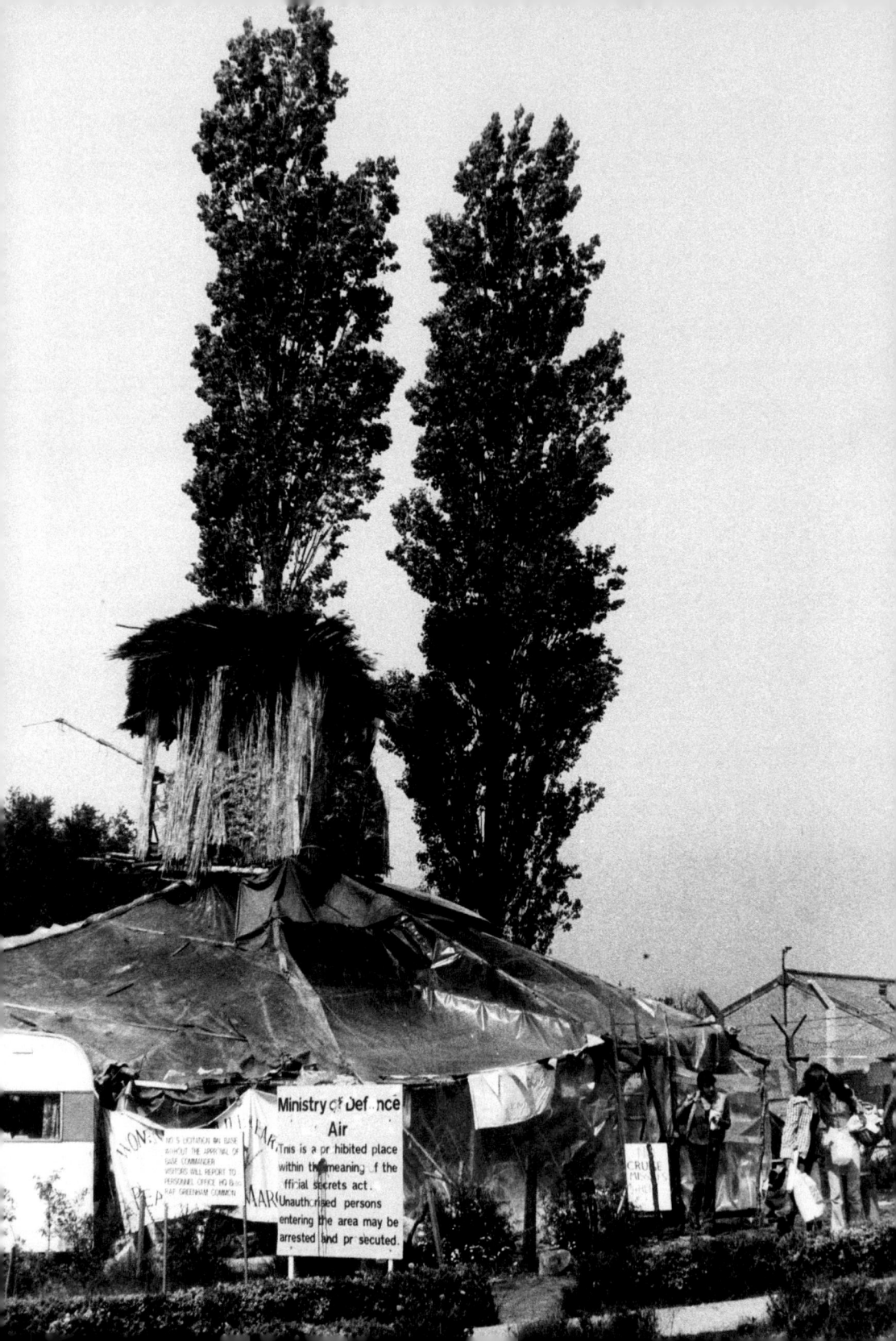

Introduction

Banners – some beautifully crafted, others spontaneously assembled – are central to the story of Greenham Common Women's Peace Camp, from its beginnings in the late summer of 1981 until it disbanded in 2000. The banners have a powerful presence in the photographs and memories of the women who campaigned against the deployment of Cruise missiles at RAF Greenham Common.

As objects, banners 'mediate social interaction as they become invested with protestors' feelings and ideas.'[1] They are a focus for the energy generated by a collective cause and a tool for conveying its messages.

The Greenham banners reveal much about the campaign's proponents, ideology, and reach. They are also evidence in a number of broader histories: the history of women-led campaigning, including the suffrage and Women's Liberation movements; the history of peace campaigning, before, during and after the First and Second World Wars; the history of women's art; and the history of the banner itself.

Opposite: Treehouse at Greenham Common Women's Peace Camp, Main Gate (also known as Yellow Gate). More substantial structures such as this and the caravan in the foreground were destroyed or removed during the evictions from the Peace Camp that started in 1982.

Next pages: *Greenham Common Women's Peace Camp*, designed by Thalia and Ian Campbell features different Greenham motifs, representing the camp, including the treehouse (left), wire cutters for snipping the perimeter fence, and a ring of women dancing on top of a missile silo (centre). Another version of this banner can be seen on pages 120–121.

Pages 12–13: Photograph by Raissa Page of women dancing on top of a missile silo, New Year's Day, 1983. Greenham women, who often favoured female journalists and photographers, had tipped-off Page, a founding member of women's photographic collective Format Photographers, about the plan to breach the perimeter fence.[2]

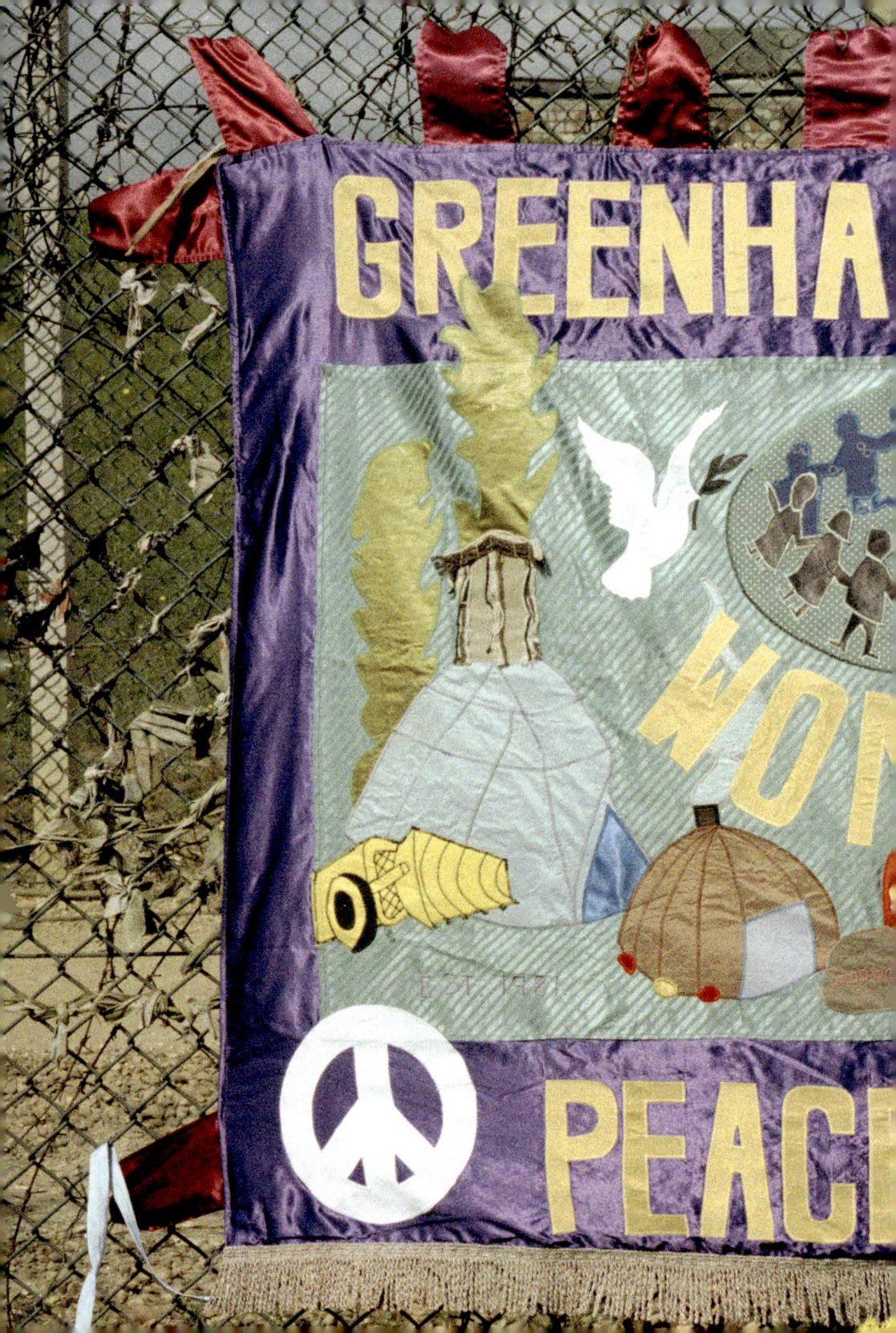

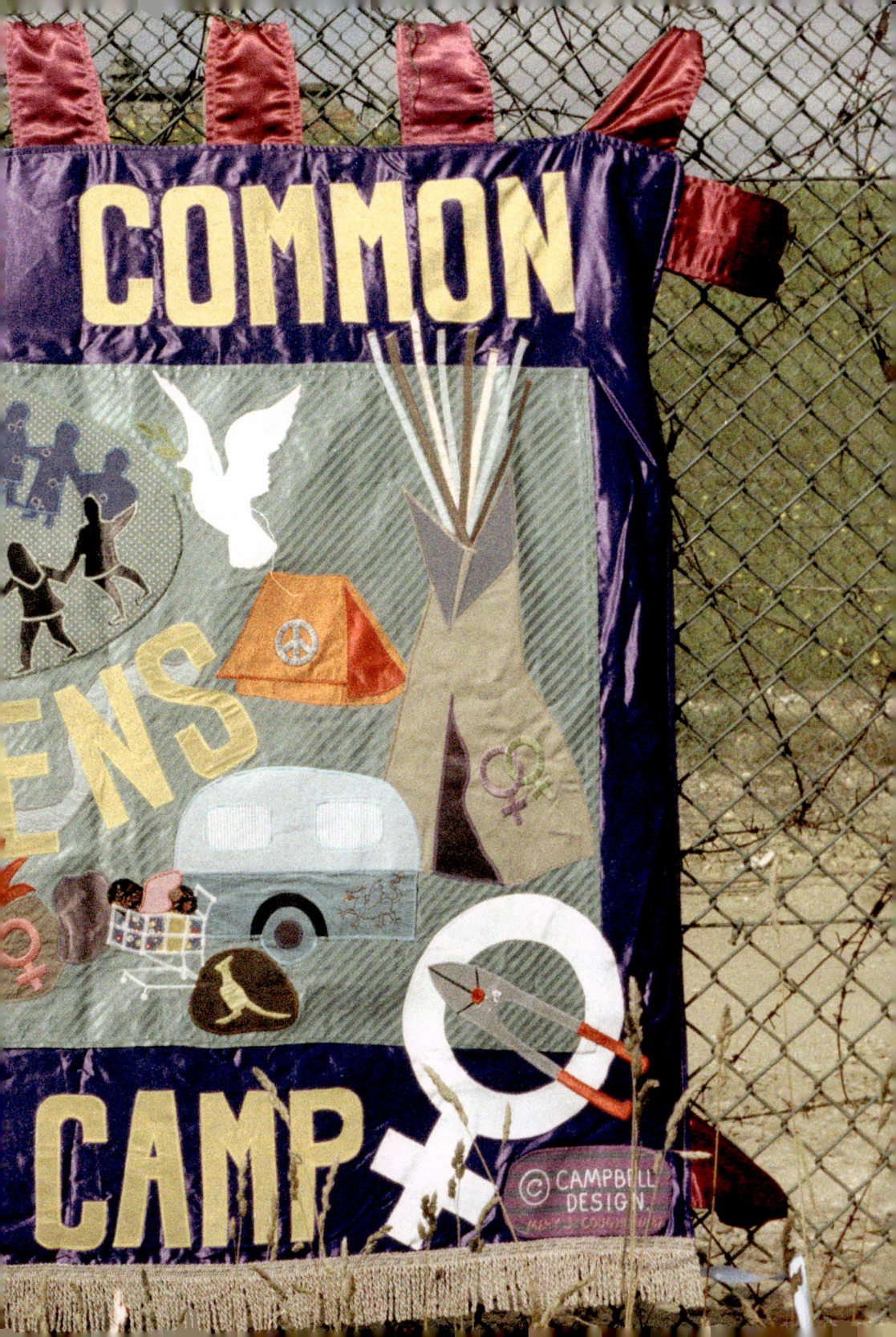

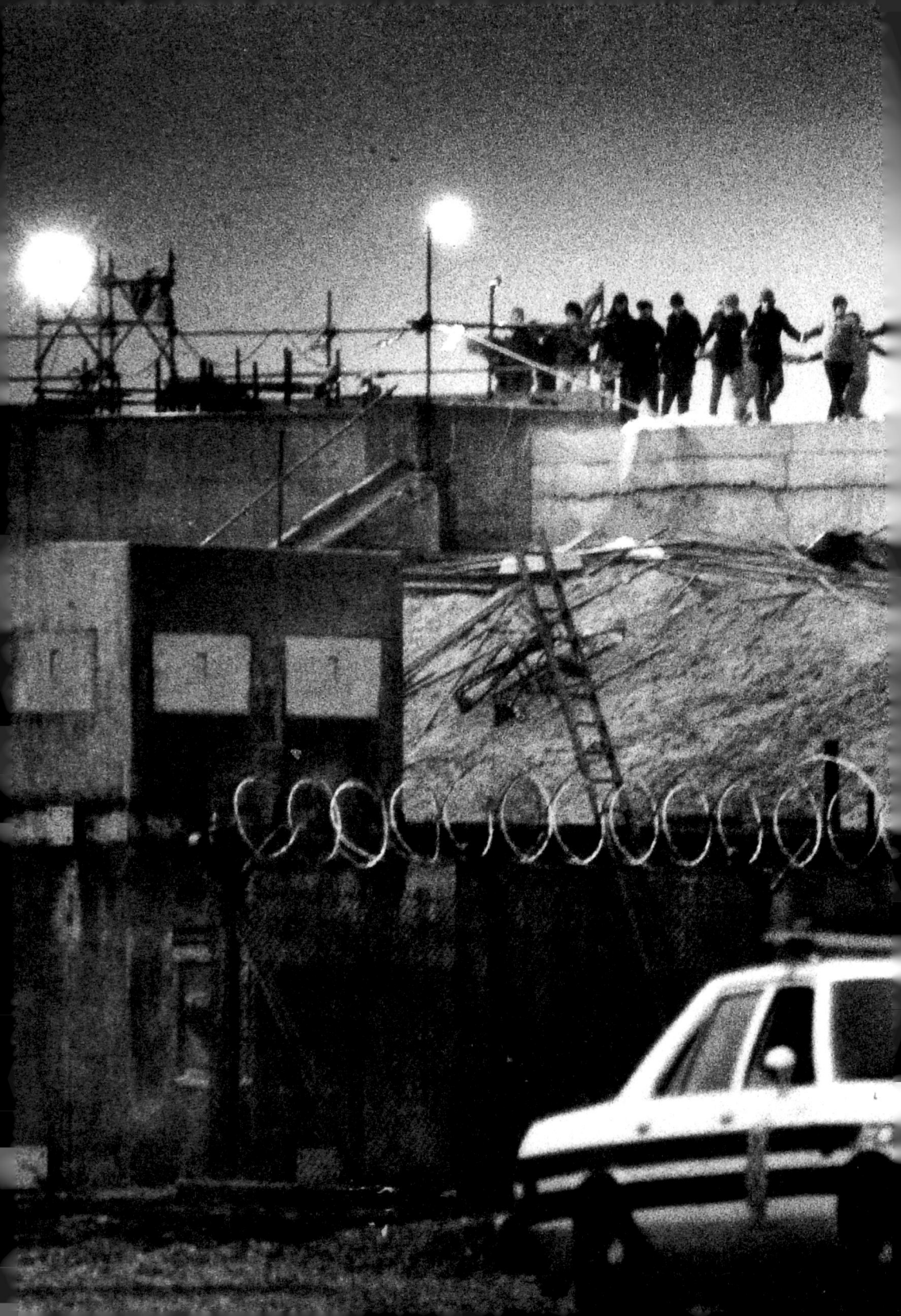

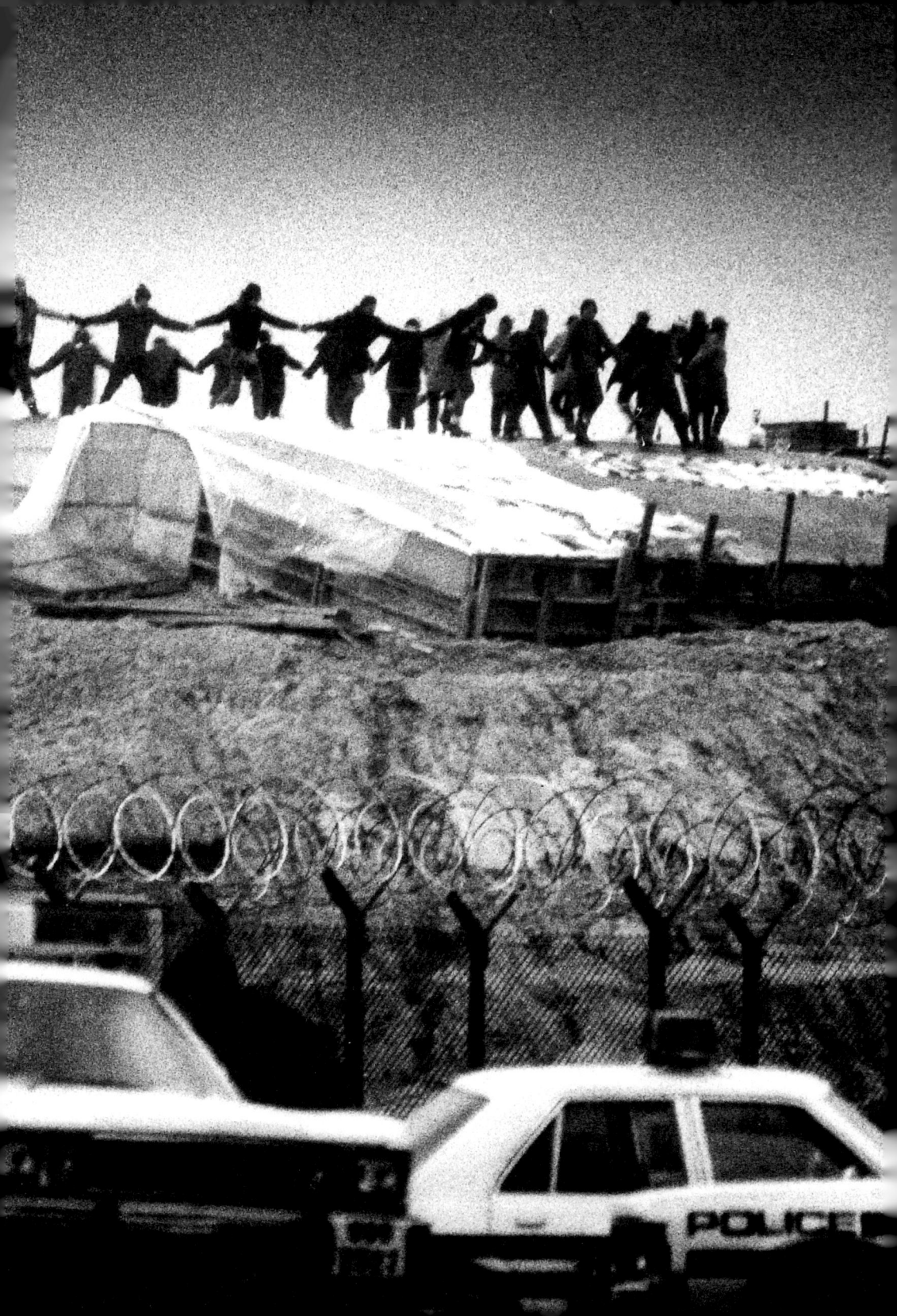

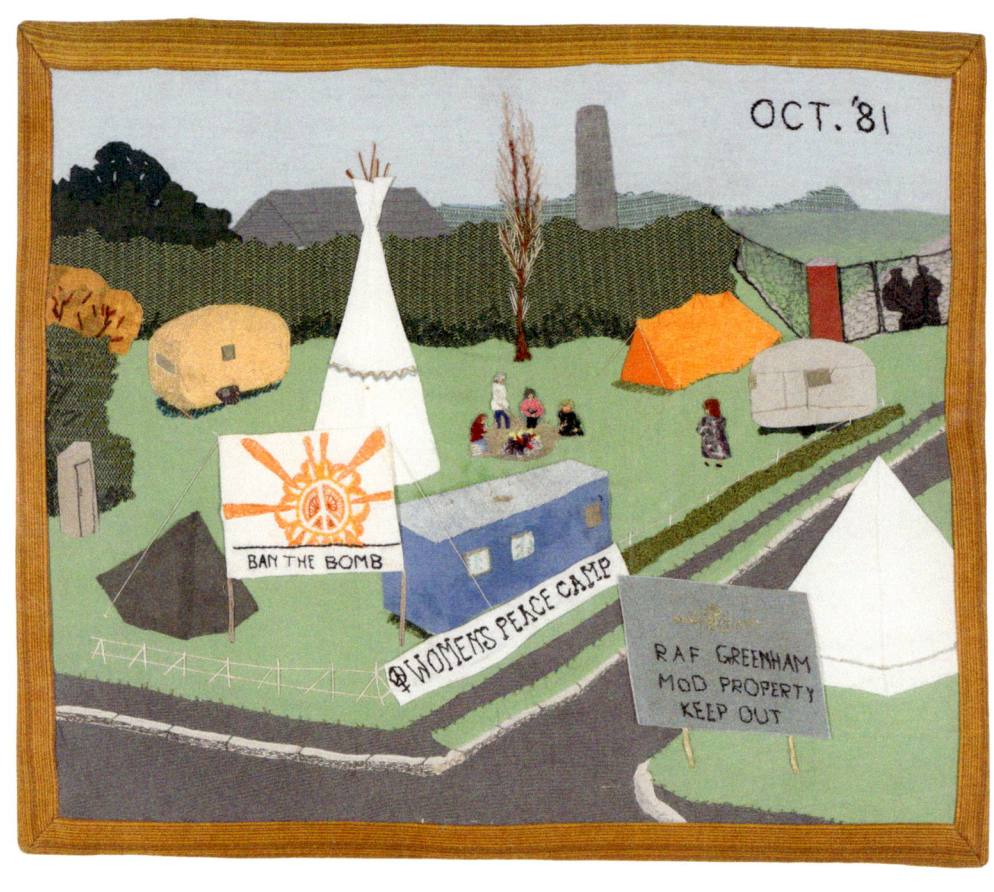

Above: Greenham Common Peace Camp in October 1981,
shortly after it was established. Appliqué by Daphne Morgan, 55 × 66 cm.

The Greenham Protests

Greenham Common, a large area of grassy heath and woodland on the edge of Newbury in Berkshire, had become a base for the United States Air Force during World War II, and in the 1950s and 60s the base was expanded, to serve the Americans' heavy bombers. In 1979, it was one of two in the UK chosen for the American ground-launched Cruise missiles. Part of NATO's Cold War response to the Soviet SS20 missiles, the Cruise missiles were ready for deployment, at bases across Western Europe; in the UK, 96 missiles were deployed at RAF Greenham Common, and 64 at RAF Molesworth in Cambridgeshire.

For some, this represented an escalation in the Cold War. The perceived threat of nuclear conflict prompted a group of women to organise a protest walk to Greenham. The march, from Cardiff in Wales, arrived on 5 September 1981, and four of the women chained themselves to the fence. This led to the idea of the Peace Camp among some of the women – a permanent presence outside the base, initially outside the Main Gate, and gradually, over the course of 1982 and 1983 at the other gates to the base. The Camp became women-only in February 1982, and many thousands of women visited and supported the camps, with some living there permanently for months and years.

The actions of these women gradually drew attention from the media and support from around the world, and despite frequent violent evictions by Newbury District Council from April 1984 onwards, the Camp continued until the year 2000 as a focus for protests against Trident, the UK's nuclear weapons programme, long after the last Cruise missiles had left in 1991.

Artist Daphne Morgan created the series of appliqués pictured here, highlighting key moments in the Greenham campaign, and this series is now held at the Peace Museum in Bradford.

Next pages: Women being removed from the woollen webbing, woven to challenge the Police's ability to remove them easily during non-violent protest. Appliqué by Daphne Morgan, 44 × 64 cm.

SEPT '82

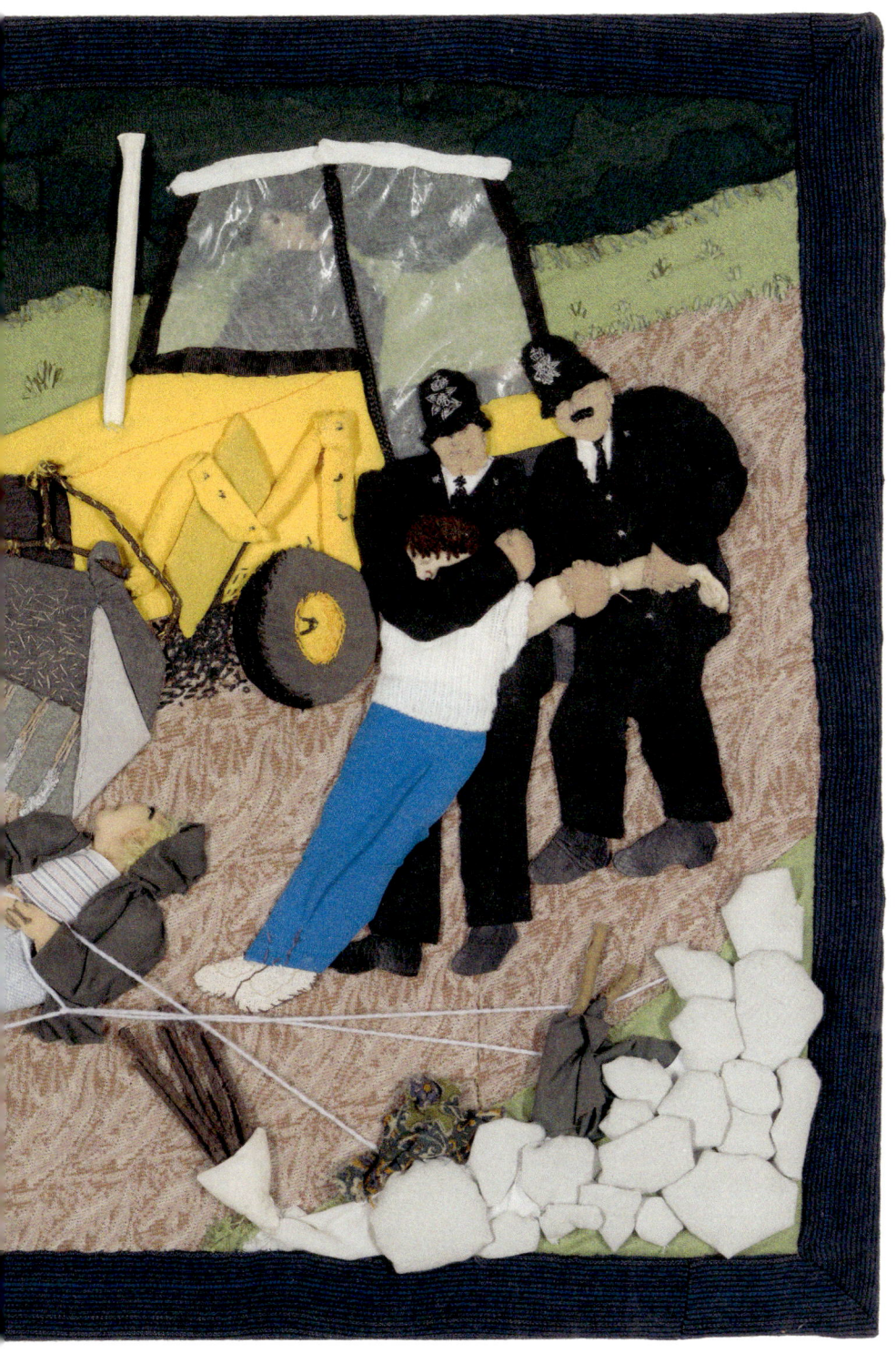

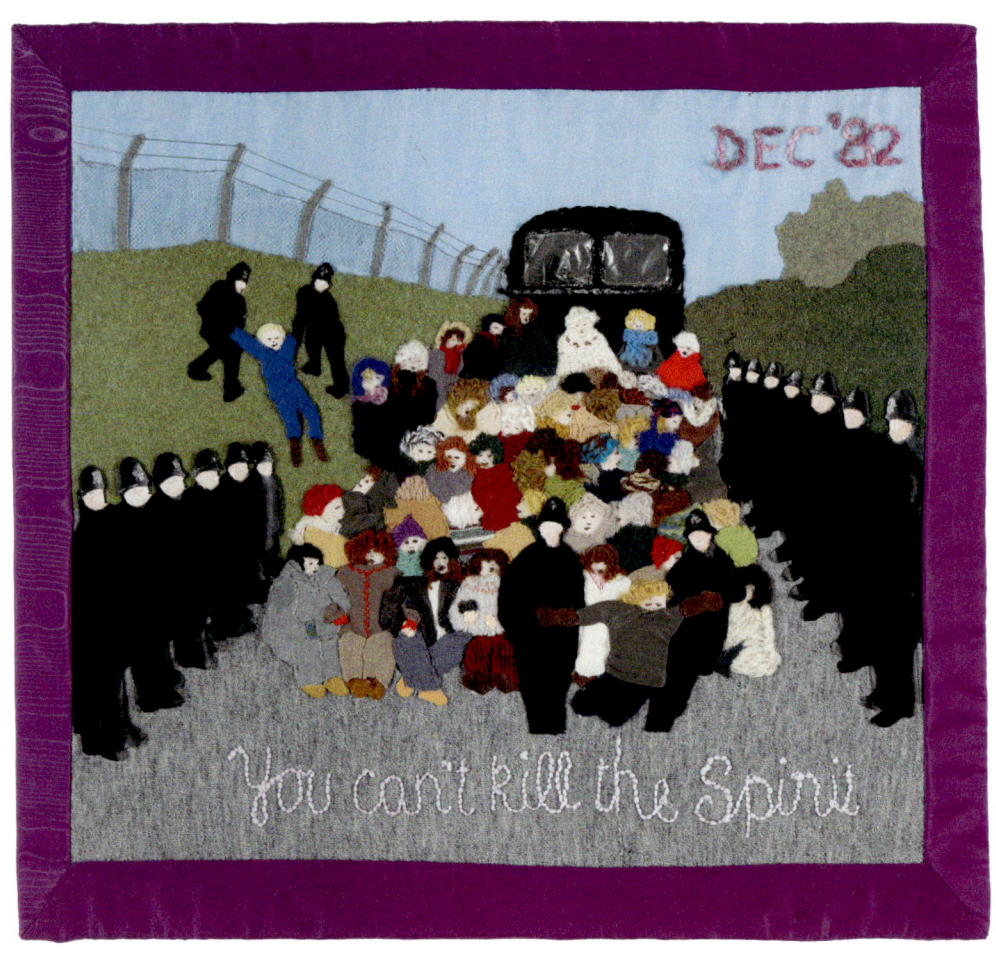

Above: *You Can't Kill the Spirit*. Protesters blocking a road at Greenham Common in December 1982. The title refers to a Greenham women's song, sung whilst taking part in sit-ins such as this. Appliqué by Daphne Morgan, 55 × 60 cm.

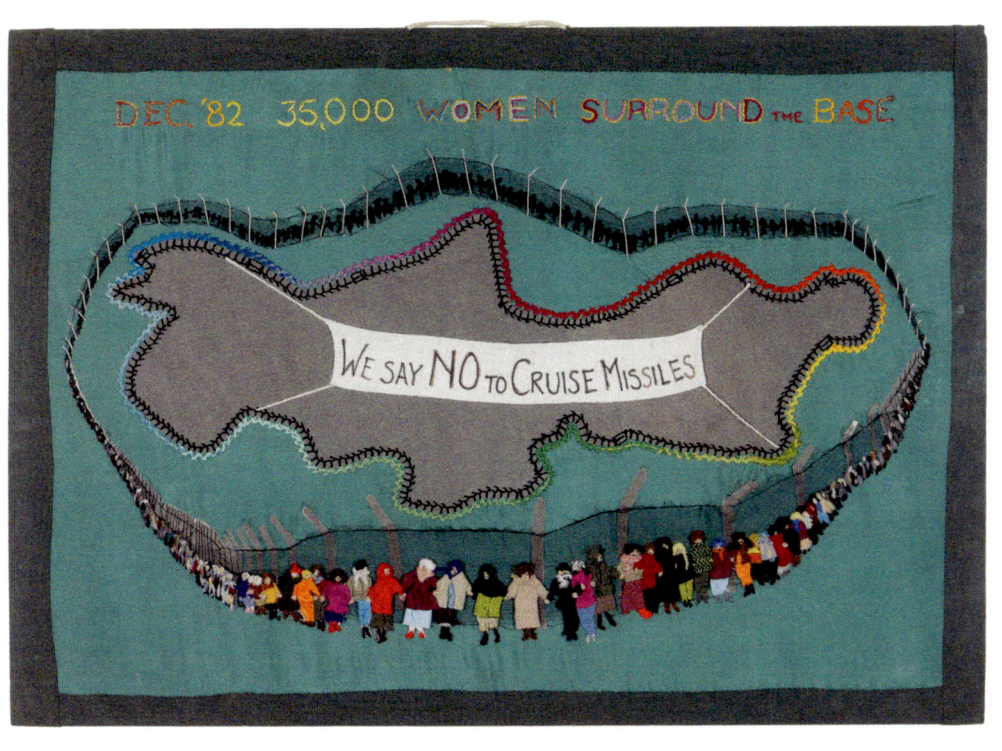

Above: *December 1982: 35,000 Women Surround the Base.* This event was known as Embrace the Base. Appliqué by Daphne Morgan, 49 × 66 cm.

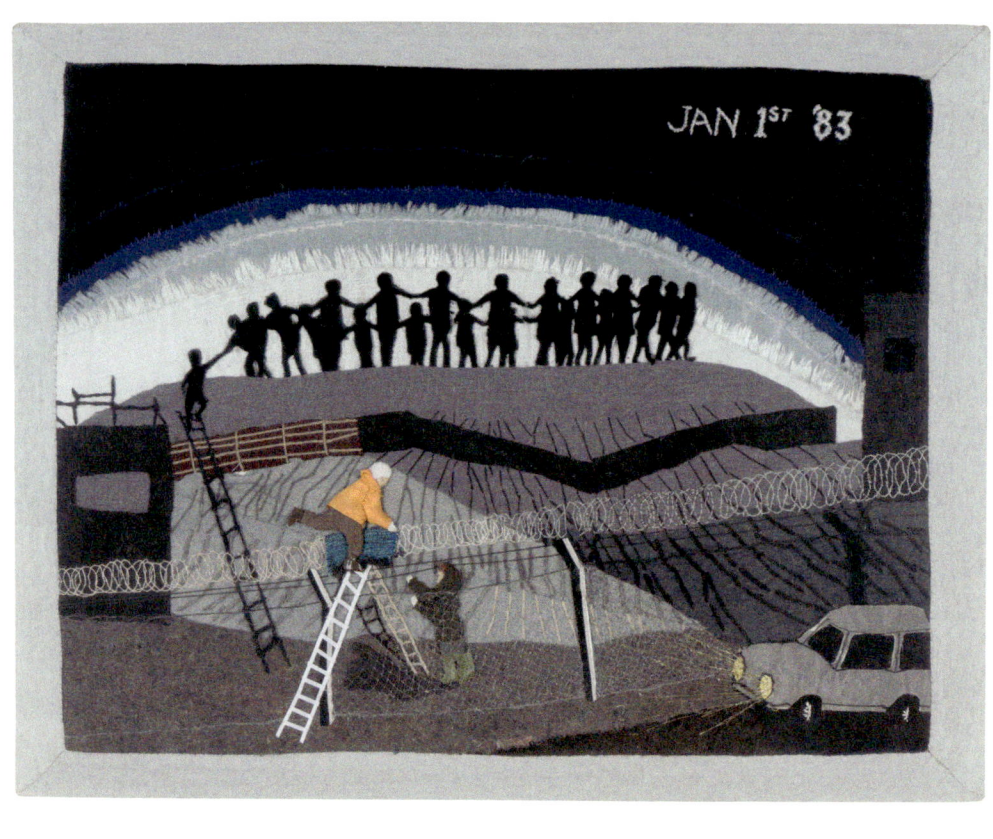

Above: 1 January 1983. Protesters cut through the perimeter fence and dance on top of a missile silo. (See also pages 12–13). Appliqué by Daphne Morgan, 53 × 71 cm.

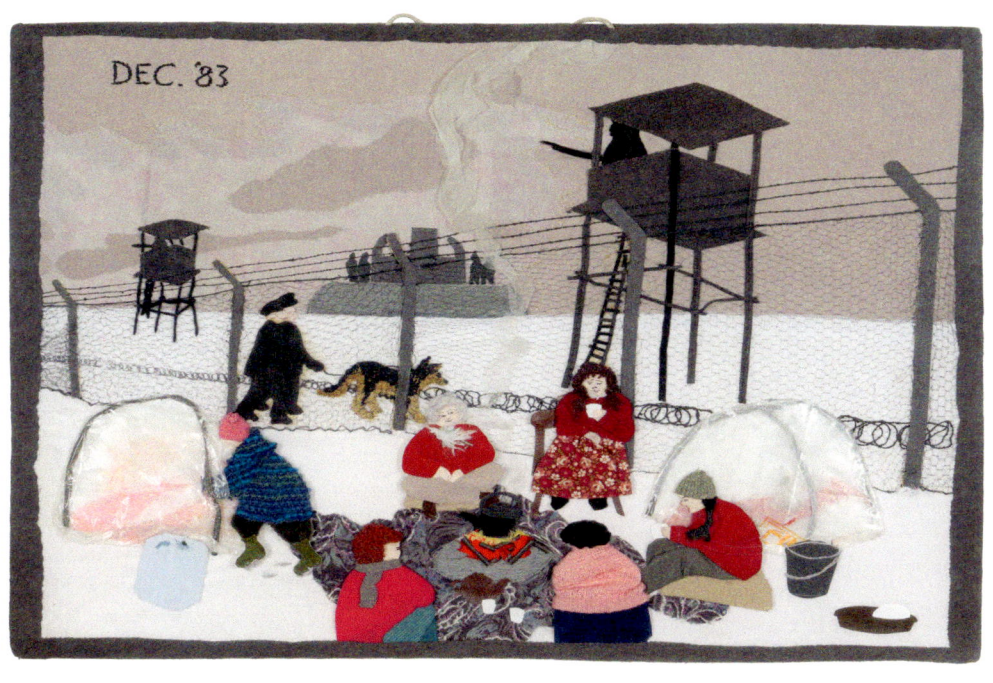

Above: December 1983. After the camp evictions started in September 1982, many women slept in structures constructed from bent branches covered in a sheet of plastic, sometimes with a wooden palette for a base. These shelters were known as 'benders'. Appliqué by Daphne Morgan, 53 × 70 cm.

Next pages: *Melting into the Countryside 1984–1990*. A major eviction of the protestors took place on 4 April 1984, but many women returned and a presence was maintained at Greenham until the year 2000. Appliqué by Daphne Morgan, 53 × 65 cm.

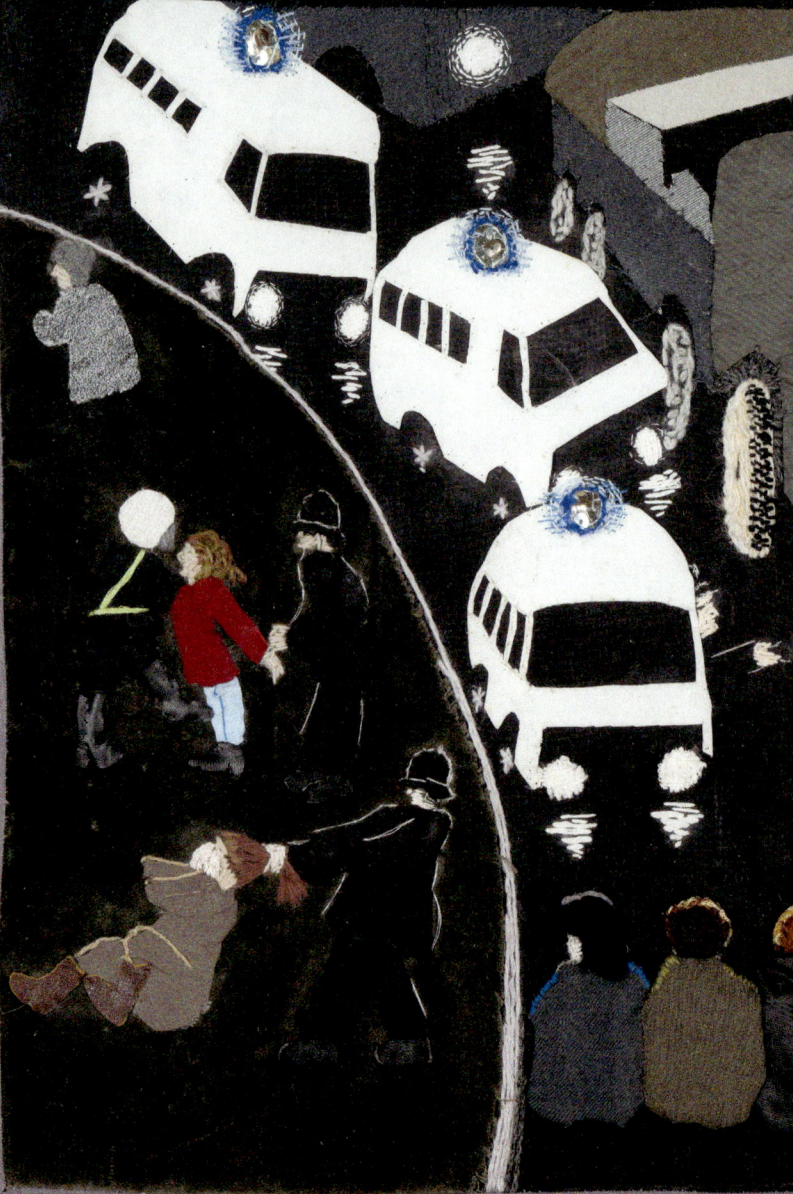

TRYSIDE" 1984-1990

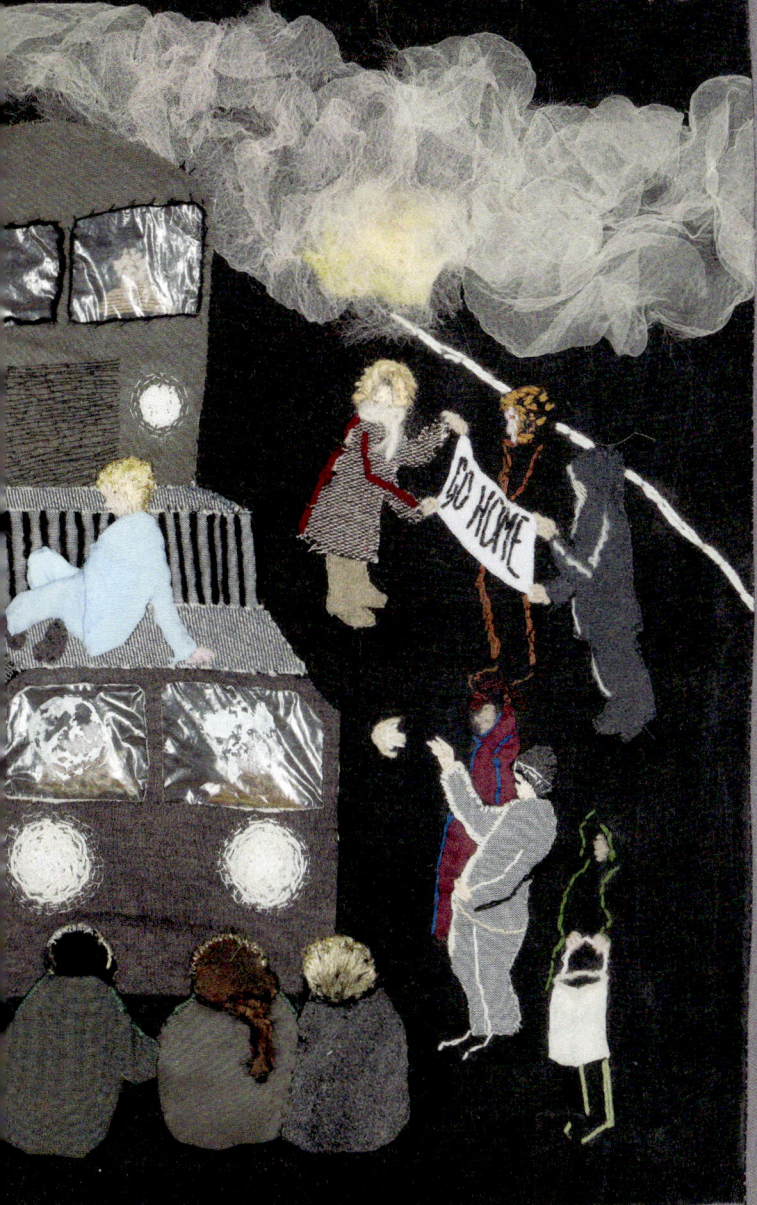

The First Greenham Banners

The women's peace camp at Greenham began at the culmination of a 10-day march from Cardiff to the airbase, just outside Newbury in Berkshire. In organising the march, Ann Pettitt, Karmen Cutler, Liney Seward and Lynne Whittemore, in a group of 36 women, aimed to 'gatecrash the closed world of the media debate on defence issues... [and] to use the media to wake up the public to what was happening'.[3]

Their actions led to a reinvigoration of women-led peace campaigning in the UK. The walk added to a lineage of 20th century peace marches, including those to the Atomic Weapons Research labs at Aldermaston predominantly between 1958 and 1965, organised by the Direct Action Committee against Nuclear War (DAC) and the Campaign for Nuclear Disarmament (CND).

The women set out for Greenham, joined in some cases by their children and with the support of partners, on 27 August 1981. They had selected Greenham as their destination as one of the two UK sites newly chosen to house Cruise missiles. Over the ensuing nights they were hosted by supportive women's, peace, and other groups on route. The walkers arrived at the airbase on 5 September.

The presence of banners is recorded in the testimony of women who took part in the protest from the beginning. Pettitt recalls the banner that accompanied them on their 110-mile march to Greenham: 'We made [it] in Lynne's field out of an old sheet dyed pink. We painted the world and a tree on it, like an upside-down CND symbol, with the prongs as branches. Later we had to cut holes in it, so the wind didn't turn it into a sail when we carried it along'.[4]

This banner included the group's name Women for Life on Earth, and 'in case this title might be mistaken for some kind of anti-abortion, religious right-to-life outfit,' Pettitt explains, 'we threw in for good measure the explanatory sub-title: "Women's Action for Disarmament"'.[5] The design of this banner and leaflets to hand out along the route were the stimulus for the group to choose a name to identify themselves and their cause.

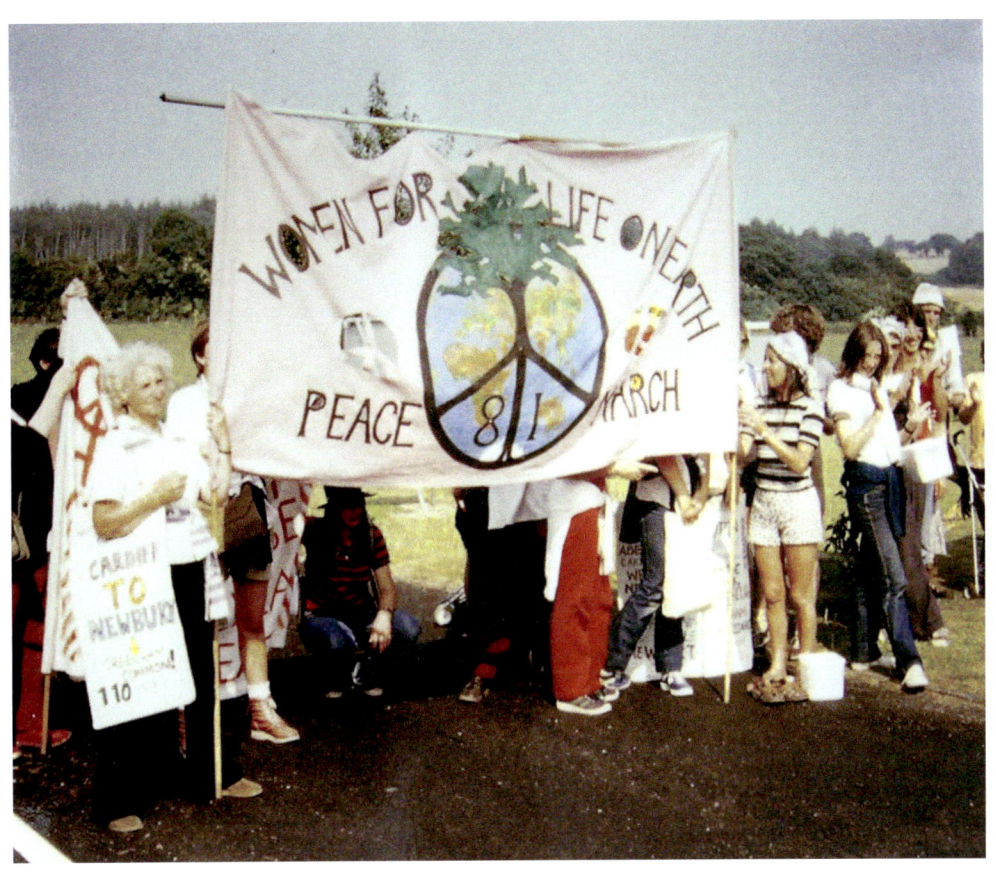

Above: The first march from Cardiff to Greenham, 27 August – 5 September 1981. Eunice Stallard is holding the banner on the left and Thalia Campbell is holding it on the right.

Next pages: One of two replicas of the second Greenham banner, now in the Peace Museum collection, 156 × 205 cm. The original (page 28), now lost, was made by Hannah Tyrrell, Lucy Campbell, Julie and other girls, assisted by Thalia Campbell, on the first march to Greenham Common.

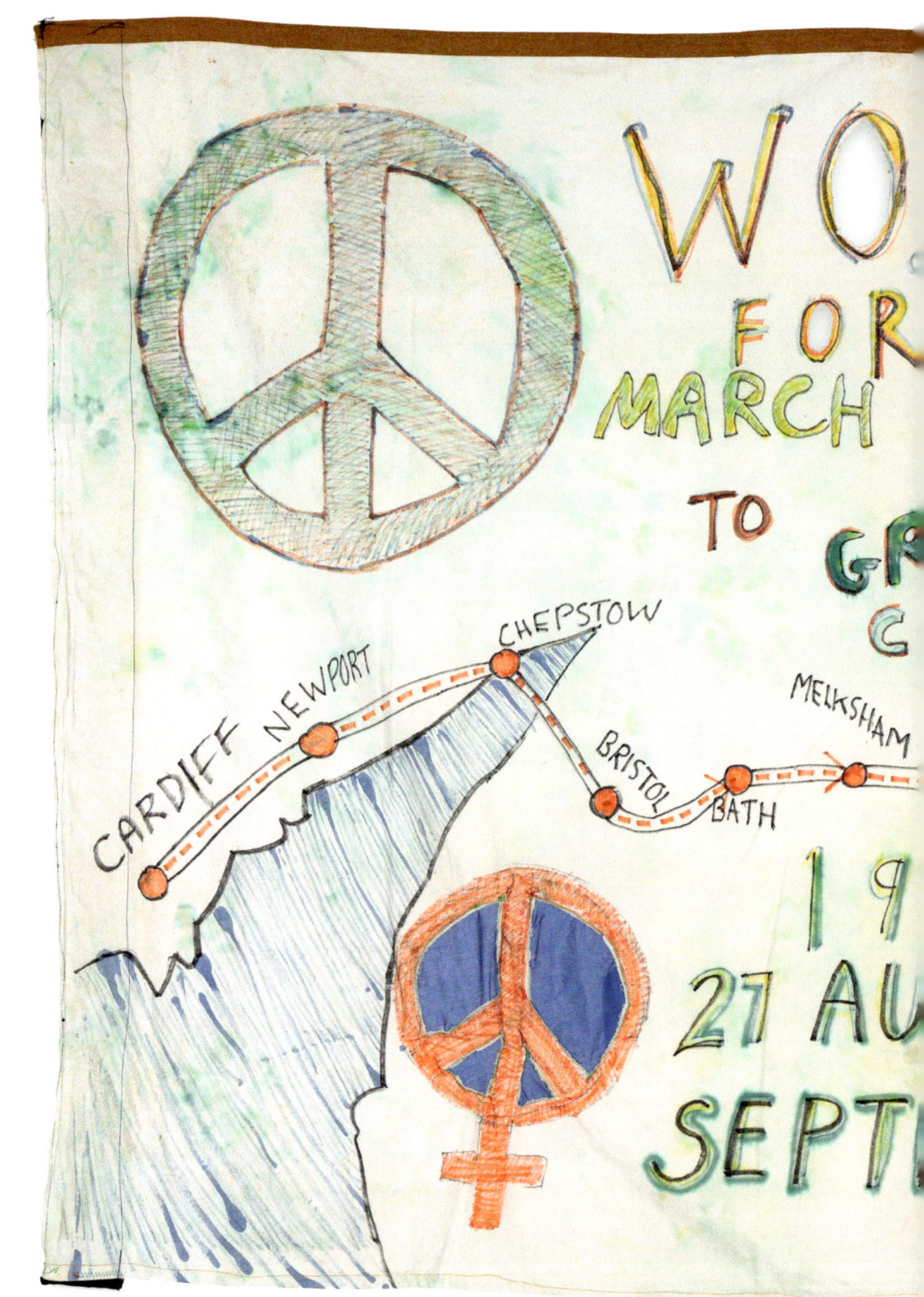

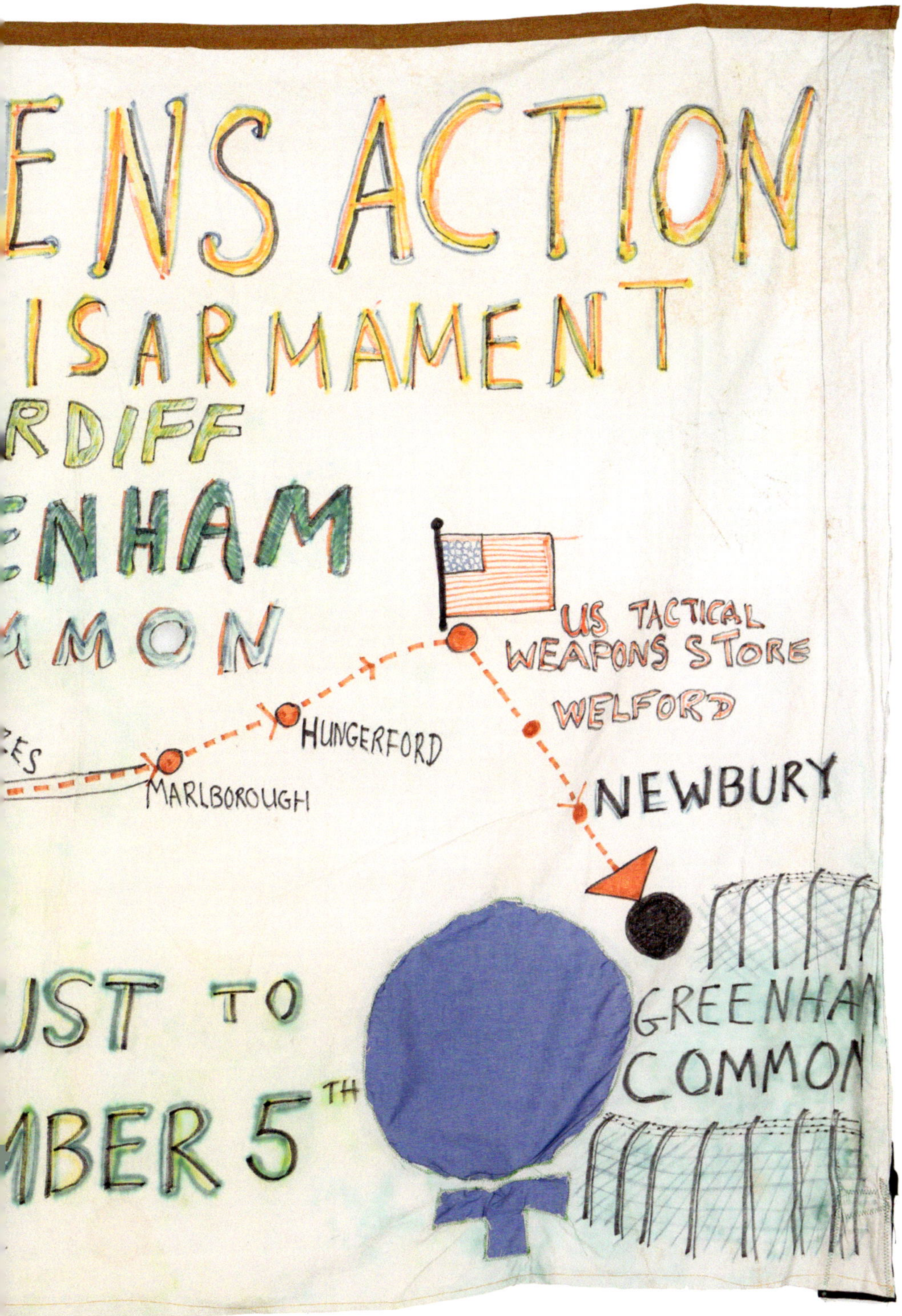

ENS ACTION
ISARMAMENT
RDIFF
ENHAM
MMON

US TACTICAL WEAPONS STORE WELFORD

HUNGERFORD
MARLBOROUGH
NEWBURY
GREENHAM COMMON

UST TO
MBER 5TH

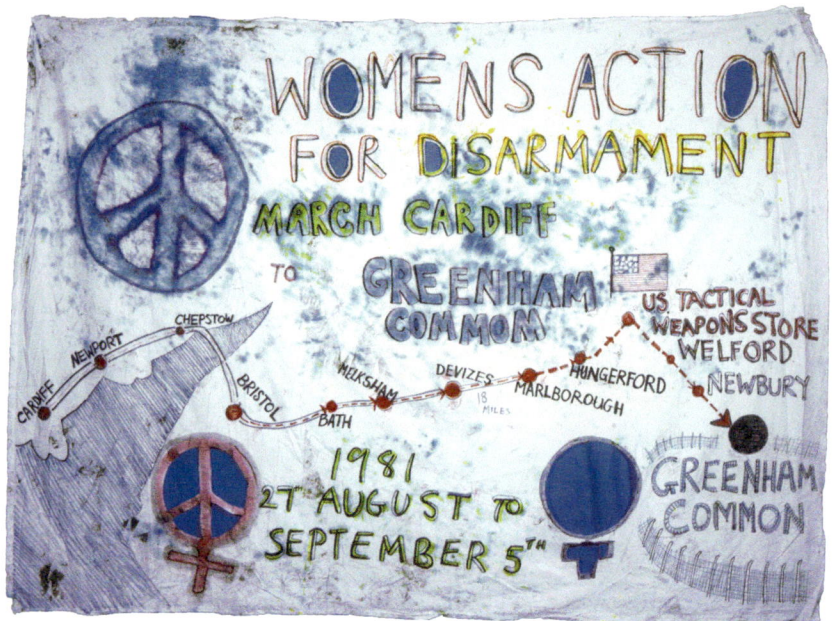

A second banner was created by four teenage girls, supported by Thalia Campbell, at the group's first overnight stop in Newport. They utilised scavenged materials: 'a white sheet' donated by a nurse and 'bamboo canes' from a gardener, which Campbell describes as 'still having mud on the bottom'.[6] This banner was made to be carried at the back of the procession, to 'explain to drivers why they were being held-up'.

Campbell went on to be the Greenham campaign's most prolific banner maker, sewing designs that were used, displayed, and reproduced all over the world. This, the first Greenham banner she was involved in making, was decorated with the slogan 'Women's Action for Disarmament' above a map of south west England and Wales, annotated with the walking route and stop-off points. It was hand-drawn 'in odd felt tips'.[7] Made quickly on the road and at the hand of the group of teenagers, this banner is atypical of her future designs for Greenham and other campaigns, which were carefully planned and executed in brightly coloured, appliquéd fabrics.

When the marchers reached RAF Greenham Common on 5 September 1981, 'a large contingent from Newbury Campaign against Cruise was waiting to greet [them]' – some with banners – as well as the Police, to keep the peace.[8]

Above: The original version of the second Greenham banner,
now lost, showing the route from Cardiff to Greenham, 1981.

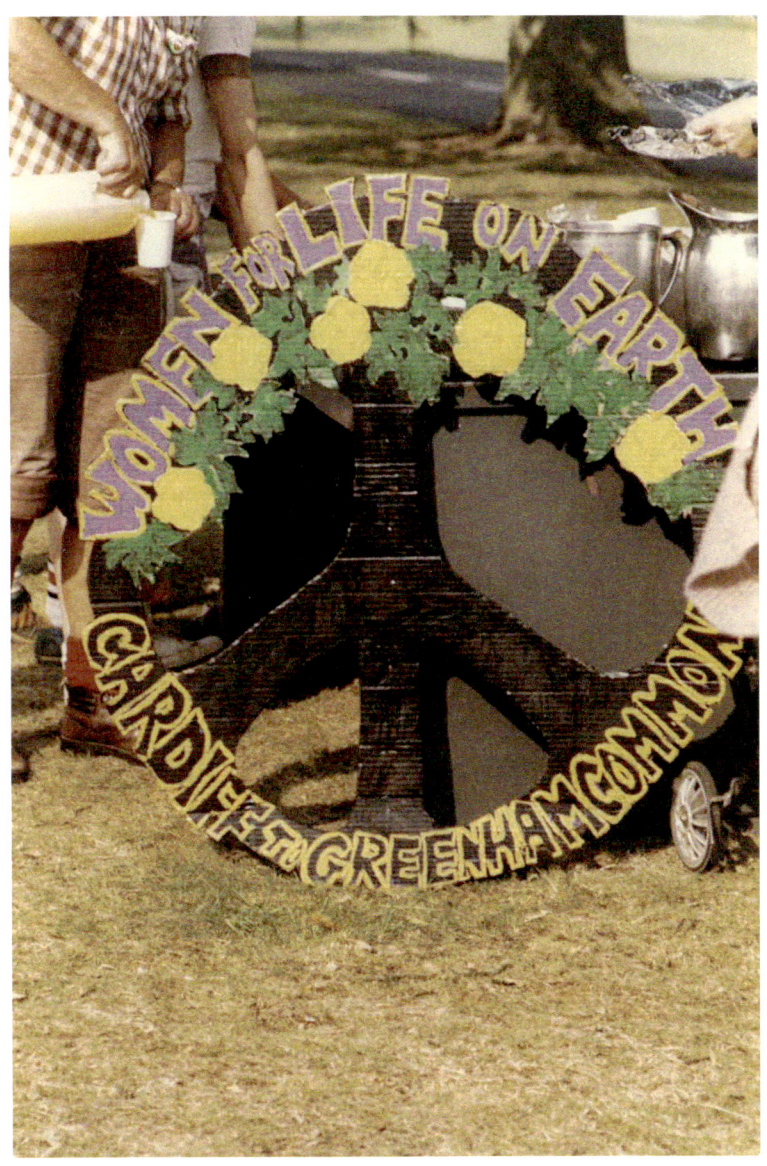

Above: An emblem from the first march from Cardiff to Greenham, 1981.

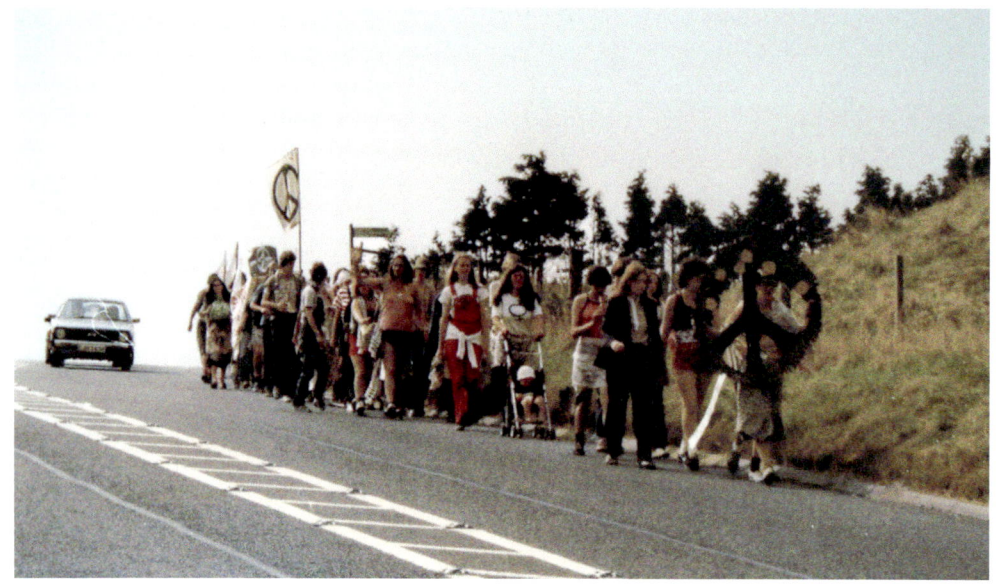

Jayne Burton, with three others, was chained to the fence to the side of the main gate, and described 'a small group of women appeared dressed in black to "keen" [sing songs for the dead]. They had a banner saying they were mourning for the children who may never have the chance to grow up.'[9]

Eunice Stallard – also chained to the fence – recalls the arrival of the main procession from Cardiff, together with a number who had joined them for the last leg of the walk: 'The marchers approached the open gates... The Base Commander was there. And then lots of MOD [Ministry of Defence] police and, following them, the civil police. It was pandemonium. We heard the Commander say, "Have you got the mug shots?" More people started arriving and kissing us. Then the marchers came led by the Fallout Marching Band with our *Women for Life on Earth* banner, and Thaila [Campbell] doing somersaults all the way...'[10]

The walk's organisers did not plan to establish a peace camp at the culmination of the protest march. However, as it became clear their efforts had failed to instigate a public debate, some of those who had made the journey from Cardiff were determined to occupy the area outside the main airbase gate, until they engaged the Base Commander, media and government in the cause for disarmament and peace.[11]

Their decision led to the continuous occupation of a camp at the main gate, later called 'Yellow Gate', for the next 19 years, as well as camps at other gates around the airbase. The peace 'camp provided an around the clock location; to observe, and to monitor the activities inside the base...', as well as conduct non-violent actions, which included cutting through the fence and entering the base, and disruption of manoeuvres to rehearse the deployment of the missiles on Salisbury Plain.[12]

The Greenham women are commonly written about as a collective, and largely they did work cooperatively. However, to describe them collectively does not acknowledge the diversity of experience thousands of women had at the camp, and the splintering that occurred between some groups. Groups differed, for example, on the presence of men, how donations were spent, and ways to address racism and class privilege that were the experience of some women.[13]

After the Main Gate camp was founded, separate camps were established at the different gates around the base, and women would often identify with and stay at a specific gate camp. Each was named after a colour of the rainbow. Their separate identities allowed for difference within the collective cause. Main Gate was renamed Yellow Gate. Others were Green Gate, located nearest to the silos housing the Cruise missiles, which was exclusively women-only at all times – male visitors were allowed at other gates during the day; Turquoise Gate; Blue Gate that had a new age focus; Pedestrian Gate; Indigo Gate; religiously focussed Violet Gate; Red Gate, known as the artists' gate; and Orange Gate.

Gates published their own newsletters and would plan actions independently, as well as taking part in larger group protests. The books that record the first-hand remembrances of the Greenham women, often represent the perspective of a certain camp or group and cannot be interpreted as representative of the experiences of all.

Throughout the different camps, during the many years of campaigning at Greenham, banners were present, as tools of protest, and a backdrop to daily life lived 'at the wire' fence, surrounding the airbase.[14]

Opposite: the first march, from Cardiff to Greenham, 1981.

The History of the Banner and its Influence at Greenham

Banners can be divided into the impulsively created and those that are carefully and expertly made. Late 20th century banners, such as those made for Greenham, embraced new materials and approaches to production: 'Ad hoc techniques have been devised to produce banners quickly such as the washing-line effect with torn sheets boldly lettered... or the use of the bias cut ribbon machine-sewn to give the flowing effect of hand written lettering. Zig-zag sewing machines are invaluable for banner makers. Felt-tip pens, spray paint, Dylon paint, indelible markers all find their place along with the deep dyed Terylene sheets which provide strong resistant and colour-fast base'.[15]

Despite sometimes using new techniques in place of traditional embroidery, appliqué, or paint, applied to a textile base, the Greenham banners often demonstrate an awareness of historic banners. In the custom of banner making, they utilise symbolic colours and combine bold text with pictorial symbols and motifs. For example, Thalia Campbell's *Remembrance is Not Enough* design, imagined during the walk to Greenham, includes traditional red poppies, white peace poppies, and green and purple ones representing the suffrage colours of the Women's Social and Political Union (WSPU).[16] The slogan is a call to action; change is needed, it is not sufficient to remember those who have been lost in conflict.

Campbell and the teenage protestors copied the slogan on their Greenham banner, from that included on walk-organiser Pettitt's first Greenham banner. The motif on Pettitt's banner evolved the Campaign for Nuclear Disarmament (CND) symbol, combining it with a tree and globe to link it to the name 'Women for Life on Earth'. Visual and textual appropriations of this nature can be traced across many of the Greenham banners made subsequently, from the present and past peace and women's campaigns.

The banner *The British People Are Prepared to Be Blown to Atomic Dust if Necessary, Lord Home 1961* is a copy of one made by a CND group in the Midlands in 1961. Campbell admired it, and considered its message to

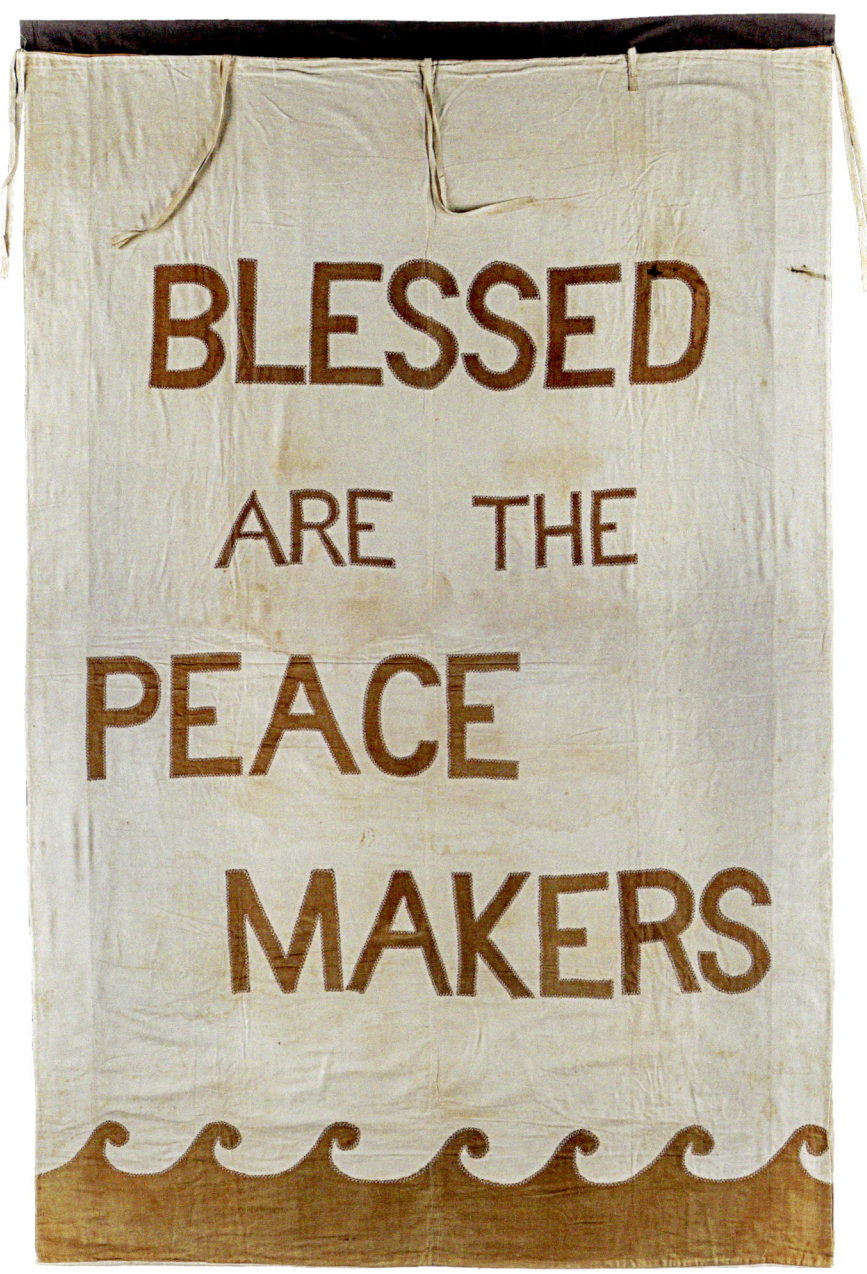

Above: *Blessed Are the Peacemakers*, suffrage banner, 1908, 219 × 149 cm.

Next page: *'The British People Are Prepared to Be Blown to Atomic Dust if Necessary'*, *Lord Home, 1961*, made by Thalia Campbell, after a Birmingham CND banner of 1961, 94 × 197 cm.

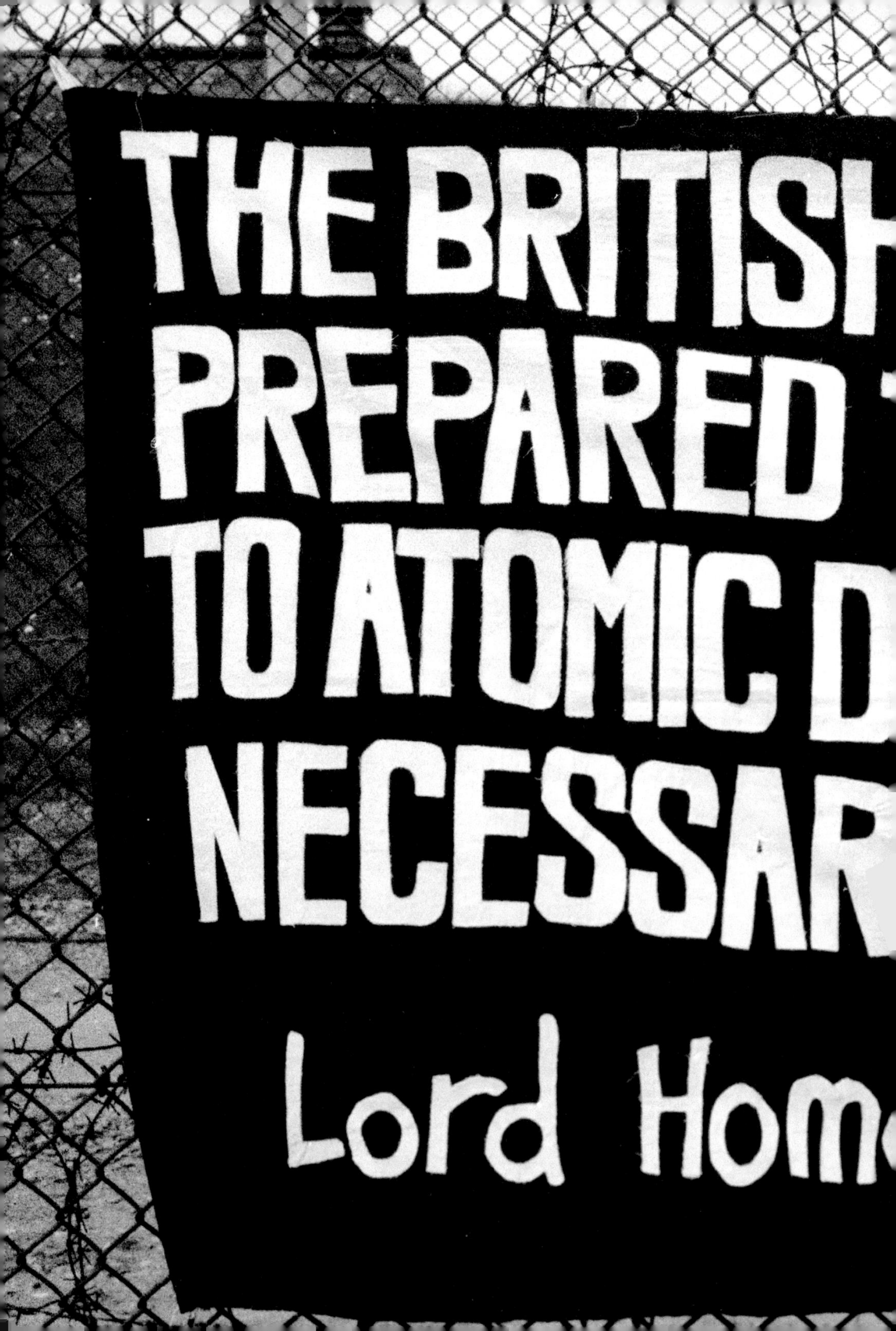

THE BRITISH
PREPARED T[O]
TO ATOMIC D[...]
NECESSAR[Y]

Lord Hom[e]

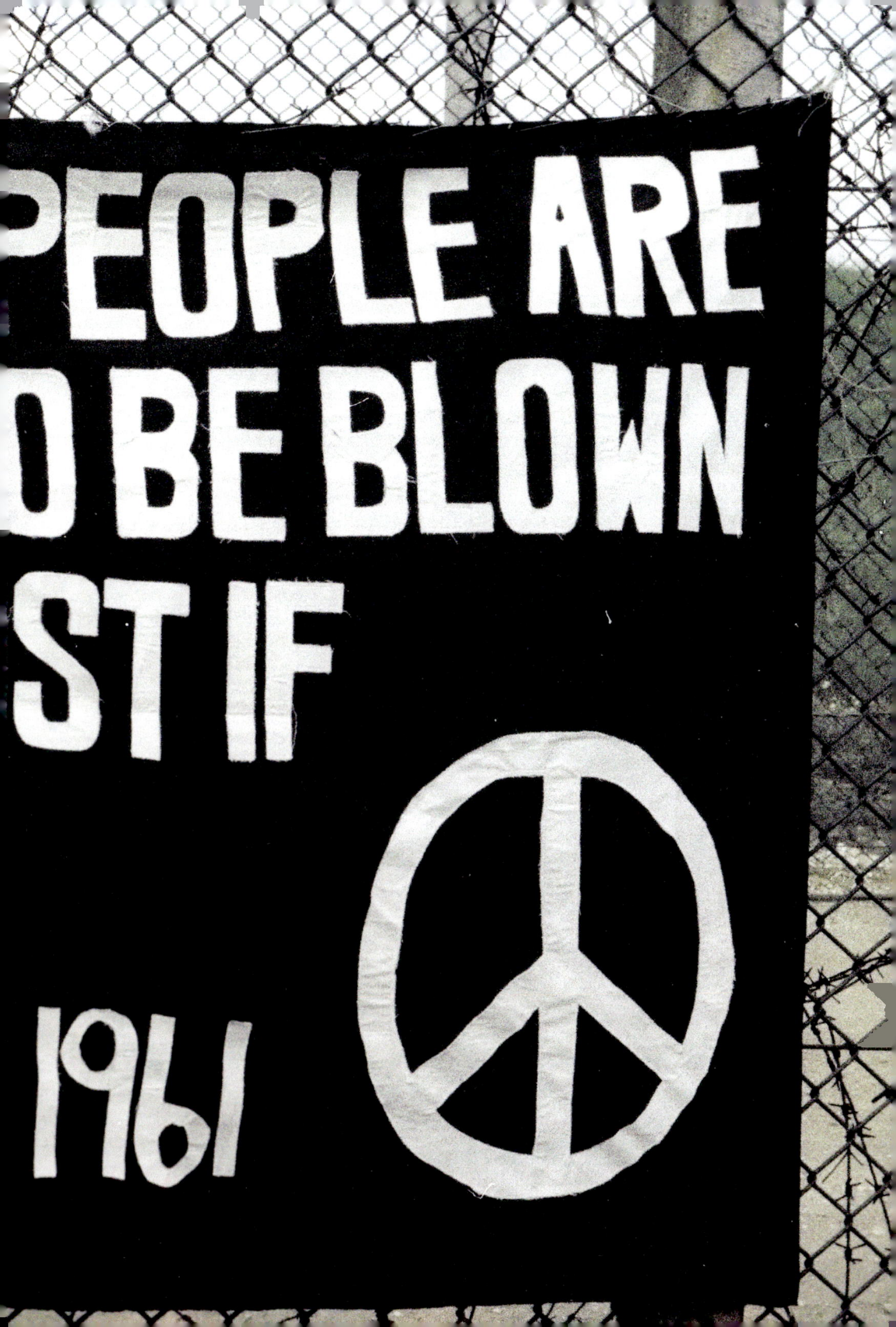

PEOPLE ARE
TO BE BLOWN
[LA]ST IF

1961

be relevant at Greenham, so made a copy. She recalls that it provoked the 'angriest responses' of all her banners at Greenham, from those not aligned with the cause.

The banner form can be traced back to antiquity, to ancient Egyptian temples, Roman standards and later the heraldry of knights. In the mid-late Middle Ages banners were made to identify the historic trade guilds.

A surge in production and use of banners during the 19th century, sprang from the significant changes brought about by the Industrial Revolution. The expanding urban population worked in factories rather than the fields. People were brought together in workplaces structured by timed shifts, and in so doing awakened ideas of social justice, healthy conditions, fair pay, and the equal right to vote and influence decision-making.

The founding of labour organisations and the trade unions gave rise to a category of banners representing the labouring classes and trades – sometimes in protest. This ran alongside the demand for banners representing the church and other organisations and societies. At this time there were commercial banner makers, such as London-based Tutill's Banners and Regalia, founded in 1837. Alternatively, the skills of a sign-writer might be employed or the sewing talents of someone involved in the movement or campaign.

Banners have played a significant role in the female-led campaigns. From those carried at the suffrage rallies and processions of the early 20th century – many designed by the Artist Suffrage League – to those held aloft by women taking part in the 1926 National Peacemakers Pilgrimage, planned by the Women's International League for Peace and Freedom (WILPF). For the latter, each of the eight walking routes converging on Hyde Park was 'headed by a great two-pole banner bearing the route name, with women carrying staffs with a dove of peace on top.'[17]

A 1908 banner bearing the slogan 'Blessed are the Peace Makers', carried in suffrage processions, is indicative of the lineage of women's peace campaigning and values during the early to mid-twentieth century. The design is believed to have been commissioned by a Somerset Quaker family.[18] Greenham banners are part of this long tradition, in the same way Labour and miner's banners from the 1980s follow those from earlier workers' campaigns.

From the 1980s, such was the demand for Campbell's banners, she and her husband Ian – both artists – made them professionally, for antinuclear, trade union and other clients, advertising: 'Be proud of your union. Campbell Design offer a complete service to organisations. We design and make painted and sewn banners.' Nevertheless, by this time, professional banner making was unusual. Many of the Greenham banners were produced by amateur individuals and groups or skilled enthusiasts like sewing teacher Eileen Scott, as well as artists, such as Katrina Howse who lived at Greenham from August 1982 to February 2000. Her creative output encompasses murals, paintings, drawings, papier-mâché puppets and forms, as well as painted banners.

How Were the Greenham Banners Used?

Following the initial march to Greenham, banners continued to be made, processed and displayed at other marches, rallies and events, and were tied to the fence and trees in the women's camps surrounding the airbase. Here they were a backdrop to Greenham life; a means of claiming the space and communicating the cause to those passing and visiting. Many banners are recorded in the photographs taken at Greenham by journalists, visitors, and the women themselves. Some appear in the background, and on other occasions are central to a posed shot.

Banners were held-up during the trial of Greenham women at Newbury Magistrates Court, and displayed outside this and other court buildings, as they faced charges for breach of the peace and trespass. They were also used at the courts between 1988 and 1997 as a group of Greenham women from Yellow Gate, including Howse, fought against the extinguishment of commoners' rights to access Greenham Common.[19] Protesters were arrested for cutting the fence and entering the airbase amongst other non-violent actions, including securing the main gate with a bicycle lock, and, on another occasion, putting super-glue in the Blue Gate padlock. All of these activities were planned to disrupt military operations and draw attention to the cause.

Sue Bolton describes the display of a banner at an awareness raising event on the Isle of Wight in 1983: 'In February, when the court cases were going on in Newbury, for the women arrested on New Year's Day at Greenham, we decided not to go to the court, because we knew there were going to be lots of women there already in support. Instead, we... held a vigil outside the court house in the Isle of Wight. Women had never demonstrated like that before on the island... When the evening came we decided to stay all night. We lit a brazier and hung our banner on the courthouse flagpole. People came to talk to us until 3am, giving us fuel for the fire and hot food.'[20]

A banner was central to a protest at the Houses of Parliament on 18 January 1982: 'We wanted to say right at the beginning of the parliamentary year, "It's enough. We've had enough"... We made trees of life.

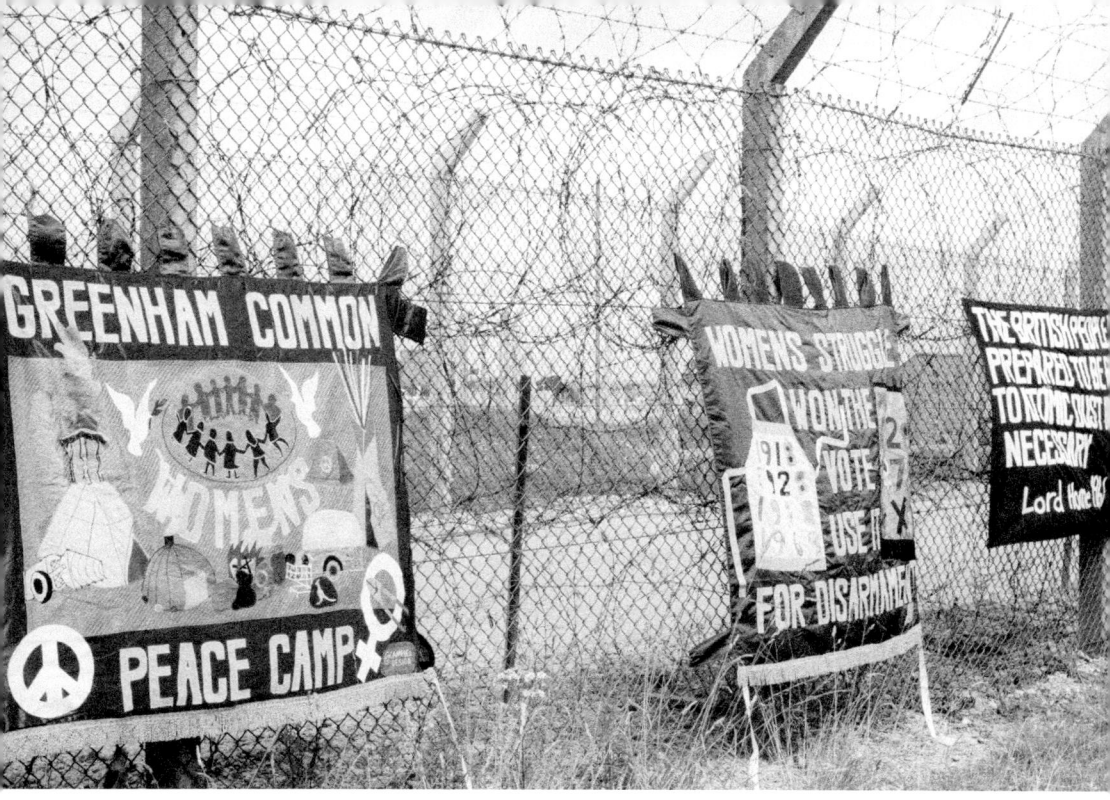

Above: Thalia Campbell banners on the fence at RAF Greenham Common.

Next pages: *Remembrance Is Not Enough* by Thalia Campbell, 119 × 204 cm. Campbell imagined the design for this banner during the first walk to Greenham. It was made by Campbell and Jan Higgs to be carried by Women For Life on Earth when they laid a wreath provided by Caernarfon CND in Suffragette colours on the Cenotaph on 13 November 1982. The banner includes traditional red poppies, white peace poppies, and green and purple ones representing the suffrage colours of the Women's Social and Political Union.

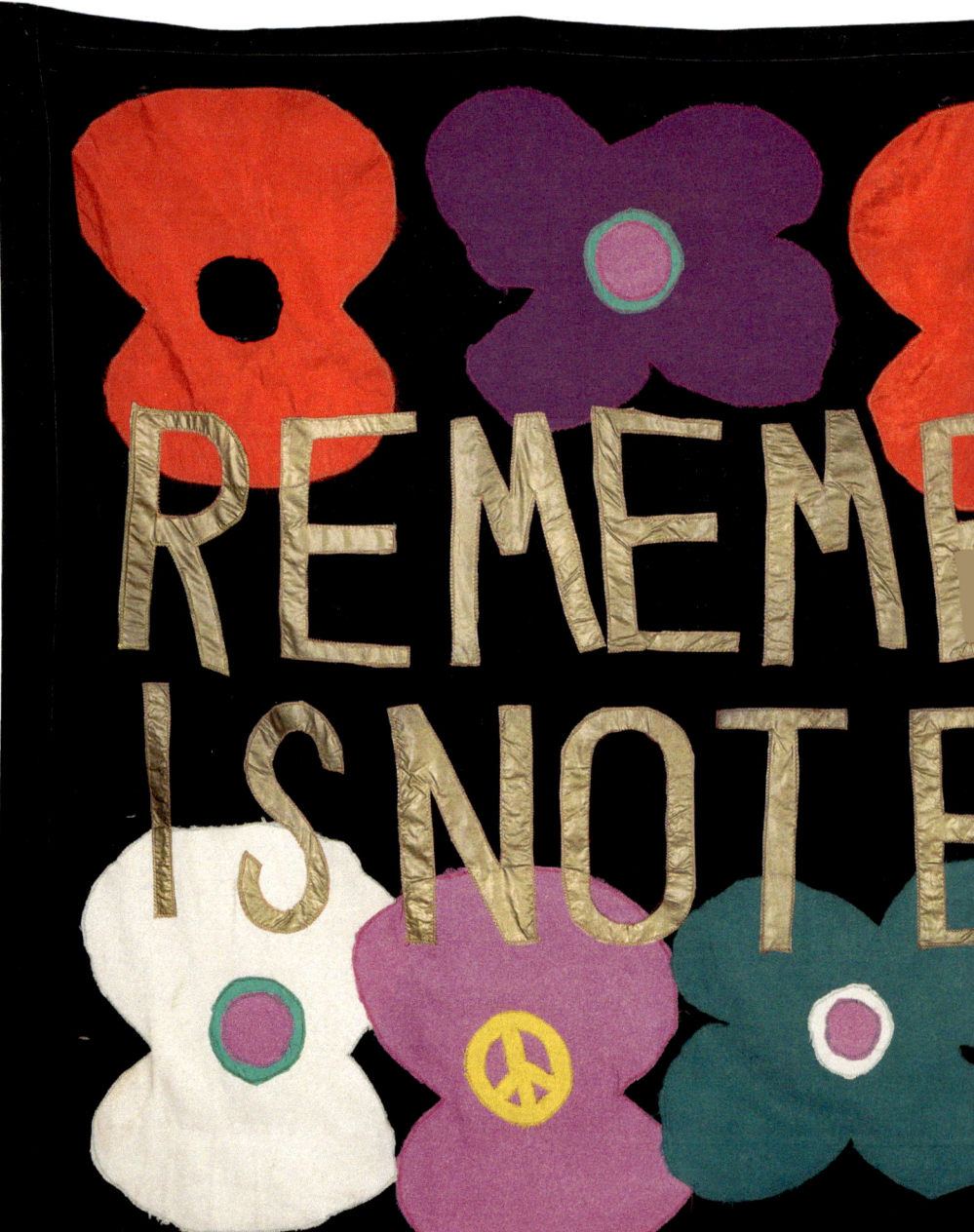

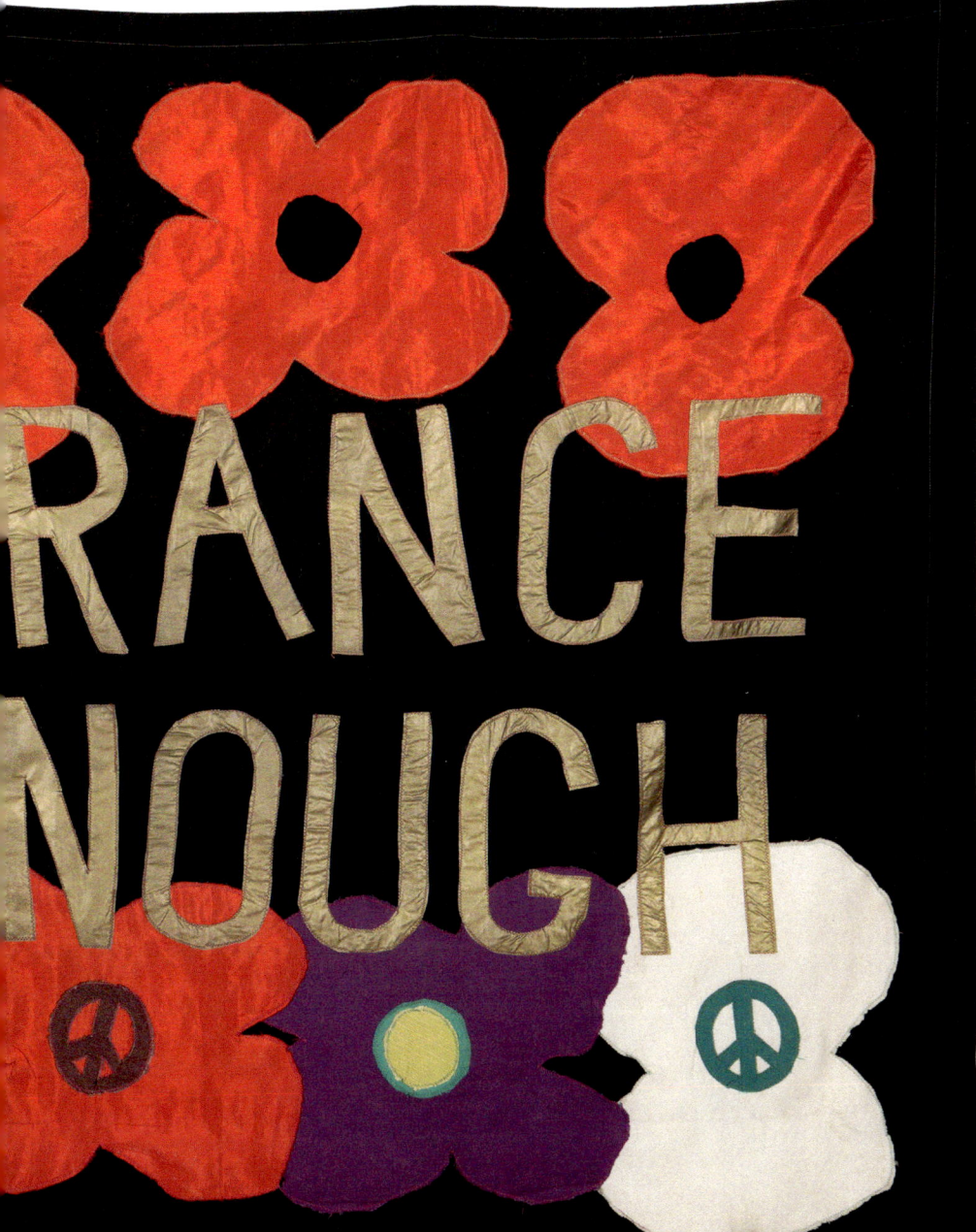

We covered twigs with ribbons in suffrage colours – purple, green and white – and hung doves of peace from them and little sequins. We made beautiful things. Our banner said: "Our hearts are breaking, you must rethink nuclear policy in 1982."'[21]

Campbell's *Remembrance Is Not Enough* banner was carried by women on the Saturday prior to Remembrance Day in 1983. The group congregated in Trafalgar Square, which had been booked for the protest, and walked down Whitehall with the banner and a wreath. Campbell recalls that their wreath was removed before the official ceremony.[22]

The first march to Greenham in 1981, was followed by further protest walks to the airbase, including the 'Star Marches', after the camp had been established. These saw 'thousands of women… simultaneously walk across the country to Greenham' illustrating 'the extent of national support', in the summer of 1983, from 30 July to 6 August.[23] The term 'star' refers to the women coming from different points in the country and internationally, converging on Greenham. Banners accompanied the women on these marches. Some groups carried designs made especially for the event, just as they were for the first walk, others held existing banners naming their group or made for a former occasion.

The design of the *Women for Life on Earth* banner (pages 44–45) made for the march is an irregular six-pointed star, decorated with representations of the solar system, sea, and natural environment. On the reverse there is a spray-painted map of the UK, encircled by the words 'We don't want Cruise missiles, do you?'

Decoration on the reverse of a banner is relatively unusual. Additional appliquéd fabric on the back can make it sag, and too heavy to be carried. If only made from a single thickness of fabric, a design on the reverse could also affect the appearance of the message on the front. This is avoided on this Star March banner as the design is applied using spray-paint. A second exception is Campbell's addition of 'Join Us' to the reverse of a banner – a slogan she copied from the back of a suffrage design. However, when reproducing the call to action, Campbell was initially unaware that in its original usage, the suffragettes were asking those watching to join 'Universal Suffrage', rather than the march itself, as she intended.

The *Bath Star March* banner, bearing the slogan 'We have a dream', was designed by Maylin Heard. In the centre a tree grows from a star; the trunk and branches forming the CND symbol. Banners made for specific events, such as the Star Marches, were subsequently used and displayed at and away from Greenham. Often an event stimulated the making of a new

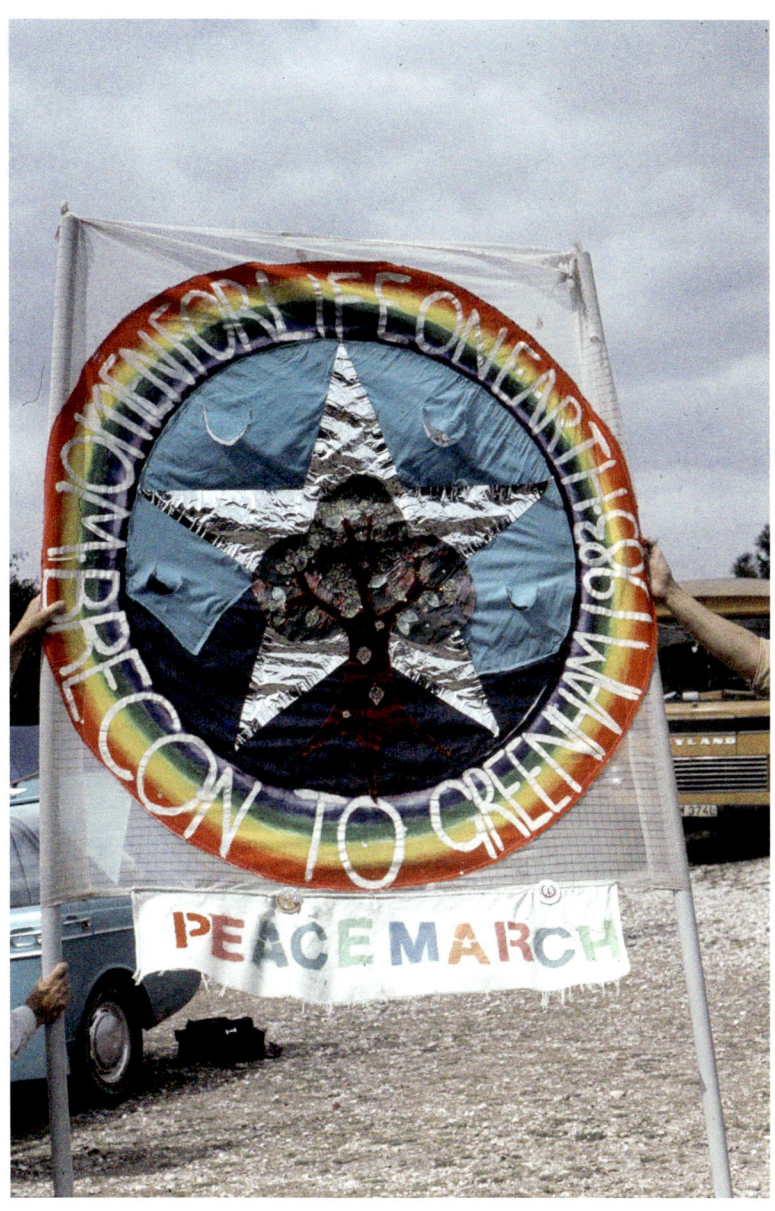

Above and next pages: Banners made by women for the Star Marches in the summer of 1983, when thousands of women protesting against nuclear weapons walked from different locations across Britain, hence the reference to a star, and converged at RAF Greenham Common.

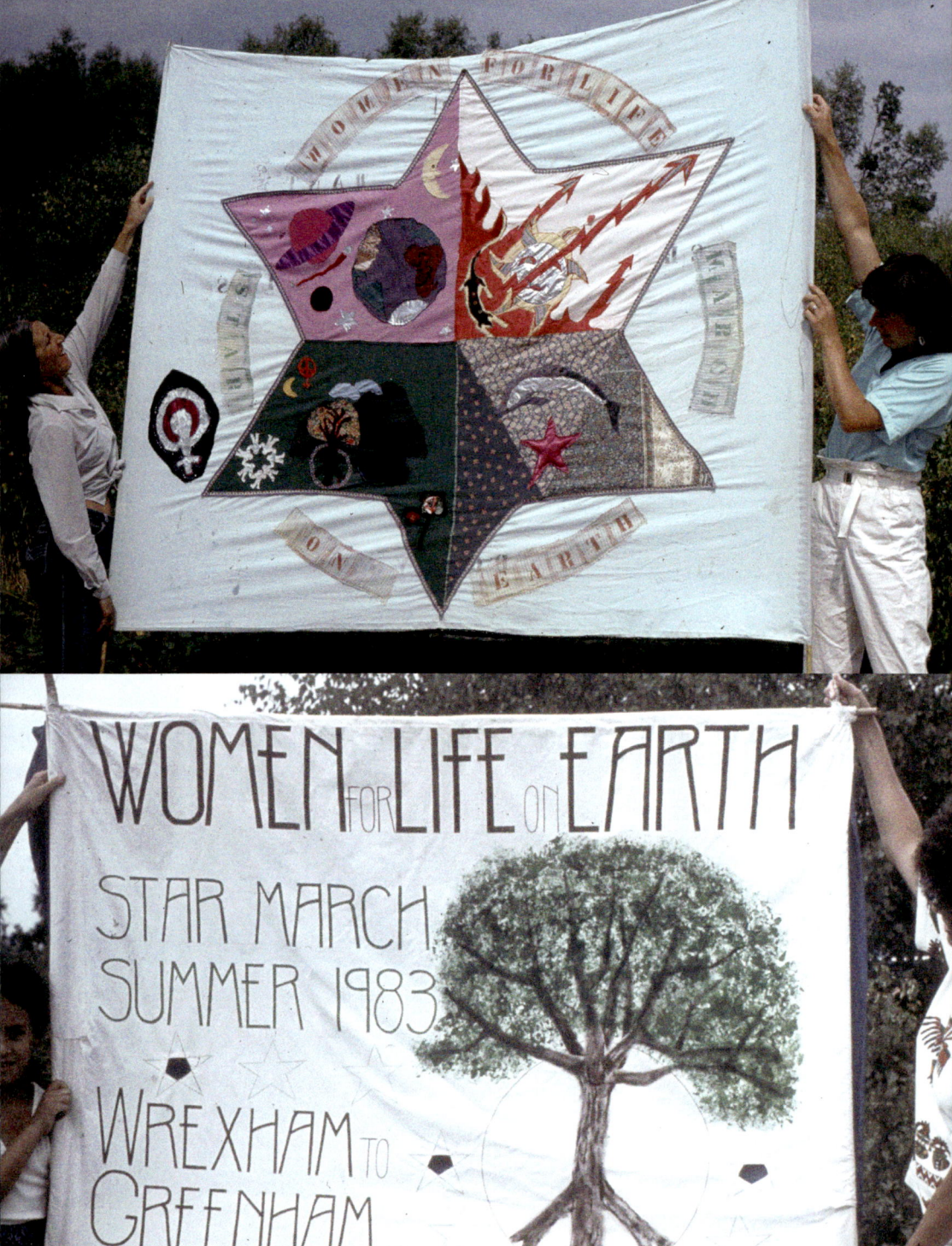

WE DONT WANT CRUISE MISSILES DO YOU?

BRISTOL – GREENHAM

STAR MARCH

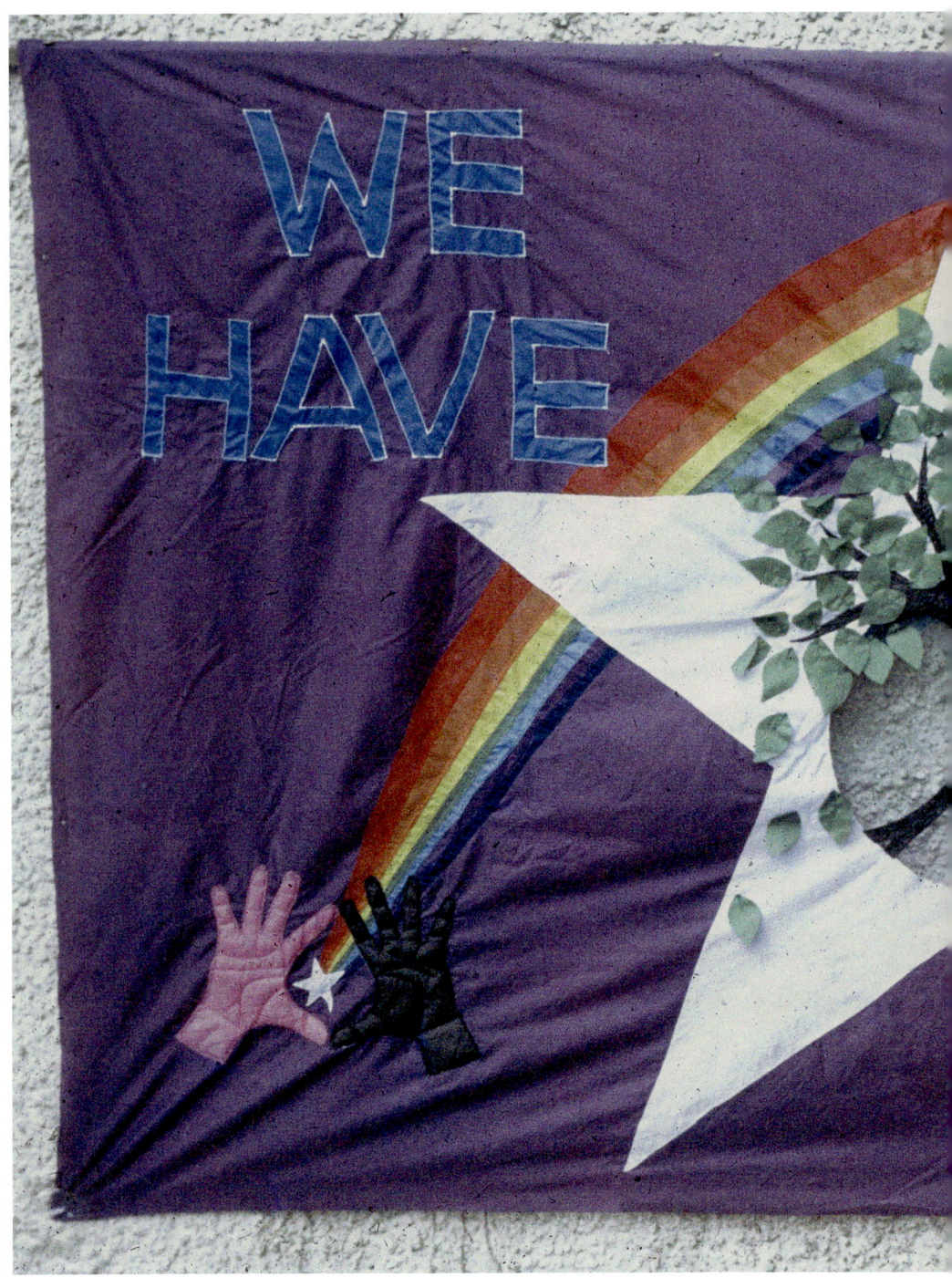

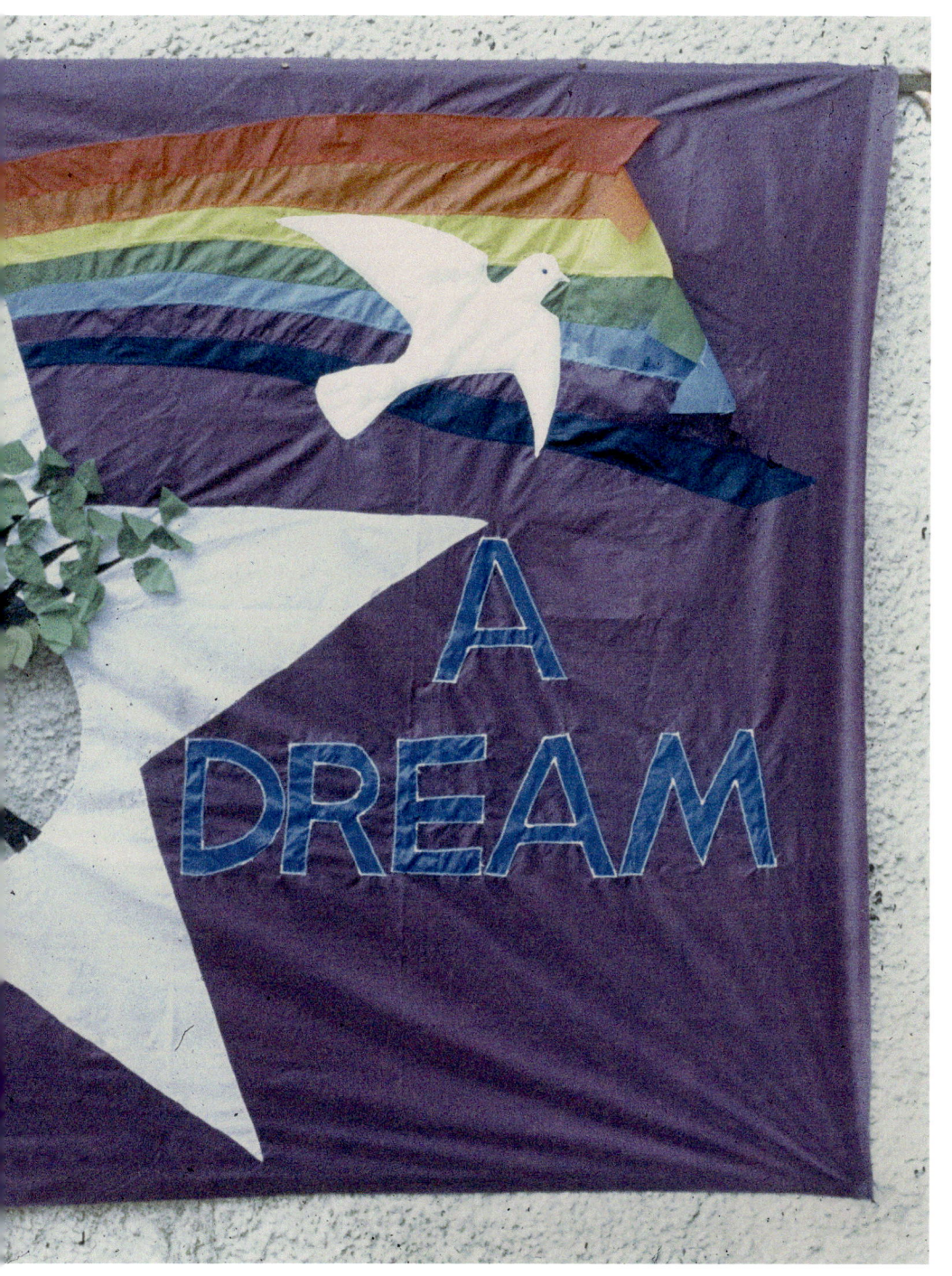

banner. It would then join the banner collections held by individuals and groups, which were brought out to represent the cause when required. In this way the banners acted as testament to participation in an event, illustrated the history and range of campaigning activity, and provided a visual reminder of the women's shared experiences.

As the camp became better known, the Greenham women travelled to domestic and international peace events, and on speaking tours, such as that embarked on in North America in 1983. A selection of banners was taken with them to these events.[24]

Campbell recalls attending upward of 80 meetings across Wales in the early 1980s, arriving early and staying after the event to hang-up and take down the banners. International interest was also stimulated by the publication of postcards of Greenham banners by Campbell and Sheila Owen-Jones. Postcard orders were posted all over the world, creating an international demand for banner commissions, often replicas of designs Campbell had made for Greenham.

Banners would 'often go missing', and some were lost or destroyed during the many years of the campaign, some in the course of camp evictions that started in 1982.[25] The evictions were carried out by Newbury Council to remove the women from the land, although their tenacity always saw them return almost immediately with the possessions they were able to save.

Campbell recalls that Maylin Heard's *Bath Star March* banner was torn-up by students who objected to the cause and a copy of the same design was subsequently made. The Greenham banner Campbell made with the group of teenage girls, on the first walk, was removed from the fence during a blockade of Blue Gate, along with other banners. Whilst the other banners were returned, after pleading with the police, the banner from the first march was lost – reported by some to have been hung in the Base mess. This stimulated Campbell and her daughter Lucy – one of the teenagers who made the original – to make two more of the same design when they returned home. The replication of designs, particularly by Campbell, was common.

Surviving banners can display evidence of their use. Campbell's first Greenham banner was used by her daughter to sleep under on the first night of the impromptu camp at the main gate, and the following day it acted as picnic rug and changing mat.

Some Greenham banners are held in museums, archives, and personal collections. They can be found at The Peace Museum, Bradford, The Women's Library collection at London School of Economics and St. Fagans National Museum of History, Cardiff.

Previous pages: *Bath Star March* banner, designed by Maylin Heard.

Of the surviving Greenham banners, the majority tend to be the more carefully designed and made. Campbell, for example, would bring a selection of banners to Greenham when she came for a four or five day stay at the Blue or Orange Gate camps. Whilst she was there, they would be tied to the fence and trees. When she left, they would go with her. They were precious and needed at other events.

Photographs and the women's testimonies reveal details of some banners that are gone. One of the most hurriedly made yet iconic Greenham banners simply read 'Peace '83', and accompanied a group of women when they entered the airbase on New Year's Day 1983. In a much-reproduced photograph of the event, the women are silhouetted in the early morning light on top of a silo housing Cruise missiles: 'We scrambled up the mud-drenched slopes to the top of the silos. Unbelieving – but knowing – we cheered, waved, jumped up and down, hugged each other in what seemed like an endless amount of energy. We had brought with us a huge piece of cloth with "Peace '83" painted across it which we held for the women to see, for the TV cameras... For an hour we danced, sang and made women's peace symbols with the stones that lay on the surface.'[26]

In the years following the disbanding of the camp, the banners together with other ephemera have been used in exhibitions and commemorations. The banners' scale, bold messages and the active way in which they were used, make them strong and potent connectors to the campaign, just as surviving suffrage and trade union banners are for those causes.

Next pages: A banner (100 × 160 cm) made by Thalia and Lucy Campbell after the original march to Greenham, within sufficient time to be able to remember the names of all of the participants who took part in the first march, and their children. The row of names along the bottom edge are people who supported, fed, and housed the marchers. Campbell made the banner in the Pentagon Peace Ribbon format. A 'yard long panel of fabric expressing the voice of an individual, family or entire community'. The Peace Ribbon project was started in the USA in 1982 by peace campaigner Justine Merritt. Tens of thousands of ribbon segments, sometimes referred to as banners, were made by individuals across America and internationally. A tab on each corner allows them to be tied to other panels of the same size, and joined to make a ribbon. The project, still ongoing, based in Princeton, USA, saw people join their banners to encircle the Pentagon on 4 August 1985. This event – the largest ribbon joining – took place two days before the 40th anniversary of the atomic bombing of Hiroshima. Merritt described this ambitious project as 'a gentle reminder to the nation that we love the earth and all its people'.[27]

Derek
Steve Elspeth
       Annie Tunnicliffe Stallard An
Liz Stocker Eunice Julia Ball Jean
Evelyn Silver Baldwin
Andrew Modres dinnie
Thomas Lynne Jones
Alan Hardman
  Karmen Cutler
    Lynne Whittemore
    Angela Phillips
    diney Seward
    Simone Wilkinson GREENHA
         Mary Crofton
Anita Gale Annie Powell Lynne Jones

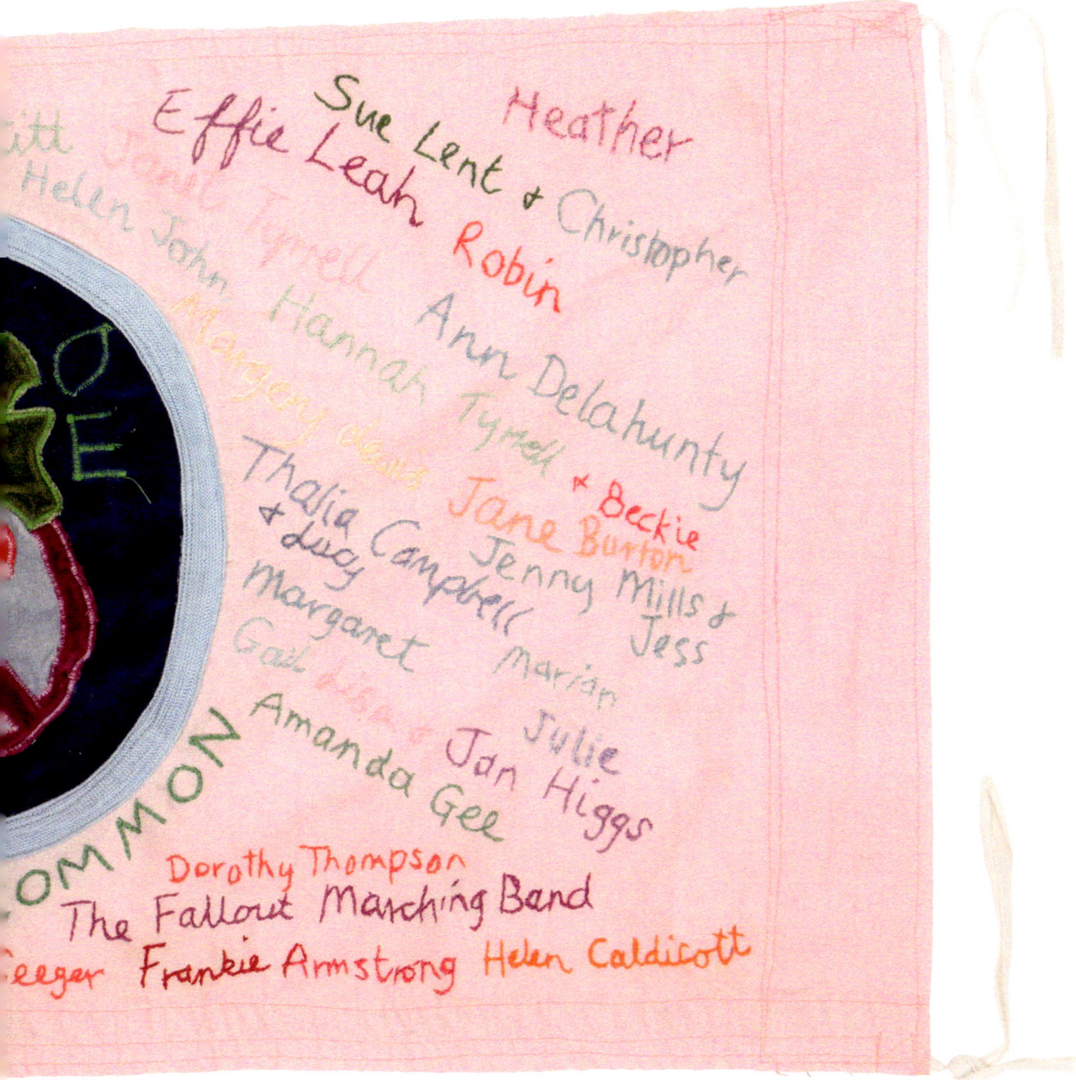

Heather
Sue Lent & Christopher
Effie Leah
Robin
Helen John Hannah Tyrrell Ann Delahunty
Margery
Thalia Campbell Jane Burton & Beckie
+ Lucy Jenny Mills & Jess
Margaret Marian
Gail Jan Higgs Julie
Amanda Gee
Dorothy Thompson
The Fallout Marching Band
Seeger Frankie Armstrong Helen Caldicott

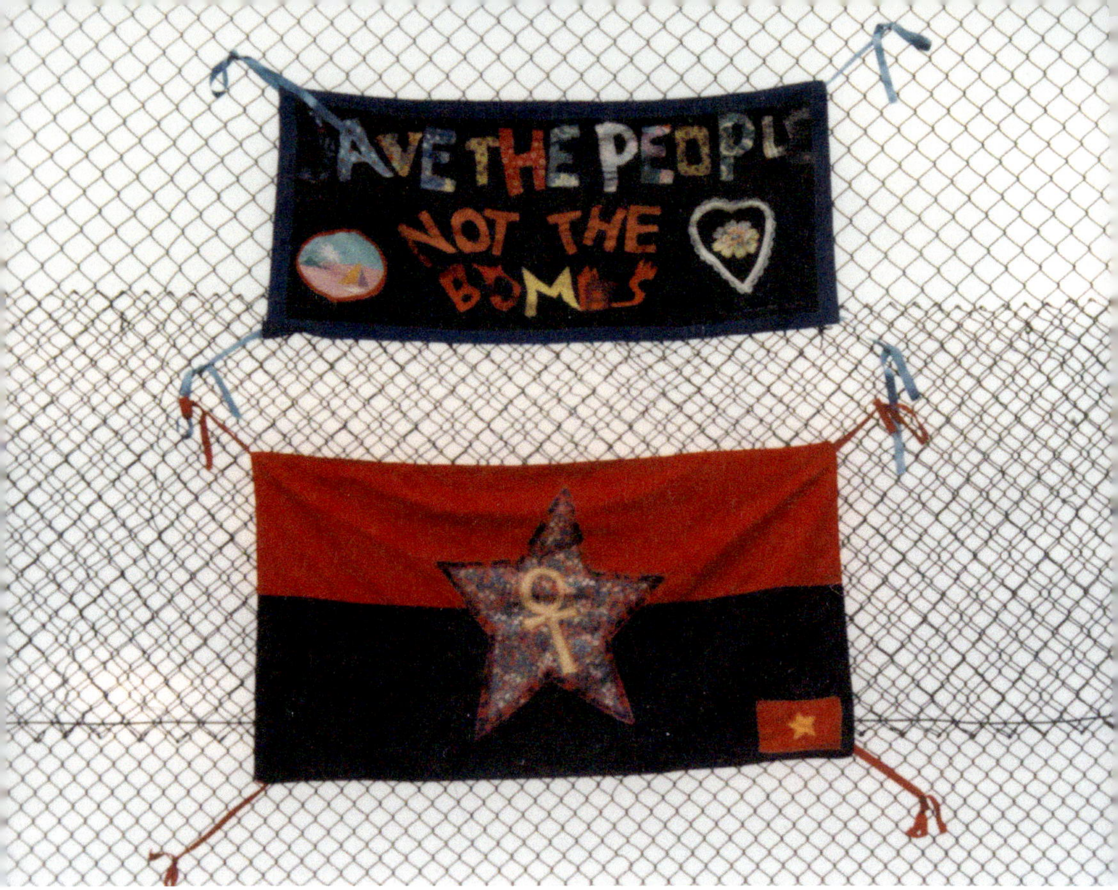

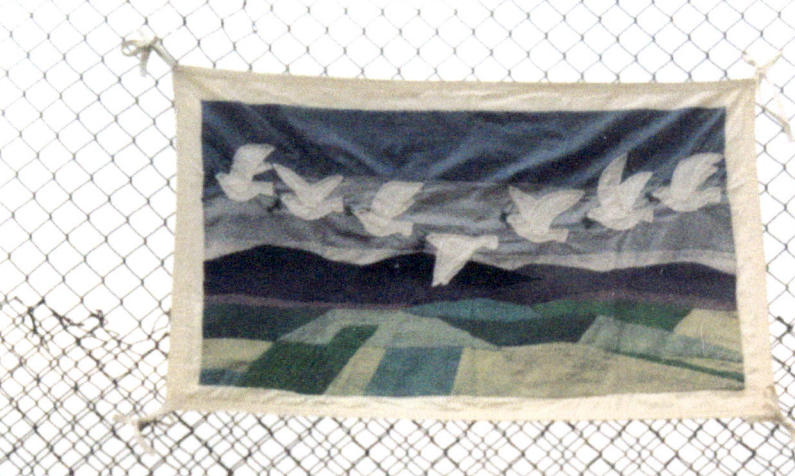

Above and opposite: Banners in the 'ribbon' format by various artists.
Thalia Campbell's 'Rachel Carson' ribbon banner incorporates her book *Silent Spring*
as well as a table mat that Campbell made with her grandmother as a child.

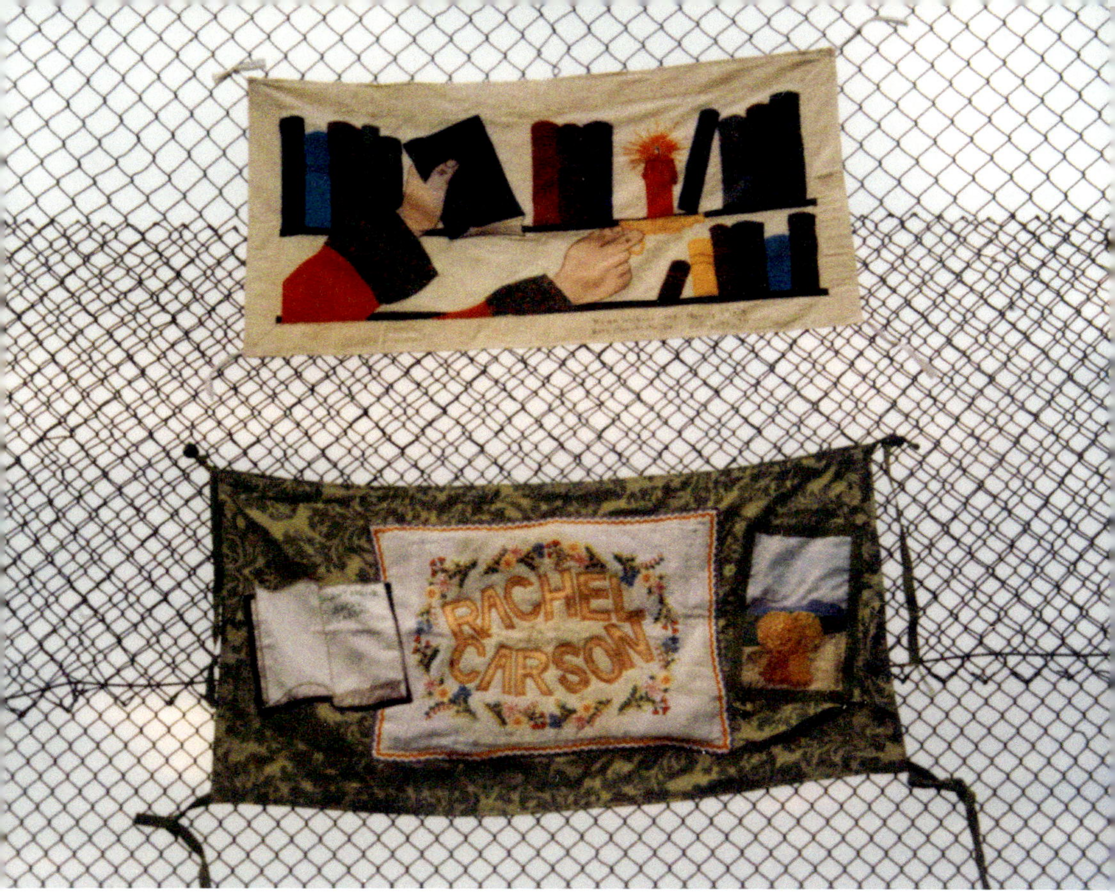

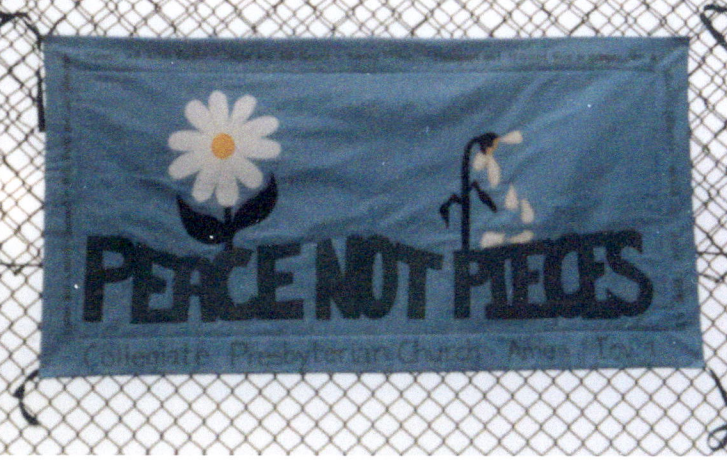

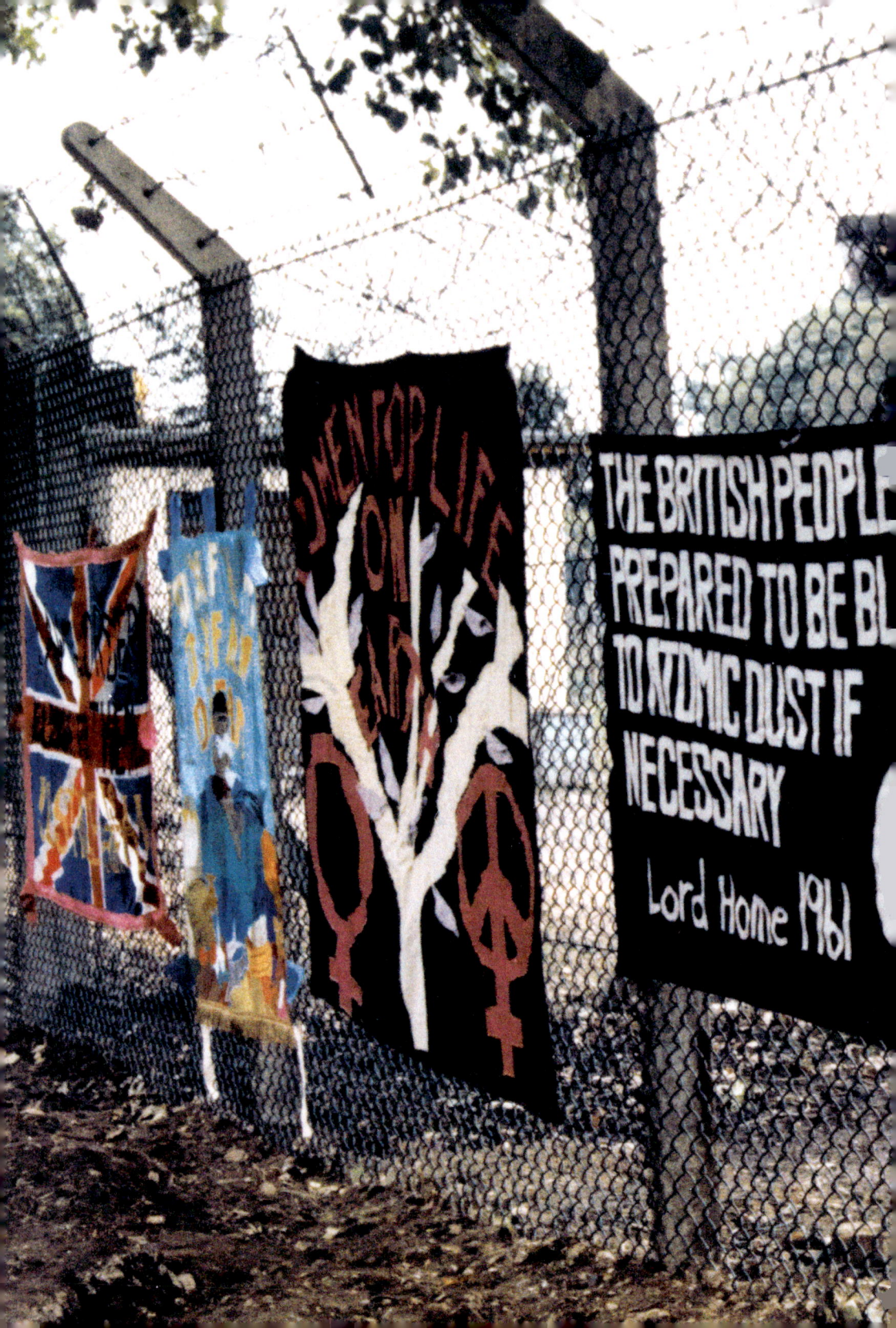

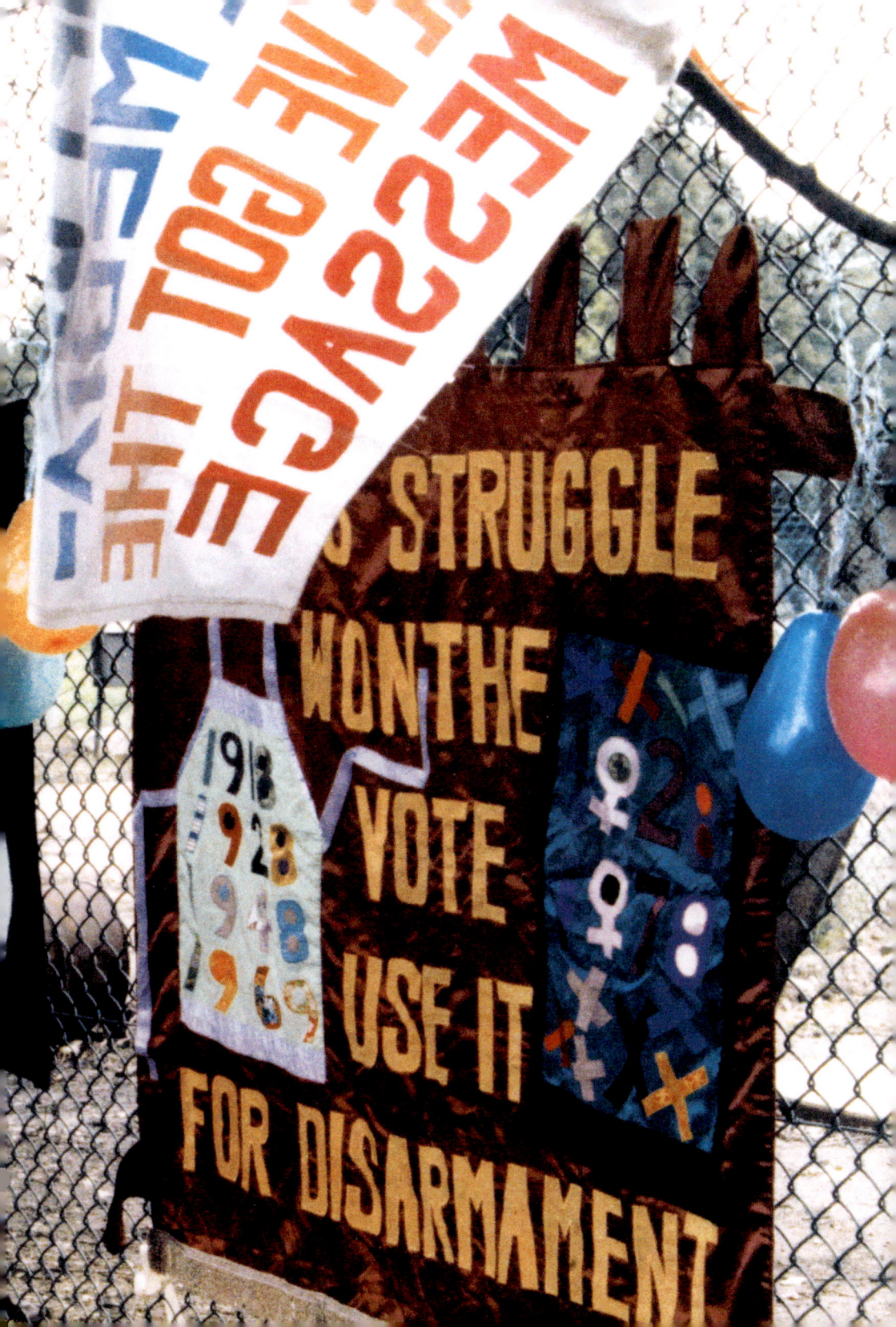

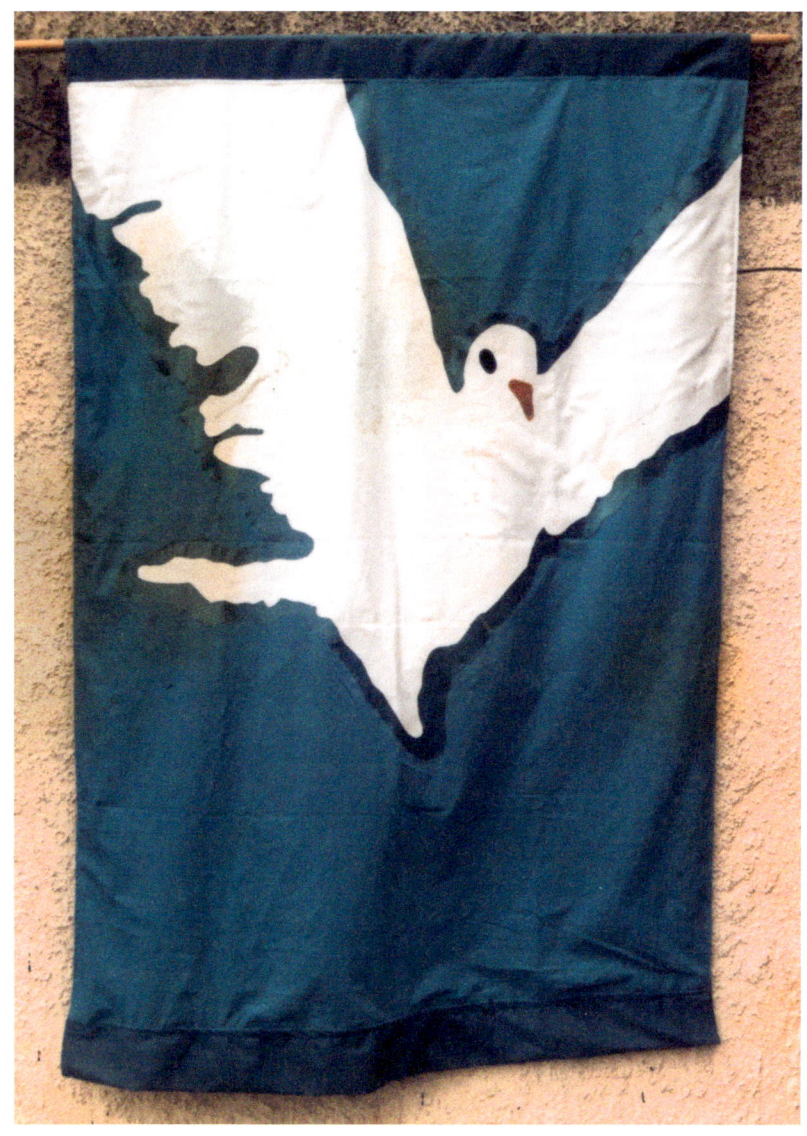

Previous pages: Thalia Campbell's banners on the fence at Greenham, 1980s.

Above: A banner made in 1982 by Ian and Thalia Campbell in support of the Manchester Nuclear Free Zone declaration of 1980. The design is based on the dove logo that appeared on posters and in other forms across the city to celebrate its decision to become the first nuclear-free city in the world. The Campbells made several banners using this design: the logo also appears in the banner on page 117.

Peace and Anti-Nuclear Banner Designs

At the beginning, when the walk and peace camp was initiated, the USA had not yet delivered the 96 Cruise missiles scheduled to be housed at Greenham. The decision to deploy them there had been taken in December 1979 and took three years to come to fruition. The women hoped that the camp and campaign could change this outcome. Banners stated: *We Don't Want Cruise Missiles Do You?*; *No Cruise*; *It's Them or Us*; *Camden Women against Cruise*; *Pay Women Not the Military*; *Greenham Women are Everywhere*; *Peace?*; *Borchester CND*.

These banners are akin to the design of contemporary and historic peace banners more broadly. The specific mention of Cruise missiles links them to Greenham and Molesworth – the only locations where this type of missile was in the UK. RAF Molesworth housed 64 Cruise missiles and another peace camp had been established there – occupied by men and women.

Most commonly, contemporary peace banners – particularly CND banners – demanded an end to nuclear weapons and bear the name of the town or city or organisation the banner represents. In this way they were designed to be carried and declare the presence of a group at any event or rally. When the Greenham women took part in another event – wherever they came from – they would usually identify as being from Greenham or part of the Greenham campaign.

The slogan 'Greenham Women are Everywhere' was used on some banners and badges. It encapsulates the belief – by some – that you did not have to be at Greenham to lend support to the anti-nuclear weapons campaign and to be called a Greenham woman. A typed and photocopied programme, made to hand out to those arriving at the airbase for an action in December 1985, explained: 'The words "Greenham Women are Everywhere" mean that all these things women do [visit, stay at weekends, live, send money and food, acting for peace in their community] are important. We need each other.'

This perspective particularly applied to women whose work and childcare responsibilities prevented them continuously camping on the Common. However, the view was not universal, and some maintained that to be a Greenham woman, it was necessary to live there.

Next pages: The first banner Thalia Campbell made after returning
from the Greenham march, using green curtain fabric to represent the fence.

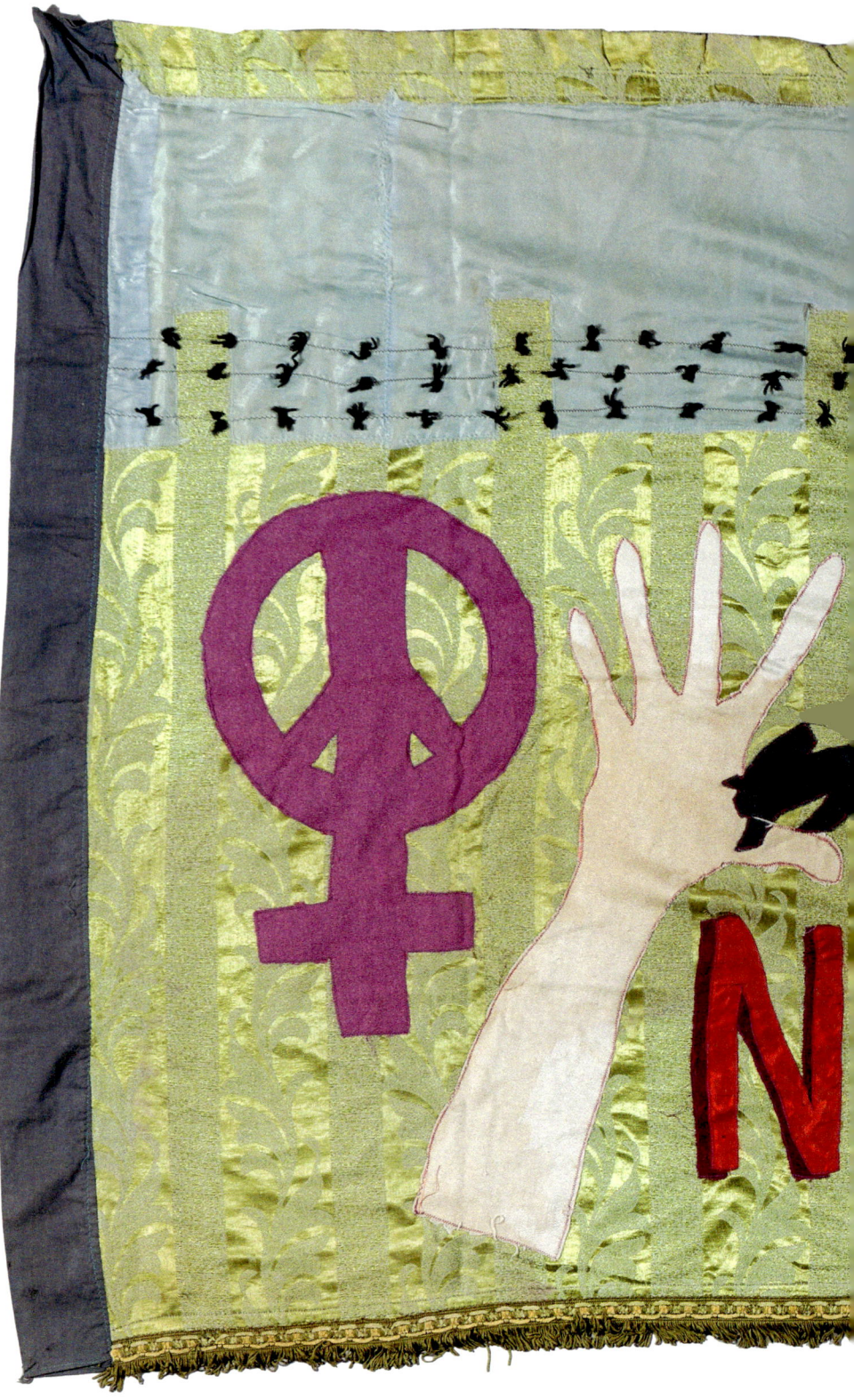

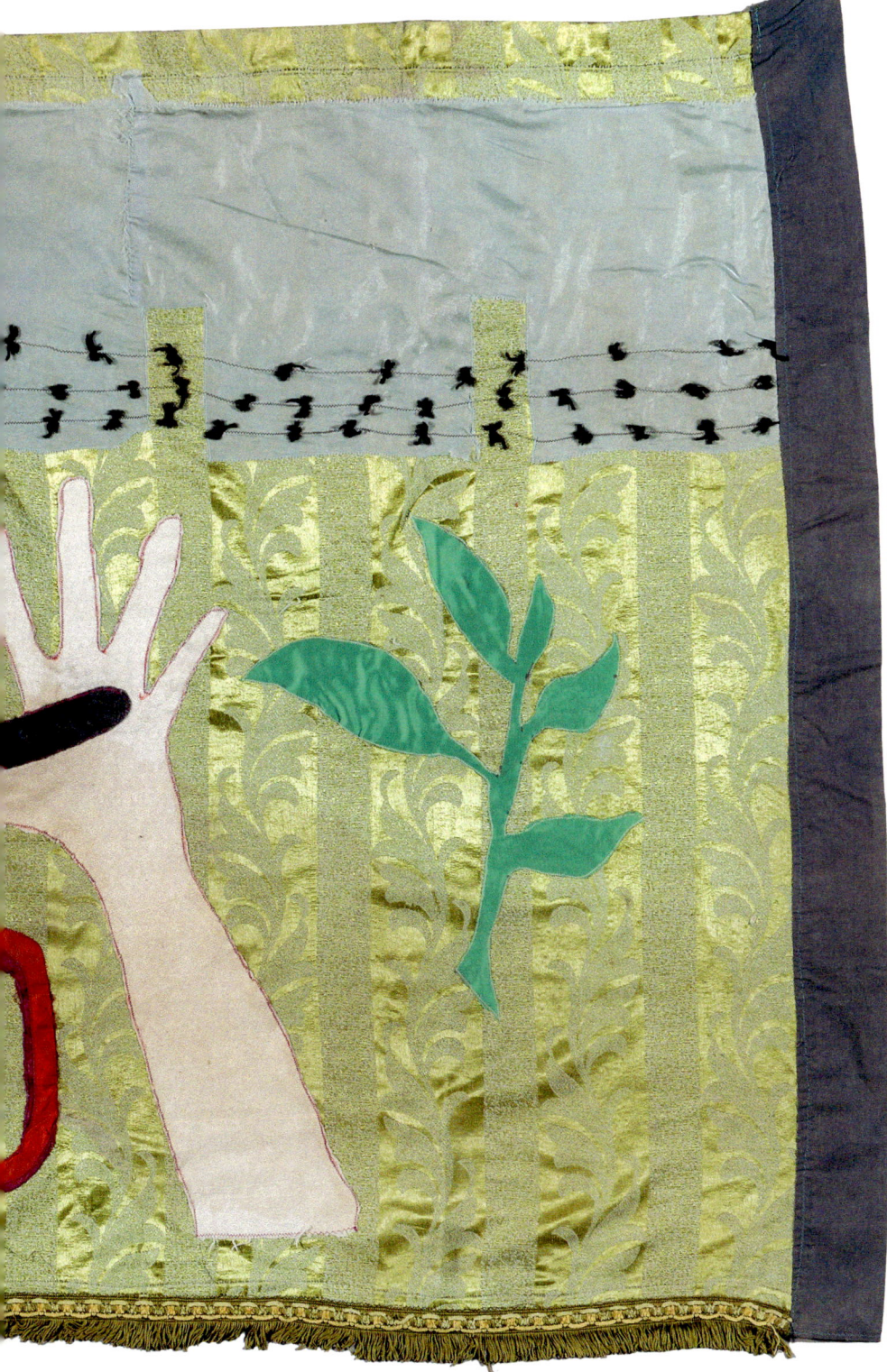

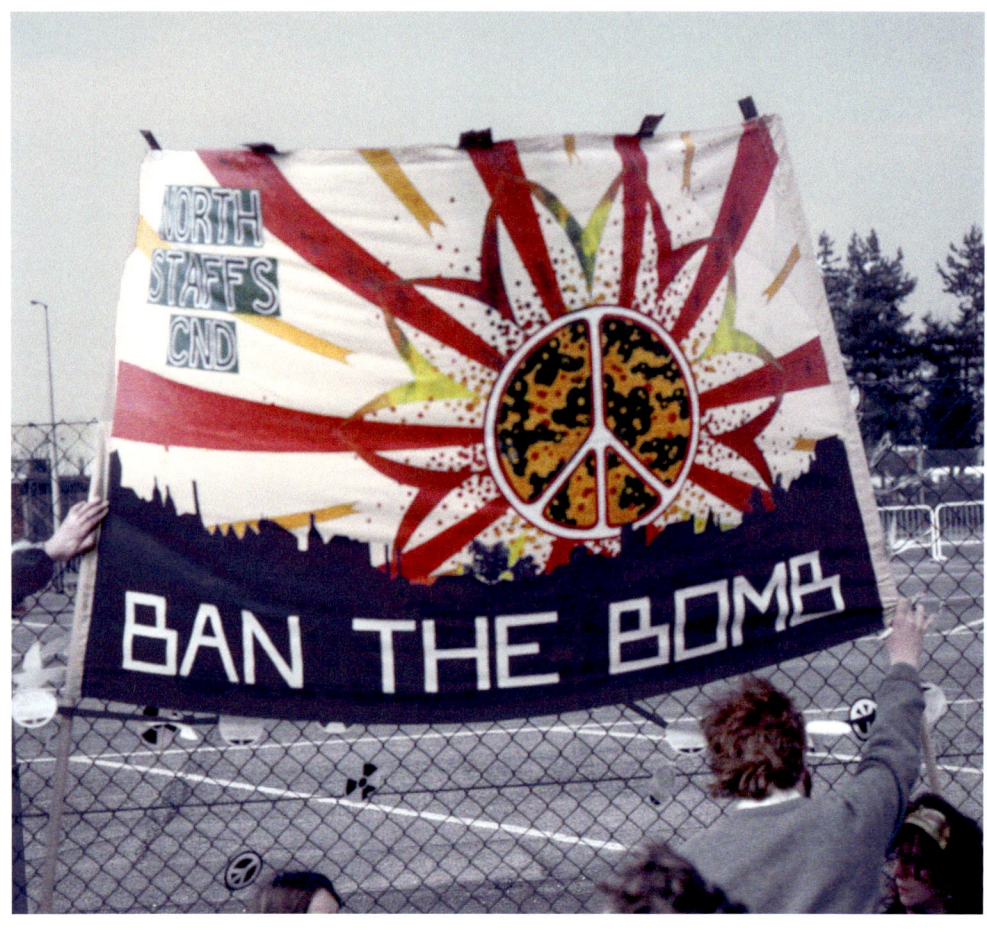

Above: A North Staffordshire CND banner, unknown artist.

Opposite: *Take a Risk for Peace Now*, designed by Andrea Kelland, Totnes Womens Centre in October 1981 originally for a CND London Rally. Thalia Campbell borrowed the banner to make a copy of the design (opposite, below), so it could be included in her touring exhibition '100 Years of Women's Banners'. She remade several banners for this reason, as they could not be borrowed for the duration of the exhibition. A postcard of this banner was often taken by women into prison, or sent to them there, serving time for actions they had undertaken at Greenham.

Next pages: *Borchester* CND banner, 112 × 174 cm. Borchester is the setting for the long running BBC Radio drama *The Archers*. This banner was designed and made by Thalia Campbell and Jan Higgs for the recording of *The Archers Christmas Concert* at Crosby on 22 October 1982. 'We gatecrashed [the] event and got all the cast except "Brian" signed up to Nuclear Free Ambridge and we gave them all pretty hand-painted badges.'[28]

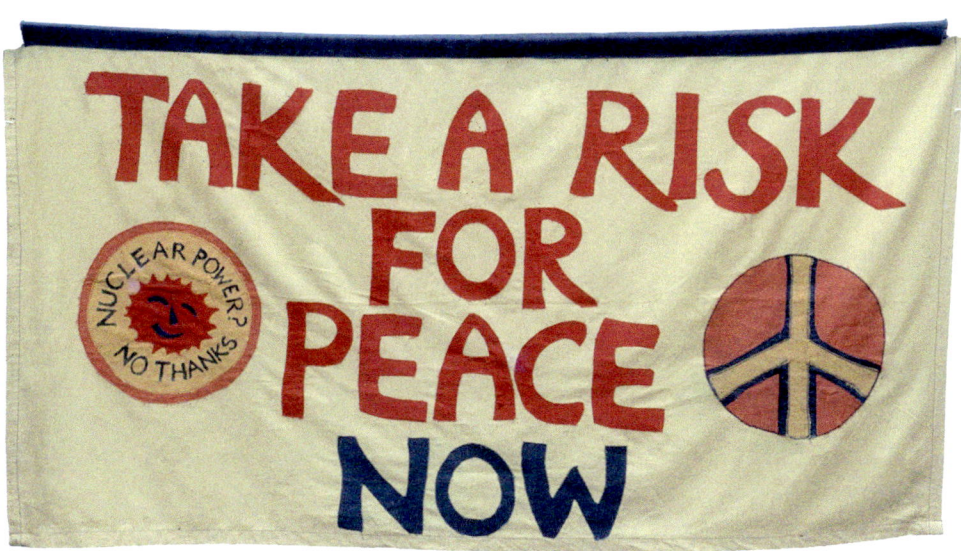

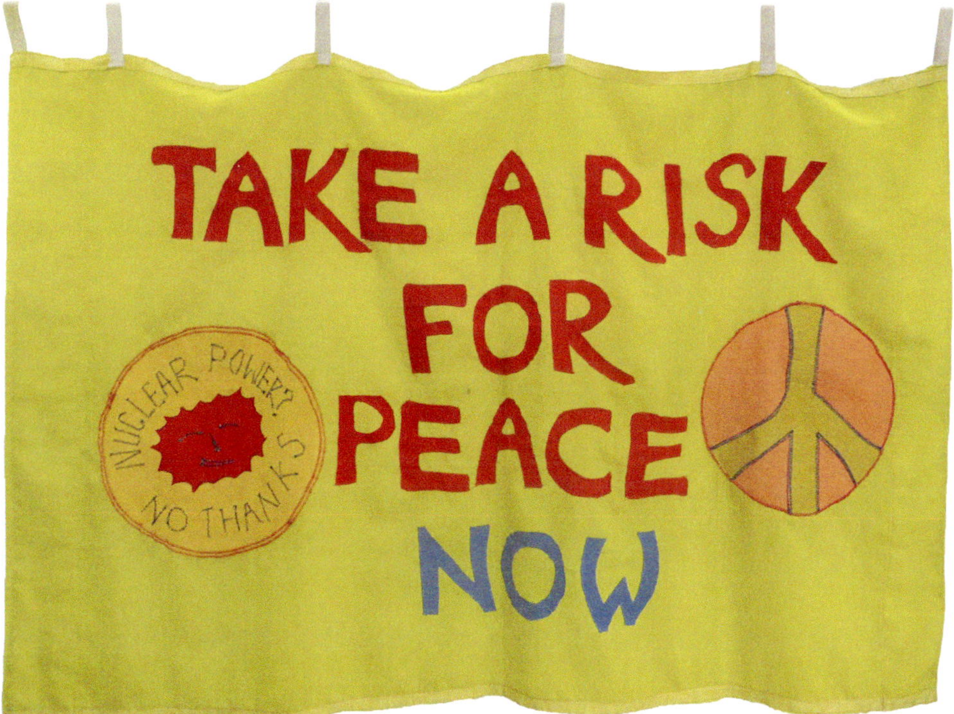

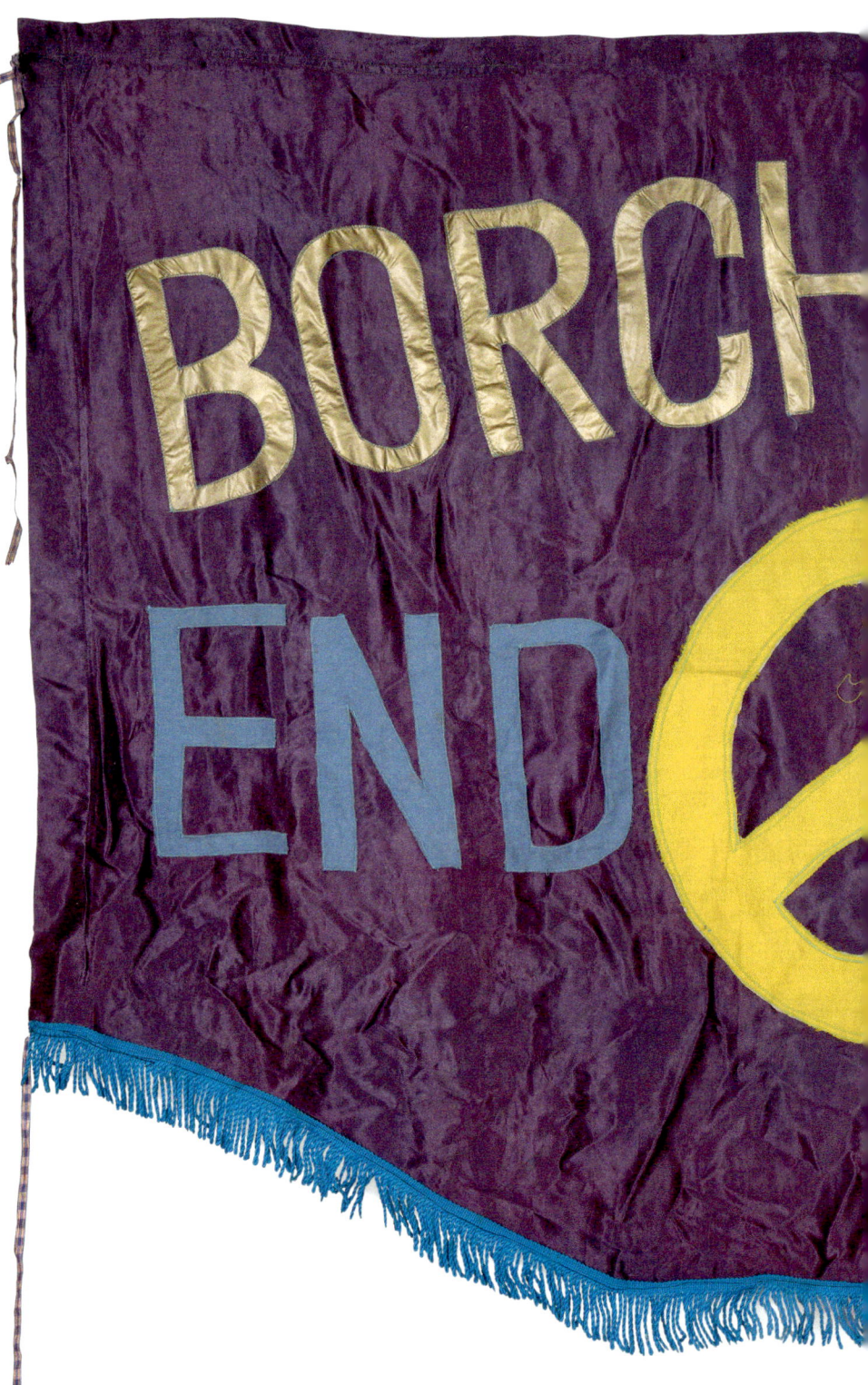

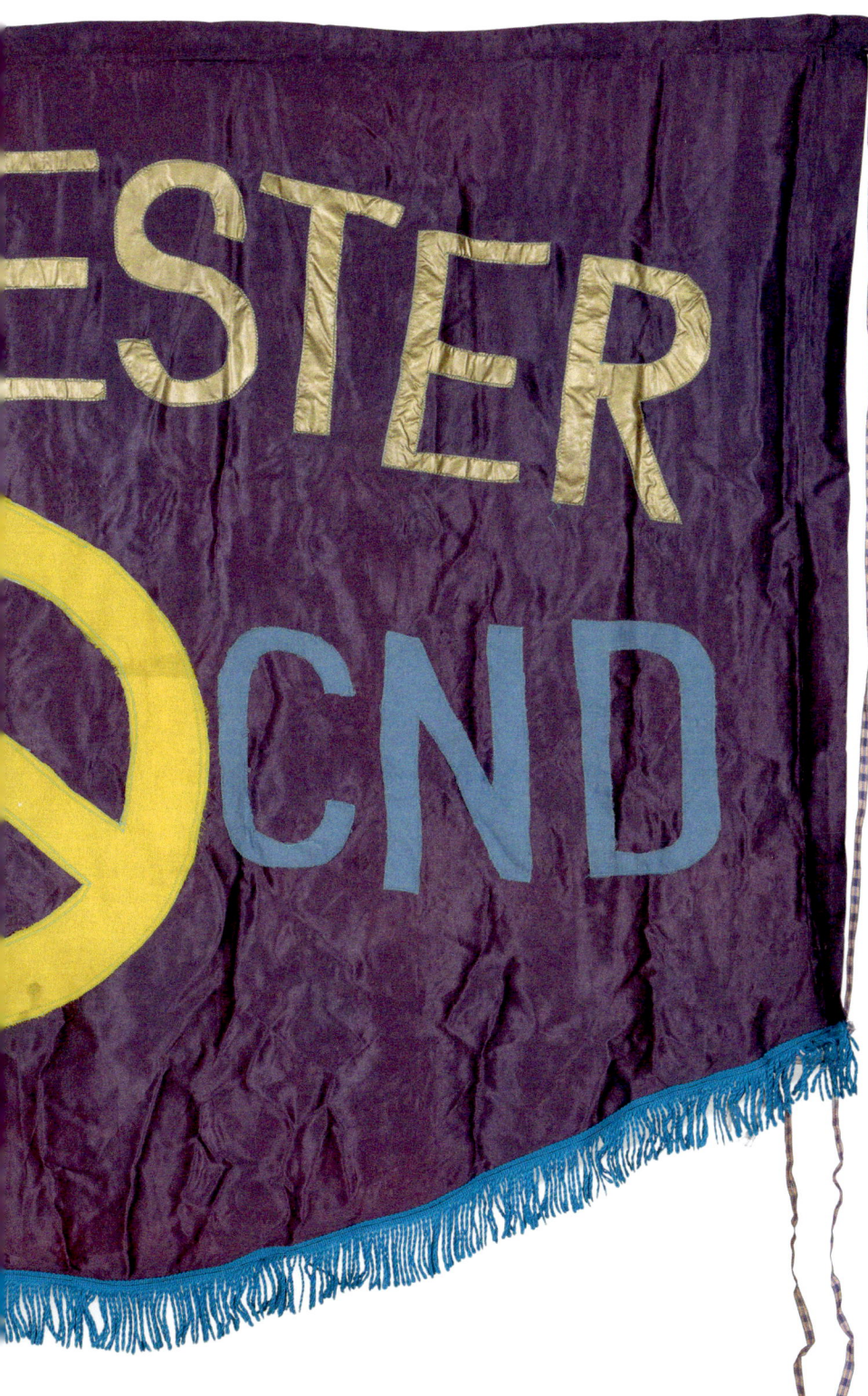

Anti-Cruise Banners

The Cruise missiles were delivered to the specially built silos at Greenham on 14 November 1983. A group of banners were made, emphasising the American military's role in the supply of weapons and occupation of the base – once common land: *US Cruise Missiles in the UK? No Way*; *F1 11 Off! to USA*; *State Terrorism. No, No, No*; *No More Star Wars*; *It's Us or Them*; *Big Bombs! Small Planet*. Similar sentiments to those expressed on this group of banners are declared on a Greenham badge that calls for people to 'Shout USA out'.

These designs frequently include an American flag. Under the slogan *Big Bombs! Small Planet* (page 91), caricatures of Russian and American military leaders sit on a cloud incorporating the colours and motifs of their country's flags. They are astride bombs, looking down on a small blue planet. On the *No More Star Wars* banner, the stars and stripes of the American flag are re-formed to create a fist, held-up against a mother shielding her child.

The *F1 11 Off! to USA* banner includes three fighter jet motifs and is made in red, white and blue fabric. It is a thinly veiled request for the United States Air Force (USAF) to 'fuck off'.[29] The text for the *State Terrorism. No, No, No* banner is appliquéd over a representation of the American flag.

The most complex of the designs by Campbell – *It's Us or Them* – labels a missile 'USA', below swastikas and National Front symbols. These appliquéd motifs are shown opposed to a bright world of plentiful food and unity.

These banners draw attention to the American military as the source of the bombs and perceived US role in the nuclear threat. They are designed to inform the viewer who the proponents of the Cold War were, as well as campaigning for change.

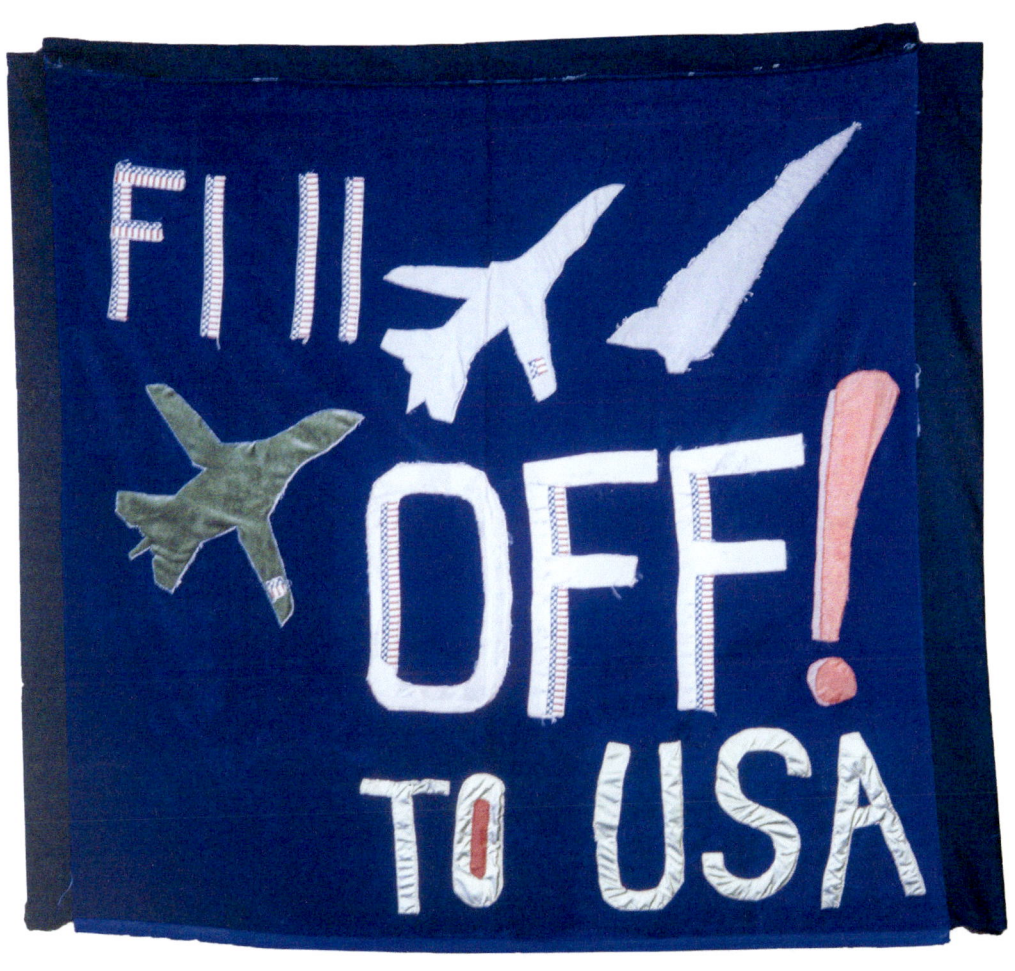

Above: *F1 II Off! to USA*. Made by Thalia Campbell, Jan Higgs and Ian Campbell for the blockade of the United States Air Force nuclear strike bomber base at RAF Upper Heyford (in Oxfordshire) on 31 December 1982.

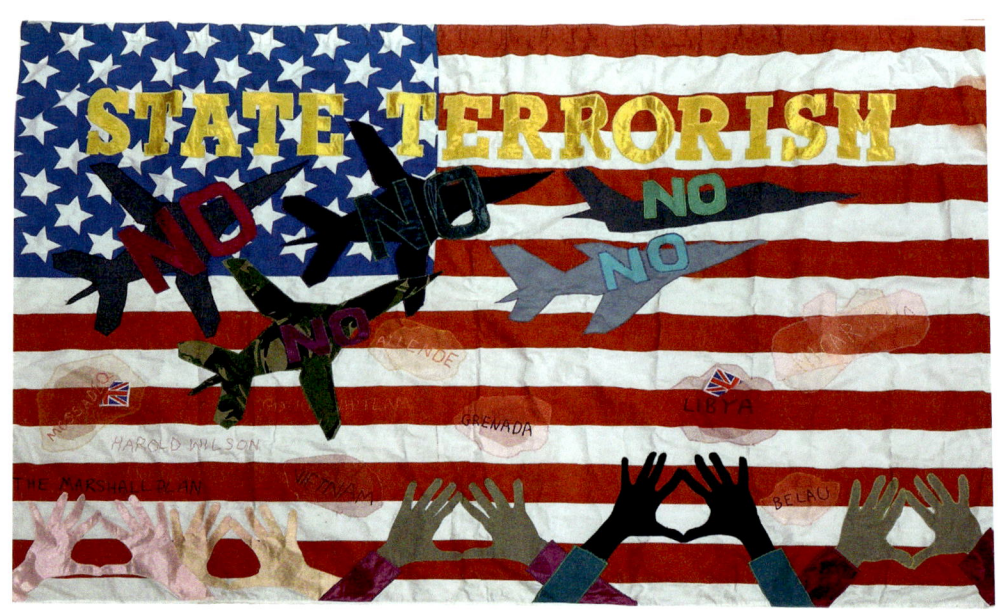

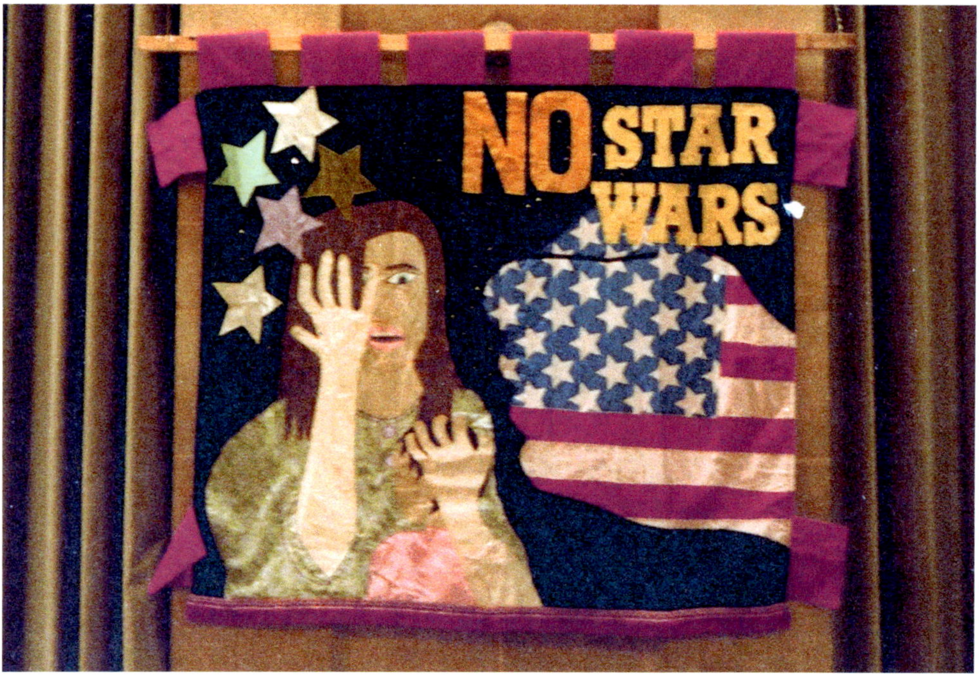

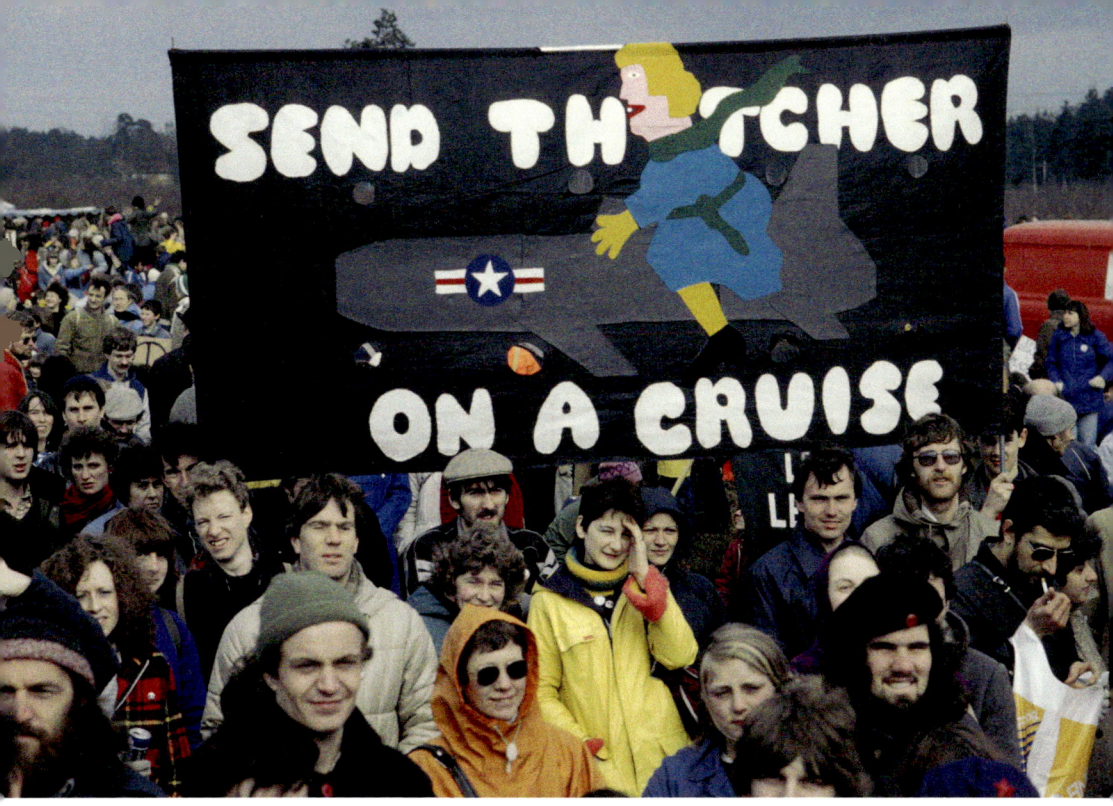

Above: *Send Thatcher on a Cruise* banner at a demonstration at Greenham on 1 April 1983. Photograph by Jacob Sutton.

Opposite, top: *State Terrorism No, No, No*. Thalia Campbell, together with other women, made this banner in response to the United States bombing of Libya on 15 April 1986 at a workshop in Leamington Spa. She made two versions of this banner; one where the hands are floating on the background, and this second one where they are attached to sleeves.

Opposite, bottom: *No Star Wars*, by Thalia Campbell. She chose the colours of the stars above the woman's head to evoke the colours of bruises, to suggest the effect of being hit by the fist of American militarism.

Fear for Future Generations

A distinct subset of Greenham banner designs expresses overt fear for the impact of nuclear armament on future generations. This same perspective is reflected in the letter delivered to the Greenham Base Commander at the end of the original protest march: 'We fear for the future of all our children and for the future of the living world which is the basis of all life.'[30] On the reverse of the leaflet handed out during the walk there 'was a picture of a baby born dead and deformed – a victim of radiation from the Hiroshima explosion.'[31]

Specific concern for their own children motivated the engagement of many Greenham protestors: 'The emotion that drove me was not so much fear as anger... That if any harm came to my children, then I would feel... an inconsolable kind of pain. I was reading in the paper about nuclear power; and how radiation affects the youngest most, starting with the embryo in a living creature's womb, because their cells are dividing fastest.'[32]

In some women, concern about nuclear power and the dumping of nuclear waste, particularly in Wales, predated a focus on the impact of nuclear weapons on children. Prior to the Greenham campaign, Campbell made a banner declaring *Nuclear Free Wales*.

Emotive Greenham banner slogans expressing concern for future generations include: *There Is No Future for Our Grandchildren in Nuclear War. Protest That They May Survive*; *Dear Margaret [Thatcher], Here's Your Christmas Cheque. Don't Spend It on Bombs for the Children. Love Mother xxx*; *It's Never Too Late to Have a Happy Childhood*; *For Our Children and for Life on Earth. South Chiltern Peace Group*. *Be Positive for Nuclear Disarmament*; *Girls Say No to the Bombs*; *I Want to Grow Up Not Blow Up*.

The last plea was taken from a child's letter and was also reproduced on a Greenham badge; the text written in a child-like script beside an image of a teddy bear. Many of those who took part in the initial march were young mothers. Four babies were recorded as part of the group. Campbell's banner *Girls Say No to the Bombs* was made with the children of

Opposite: Letter fastened to the fence at Greenham (see also the badge on page 197).

Next pages: *It's Never too Late to Have a Happy Childhood*, unknown artist, 98 × 254 cm.

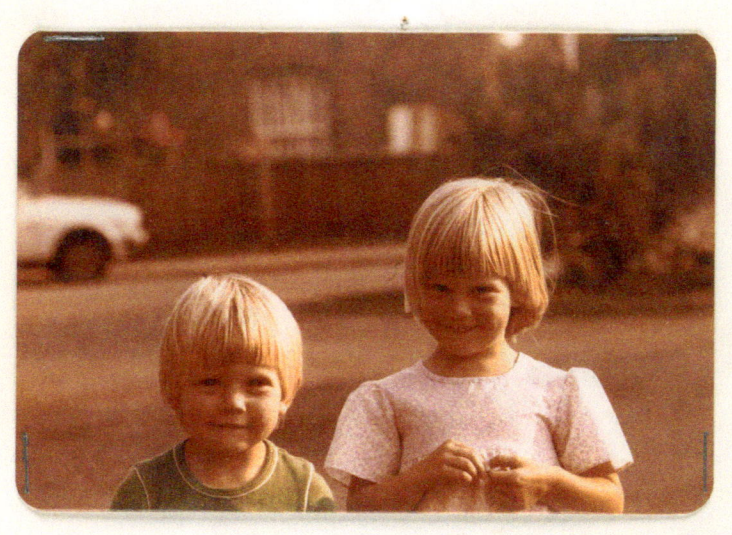

we want to grow up
not blow up.

love

gayle and sam
++++   ++++

4   2

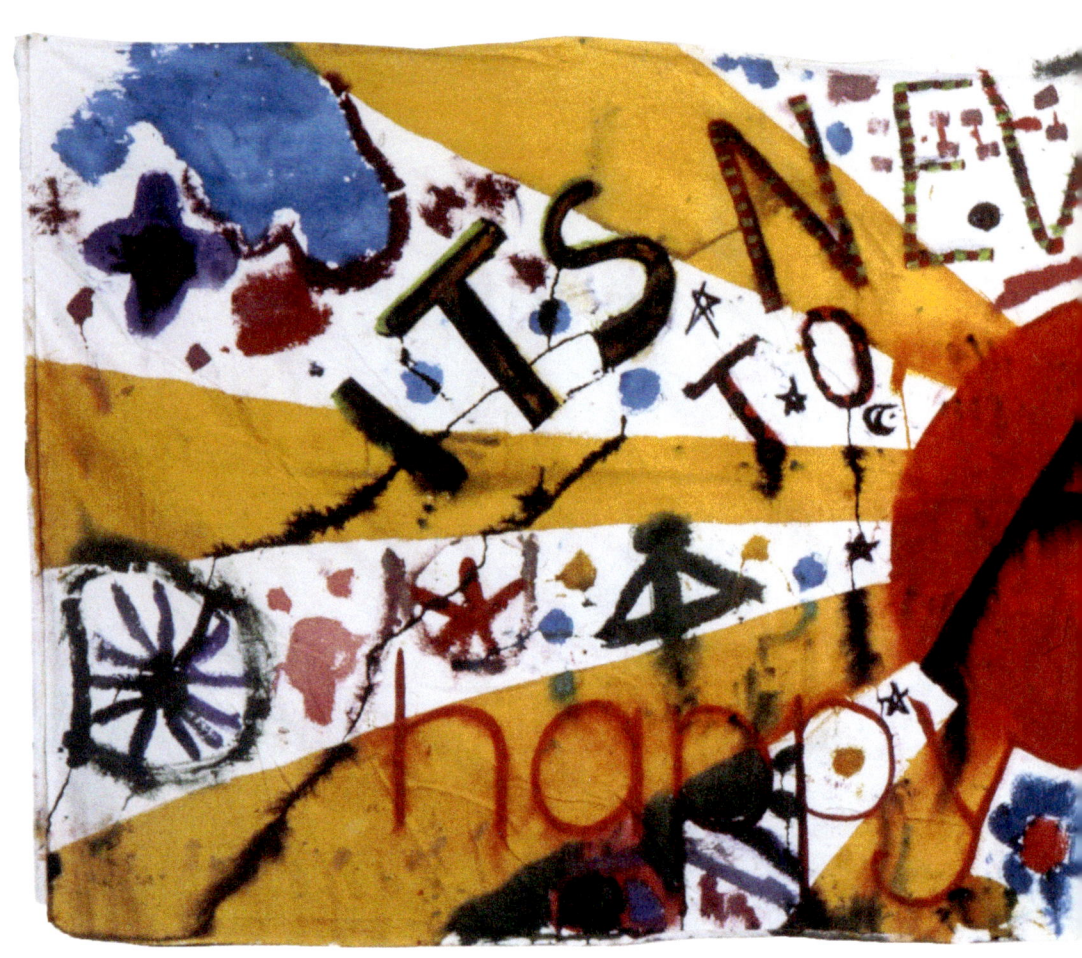

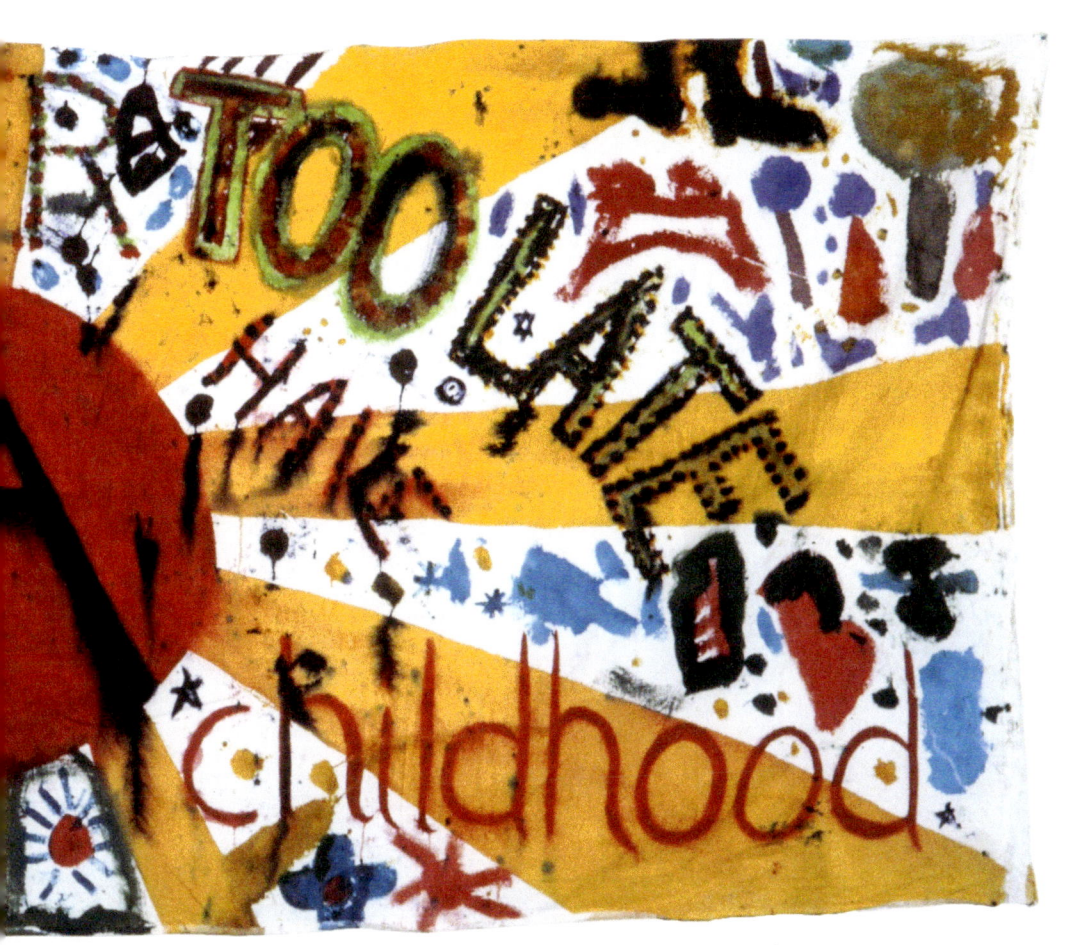

women at the camp in mind. A row of tactile objects is sewn to the bottom edge of the banner, in place of traditional tassels, which children could play with and be entertained by when the banner was hung on the fence.

The link between children and the nuclear threat was a principle narrative in Greenham's largest protest event Embrace the Base in December 1982, when more than 30,000 people linked arms around the length of the airbase and attached personal effects, especially children's clothes and toys to the fence.

The banners expressing a fear for future generations asked people to see the nuclear threat from a mother's or child's perspective. This narrative was sometimes turned against the Greenham women in the press and by members of the public who were against the camp. They faced criticism for abandoning their families to live at Greenham, just as the anti-suffragists represented suffragettes as neglectful mothers and wives.

Grave public concern about the deployment of nuclear arms was not universal. Opinion differed regarding the likelihood of war, as well as in respect of the country's readiness to instruct and help its inhabitants if a nuclear bomb was dropped. From one perspective, the Government's preparations were inadequate and futile: bunkers for the powerful, and little or no resources for most of the population, except instructions in home-made shelter building, barely changed from those issued during World War Two. An alternative view saw the readiness of nuclear weapons in both Soviet and NATO territories as sufficient deterrent to engagement by either side; the risk reduced by the weapons themselves.

The BBC *Panorama* episode 'If The Bomb Drops', aired in March 1980, exposed the inadequacies of the *Protect and Survive* guidance and infrastructure developed by the Government. The Greenham women felt the nuclear threat keenly, and exposure of the lack of preparedness fed their view.

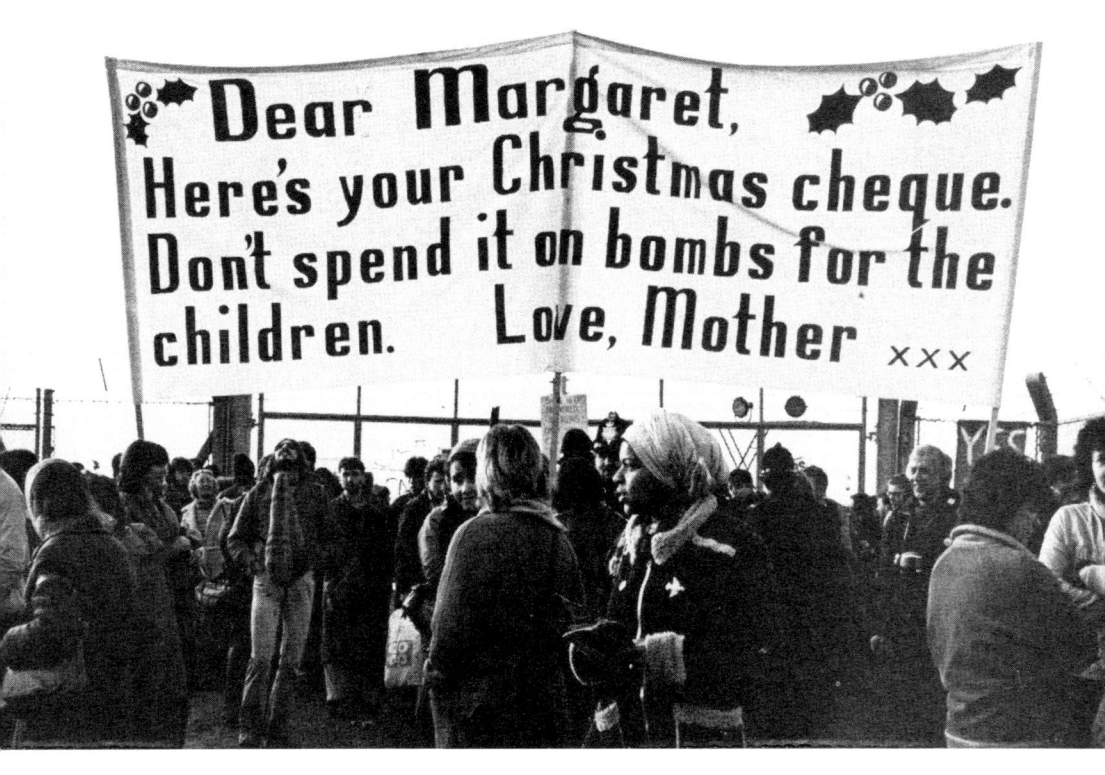

Above: A banner at the Embrace the Base event, Greenham Common, December 1982, unknown artist. Photograph by Brenda Prince.

Next pages: *Girls Say No to the Bombs*, 117 × 156.5 cm. Thalia Campbell had the children at the camp in mind when she made this banner. A row of tactile objects is sewn to the bottom edge of the banner, in place of traditional tassels, which children could play with and be entertained by when the banner was hung on the fence.

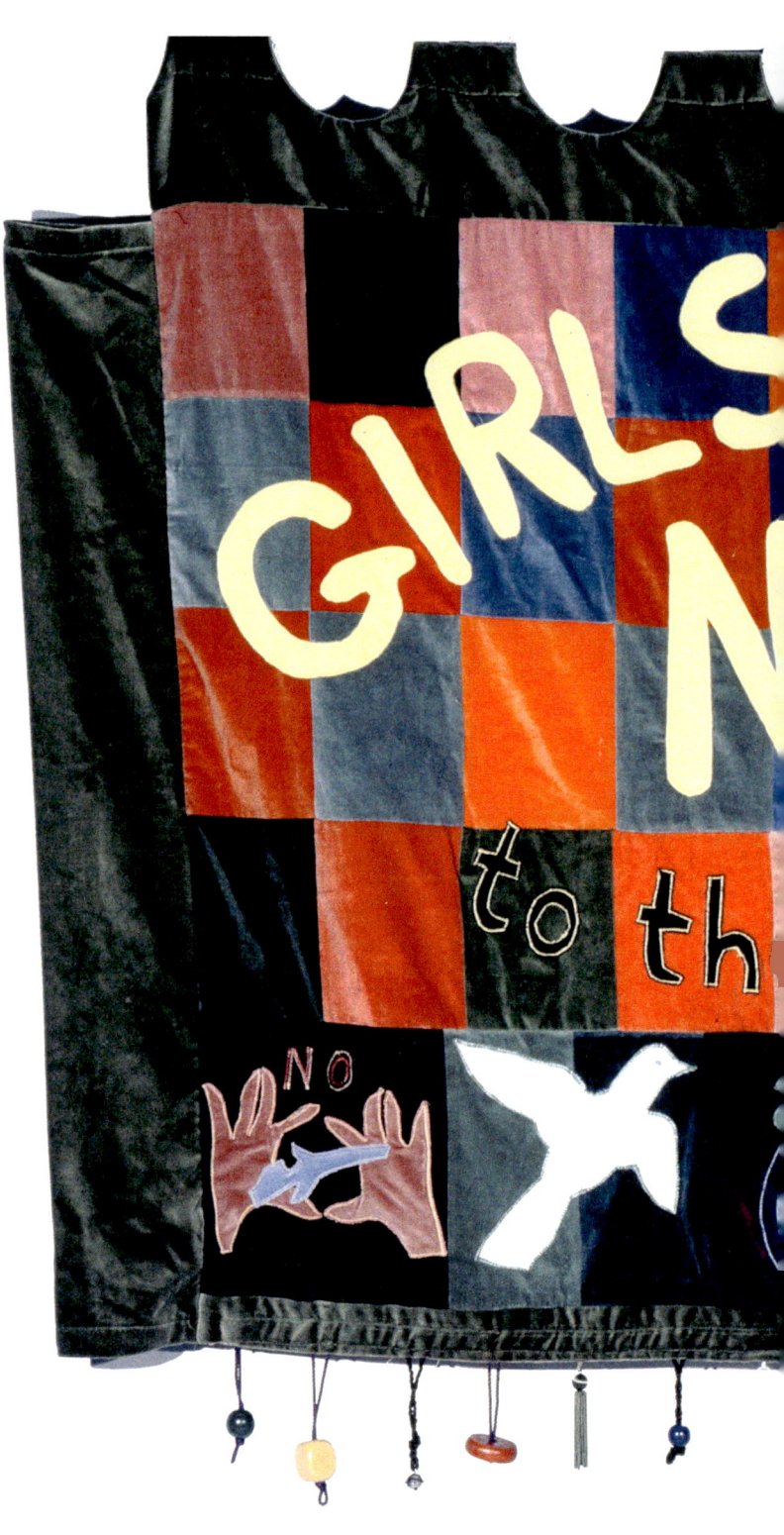

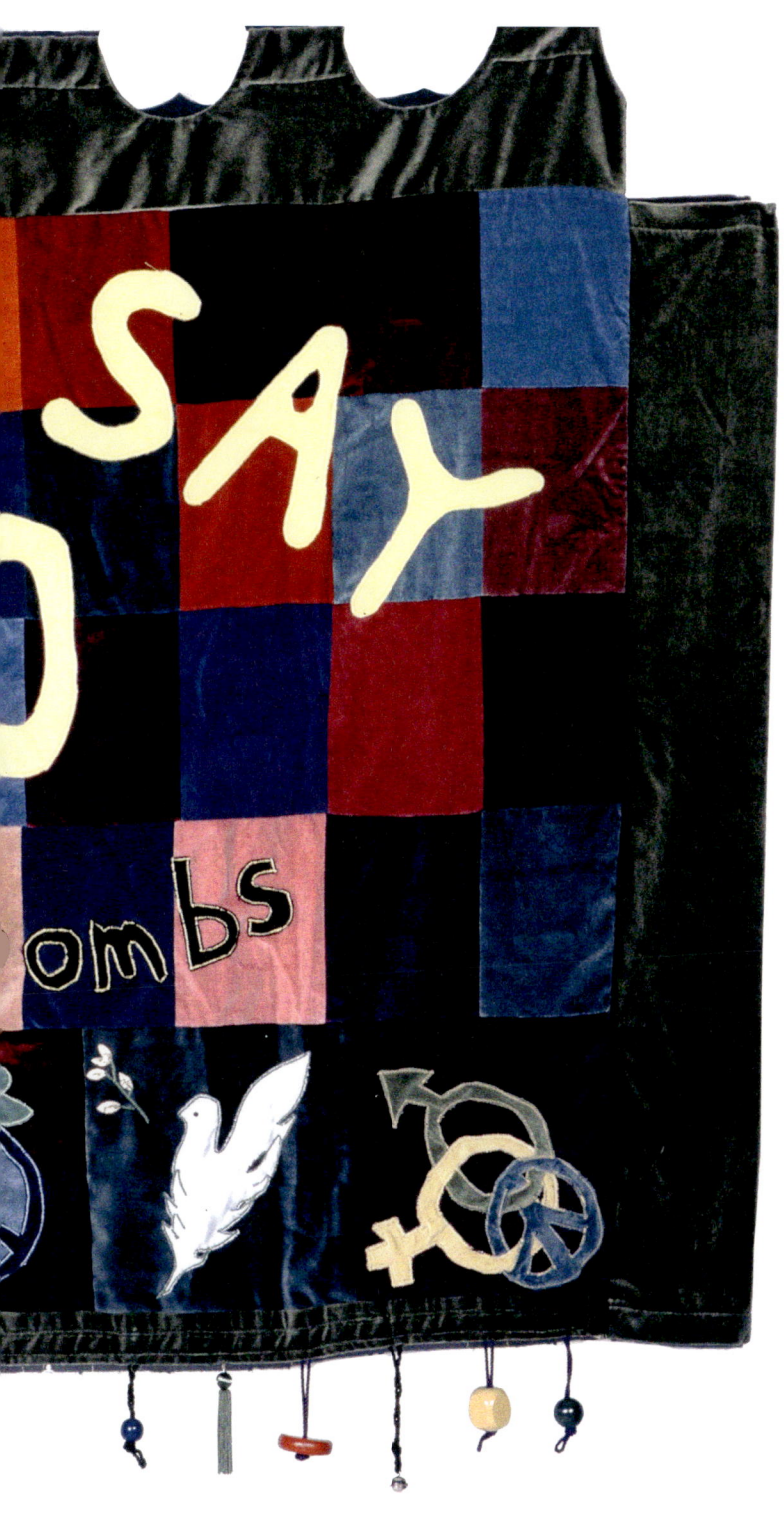

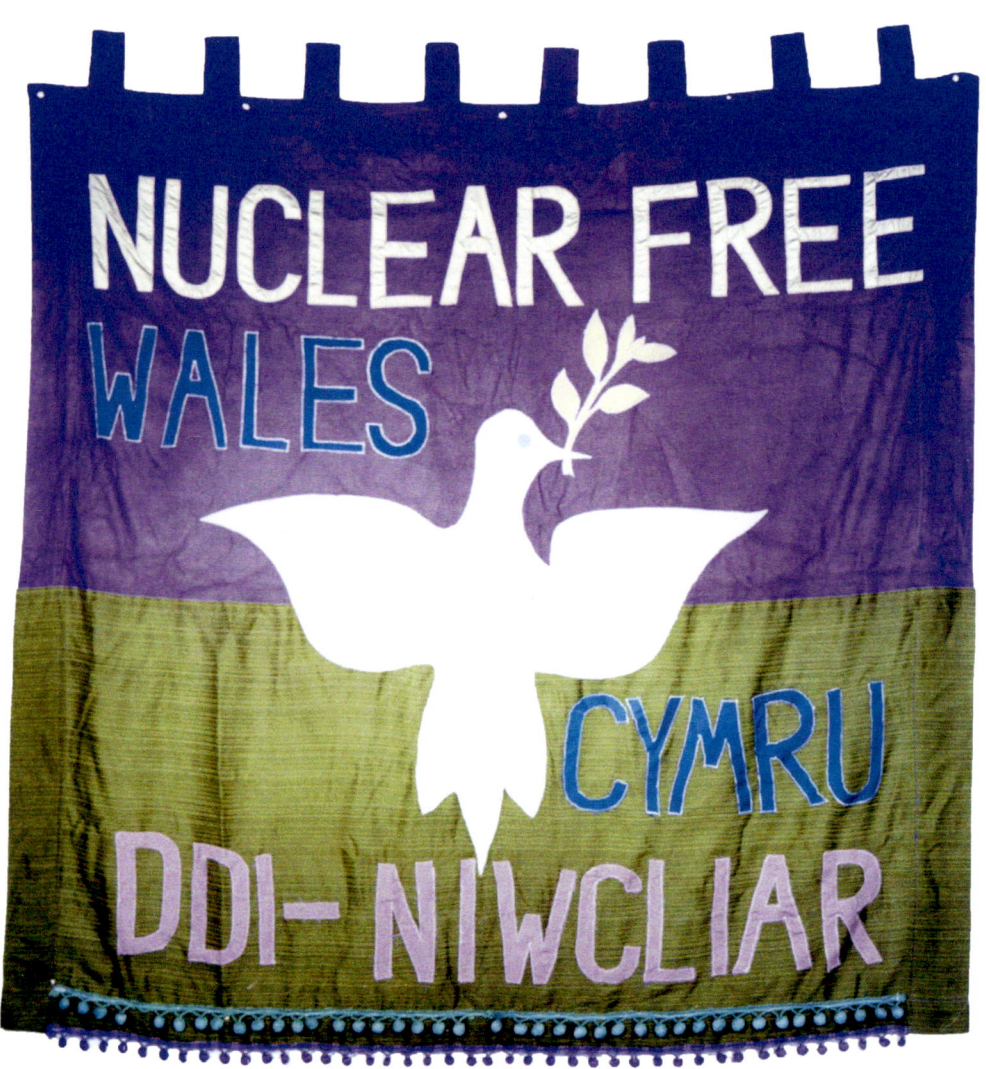

Above: *Nuclear Free Wales*, c. 1979, 196 × 196 cm. Designed and made by Thalia Campbell with help from Ian Campbell and Jan Higgs. Suffragette colours are employed: purple symbolising dignity, white for purity and honour, and green for new life. The banner was made in protest against proposals (eventually dropped) to dump nuclear waste in locations across North Wales.

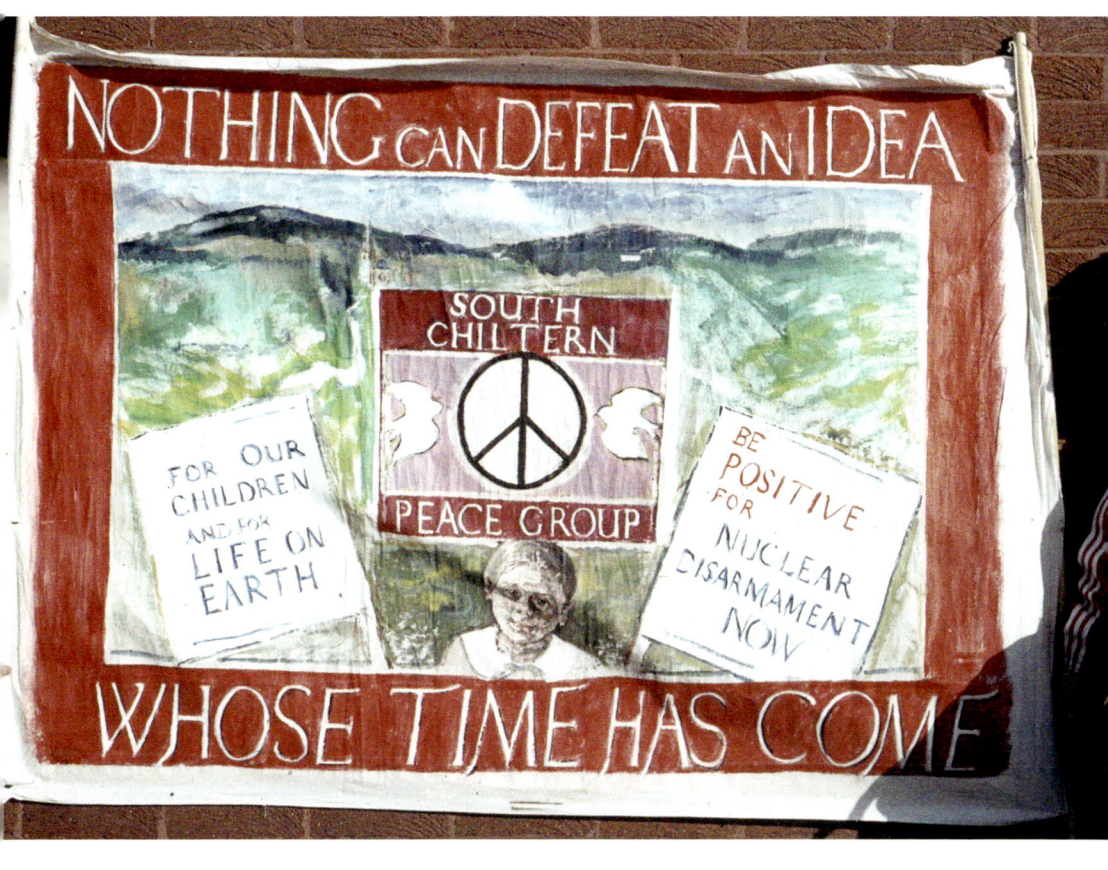

Above: *Nothing Can Defeat an Idea Whose Time Has Come*, South Chiltern Peace Group.

Next pages: *Ni Neu Nhw / It's Us or Them*. Made by Thalia Campbell, Ian Campbell and Jan Higgs for the blockade of RAF Greenham Common, 4–8 July 1983.

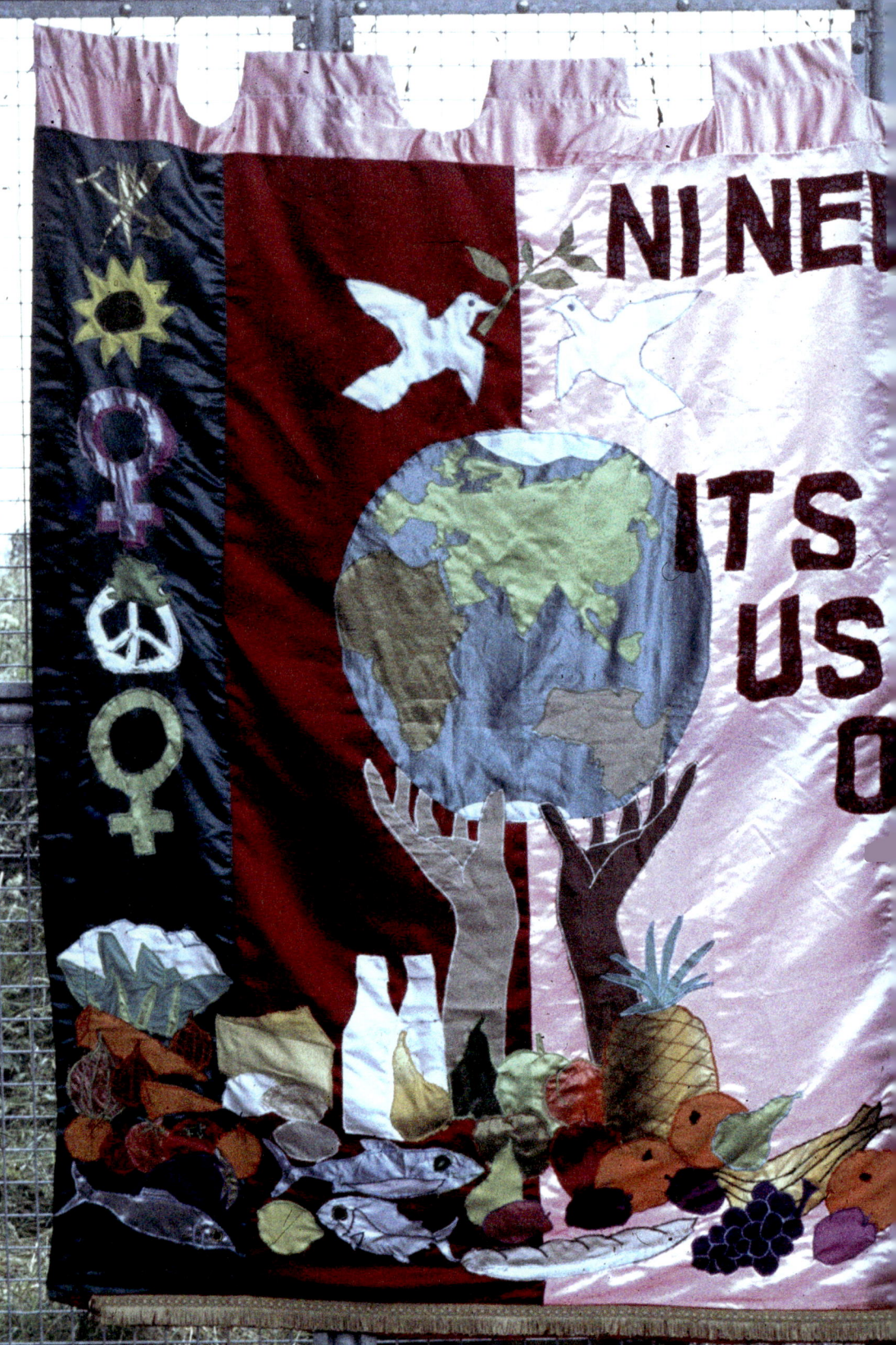

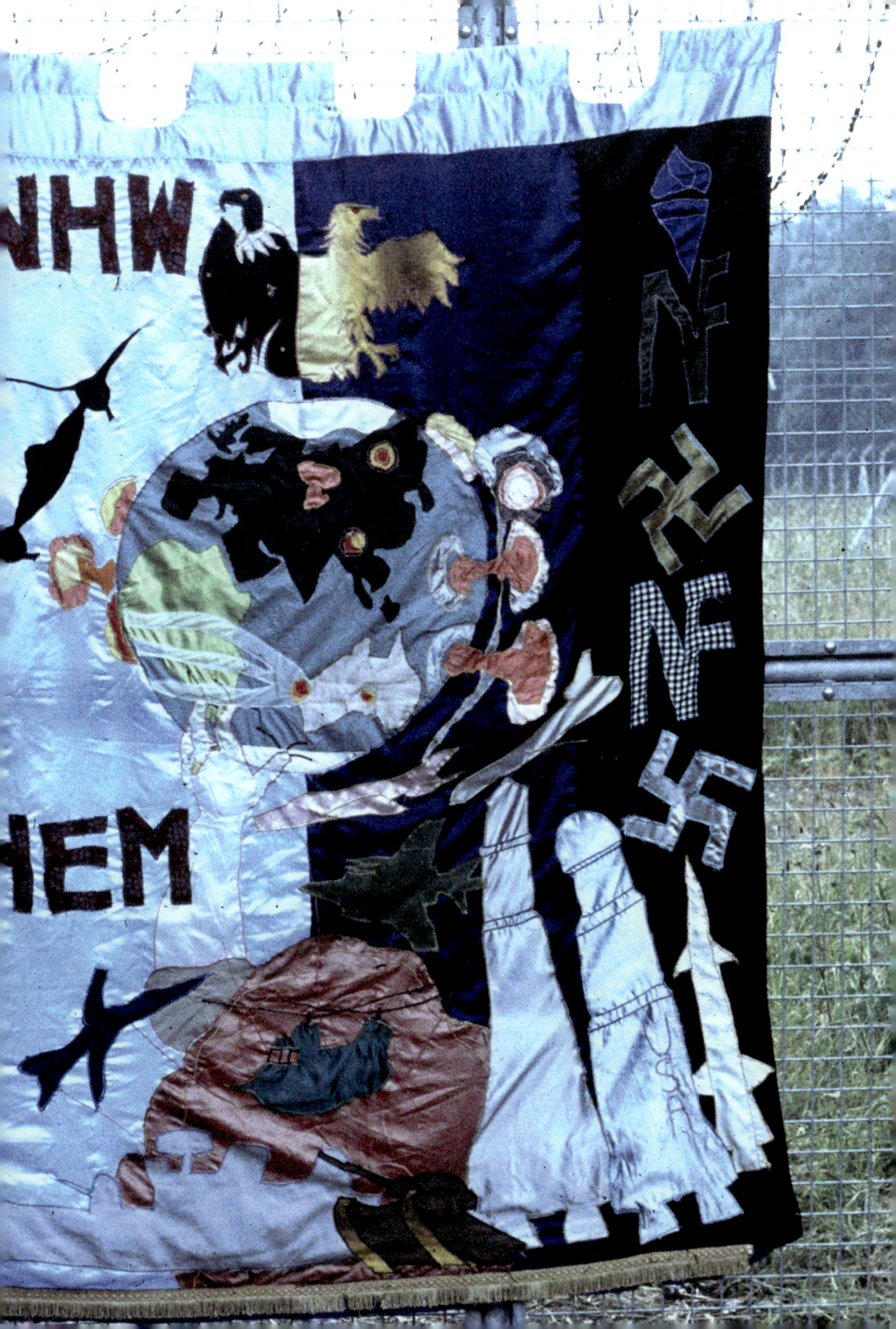

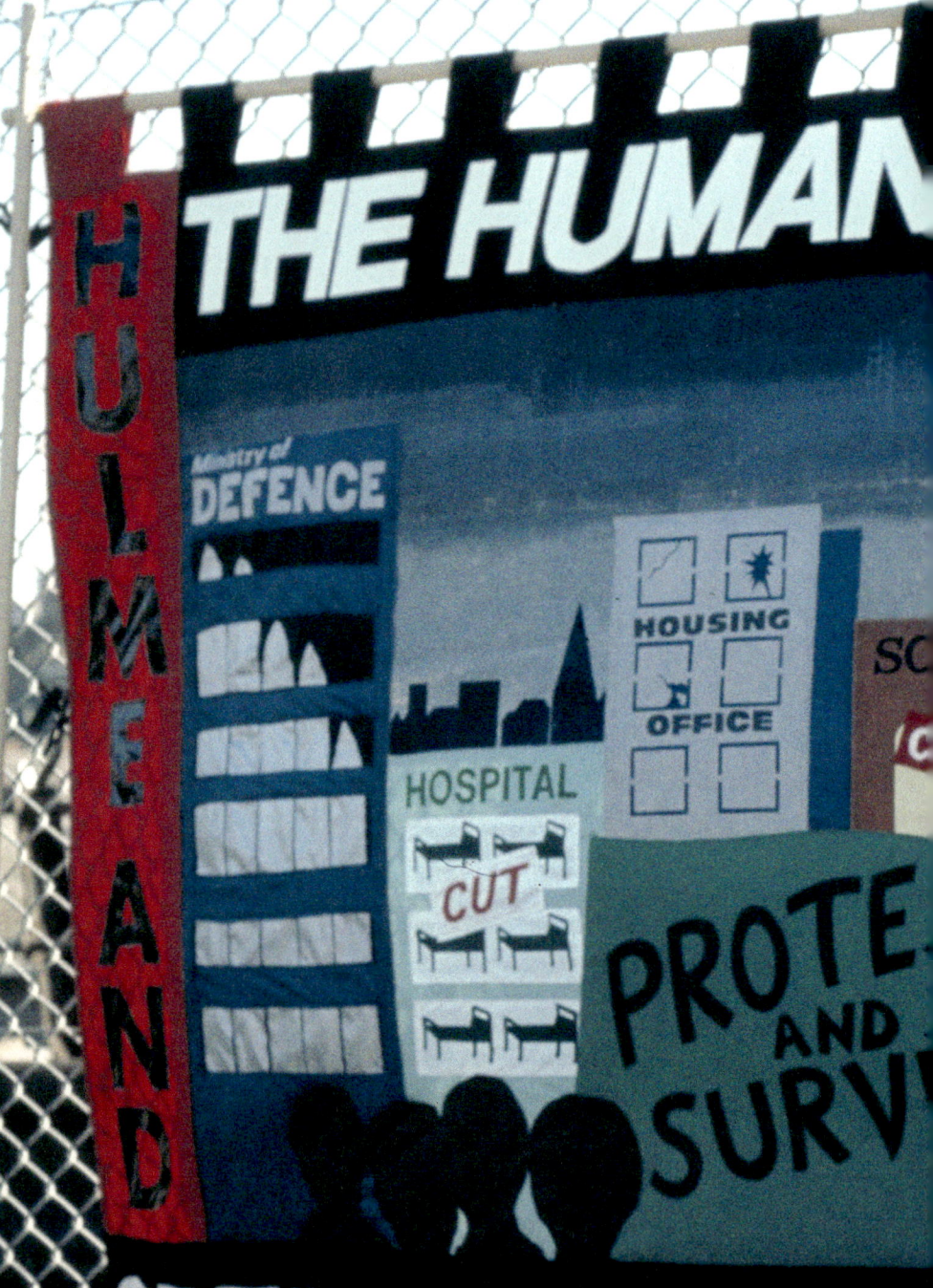

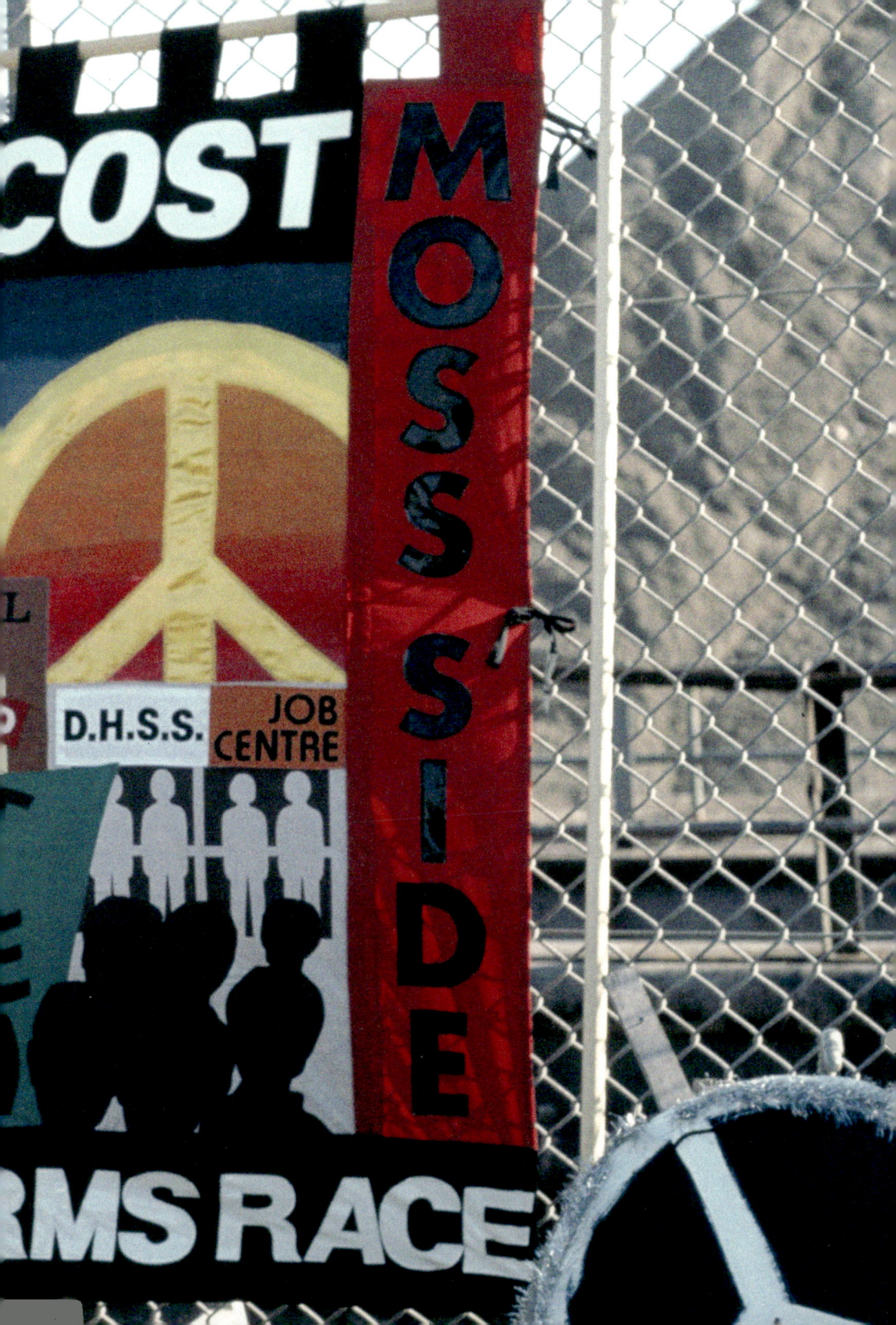

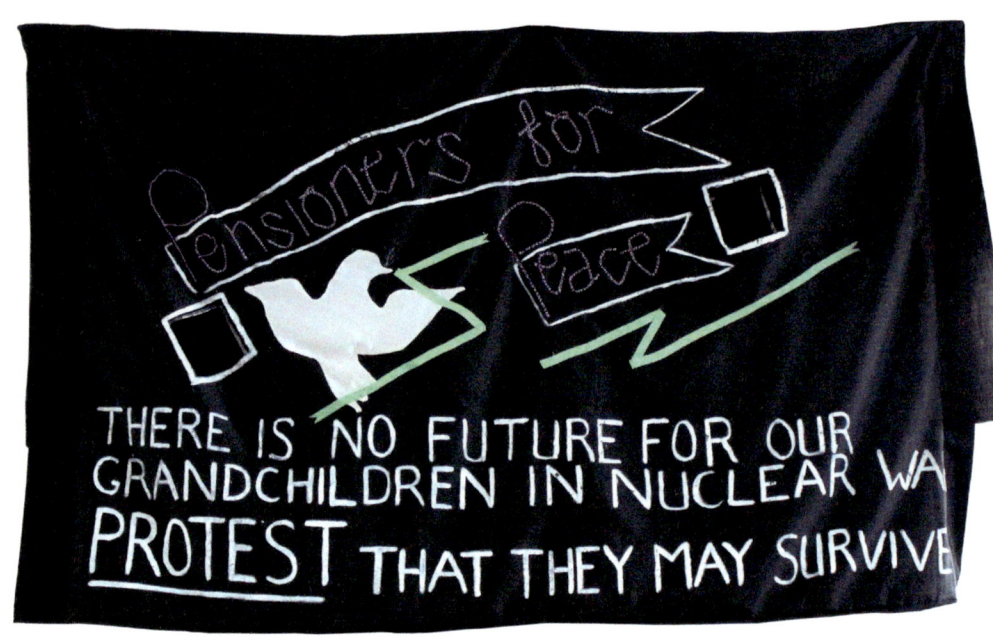

Previous pages: *The Human Cost of the Nuclear Arms Race. Hulme and Moss Side.* Design by Thalia Campbell.

Above: *Pensioners for Peace* banner, unknown artist.

Opposite: Pensioners Vigil at Greenham Common on 20 May 1984. Photograph by Raissa Page.

Next pages: Protesters at Greenham Common, 1983. The phrase *Protest, Survive* satirises the government's official advice for nuclear war, *Protect and Survive*. Photograph by Raissa Page.

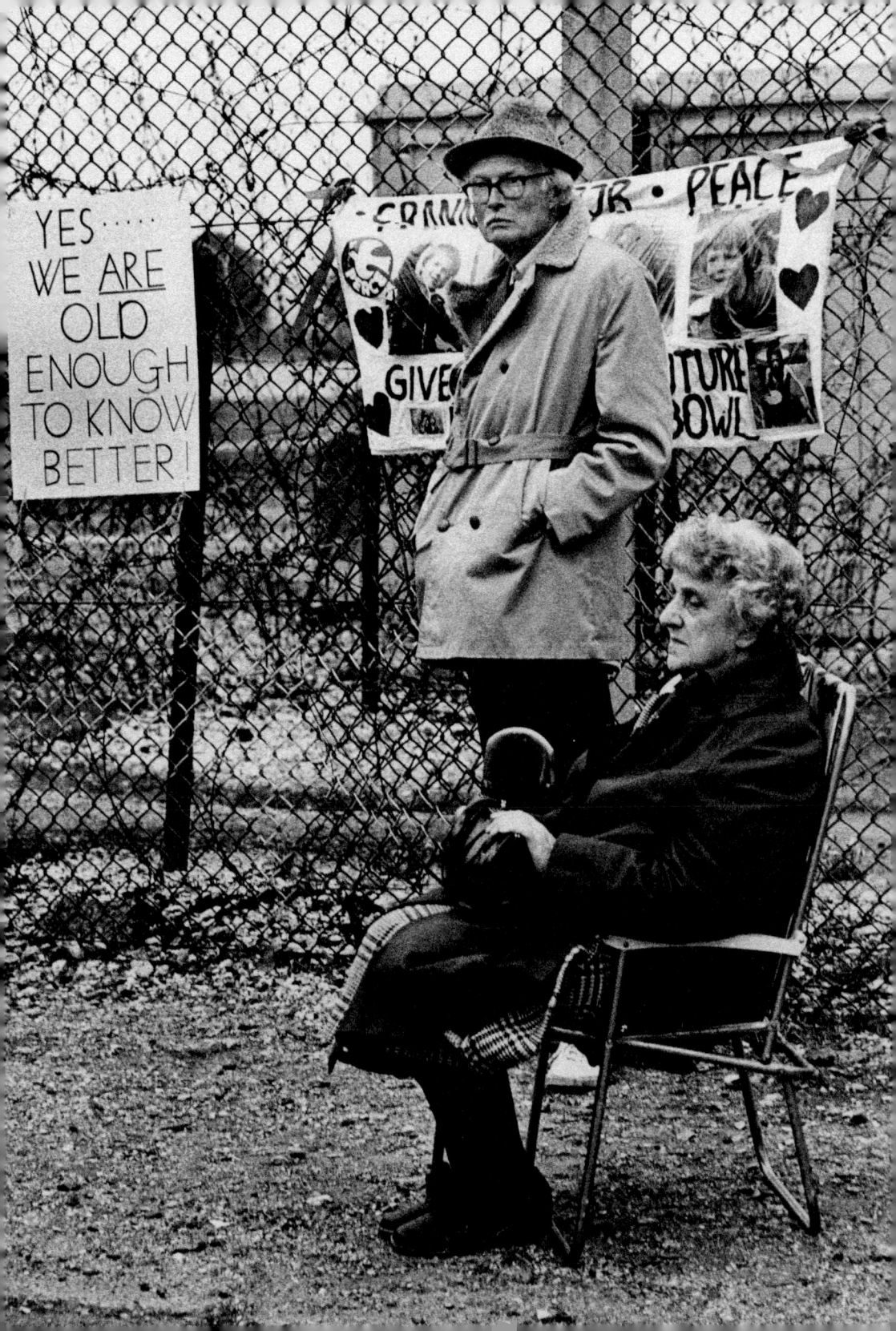

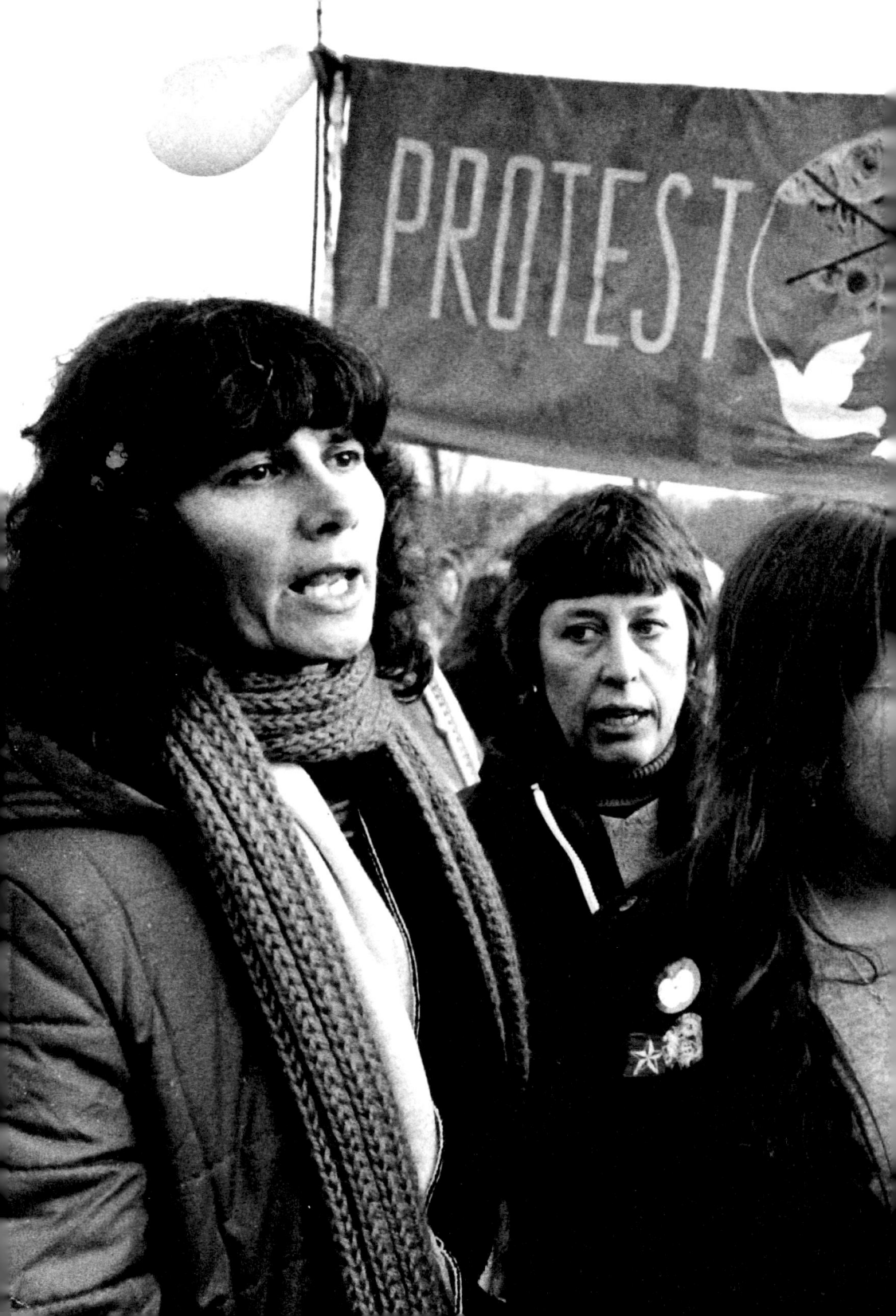

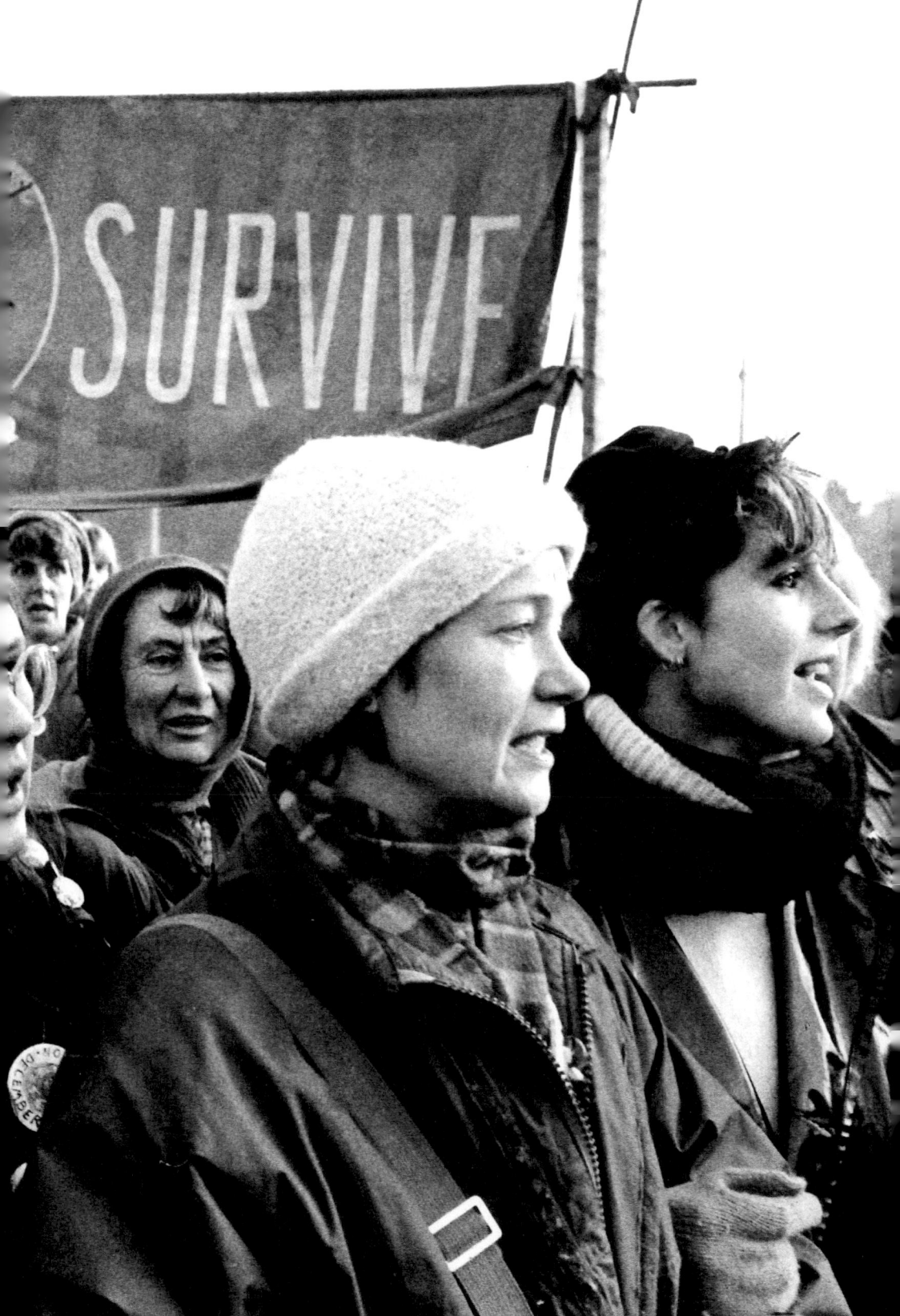

Banners against Male Dominance and Aggression

The peace camp was not initially strictly women-only, although predominantly women-led. Men had taken a supporting role during the first walk to Greenham and continued to do so at the camp in its early months. The situation came to a head early in 1982. In advance of the Equinox Festival on 21 March, the decision was taken that no men be allowed to live or stay overnight at the camp.

In *Greenham Women are Everywhere*, published in 1983, Katrina Howse explained her belief in the decision: 'I want to say very strongly that having women's actions in my view has got nothing to do with excluding men. It's got to do with – for once, just once – giving women a chance, including women. It's so women – who have been kept out of politics and all walks of life for so long, who've been pushed back into the home and told that they can only function in one small closed-in area to do with children and nurturing – can come out of those areas and take part in politics and actually begin to affect and change the world, and that's Why Women... It's positive.'[33]

A further argument for a women's only camp was that the commitment to non-violence was more likely to be maintained during actions, if the participants were all female. This determination created some divisions amongst Greenham women but did little to change the narrative of the camp's campaign, as the focus had always been on representing women's perspectives on nuclear warfare.

The sense that decisions concerning war and armament were made by men, against the wishes of women, is the narrative stance of a group of banners. These designs focus on perceived male political dominance and a masculine predisposition towards war and aggression. They argue: '*Coercion Is Not Government*', *Sylvia Pankhurst, Then or Now*; *Not In Our Name*; *Women's Struggle Won the Vote Use It for Disarmament*; '*The British People Are Prepared to Be Blown to Atomic Dust If Necessary*', *Lord Home, 1961*; *Did You Vote to Become America's Largest Aircraft Carrier? Support the Women's Peace Camp*; *War Is Menstrual Envy*; *No More Toys for the Boys*; *Remembrance Is Not Enough*; *No Cruise Please. There Are Better Ways to Prove Your Virility.*

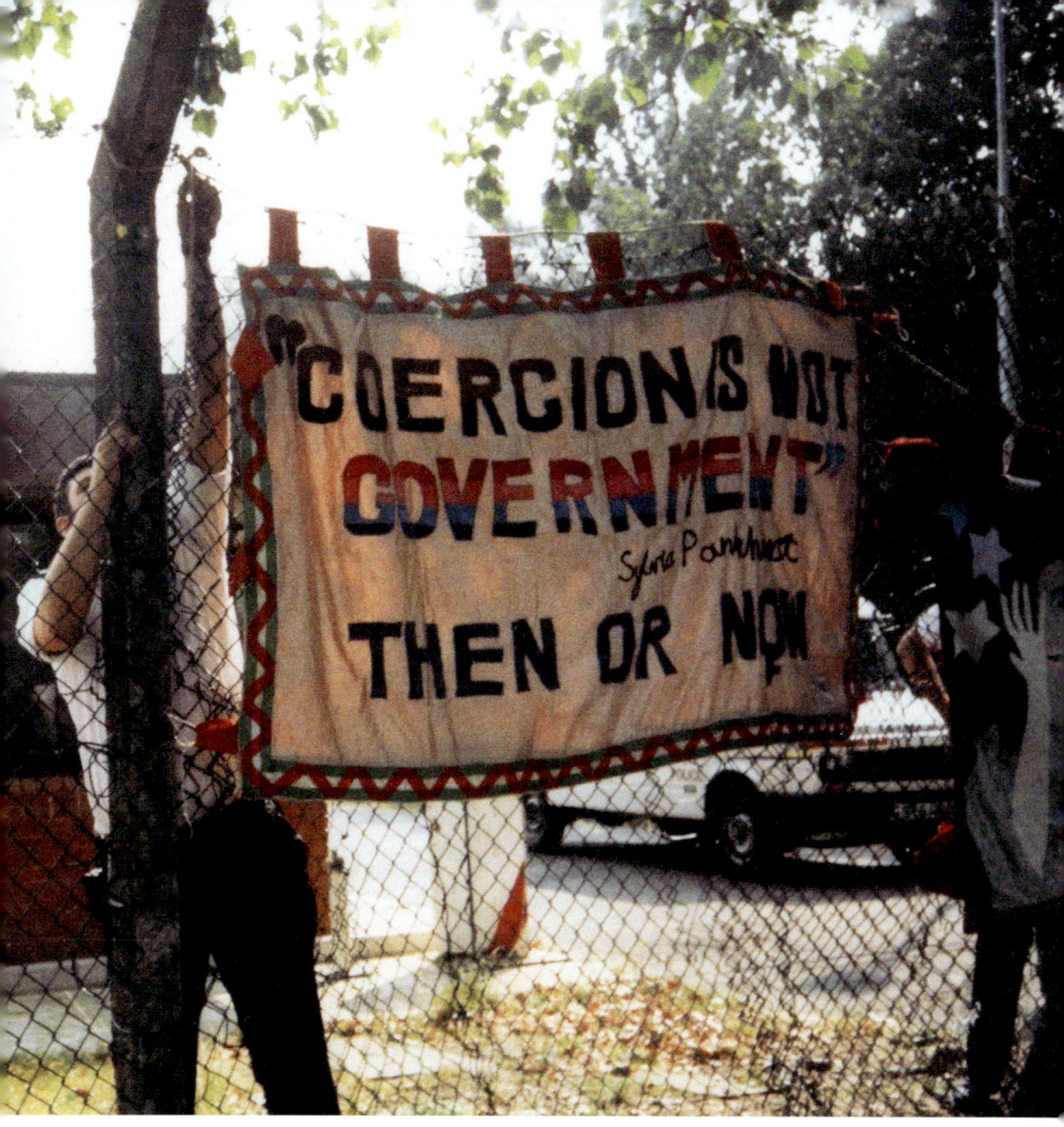

Above and next pages: *'Coercion Is Not Government'*, Sylvia Pankhurst, *Then or Now*, 1985, 104 × 183 cm.

Thalia and Ian Campbell's design makes overt reference to the women's suffrage movement, a campaign which called for the right of women to vote in national and local elections. The banner quotes prominent suffrage campaigner Sylvia Pankhurst at the time of the 'Cat and Mouse' Act, 1913. Using this act, the government sought to deal with women on hunger strike by releasing them from prison early and re-arresting them when they had recovered their health. The Campbells view this statement as still relevant now, decades later.

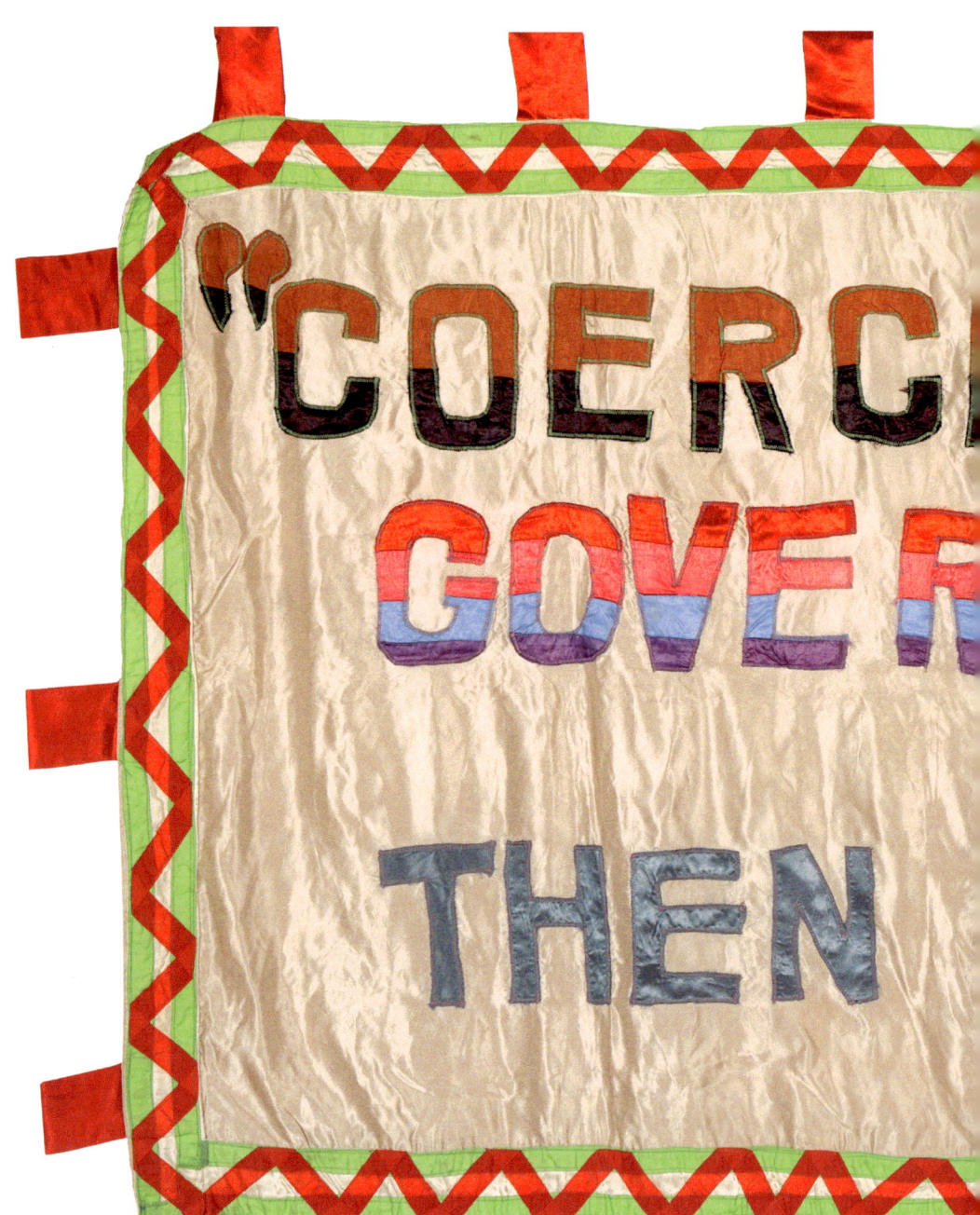

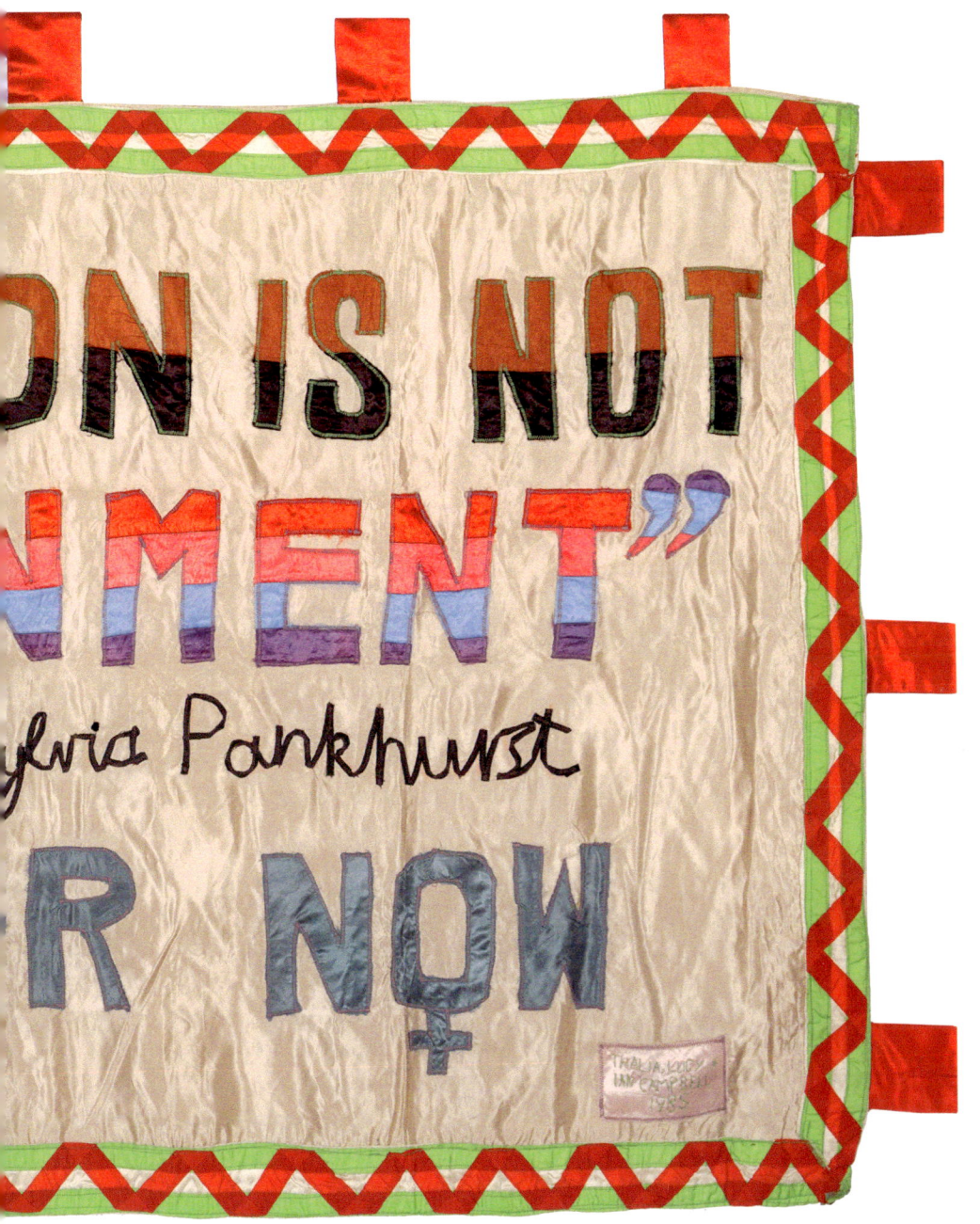

Two of the slogans used on these banners are drawn from contemporary feminist literature; *War Is Menstrual Envy* is taken from the Winter 1982 and Spring 1984 editions of *Lysistrata*, and *No More Toys for the Boys* from an October 1980 *Spare Rib* article about Cruise missiles and CND's strategy – originally the line read 'Take the toys from the boys'.

The women-only nature of the camp led to comparisons between the Greenham women and early 20th century suffragists and suffragettes, as well as members of the 1970s Women's Liberation movement, in which some Greenham women had played a part.

However, the Greenham campaign did not receive support from all women concerned with women's rights. Sections of the Women's Liberation movement believed that the Greenham campaign 'divert[s] our attention from the all too familiar threats of male violence and dominance in our homes, at work, in the streets, schools etc. The lives of one woman, then women or all women are not changed by 30,000 women surrounding a military base.'[34] The statement illustrates the fear by some that Greenham was eclipsing wider women's issues.

In her 1983 book *Black Women and the Peace Movement* (expanded and republished in 1984), campaigner Wilmette Brown argues that for Black women peace campaigning cannot be isolated from broader issues: 'From the point of view of women of colour... the threat of nuclear war and nuclear power is inseparable from day-to-day military-industrial repression: "sex", "race" and "class" issues are "peace" issues.'[35] That poverty, born of racism, can restrict the ability of Black women to participate in the peace movement is emphasised, as well as the link between repression of Black communities and military recruitment.

Brown connects spending on armament to reduced welfare funding and recognises a synergy with the argument put forward in Virginia Woolf's 1938 book *Three Guineas*: 'The common strategy of Virginia Woolf and Black welfare mothers which speaks to most women at the bottom is: pay women not the military'.[36] In October 1986, Brown spoke at Greenham Common in front of a banner bearing the slogan *Pay Women Not the Military*, representing the International Wages for Housework and International Black Women for Wages for Housework campaigns.

Some of the banners addressing male power overtly reference past women's campaigns, for example referring to the female vote and quoting Sylvia Pankhurst. A *Guardian* newspaper report from 13 December 1983 describes a 'Cat and mouse game at Greenham', equating cutting and entering the Greenham perimeter fence and being arrested for trespass,

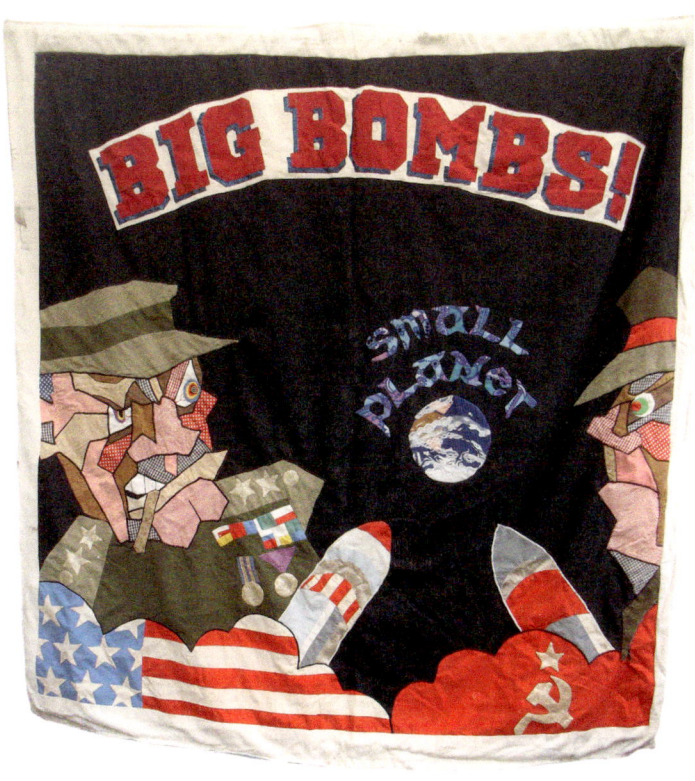

Above: *Big Bombs!, Small Planet* by Jo Pate.

Next pages: *Women's Struggle Won the Vote Use It for Disarmament*, 105 × 163 cm. Designed and made by Thalia Campbell, with help from Ian Campbell and Jan Higgs. Campbell says she made three versions of this banner – the first from her son's bedspread. The dates on the apron on the left-side of the banner referred to different voting milestones in British history. 1918: Representation of the People Act; 1928: Equal Franchise Act; 1968: the voting age right was reduced from 21 to 18 years; 1978: 50th anniversary of the Equal Franchise Act. On the right of the design, there is a small banner with a black border. This is a funeral banner, and serves to represent when women have not utilised the vote.

WOMENS

WOM
WON
US

FOR DISAR

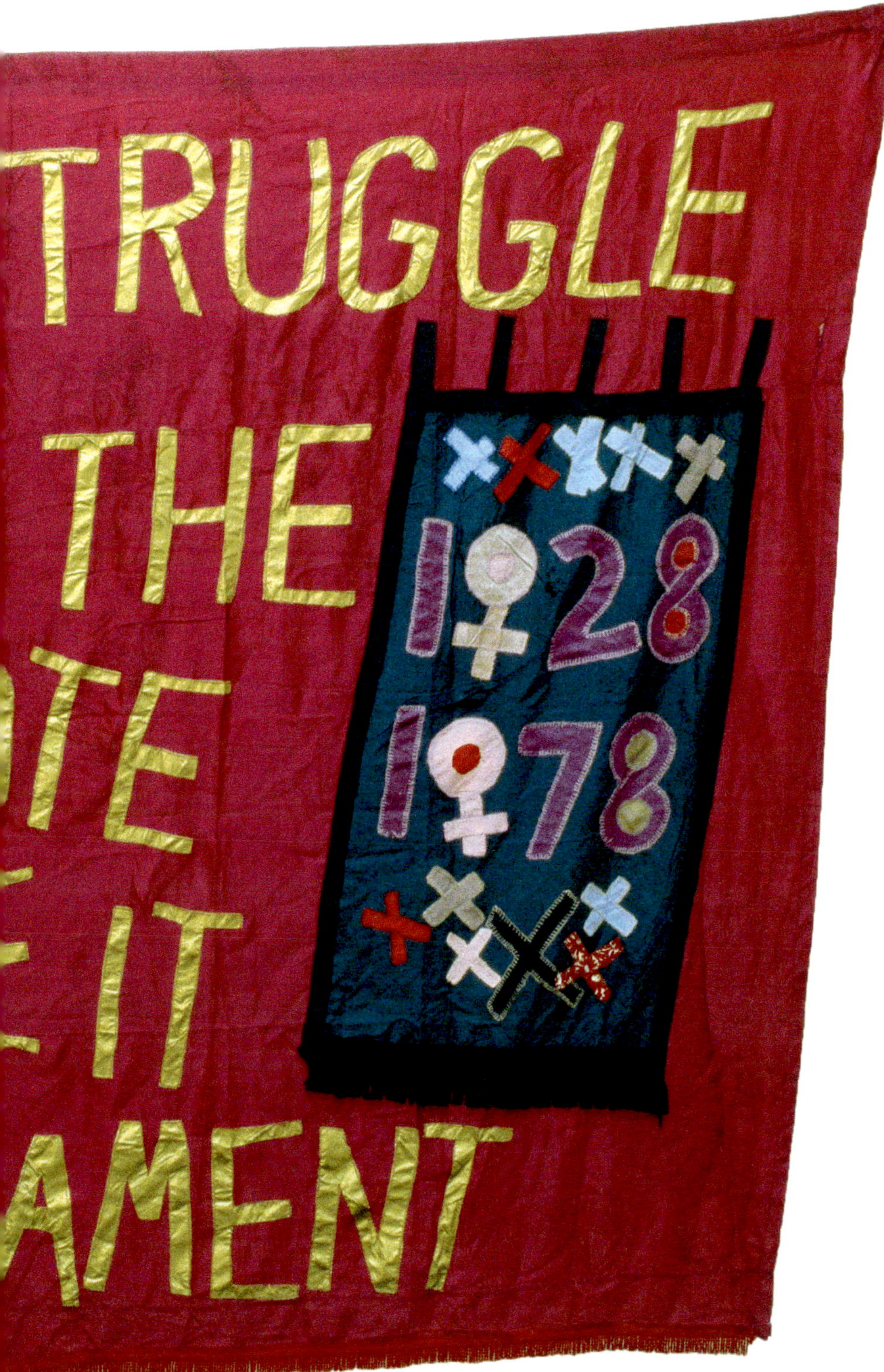

TRUGGLE

THE
TE
E IT
AMENT

1928
1978

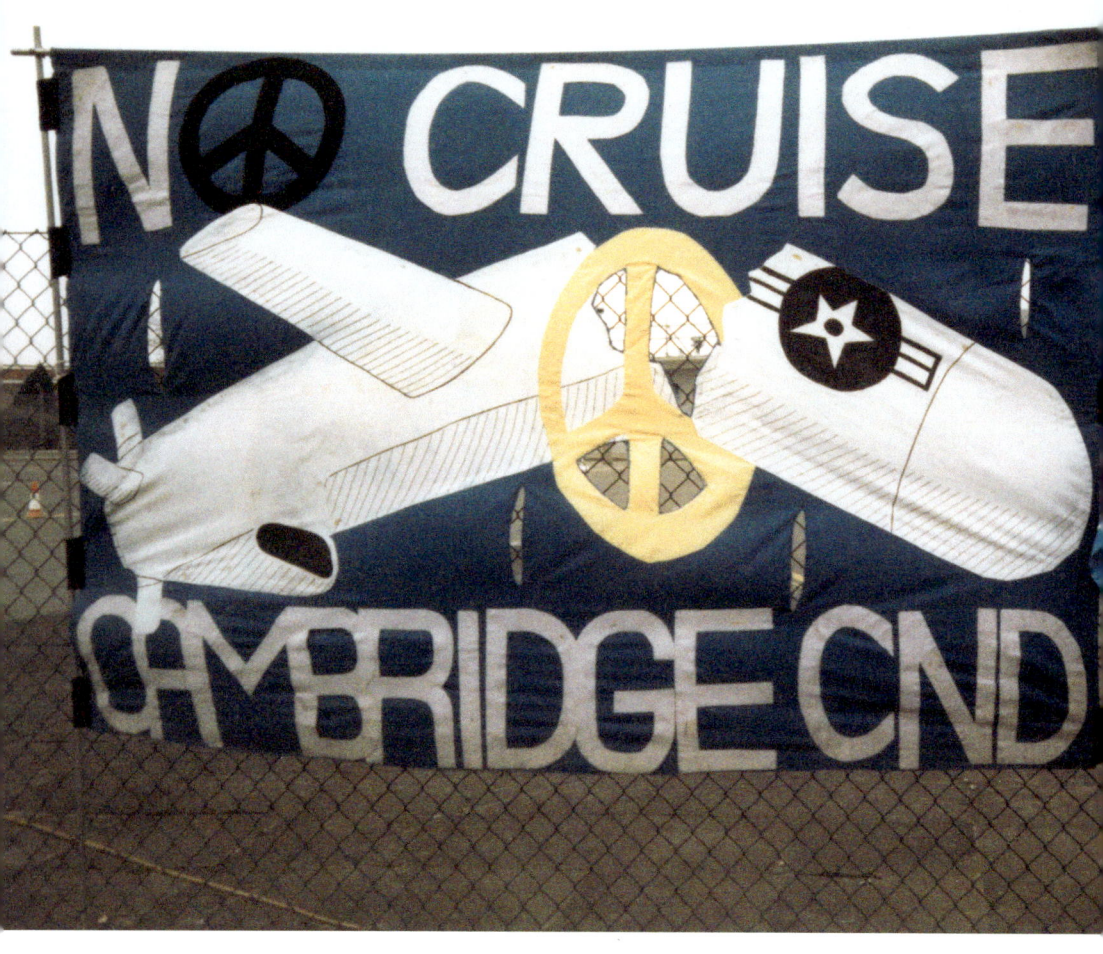

Above: *No Cruise Cambridge* CND.
Next pages: Greenham Women's Peace Camp, late 1980s.

to a so-called 'game' suffragettes played. This saw suffragettes go on hunger strike in prison, effecting their release, only to be returned to prison when physically well enough. The practice stopped when force feeding was introduced.

Concern about the impact of nuclear warfare on future generations and the gendered nature of war policy and aggression – as expressed in the banners discussed in this and the previous chapter – are recognised arguments from past feminist and peace campaigns.

In her book *The Long Road to Greenham: Feminism & Anti-Militarism in Britain Since 1820*, Jill Liddington defines the first argument as 'maternalist feminism' and describes it as the oldest strand of 'peace propaganda', initially practiced in the domestic sphere, and from 1820 onwards through the formation of 'small women's peace groups'.[37]

The argument used by the National Council for the Abolition of Nuclear Weapon Tests, in a demonstration organised by women on 12 May 1957, can be defined as 'maternalist feminism'. Protestors carried banners reading: 'Stop the Tests' and 'Save Your Child'.[38]

The other campaigning standpoints Liddington recognises are 'equal-rights feminism... rooted in a recognition of women's traditional exclusion from power and in the optimistic belief that once this was rectified war would cease' – as expressed in Woolf's *Three Guineas* – and 'maleness = violence... [which] links military aggression with domestic and sexual violence'.[39]

The extent to which the same arguments as used historically were knowingly adopted by the Greenham protestors, in their banners and more widely, is arguable. However, Wilmette Brown's writing about black women's peace campaigning makes clear her appreciation of Woolf's earlier arguments, and Thalia Campbell stands out as a banner maker with a strong interest in history. She recalls sitting around the campfire at Greenham discussing the suffragettes.[40] Respect for the banner designs of the past, such as those of the Women's Cooperative Guild, is expressed through her reproduction of some historic banners on the postcards she printed, alongside postcards of her own and other Greenham banners. It is most likely that some Greenham women were aware of the historic context of their arguments and others were not.

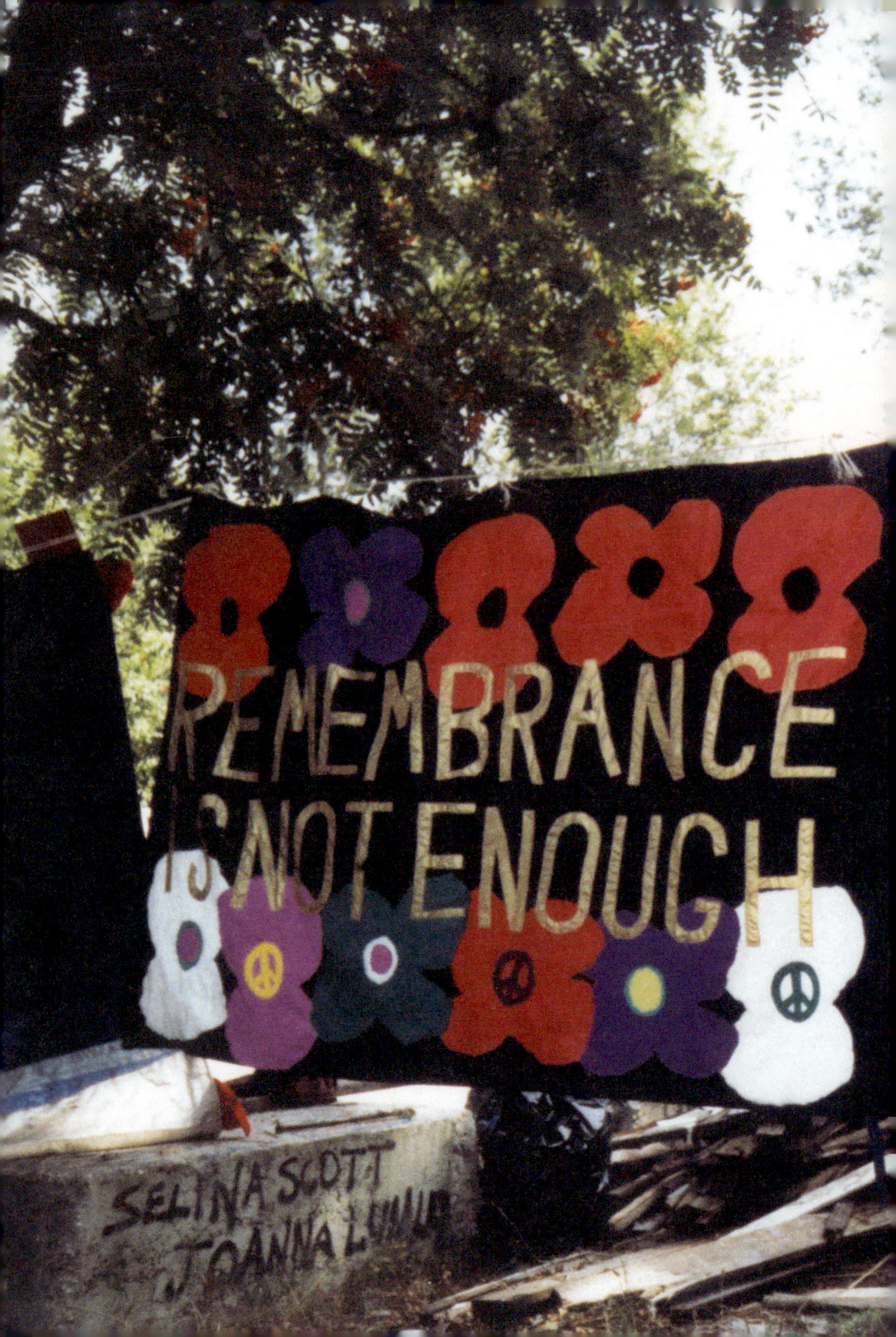

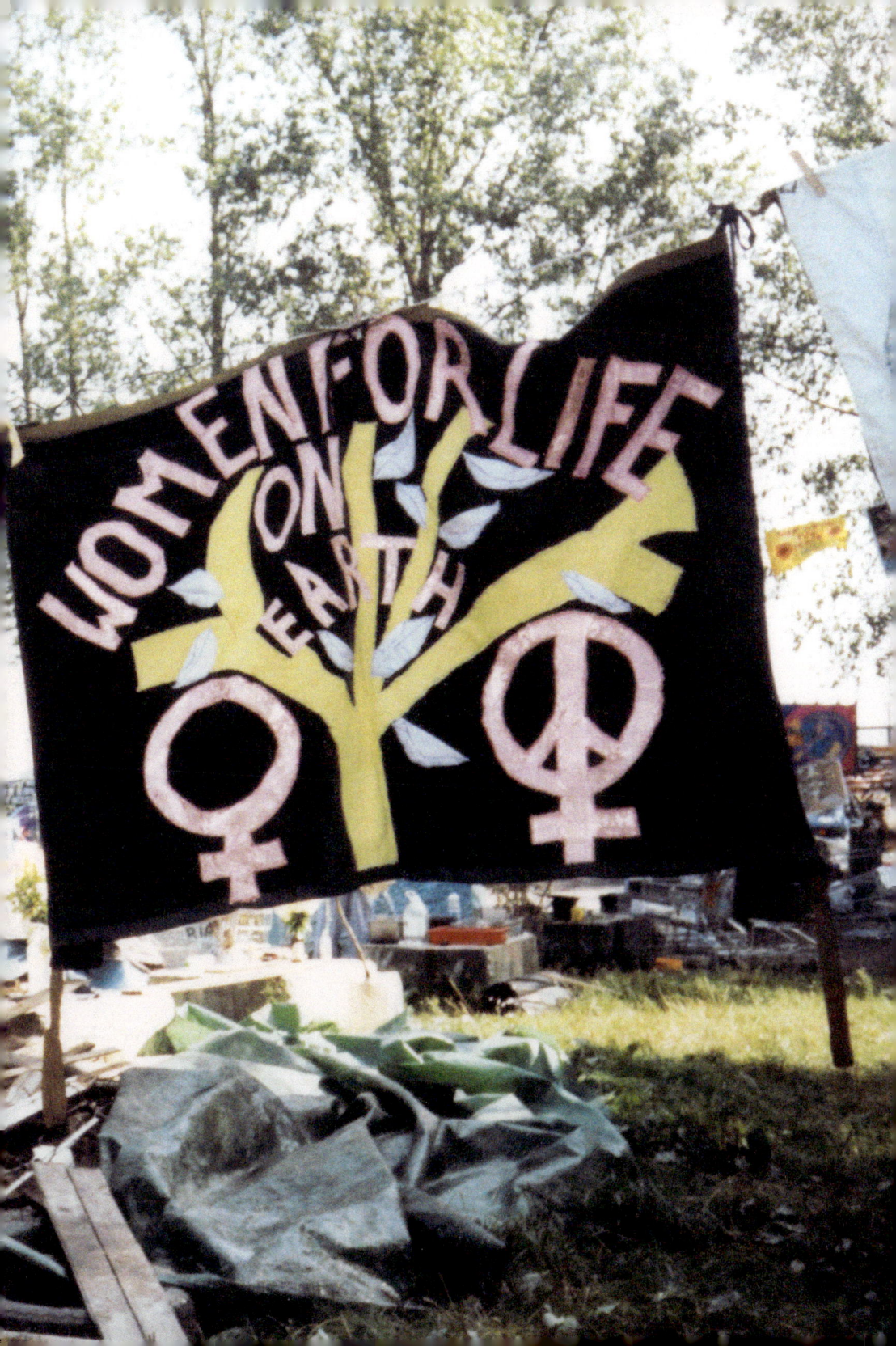

Embrace the Base

250 Greenham women had blockaded the base in March 1982, causing a great deal of disruption, but their next major action was many times larger. Attracting international attention due to its scale, Embrace the Base took place on 12 December 1982, and was repeated in subsequent years on the same weekend in December. Extensive organisation saw participants distributed around the full distance of the nine-mile fence enclosing the airbase, and link hands. In 1982 more than 30,000 women travelled from across the UK and around the world, informed by chain-letter, to join the core camp of campaigners. This number rose to 50,000 women in 1983.[41]

The typed, hand-illustrated and photocopied programme for the first event, created by the women at Main Gate (Yellow), tells those taking part: 'You have arrived at one of the eight gates of RAF Greenham Common, once beautiful common land, now a nightmare. We are here to come to terms with this place, on our terms, the terms of life. Listen to your feelings, hang banners, spin webs, write messages in the mud, make yourselves at home.'

An illustration by artist Katrina Howse, resident at Yellow Gate, was reproduced on the 1982 event poster. Titled *Punishment Cell* (page 105) it was drawn in ink on flower paper in the punishment cell of Drake Hall Prison, Staffordshire. It graphically describes the containment of women and illustrates that many Greenham women were prepared to be arrested and imprisoned for the peace cause.

In the invitation to Embrace the Base, women were asked to 'bring personal things that represent the threat of nuclear war to us and express our lives, our anger and our joy'.[42] Consequently 'the fence around the military base was both 'embraced' and transformed into a 'Women's collage for life'. Women brought clothes, photos, weaving, pictures, objects of various kinds, and pinned them onto the fence in order symbolically to block out the base', as well as banners.[43]

A sharp contrast was created by juxtaposing personal effects with the metal, barbed-wire topped fence: 'Displayed at Greenham, the banners [and other objects] declare the fence as a boundary between femininity

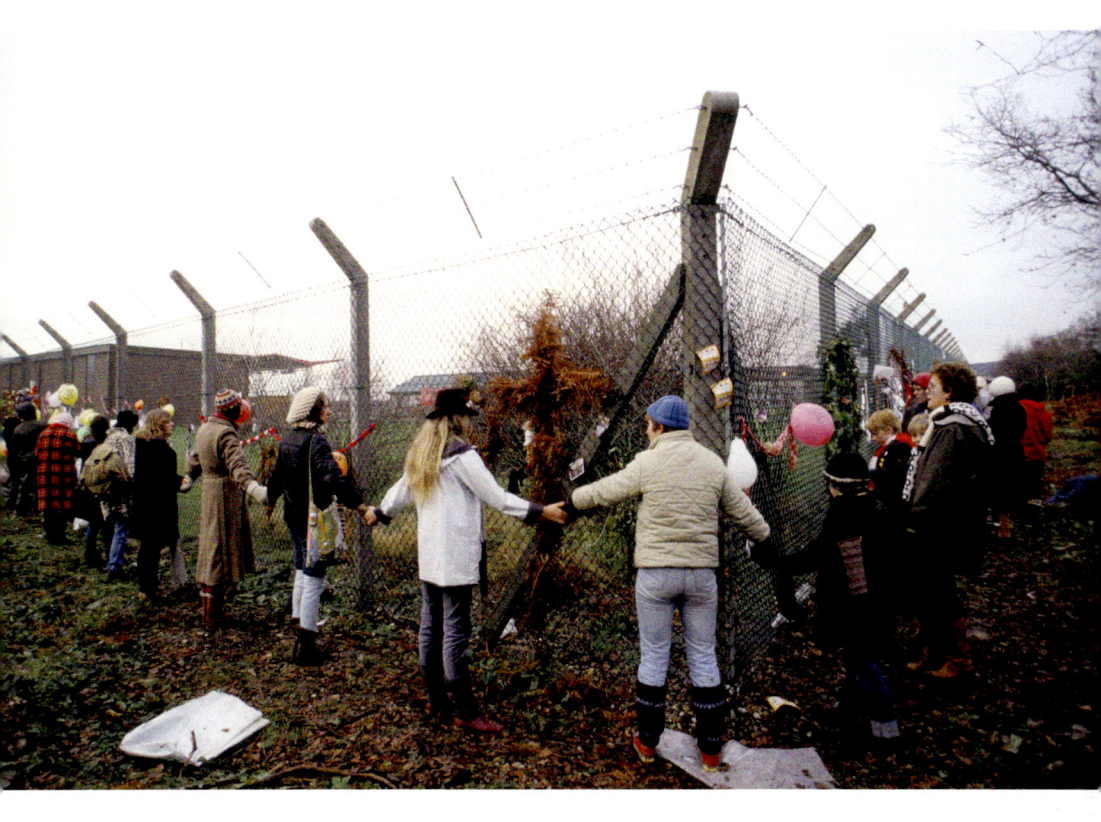

Above, and next pages: Embrace the Base at RAF Greenham Common, December 1982. Photographs by Homer Sykes.

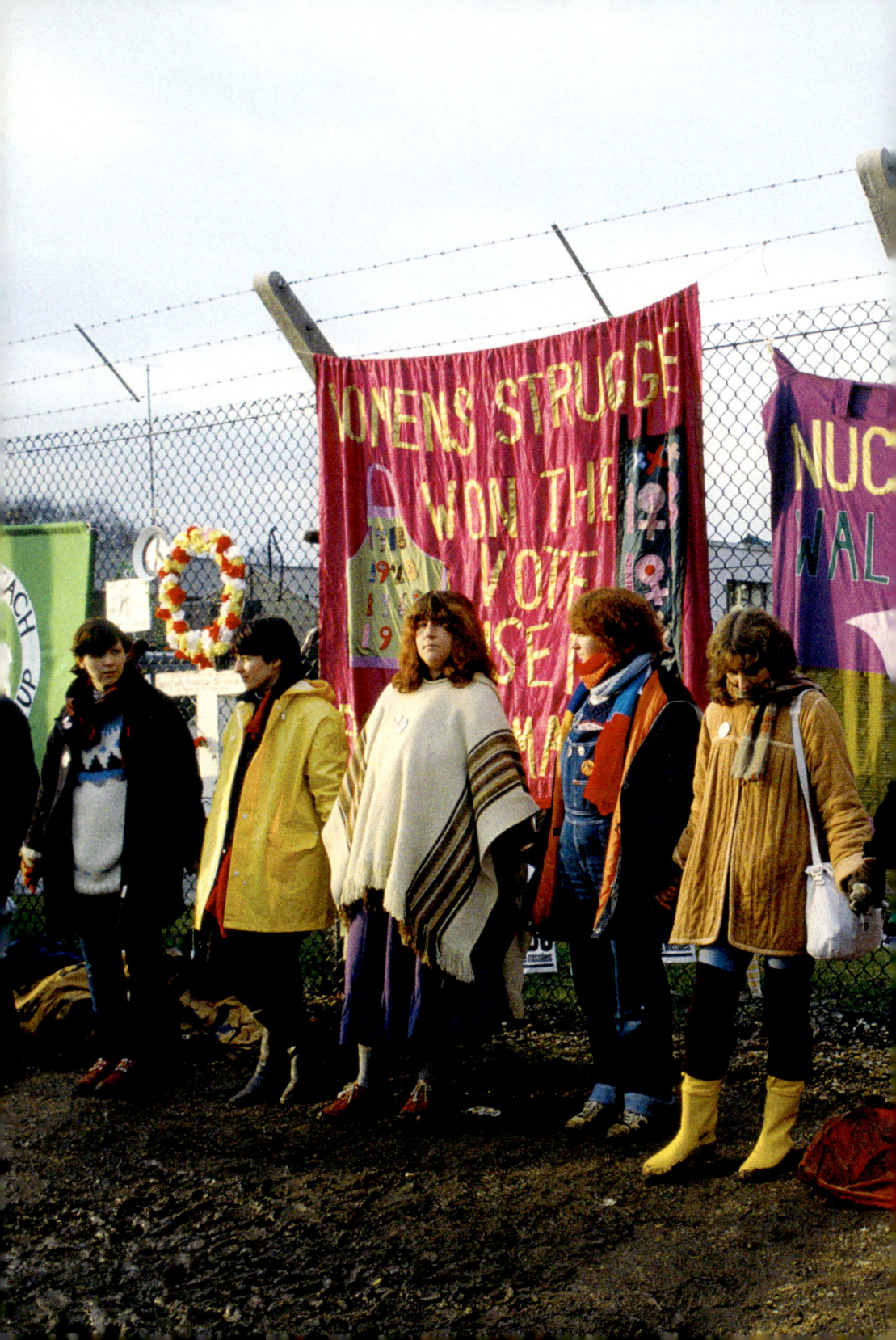

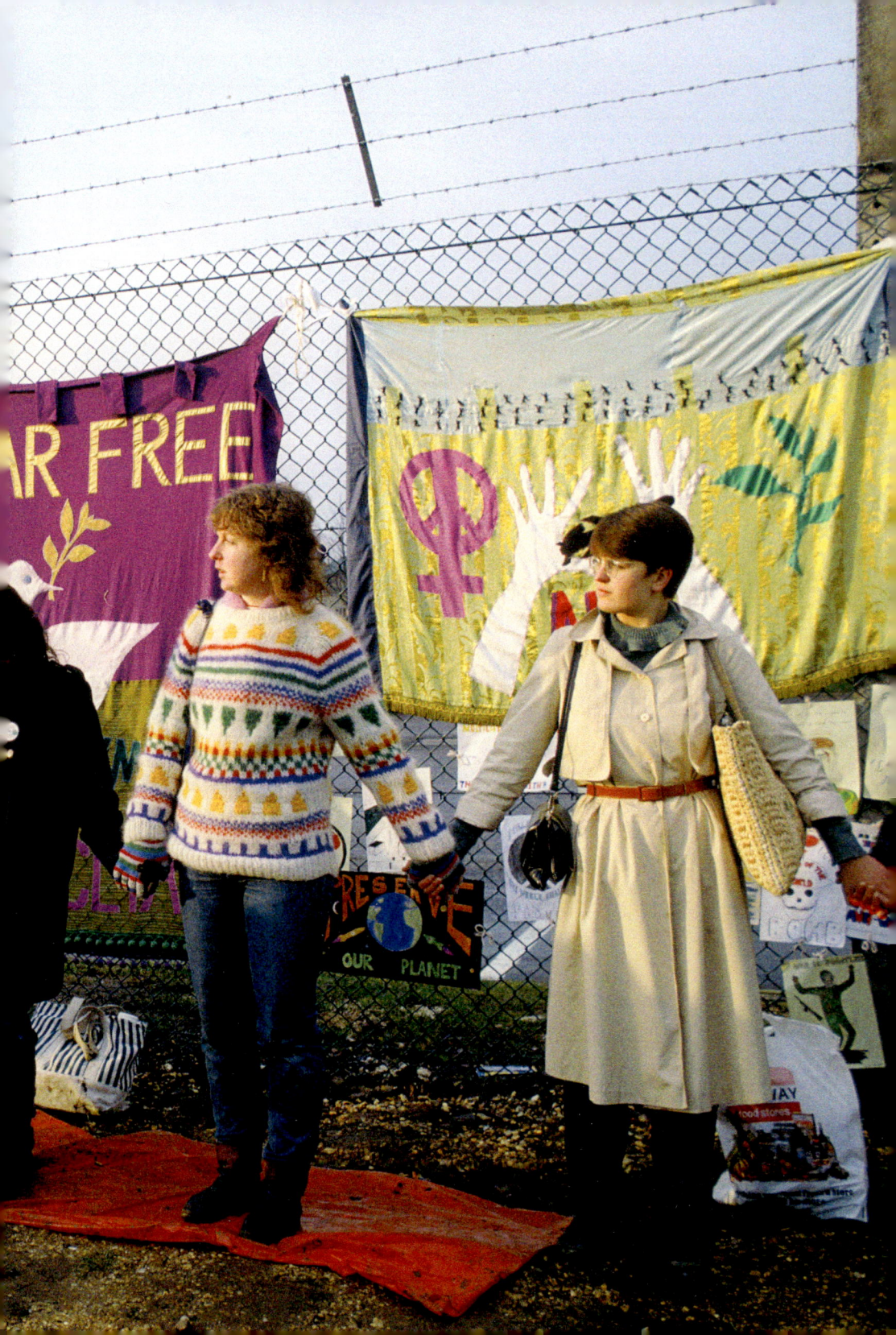

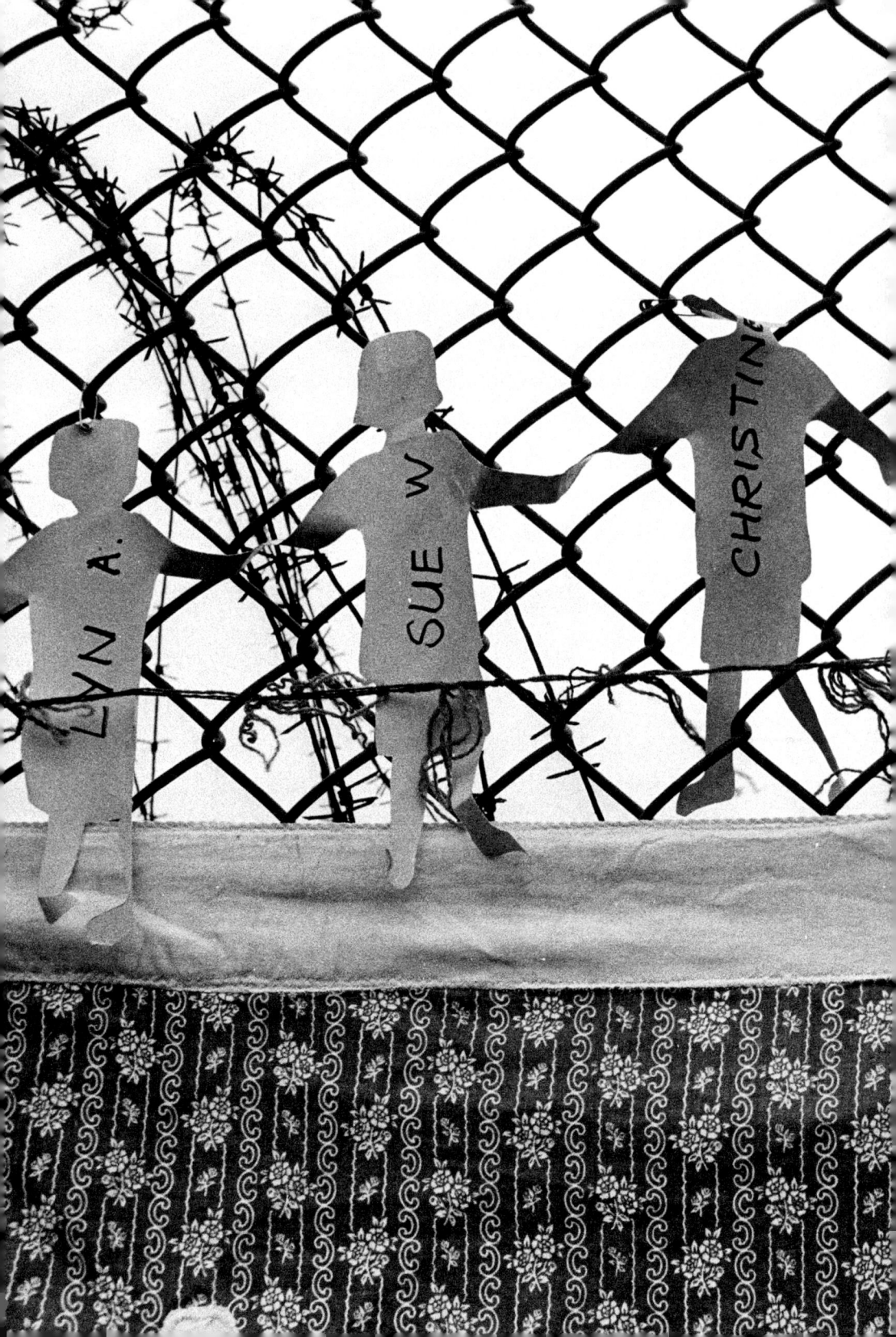

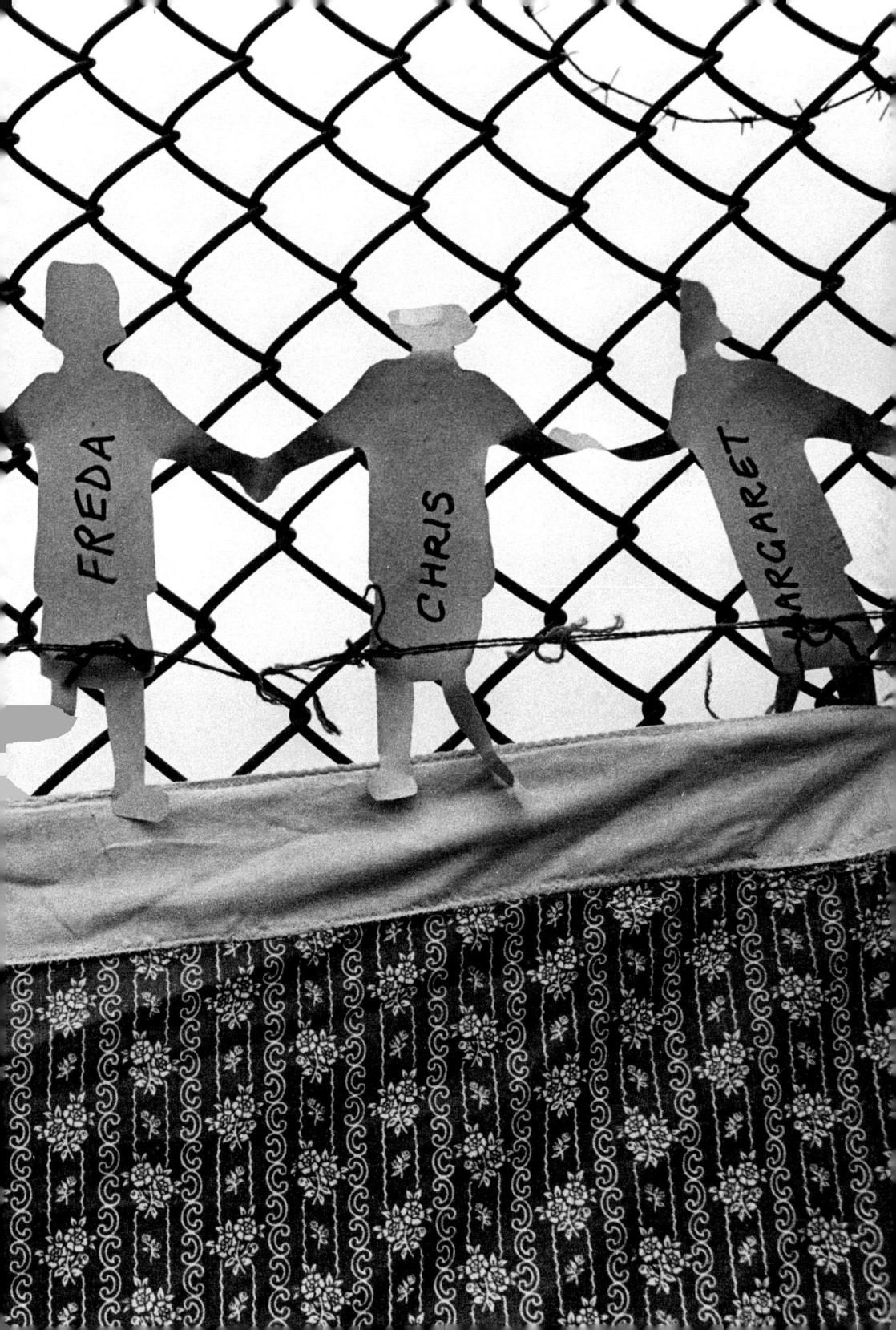

and masculinity, between life and death, technology and nature.'[44] The action brought objects representing life and future generations to the locality of the perceived threat.

A significant number of women camped overnight after embracing the base, and the following day took part in non-violent actions, which included blockading the base gates between 2pm and 6pm. A map in the middle of the event programme illustrates the amenities that the women had arranged for those travelling to take part, including a bus/coach station, creche, rest tents and food and information points. Those taking part were told: 'The 13th is a women's day of Action... There are many things we can do. None are more important than others: camping on the common, talking to workers, singing, blockading, letting our imaginations and humour work – all are direct actions... some may [be] legal, some illegal.'

The event stimulated women to make new banners, as well as bringing existing designs. Some banners, together with many thousands of personal possessions, were left on the fence after the event. Campbell rescued several international and other banners before Newbury Council disposed of them in the large clean-up that followed.

Previous pages: Greenham Common Women's Peace Camp, 1983.
Photograph by Janine Wiedel.

Opposite: *Punishment Cell*, 1982, by Katrina Howse. Ink on paper drawing.

Next pages: Banner made by Swedish women and sent to Greenham in 1982 for the Embrace the Base event. The design was intended to represent them, as they could not attend in person.

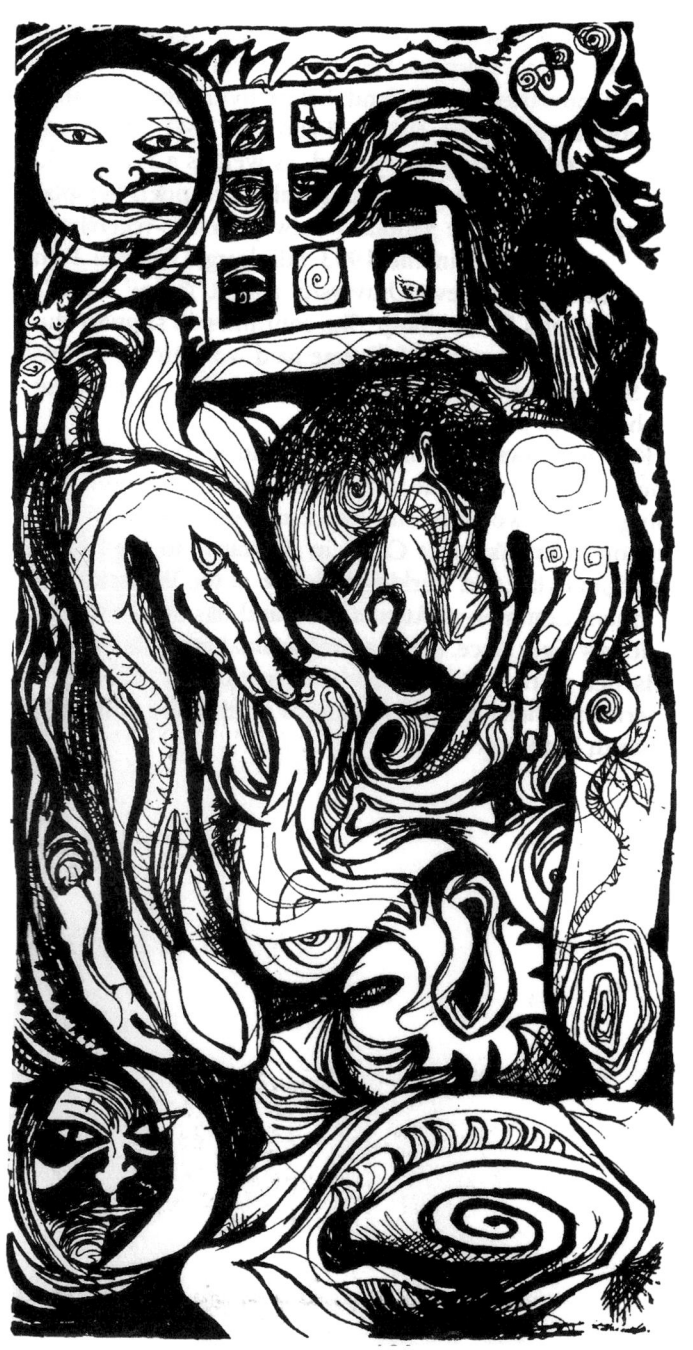

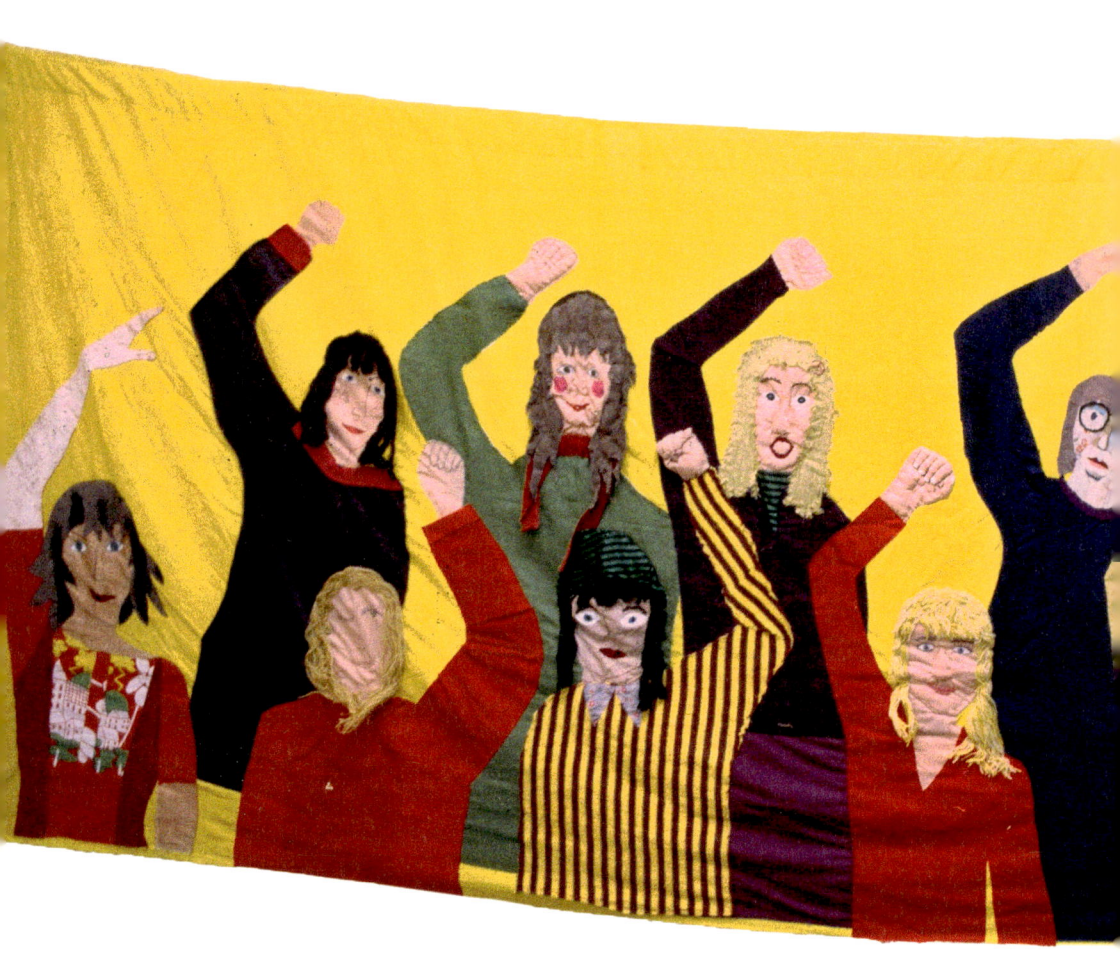

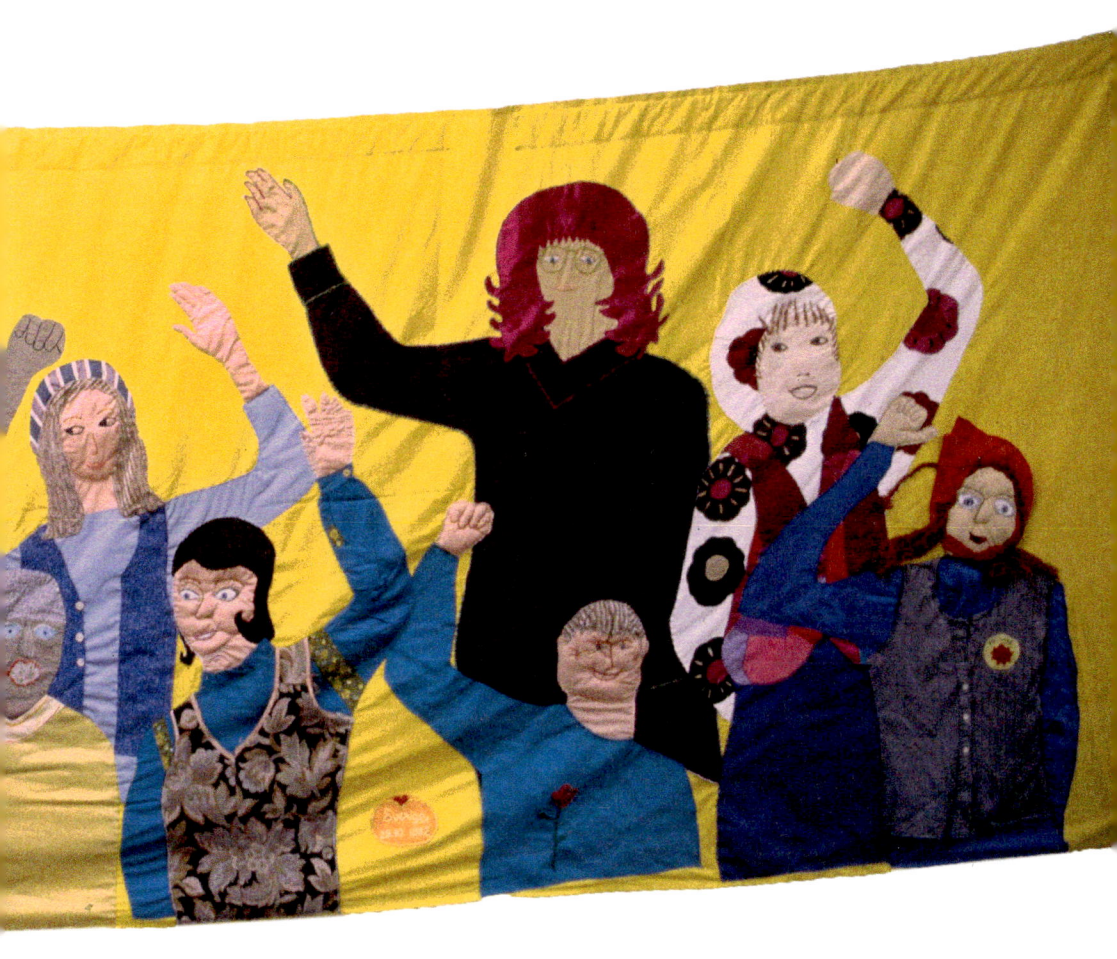

International Banner Designs

A group of banners, of which only a small number survive in UK collections, illustrates international engagement in the Greenham campaign. Women travelled from across the world to stay at Greenham, others came for specific events. When they visited some left banners behind. Half of a Russian banner was rescued from the Greenham fence by Campbell. It is reputed to have been torn in half by the Ministry of Defence during the first Soviet inspection of the Greenham base in 1987. The visit followed the signing of the Intermediate-Range Nuclear Forces (INF) Treaty (that reduced and limited missile stocks) in December of the same year.

Four international peace banners that were used at Greenham are in the collection of the Peace Museum in Bradford and were donated by Campbell, including the Russian design. Another bears a message of peace in Esperanto, applied in green paint on a thick cream cotton. A third, from the Netherlands, depicts a large, uplifted hand, holding a rainbow coloured world. The fourth, from the USA, uses batik – a wax-resist dying technique – on cotton fabric and is addressed: *To Sisters Womens Peace Camp Greenham Common in Solidarity from the Mink Hills New Hampshire, USA*. Mink Hills is just over an hour's drive from the Seabrook Station Nuclear Power Plant, completed in 1986, after permission to build it was granted in 1976. A link between campaigning against nuclear power and weapons is not unusual, as illustrated by the banner made by Campbell demanding a *Nuclear Free Wales*, prior to her participation in the Greenham campaign.

As banners from international supporters were being made for Greenham and left there in some instances, Campbell was responding to international orders for her designs; commissions and requests to borrow banners for exhibitions and events.

The campaign had a global reach, and Greenham protesters were conscious of peace campaigning – particularly by women – worldwide. Articles included in the Greenham women's newsletters, authored and produced by different gates, report on international peace camps,

Opposite: Torn Russian banner salvaged from Embrace the Base, 88 × 78 cm.

ДОЛ

АМЕРИК

БАЗЫ

campaigns and conferences. They include accounts of trips made by the women, sites where nuclear testing was being undertaken and mark events such as the anniversaries of the bombings of Hiroshima and Nagasaki. The women's global awareness is illustrated by the banner series made by Howse titled *Women Are Angry About the Bombing of Libya*, painted outdoors in 1986, at a friend's house near Greenham. One banner slogan reads *Bombing Of Libya – It Is Murder*. Howse went on to make a banner in 1991 protesting the Gulf War, while still living at Greenham.

Opposite: *In Solidarity from the Mink Hills New Hampshire*, USA, 173 × 97 cm.

Next pages: *Esperantistoj por Mondpaco* (Esperanto Speakers for World Peace), 60 × 180 cm.

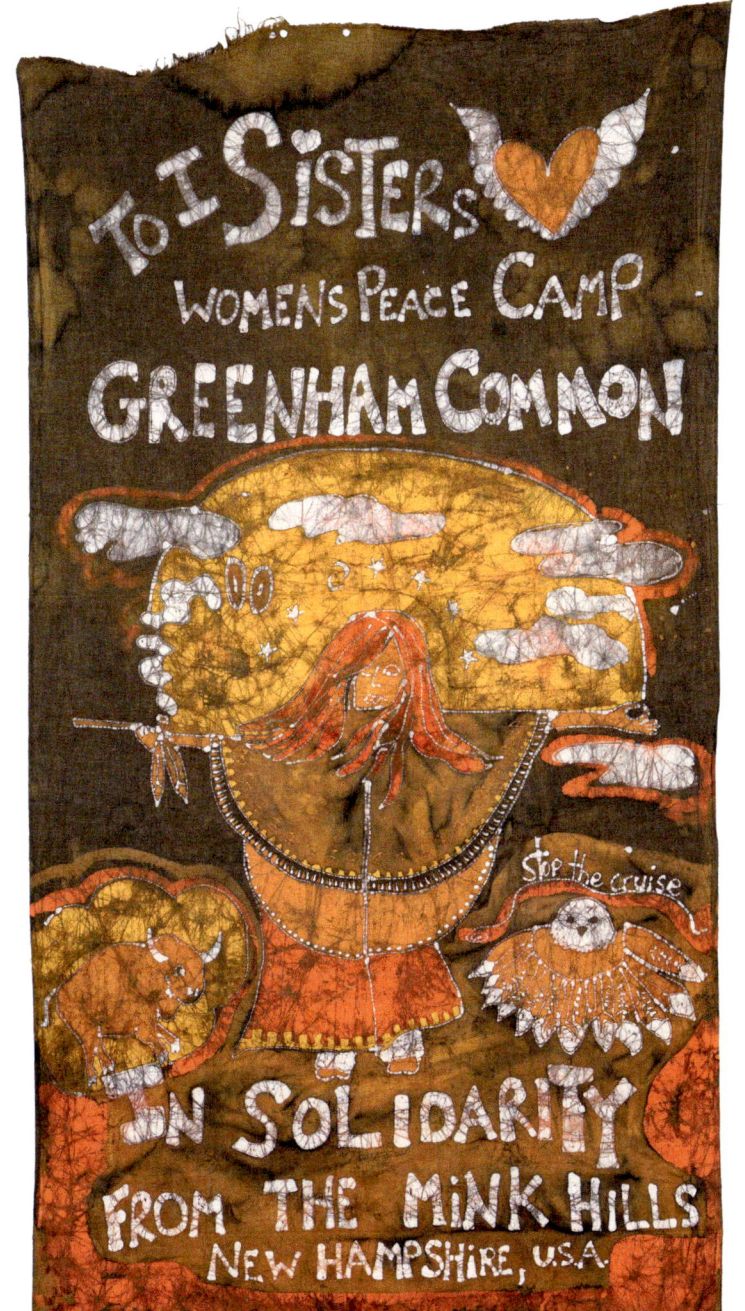

ESPERA
POR MO

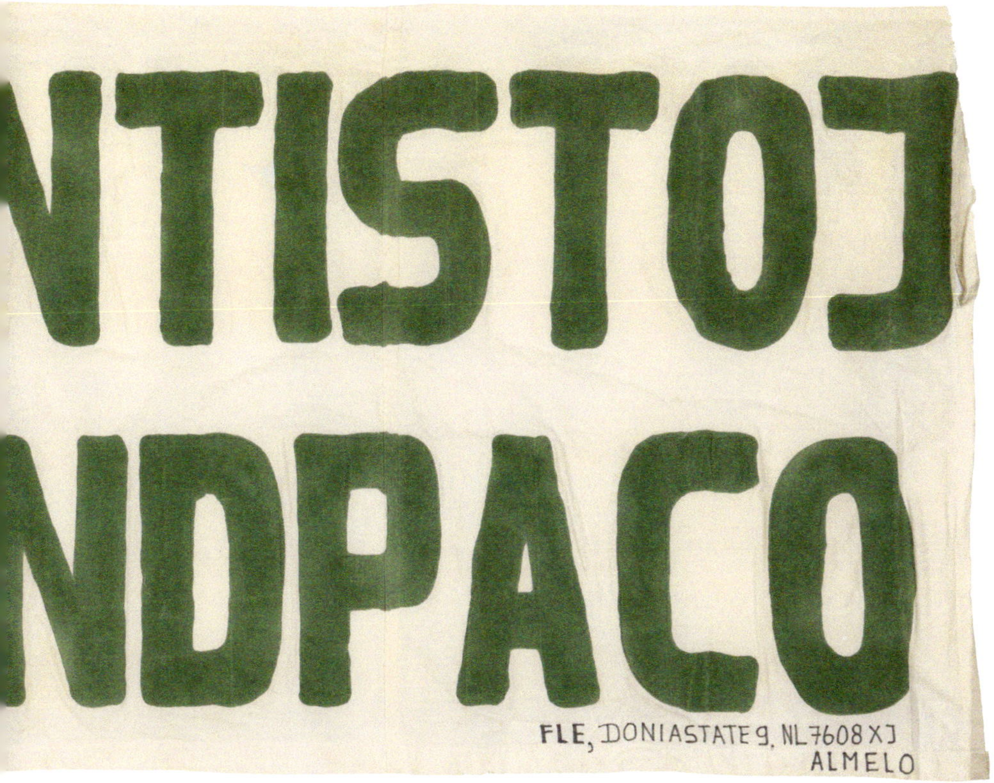

NTISTO[
COTSITO]
NDPACO

FLE, DONIASTATE 9, NL 7608 XJ
ALMELO

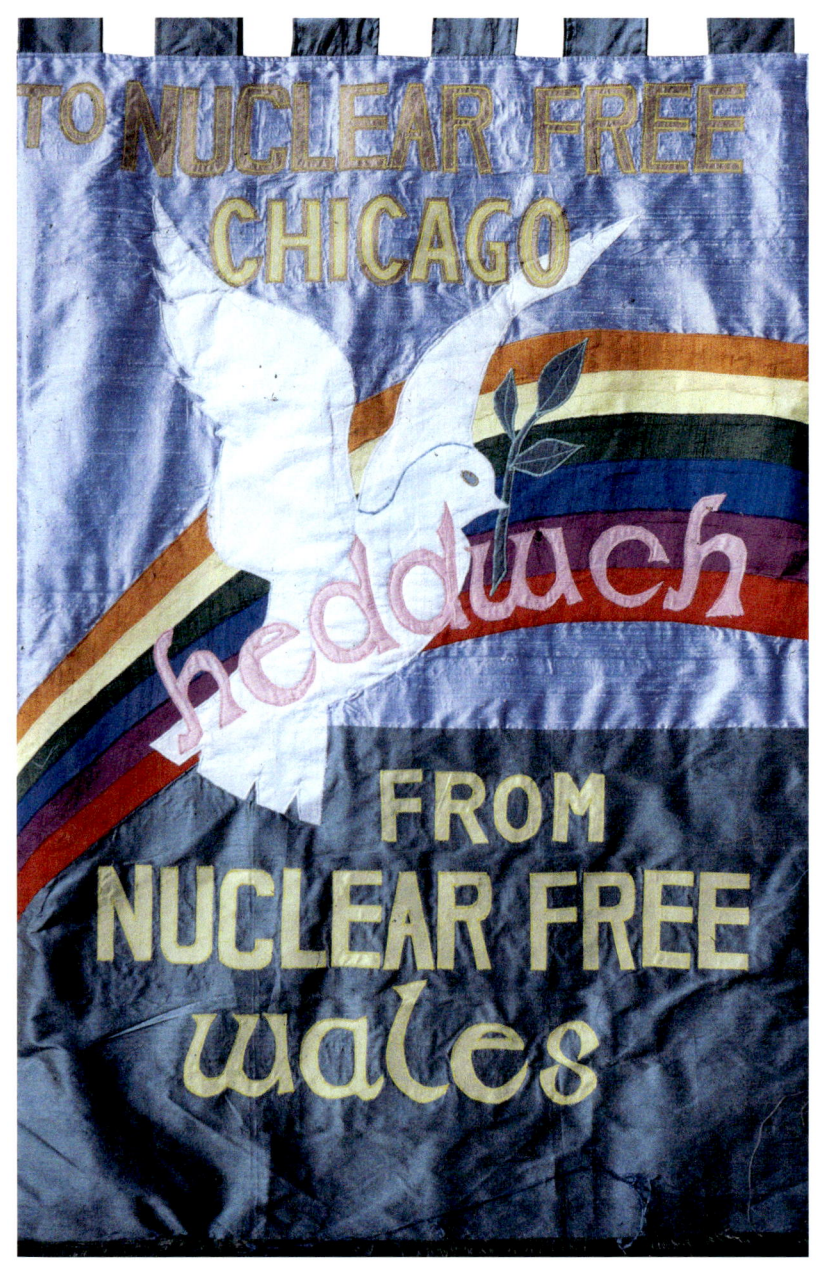

Above: *To Nuclear Free Chicago Heddwch [Peace] from Nuclear Free Wales.*
Opposite: *Nederland P.*, 198 × 173 cm.

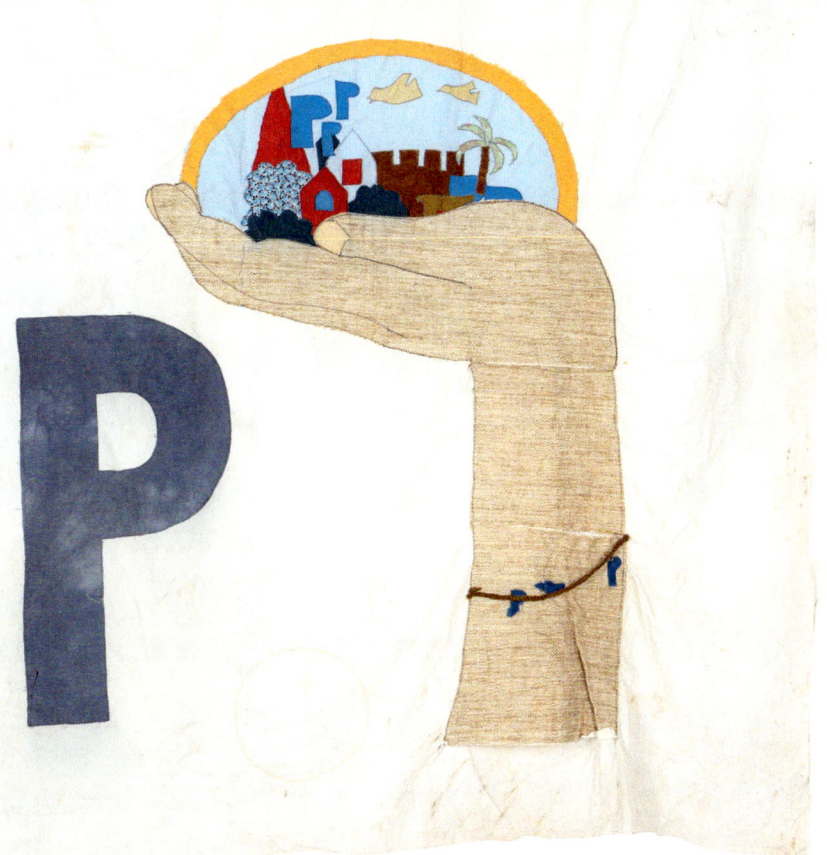

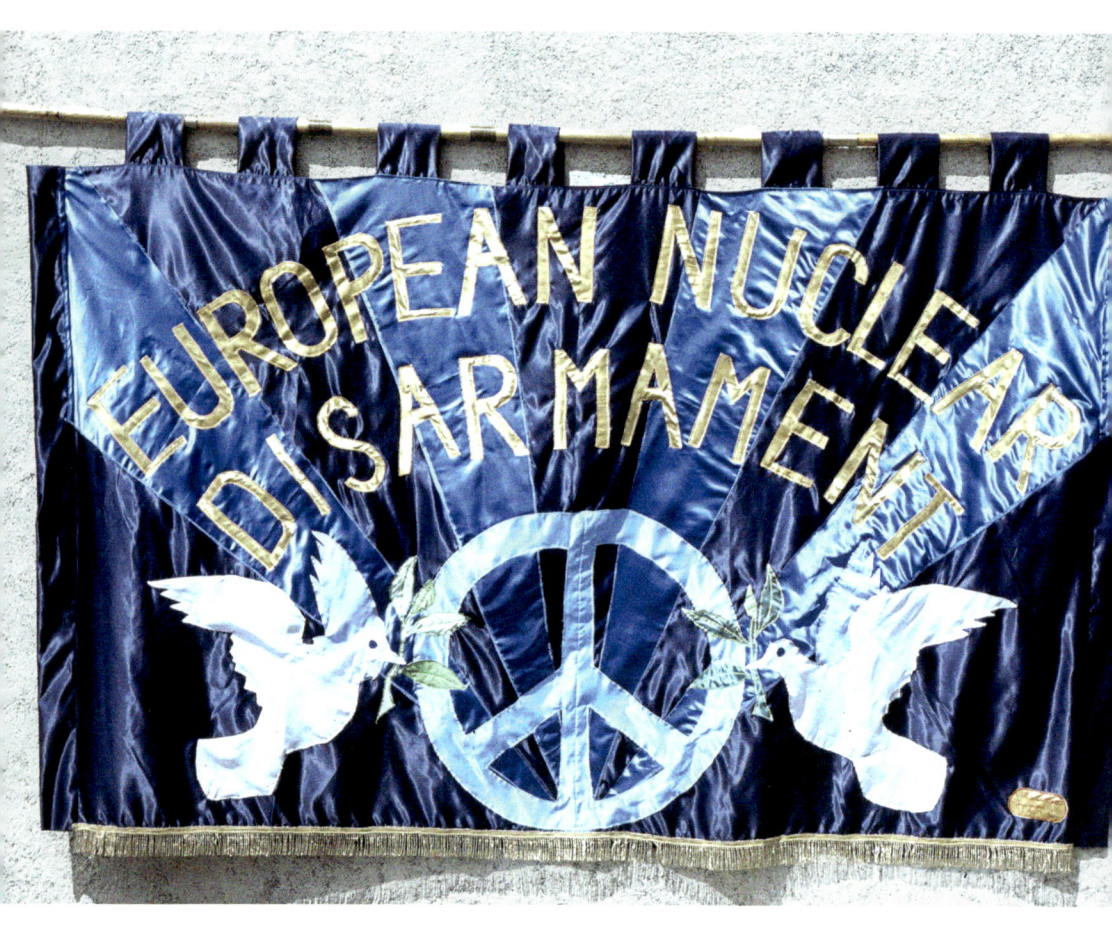

Above: *European Nuclear Disarmament*, 1984, by Thalia Campbell.

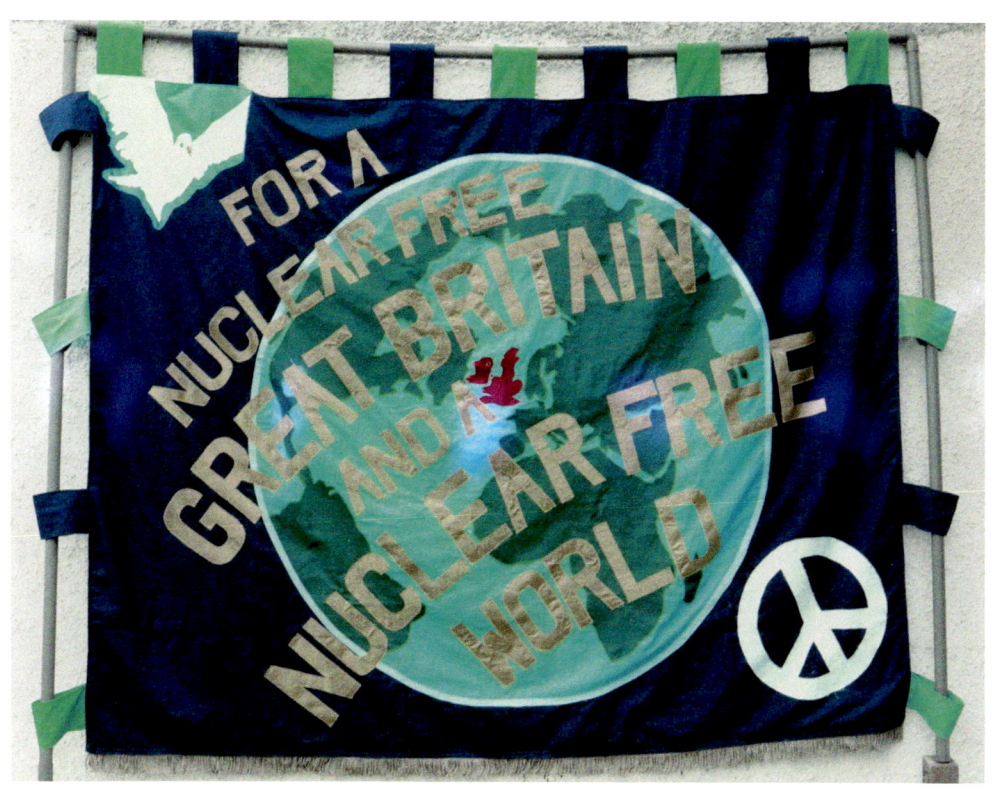

Above: *For a Nuclear Free Great Britain and a Nuclear Free World*, c. 1980s, by Thalia Campbell.

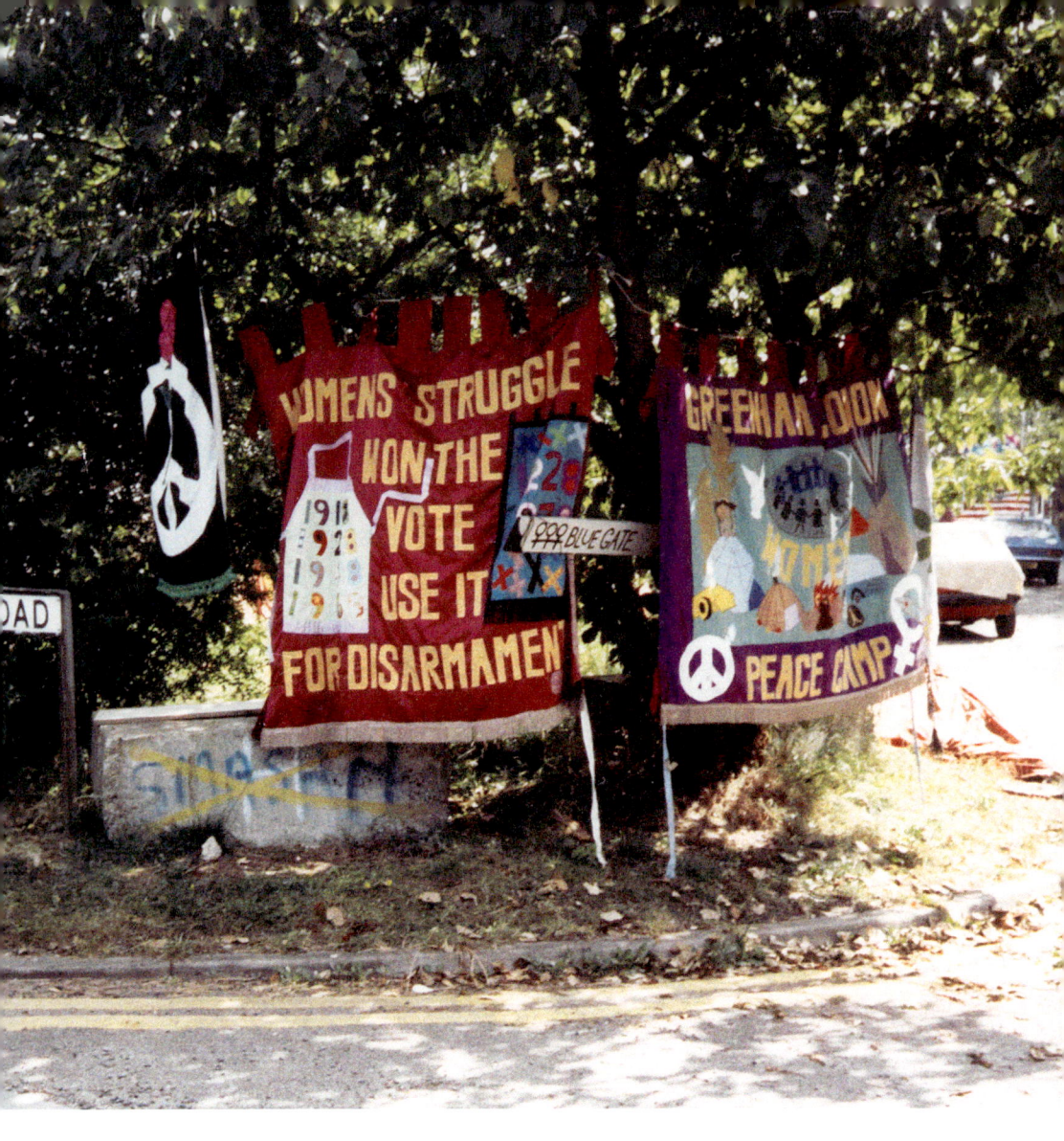

Above: Approaching Blue Gate camp, Greenham Common, c. 1990.
The banner on the right is one of four designed by Thalia and Ian Campbell illustrating details of life at the camp; small details differ in each banner. They were made in Thalia's workshop; the one on pages 10–11 was sewn by Mary Coughlin, while the one on pages 120–121 was sewn by Jan Higgs.

Greenham Women's Peace Camp Banner Designs

A desire to share and record the story of the Greenham women's peace camp inspired the creation of a group of banners that represent the life and activities of the resident women. By 1983, thanks in part to the Embrace the Base event, Greenham had become an internationally recognised symbol of the anti-nuclear weapons campaign. It was a focus and by-word for women's peace campaigning around the world.

A core group of campaigners were in permanent residence at Greenham – they received post and were registered to vote from the camp address. These women were joined by short and medium term residents from the UK and abroad. Family and work commitments meant that some women could stay for a few days at a time and kept returning, and others were there for a fixed period.

In her 1985 essay 'Banners and the Women's Peace Movement' Moira Vincentelli suggests that 'Greenham Common is not just a political phenomenon... it stands for a whole alternative culture and just as it has forced some women to take on an alternative lifestyle it has also inspired a new women-centred folk art in the poems, songs, ad hoc architecture and banners.'[45]

On this basis it is not surprising that the lived experiences of the women who camped at Greenham were expressed and represented through some of the banners they made. Examples include: *The USAF Base Is Illegally Erected on Common Land. Restore Greenham Common; Justice. Yellow Gate. Autonomous Women. Non Aligned; Greenham Wimmin Cut Defence!; Reclaim the Base; Yellow Gate. Greenham Common. Here to Stay Here to Verify; Yellow Gate. Greenham Women's Peace Camp. The Struggle Continues; Greenham Common Women's Peace Camp; We Are Mourning the Death of Helen Thomas, Killed by a Police Vehicle, 5th August 1989; 9 Years Yellow Gate Greenham Common. We Stand Alone; Yellow Gate Greenham Commmon Peace Camp. 10 Years.*

Before making the *Greenham Common Women's Peace Camp* design, with encouragement from South Wales academic Sheila Owen-Jones, Campbell recalls thinking 'why don't we make a banner about everything that's happened so far?'[46] She went on to make several versions evolving this theme.

Next pages: *Greenham Common Women's Peace Camp.*

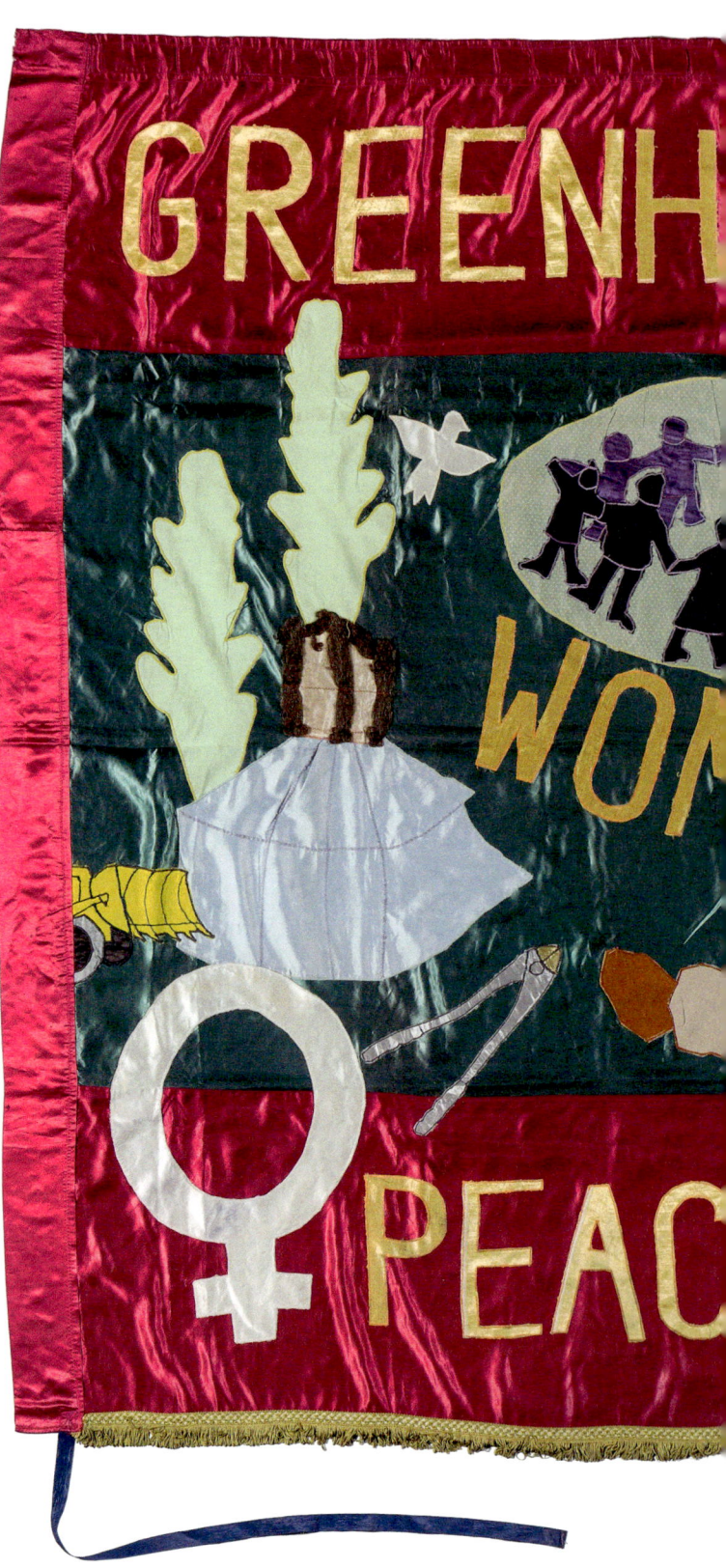

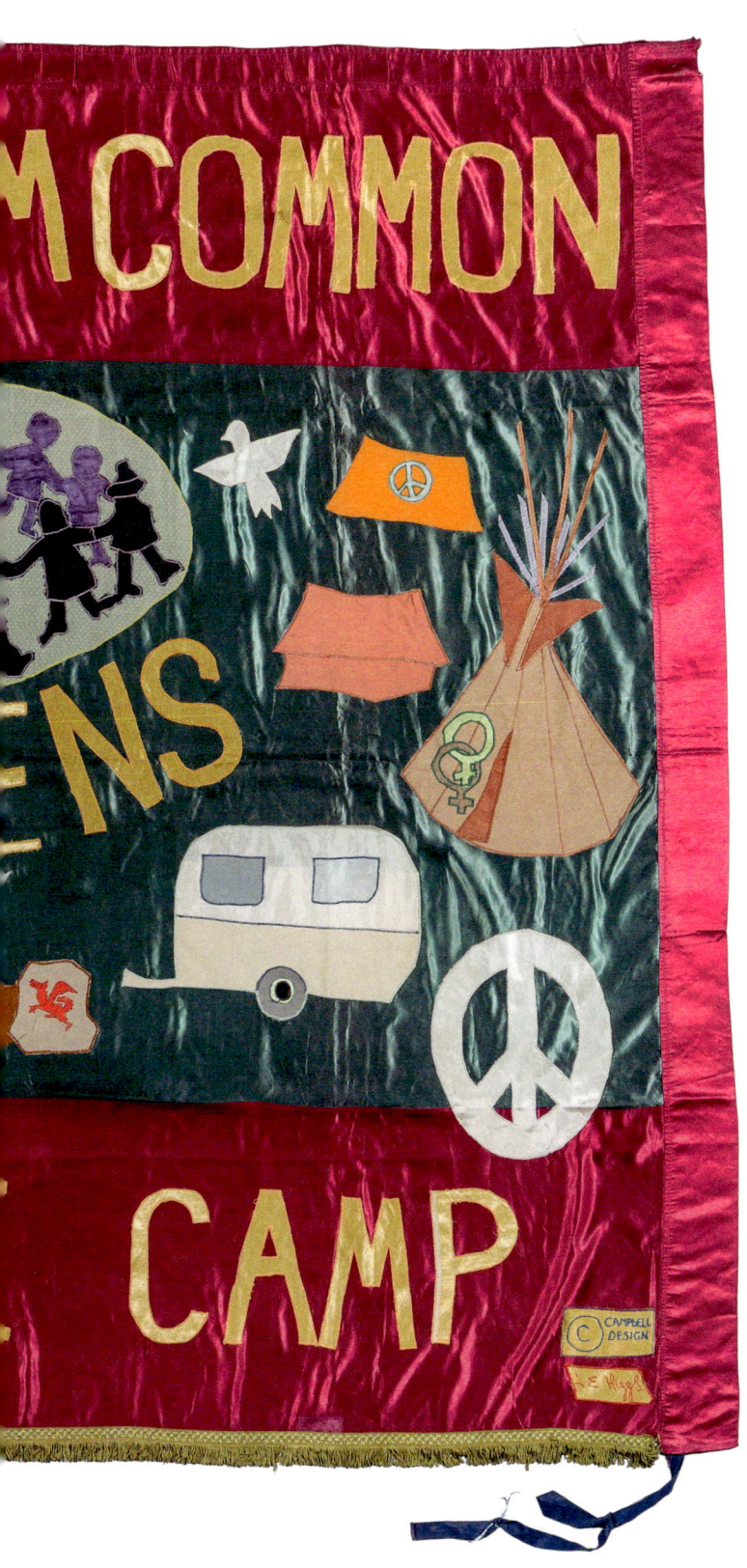

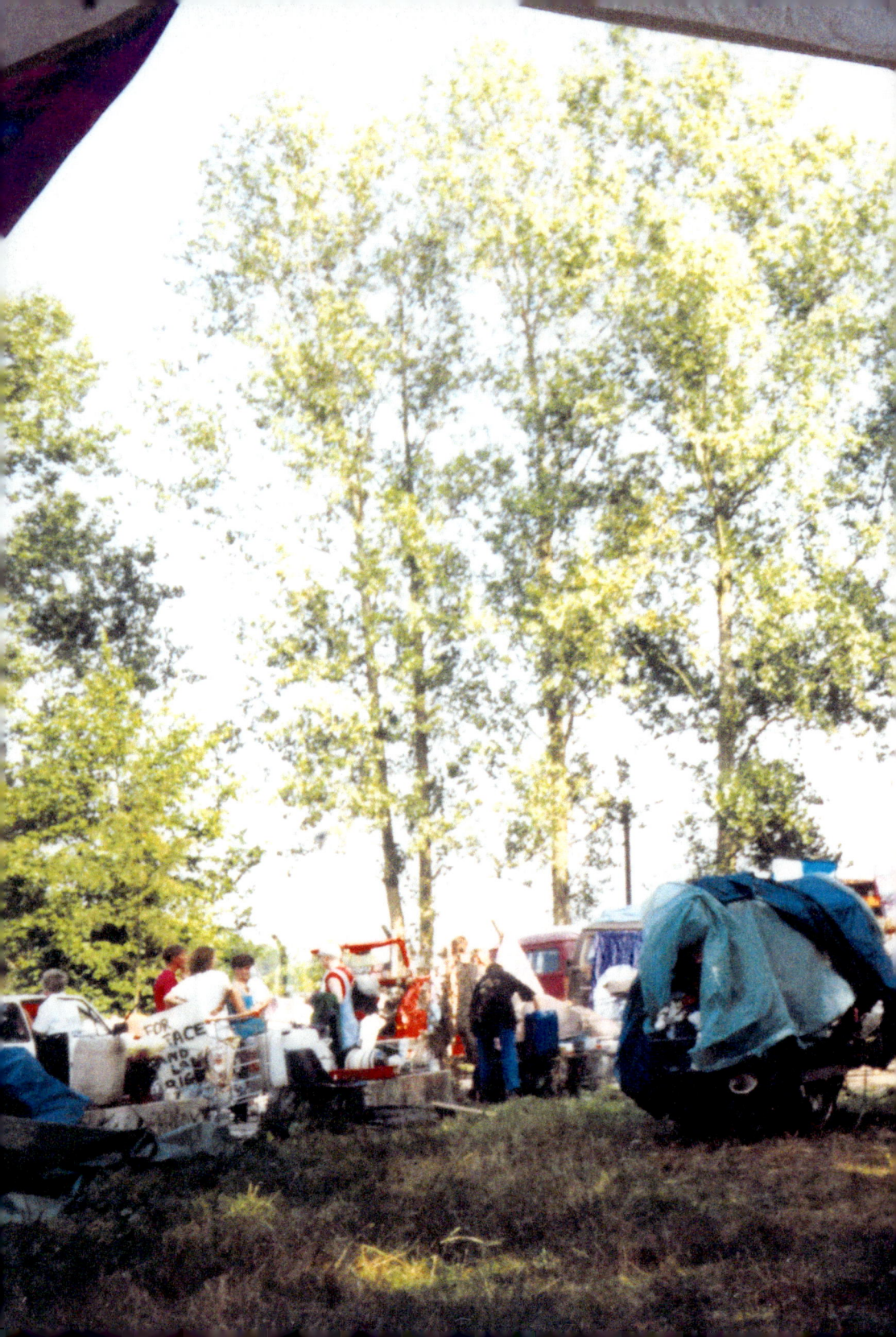

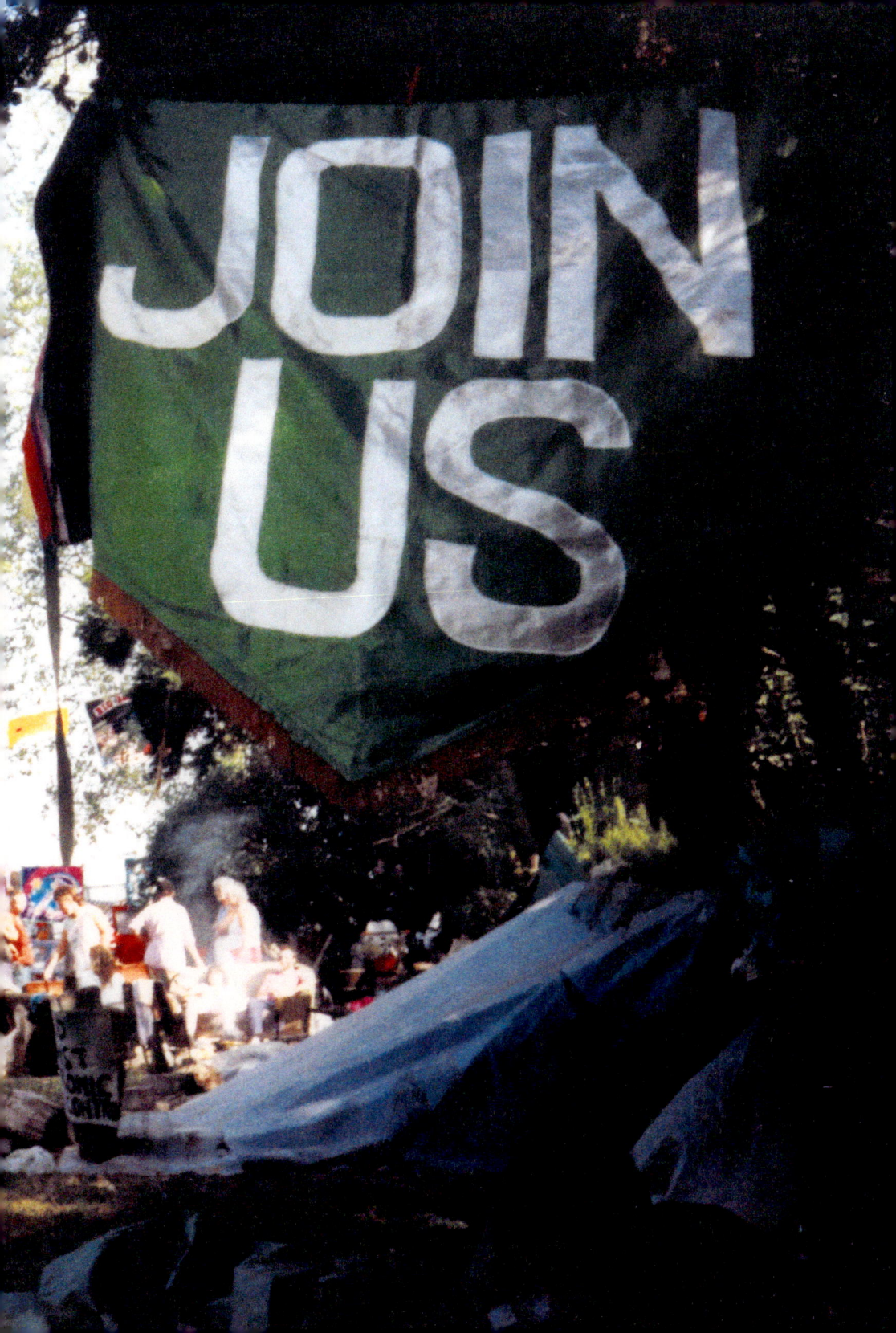

The designs for these banners include motifs that link the campaign to other peace and women's causes. Most commonly they combined the CND logo and female symbol, or the CND logo and the female-power clenched fist, itself evolved from a civil rights movement symbol. Doves, hands, and rainbows are also frequently incorporated. In addition to these more generic symbols, a range of motifs that represent the camp itself are often included.

Greenham women kept-up a campaign of non-violent actions to disrupt the operation of the base and the missile deployment practice exercises on Salisbury Plain. They cut the fence and repeatedly entered the base, blockaded the gates, tied the gates together, filled gate locks with super glue and on one occasion barricaded themselves in the sentry box at Yellow Gate. They also sought to demonstrate that USAF occupation of Greenham Common was illegal, through exhaustive research and a protracted court case to illustrate that it should be common land.

All these activities are symbolised on the Greenham banners and other artworks that take the camp as their subject. A wire fence motif and representations of wire cutters are often included, as well as depictions of the women's sleeping 'benders' – a bent wood frame covered in thick plastic – campfires, the caravans originally parked there that were removed during the evictions and each of the occupied gates.

A further motif – that of a web – is also included on banners. The creation of woollen webs, was a creative, disruptive, and symbolic activity undertaken by the women. 'For women of Greenham [the web] represents connections between women, or between ideas; it can be started at any point; it is fragile yet strong, and very beautiful. Moreover, weaving is traditionally women's work, individual yet also essential, constructive and beautiful. No two women will necessarily give the same interpretation. The web may be valued by some women not for its messages, but just for its practical ability utterly to bewilder police, or construction workers.'[47]

What is striking about these banners representing the camp, and Greenham banners generally, is that they rarely celebrate specific women who were part of the campaign; they focus on the shared experiences, actions and demands. The small number of exceptions commemorate the participation of a group of women in an event or activity, rather than a singular woman. For example, a small pink banner embroidered with the names of the women, partners and children who participated in the first

Previous pages: Greenham Common Women's Peace Camp.
Opposite: *Justice. Yellow Gate. Autonomous Women. Non-Aligned. Non-Violent. Anti-Racist.*
Next pages: Obstruction, RAF Greenham Common, October 1982.
Photograph by Edward Barber.

YELLOW GATE

AUTONOMOUS WOMEN
NON-ALIGNED
NON-VIOLENT
ANTI RACIST

JUSTICE JUSTICE JUSTICE

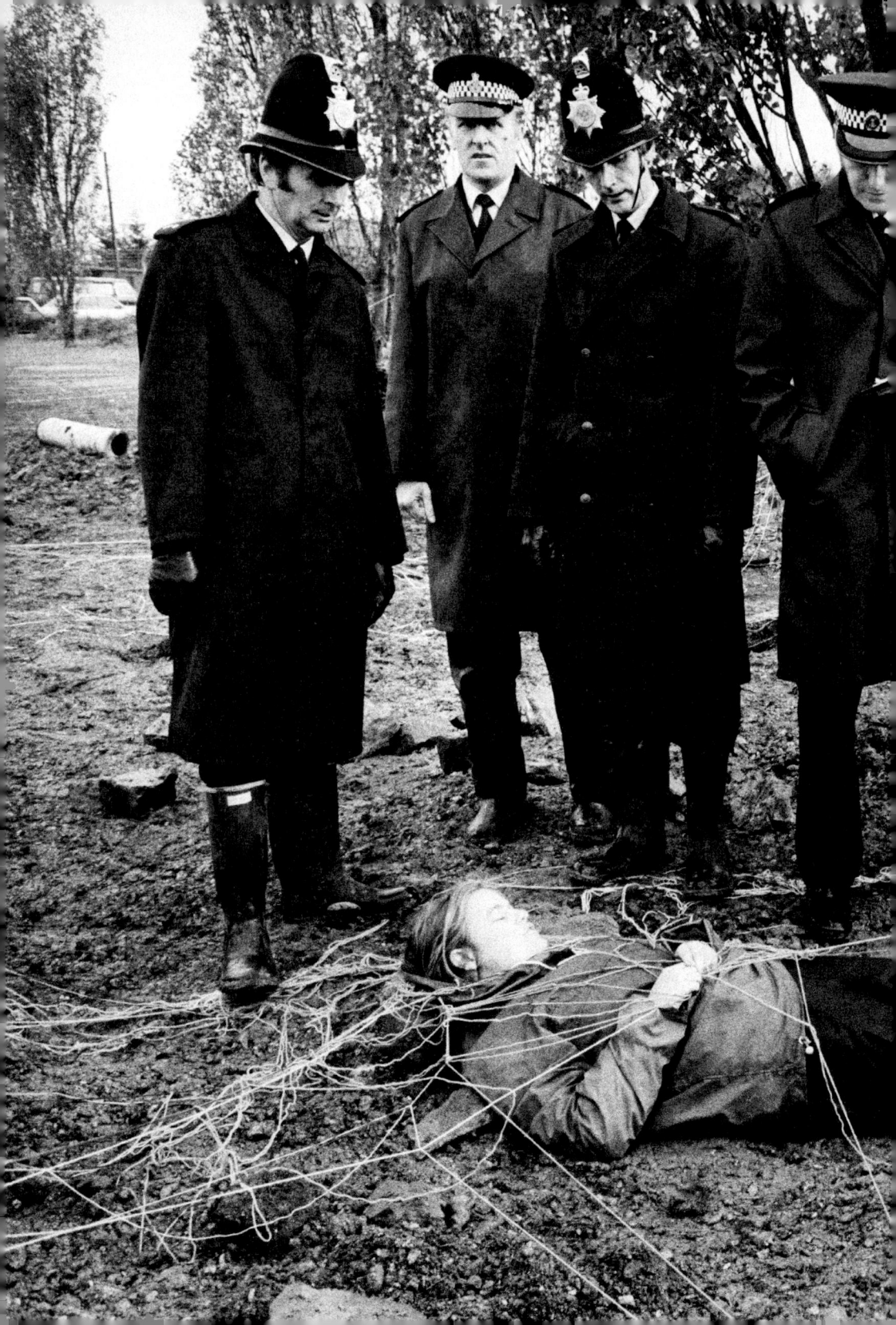

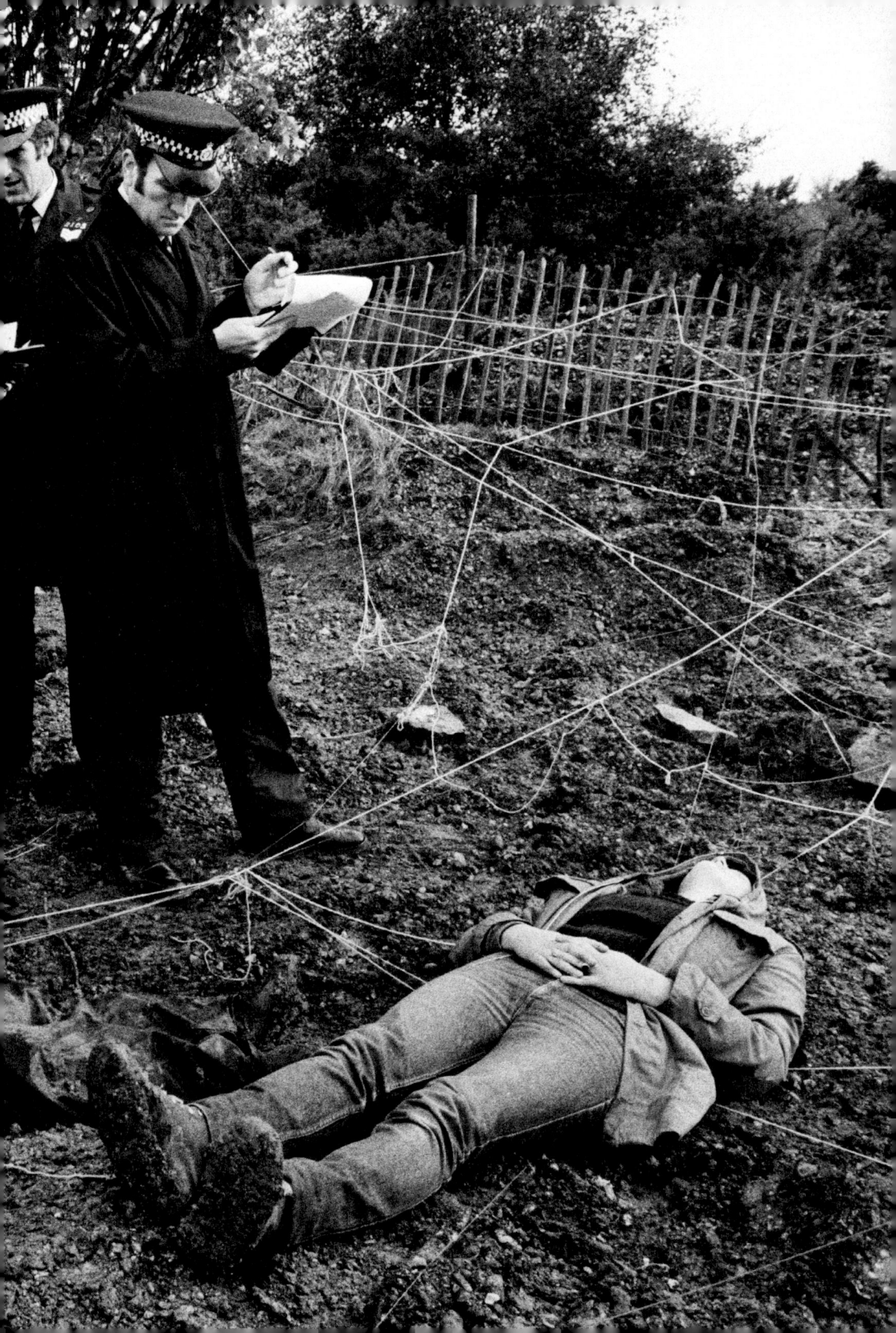

walk to Greenham, made by Campbell in the Pentagon Peace Ribbon format. The names of the people who housed and helped them during the walk are also inlcuded along the bottom edge of the banner. In the centre there is a CND symbol overlaid with a leaf, and the acronym 'WFLOE [Women for Life on Earth] 1981'.

A further exception is Howse's banner dedicated to Welsh Yellow Gate resident Helen Thomas. She was tragically knocked down and killed at Greenham by a police horsebox, in the summer of 1989. Her death significantly affected the women with whom she lived and worked. There is a permanent memorial to Thomas in the peace garden that was erected on part of the site of the Yellow Gate camp, opened on 5 October 2002.

Predominantly, the designs that represent the camp signify its flat structure for decision making, publicity and activity. All women were considered equal and decisions were made by consensus: 'In consensus decision-making... Everyone has the opportunity – some would say responsibility – to say what they think. As each person speaks, everyone's understanding of the decision deepens. The discussion is continually refined and reworked to assimilate each person's ideas and feelings...'[48] There were disagreements and arguments, and the establishment of separate camps at different gates reflected this, but there was no overriding spokesperson or peace camp leader.

In this way, Rozsika Parker proposes that the Greenham banners differ markedly from some suffrage designs and their campaign philosophy: 'The set of [suffrage] heroine banners reflects the organisational ideology of the Suffrage movement, which unlike present-day feminism with its insistence on a collective structure, set up its leaders as sources of inspiration and devotion. Thus, a banner commemorating members of the WSPU (Women's Social and Political Union) who were forcibly fed in prison is embroidered with the names of Mrs Pethick-Lawrence, Christabel Pankhurst, Mrs Pankhurst and Annie Kenney in art nouveau lettering.'[49] None of the 'heroines' of Greenham are celebrated on their banners, only the activities and beliefs of the camp.

The approach taken to the design of Greenham banners illustrates the women's shared ideology. To find most of the names of the women behind the campaign and the banners, you must look beyond the objects themselves, as they are seldom mentioned or glorified.

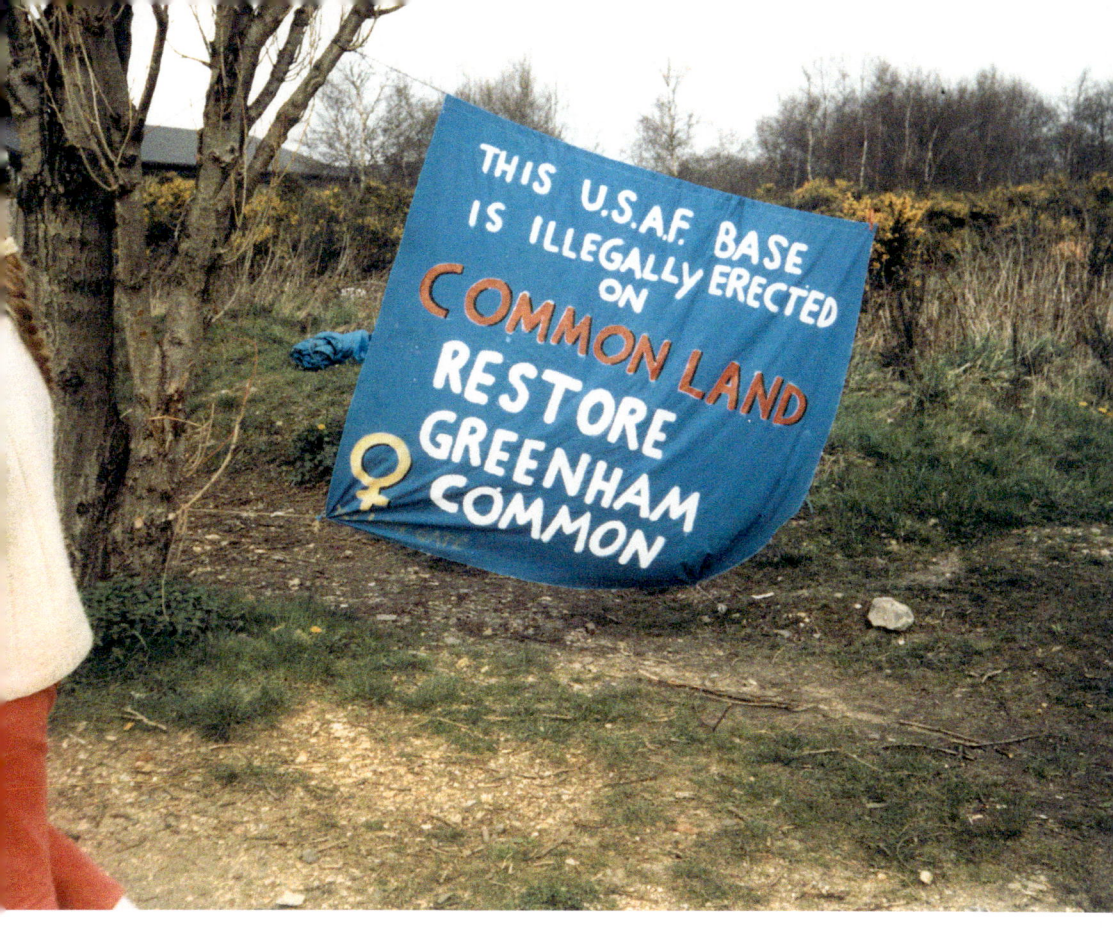

Above: *This USAF Base Is Illegally Erected on Common Land. Restore Greenham Common.*

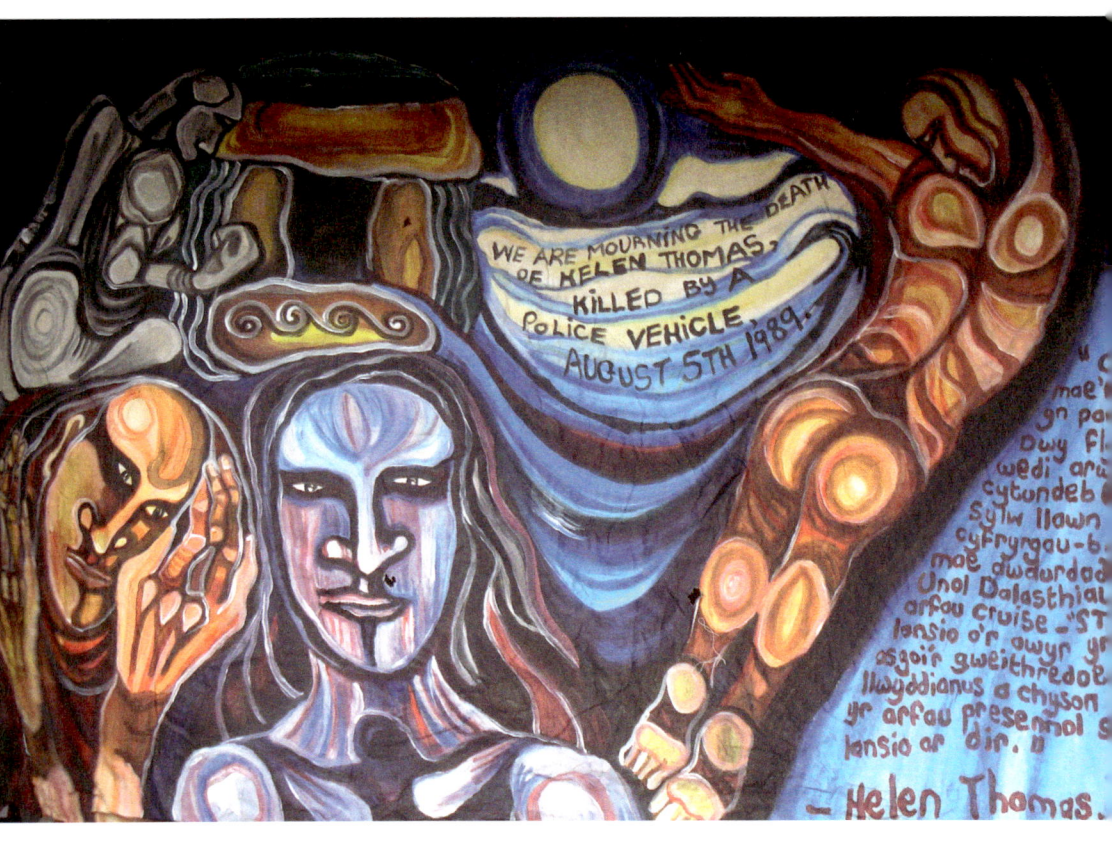

An ink on paper drawing by Katrina Howse (opposite) and a detail from one of her banners (above), both dedicated to campaigner and writer Helen Thomas, who was killed, while waiting to cross the road, by a West Midlands Police horsebox, at Greenham on 5 August 1989.

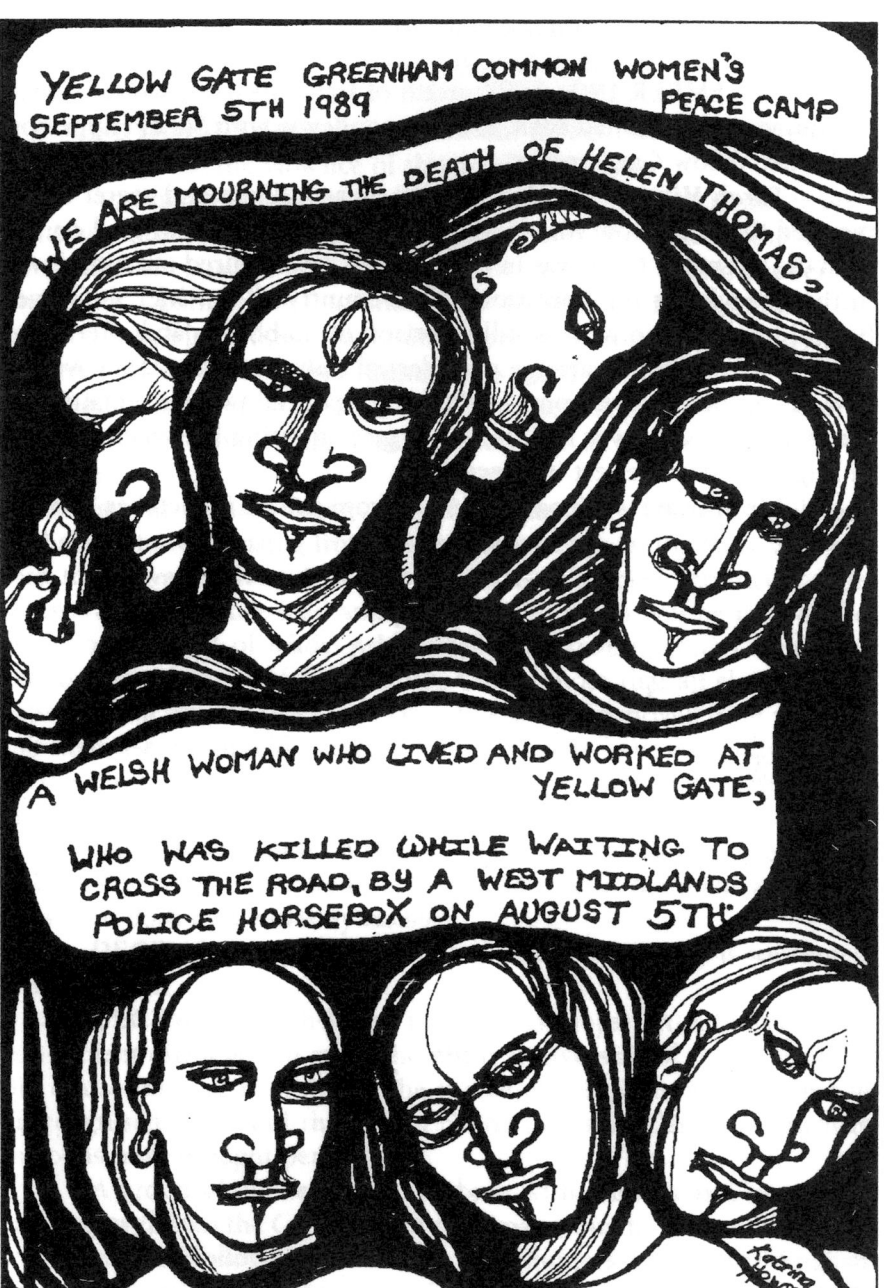

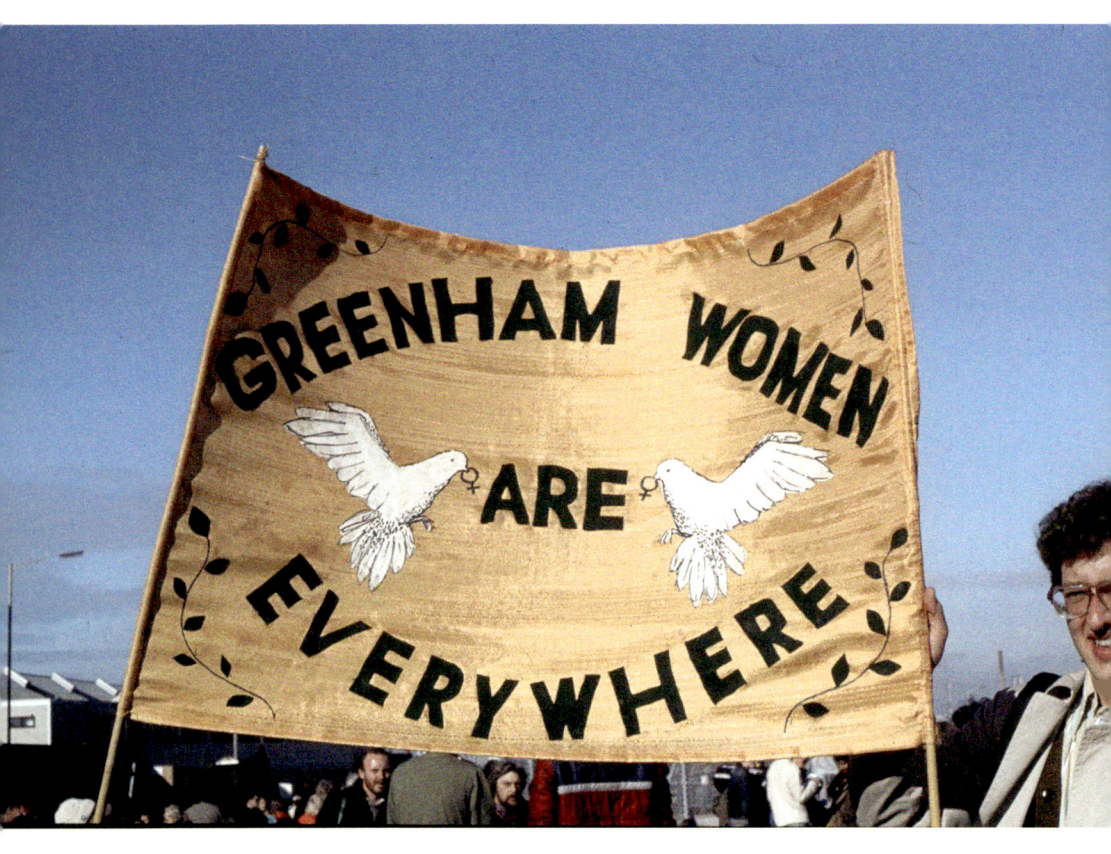

Above: The notion *Greenham Women Are Everywhere* caused much debate at the camp and beyond. Some believed that you could be a Greenham Woman if you shared the values of Greenham women, campaigned for peace in other ways, but did not live at Greenham. Others maintained that to be a Greenham Woman, you needed to live there. The latter view upset women who had jobs and children, so could not live at the camp.

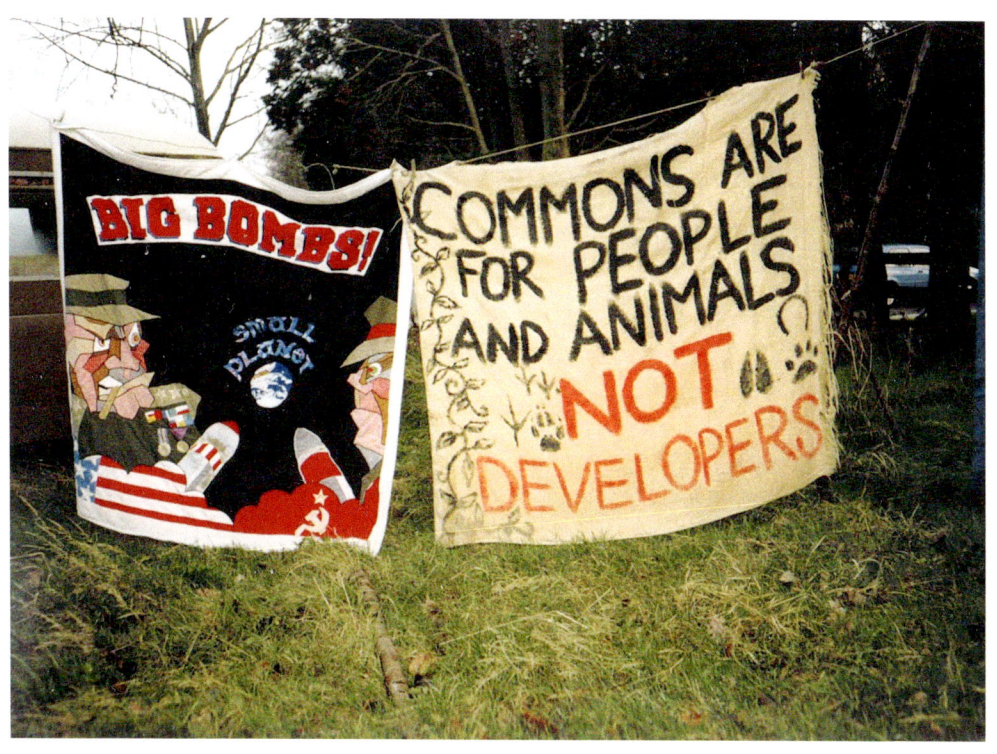

Above: Greenham Common, c. 1990.

Other Marches and Protest Sites

When the walk to Greenham, in summer 1981, was arranged, the women involved joined a long and ongoing tradition of marches to peacefully raise awareness and support for a cause. In April 1981 its four organisers heard that a group of Scandinavian women were planning to walk from Copenhagen to Paris during the summer of that year, to draw attention to their anxieties about the nuclear threat overshadowing their lives. They chose to coordinate a similar walking protest with Greenham Common as their destination.

The undertaking of these campaigners is akin to that of the women who took part in the Suffrage Pilgrimage of 1913. This saw non-militant suffragettes from the National Union of Women's Suffrage Societies (NUWSS) join one of six marching routes, starting from destinations including Newcastle, Bangor and St. Austell, to London. Walking over a five-week period, they held public meetings and gathered support along the way. All the routes converged on Hyde Park for a rally on 26 July 1913.

On the first march, the group took nine days to walk from Cardiff to Greenham Common. The subsequent Star Marches to Greenham, in the summer of 1983, saw women from a range of starting points walk for a number of days, to converge on the Common.

Protest marches and walks were a regular focus of activity for Campaign for Nuclear Disarmament (CND) members from the organisation's founding in November 1957. Their events often culminated or commenced from sites connected to nuclear science and military activity, in regional and rural places – like Greenham – where the nuclear arms were developed and later stored, including Aldermaston, RAF Molesworth, RAF Upper Hayford and RAF Brawdy. The Easter marches to the Atomic Weapons Research labs at Aldermaston started in 1958 and repeated at scale until 1965, attracting thousands of campaigners. A fiftieth anniversary march was held on the route in 2008.

Cold War nuclear developments provoked the establishment of peace camps at many of the sites to which marches were organised. The reputation

Opposite: Protests at RAF Brawdy.

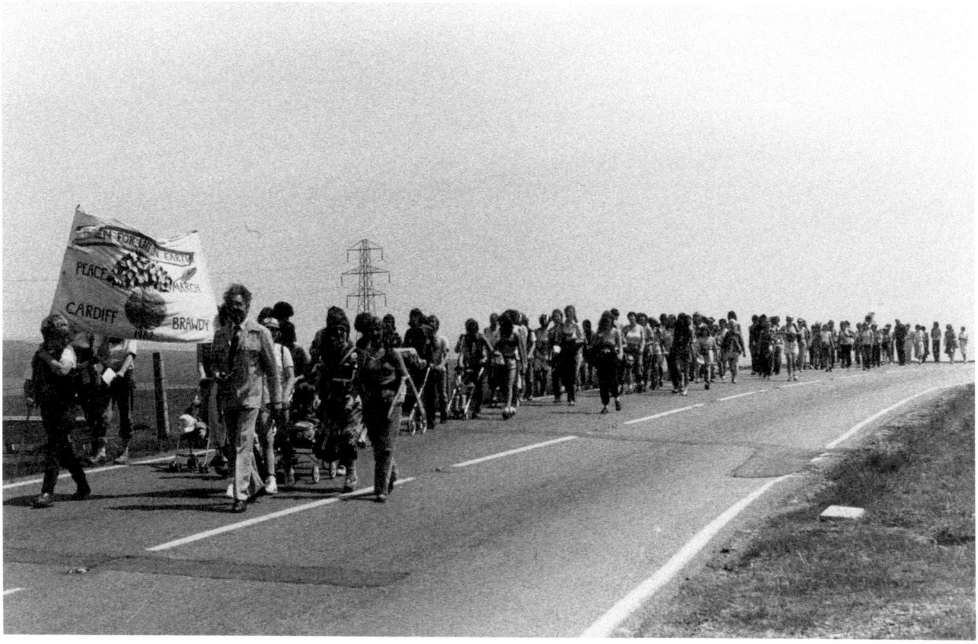

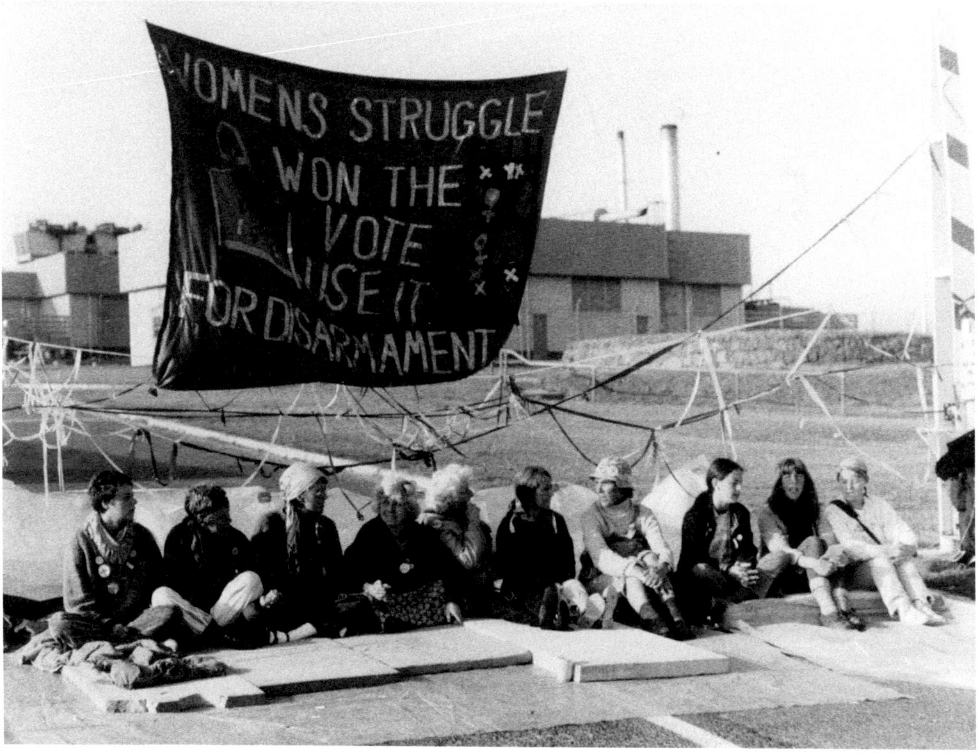

and profile of Greenham was raised by its women-only status, the scale of the camps at different gates – particularly in the early years – and the women's profile-raising campaigning. Katrina Howse was involved in the setting-up of the RAF Waddington Women's Peace Camp prior to moving to Yellow Gate at Greenham. A camp a Burghfield, the site of a nuclear ordnance factory in Berkshire, was a close neighbour to the Greenham Camp and home to men and women.

Greenham campaigners were involved in other camps, sometimes resident there, and participated in walks and marches to them. Photographs in Campbell's archive show her taking part in the March 1982 march from Cardiff to RAF Brawdy. Liz Forder created a banner that Thalia later made a replica of (opposite). In Forder's design, the 'Women for Life on Earth' symbol is appliquéd on to a pink baby blanket, with the year and start and finish point for the march. Campbell and her husband Ian were commissioned to make three banners for the CND organised March to Molesworth, 1985. The banners were designed by Ian and sewn by Thalia. A family photograph shows them being tested in the wind on the cliffs above Aberystwyth; one had to be reinforced following this outing. Banners and placards of extraordinary variety are present in the photographs that record the proliferation of peace camps and marches throughout this time.

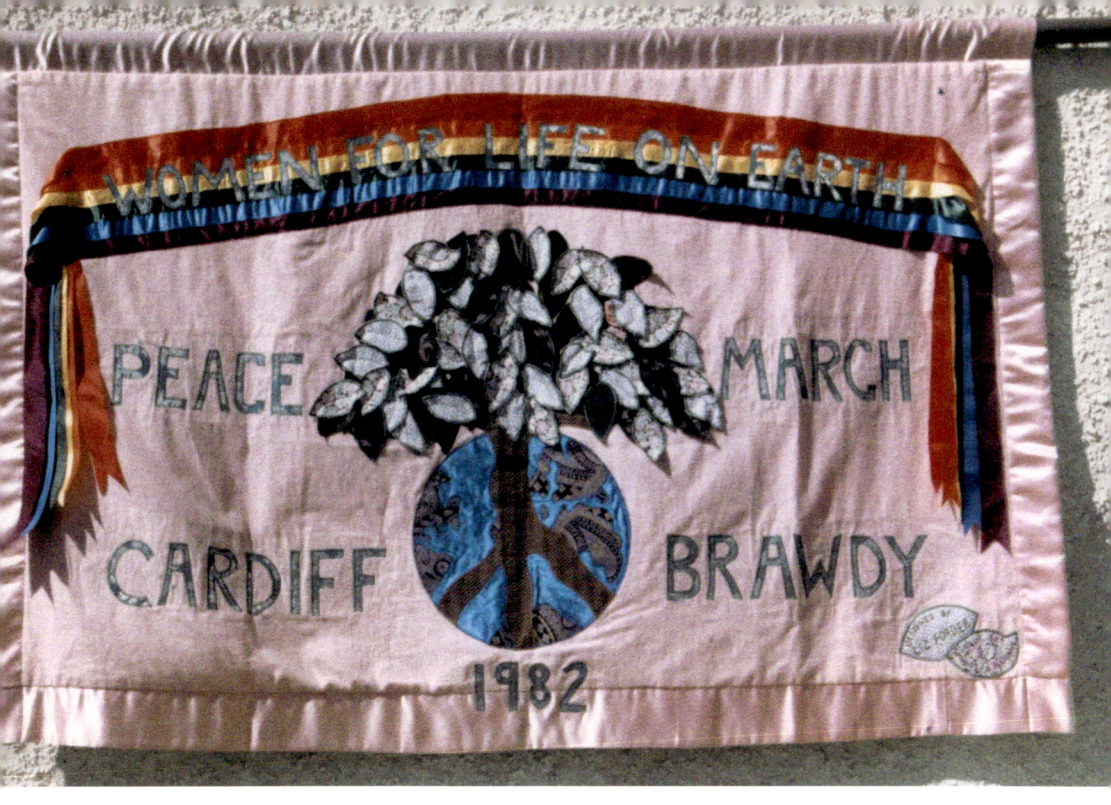

Above: Thalia Campbell's replica of Liz Forder's banner for the March to Brawdy, 1982.

Next pages: Campbell was commissioned to make three banners for the Easter 1985 March to Molesworth. Here Campbell is photographed by her husband Ian, with her children Angus and Lucy, testing the banners on a beach in West Wales. The pink fabric of the banner Campbell is holding tore and had to be repaired before it was used for the march. RAF Molesworth was chosen as the second site to house Cruise missiles, along with Greenham, and was home to a mixed gender peace camp.

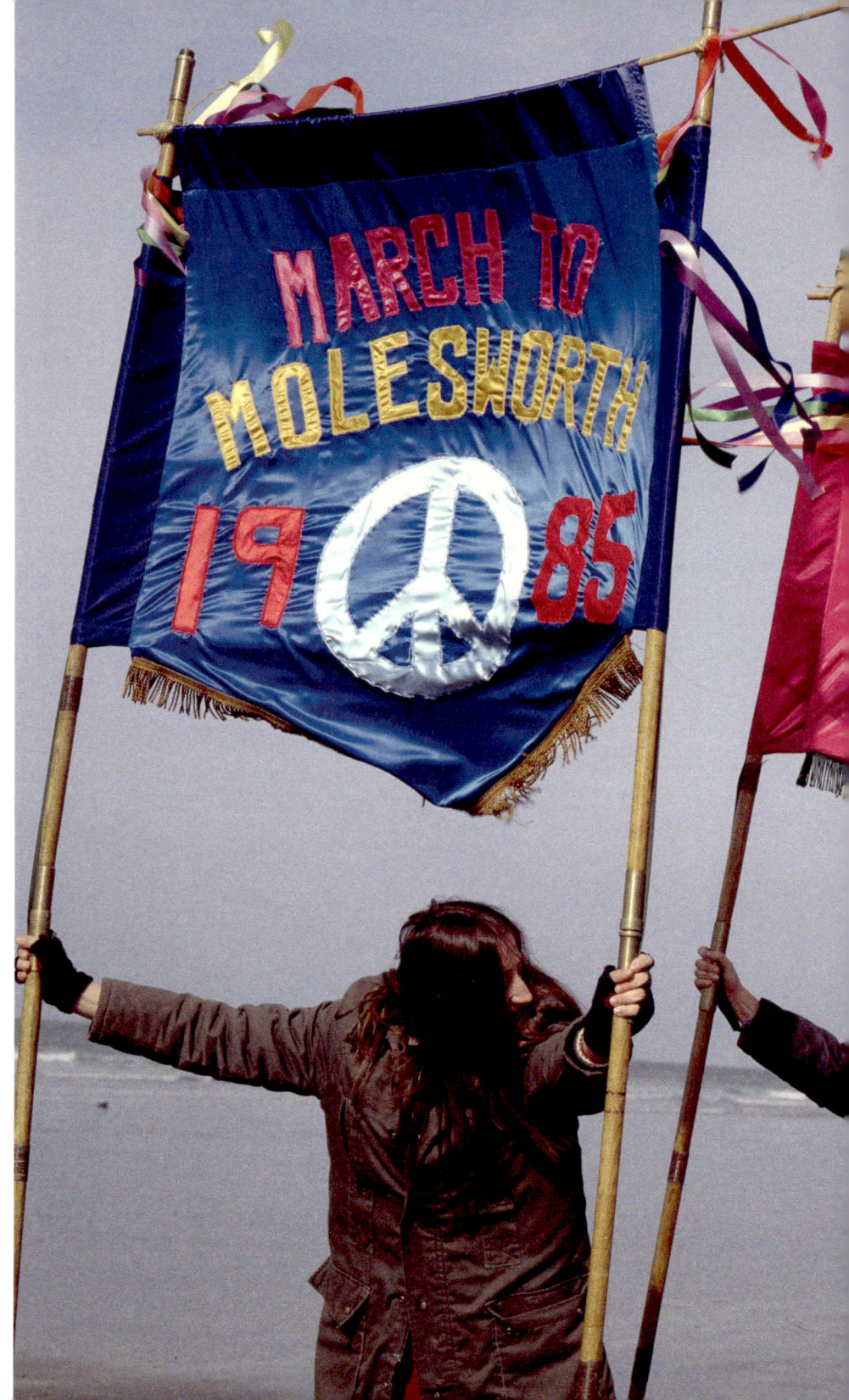

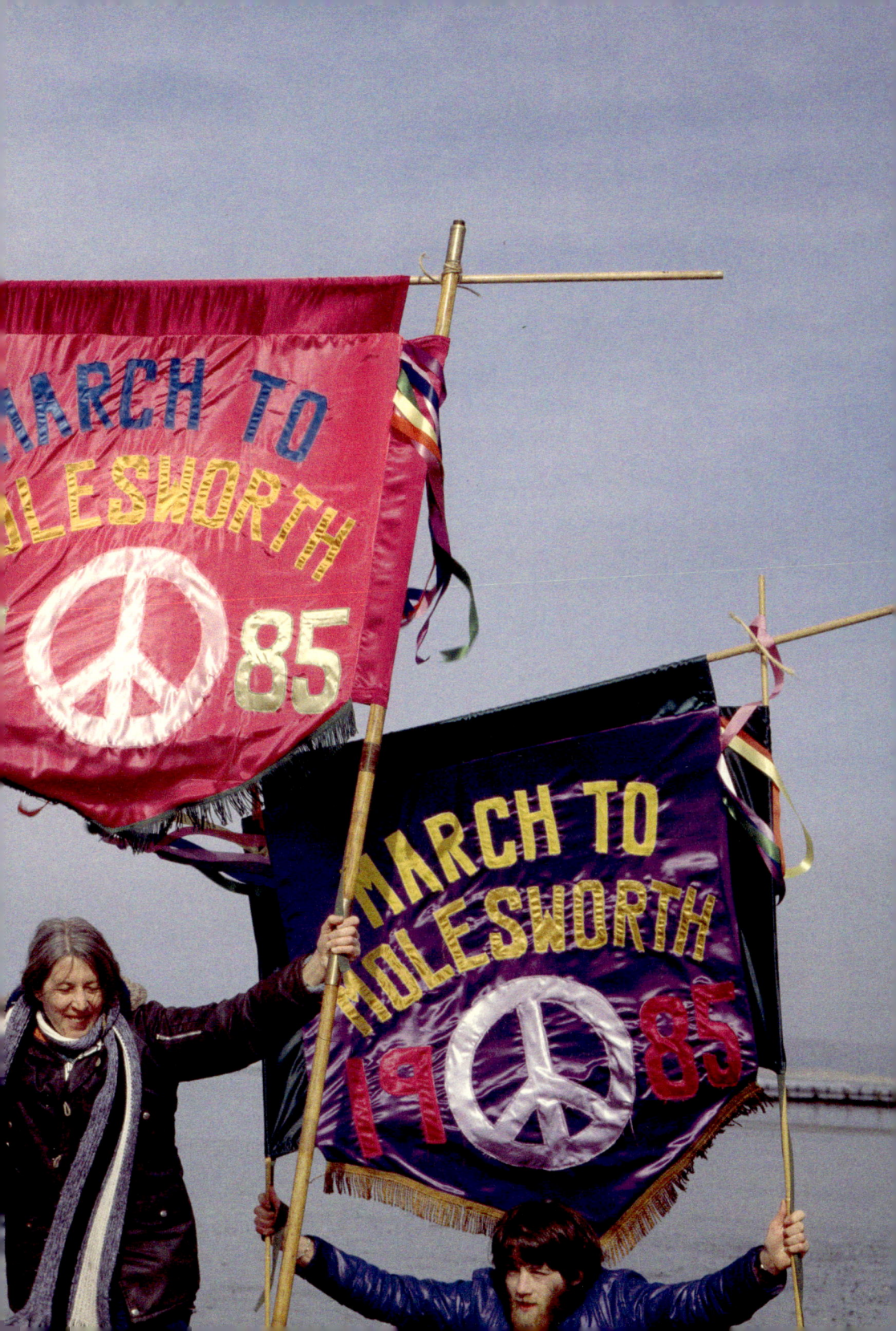

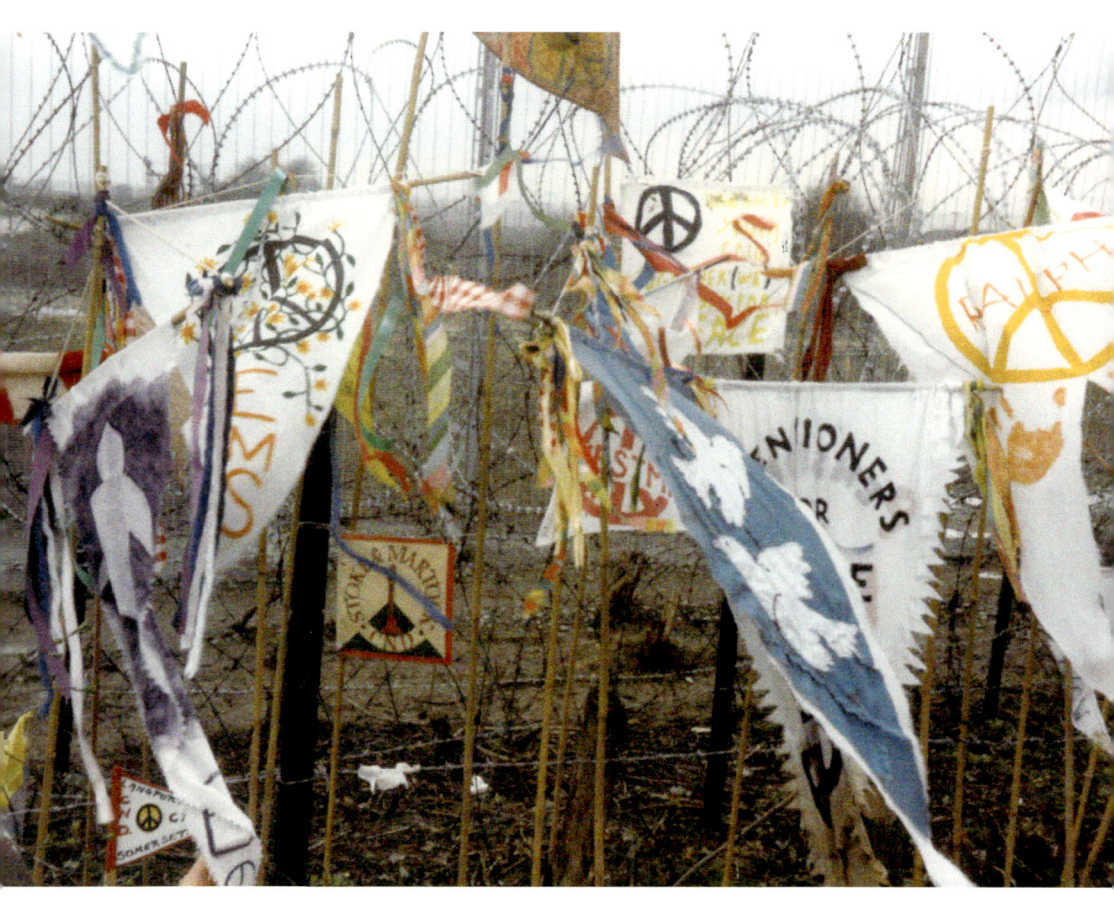

Above: Pennants hanging from the fence at RAF Molesworth.

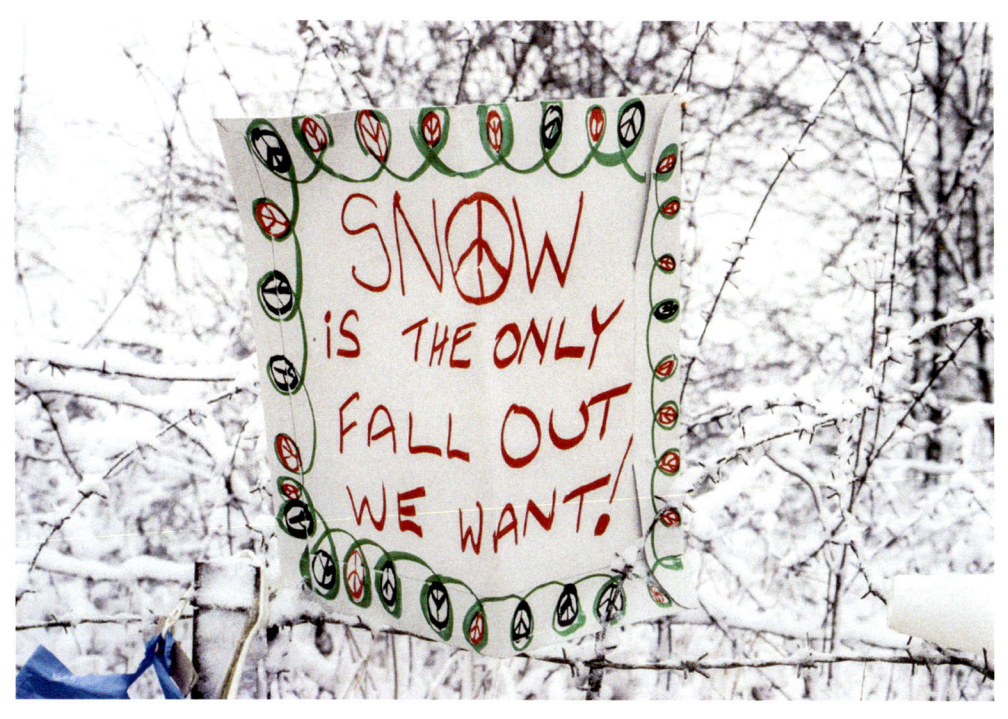

Above: *Snow Is the Only Fall Out We Want!* banner at Anti-Cruise missile demonstration at RAF Molesworth on 2 February 1986. Photograph by Phil Crean.

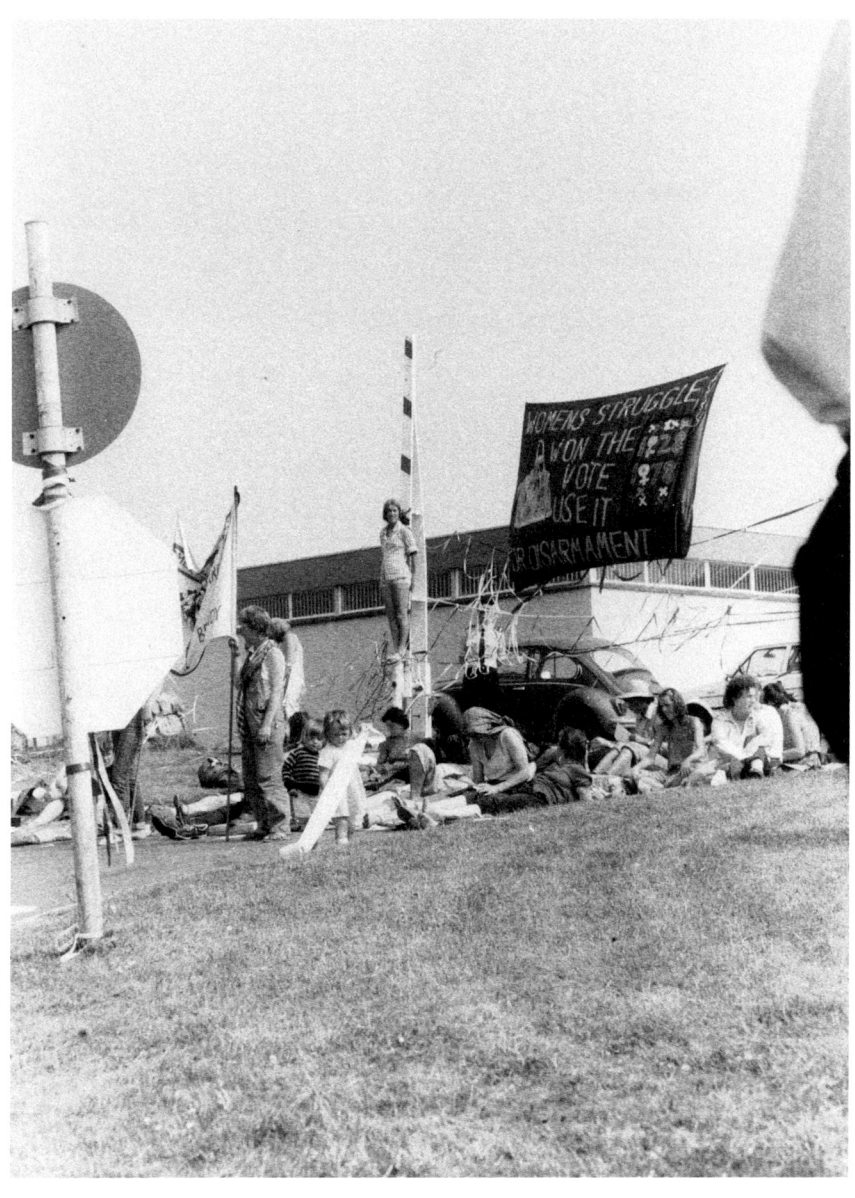

Above: RAF Brawdy.

Opposite: RAF Upper Heyford in Oxfordshire was used as a base by the US Strategic Air Command, including for their F-III strike aircraft.

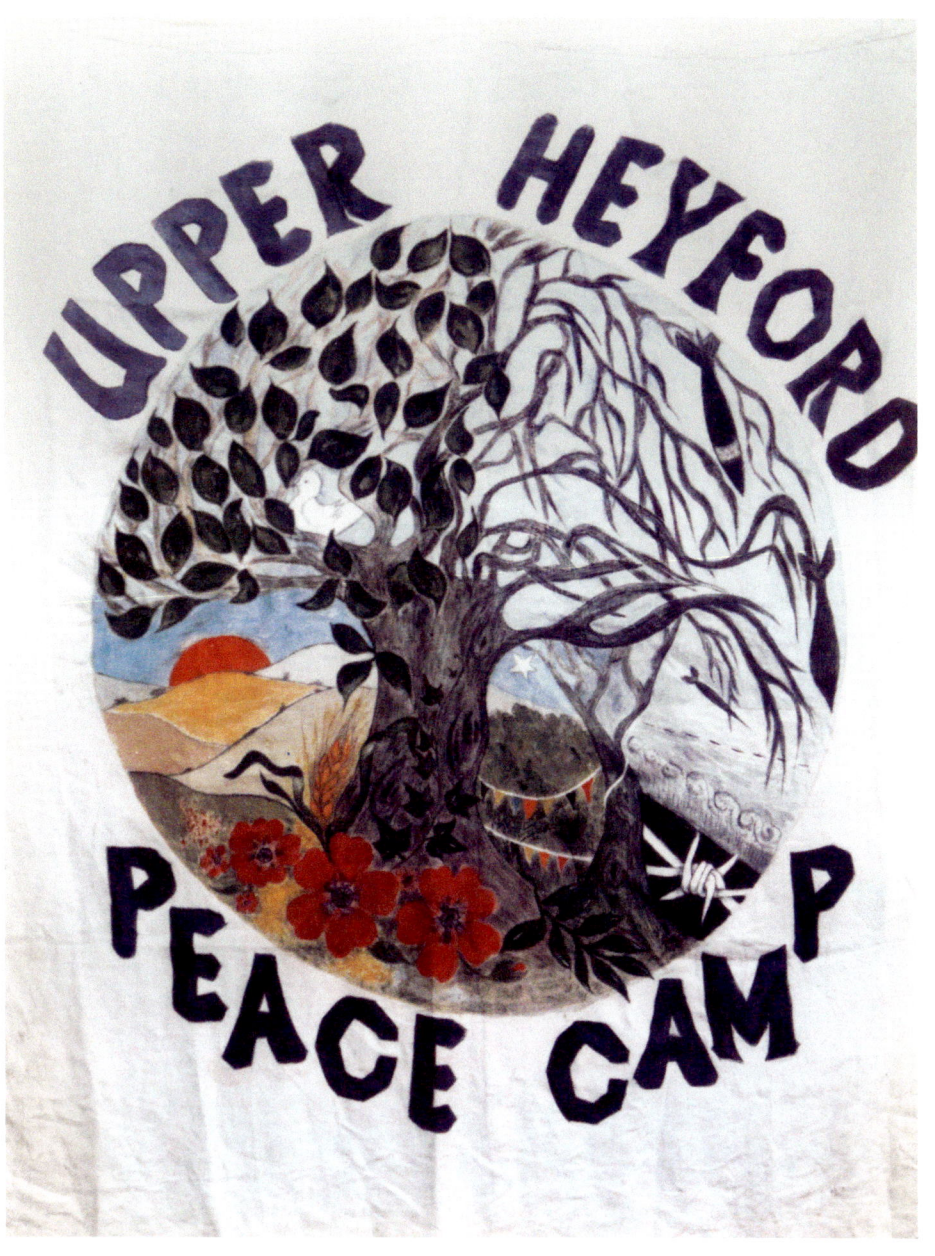

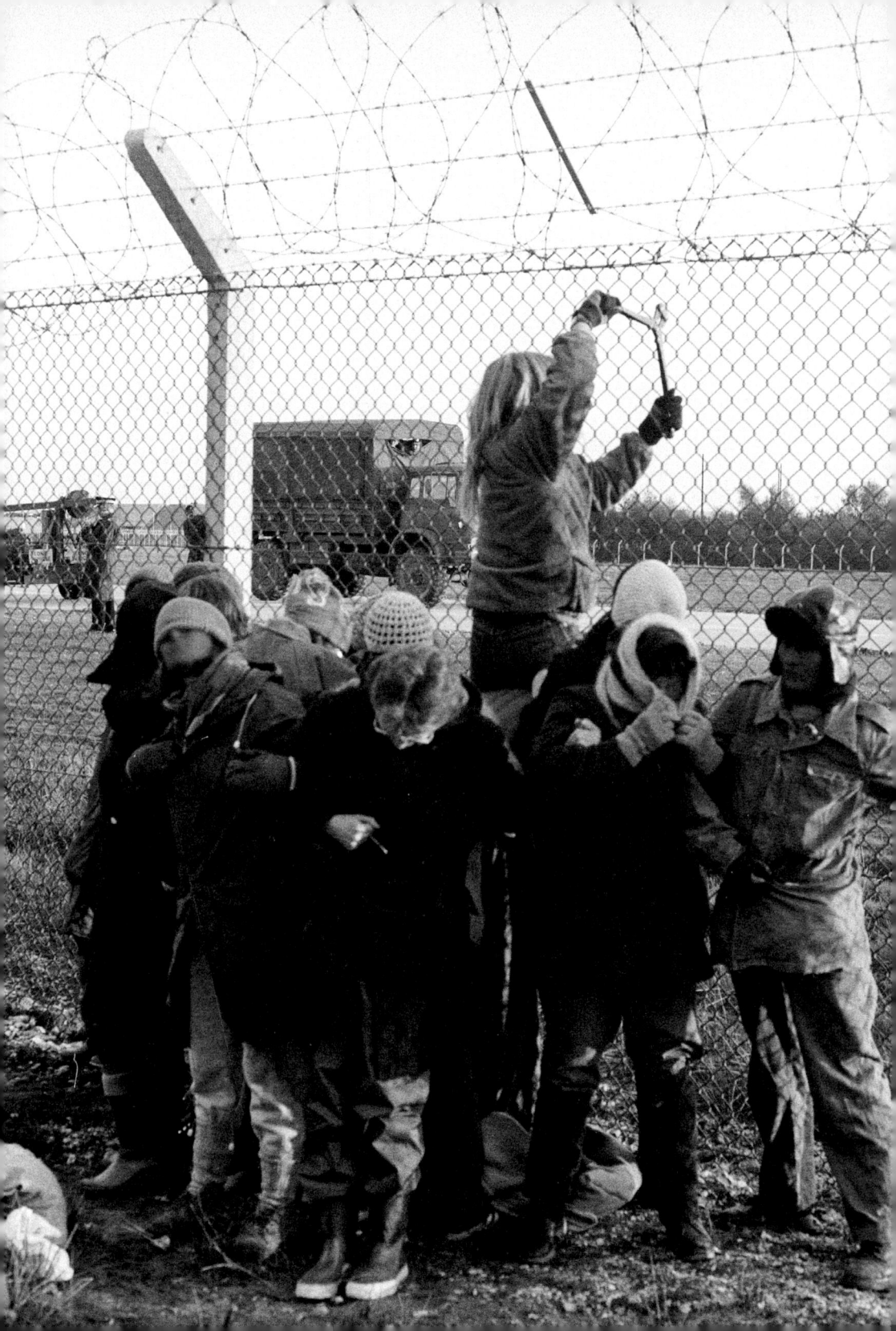

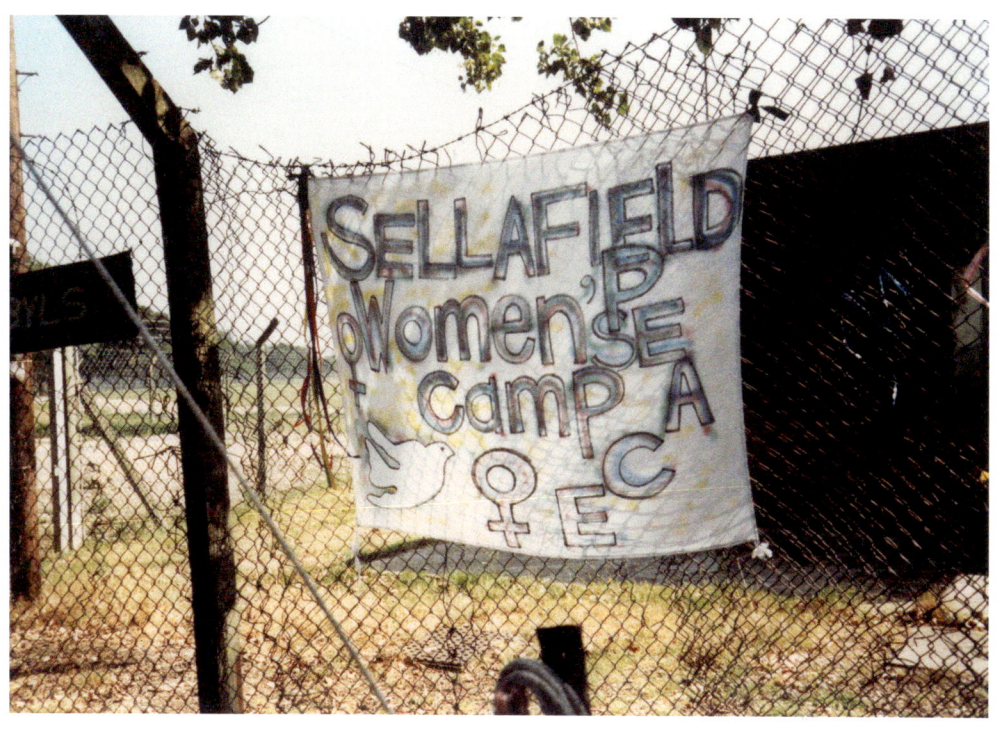

Opposite: Cutting the fence at RAF Brawdy.

Above: Banner at Greenham, c.1990s. Sellafield, a large nuclear site in Cumbria, was the focus of a long running protest camp in the 1990s.

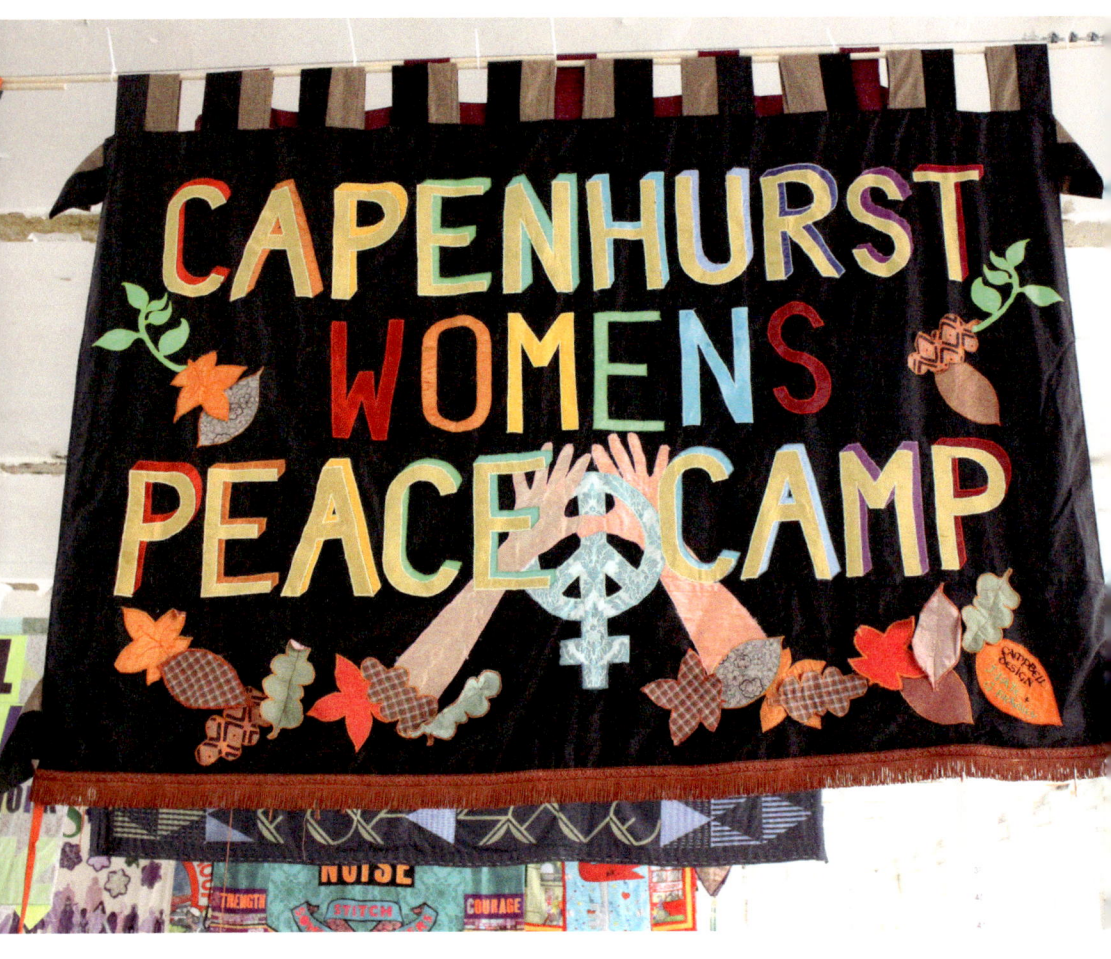

Above: *Capenhurst Women's Peace Camp*. This camp, at a nuclear site for uranium enrichment, ran from October 1982 to March 1983. Photograph by Melanie Diggle, taken at *Banner Culture*, an exhibition by Mid Pennine Arts at Brierfield, Lancashire, in 2019.

Opposite: Protesters at the Atomic Weapons Establishment at Aldermaston.

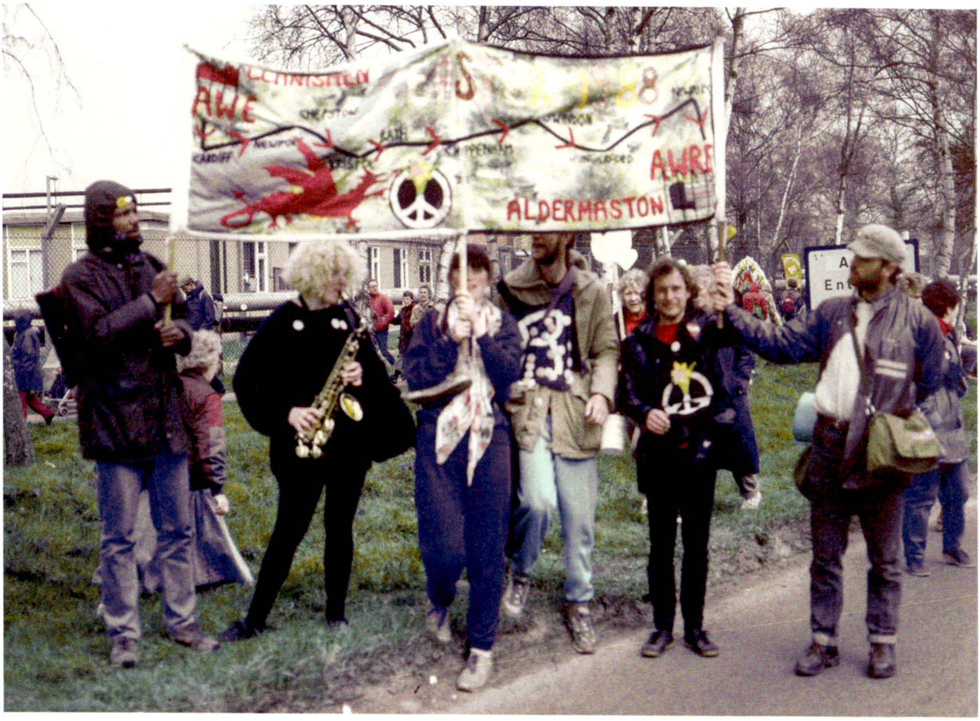

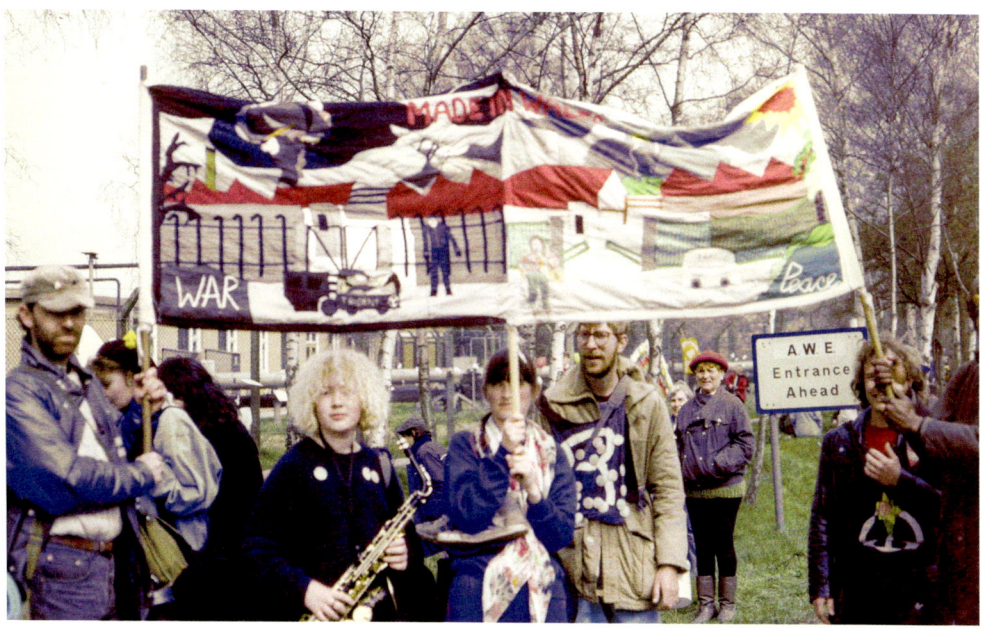

Banners Representing Groups and Organisations

Banners representing specific groups, often regional branches of a national organisation, or people from a specific place united in fighting for the same cause, were used in peace events, organised by the Greenham women, and more widely through CND and other networks. Their designs most closely follow the form of historic banners, commissioned for a specific church or branch of an organisation such as the Girl's Friendly Society, Women's Institute, Co-operative Society, Union, or Mason's Lodge. They commonly combine the group's name or cause, and the name of the place they come from, with an image related to this place or the focus of their interest or protest. Such banners could be used at any event to inform people of a group's participation and support for a march or action. In photographs of events at Greenham, and CND events, this type of banner gives a sense of the extent to which campaigners travelled across the country to take part and demonstrate their support for a campaign.

As professional banner makers, Thalia and Ian Campbell were commissioned to make several banners of this type, including designs for the Christian CND group, the Medical Campaign against Nuclear Weapons national organisation as well as its group in Sussex.

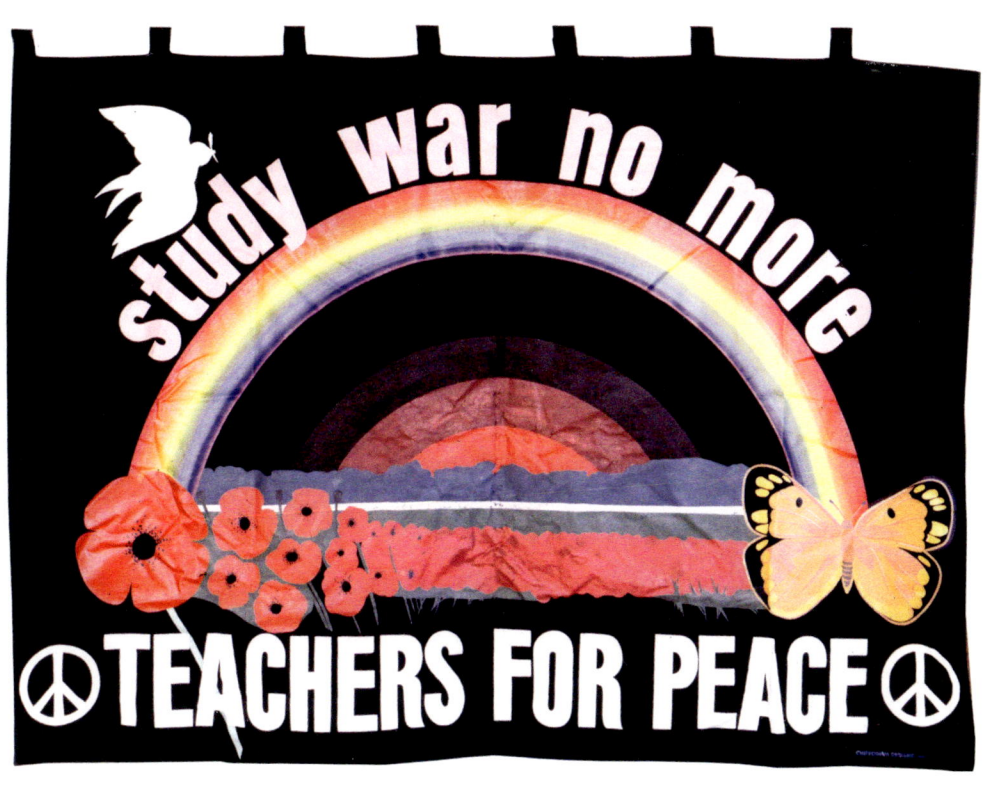

Above: *Teachers for Peace, 1982*. A contemporary postcard of the banner attributes it to 'Mike, Hilary, Maggie and John'.

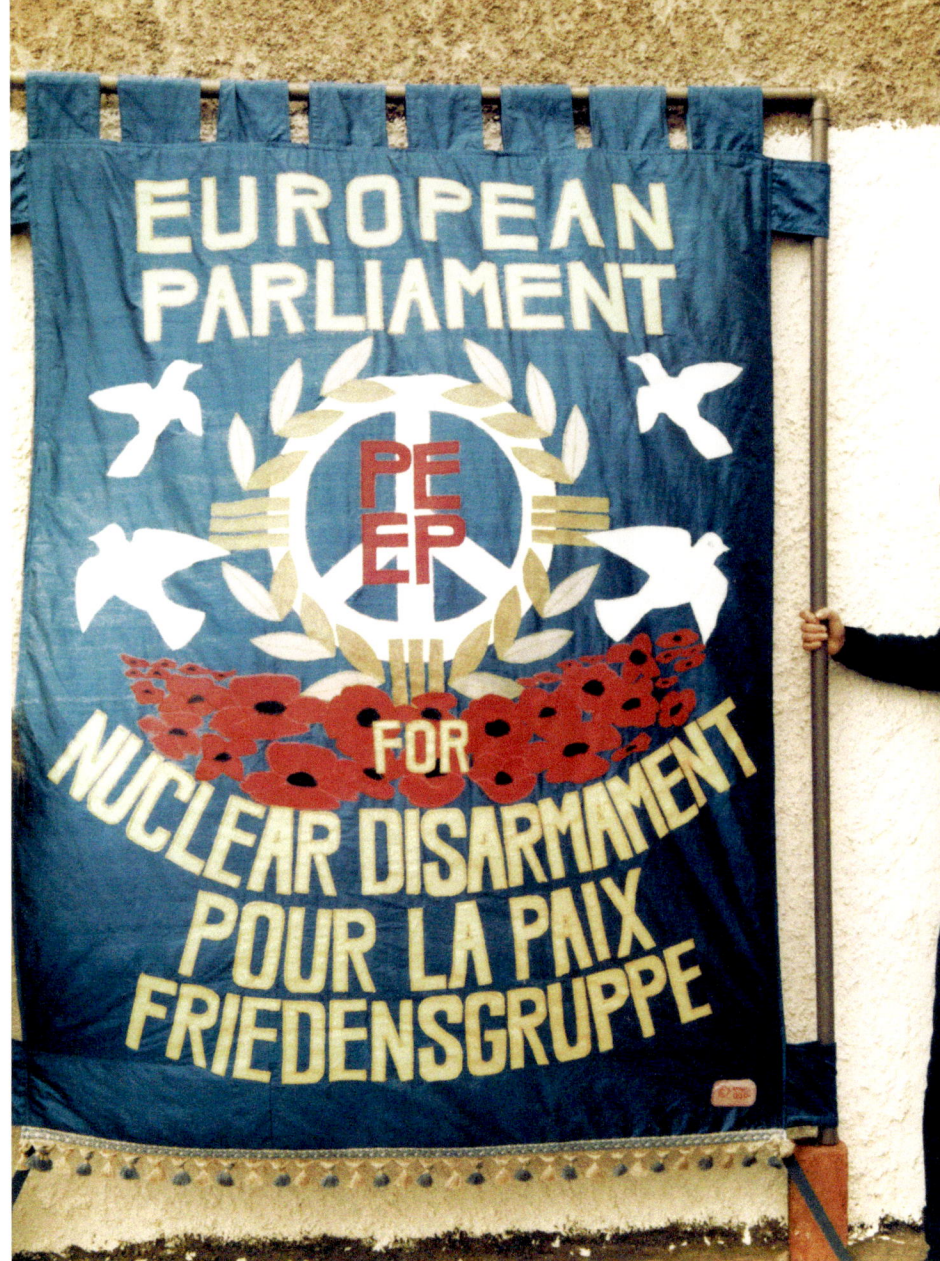

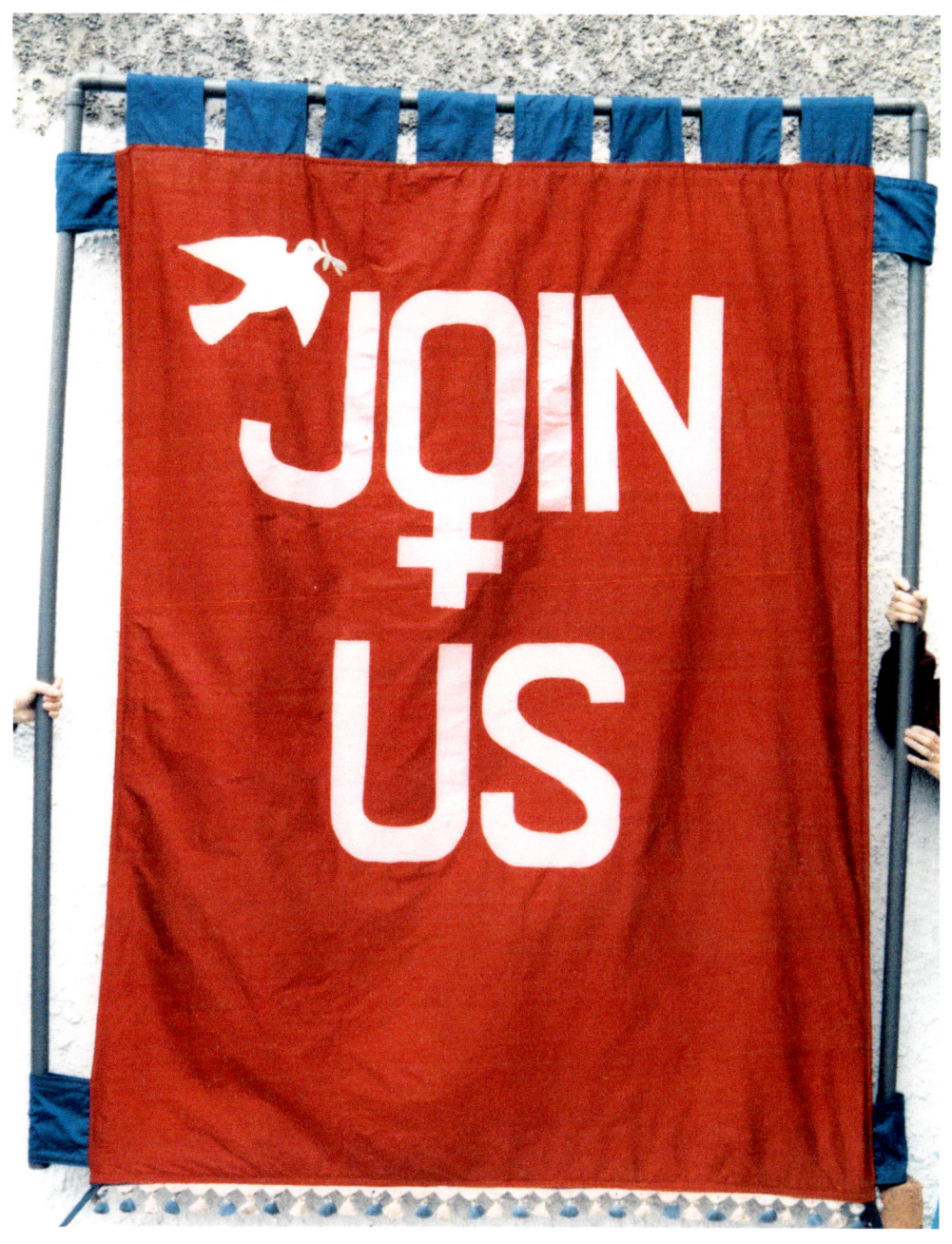

European Parliament for Nuclear Disarmament banner, by Thalia Campbell,
front (opposite) & reverse (above).

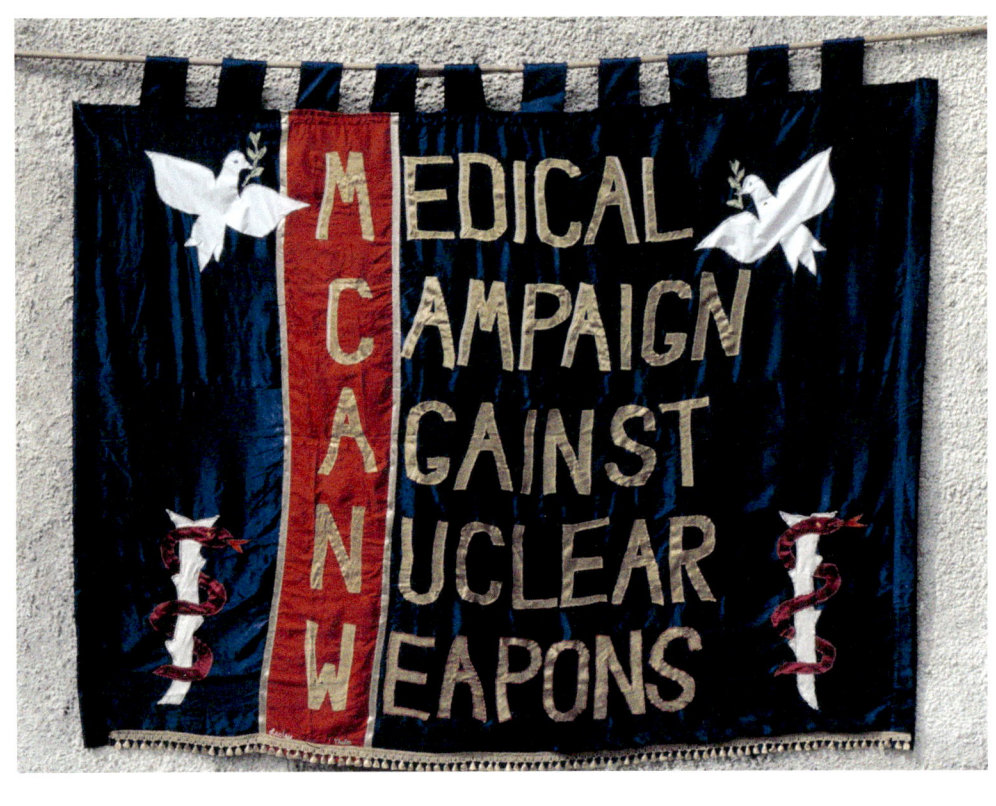

Above: *Medical Campaign against Nuclear Weapons*, 1983. Both banners on these pages were designed by Thalia Campbell. This one was made with help from Jan Higgs and Lesley Owen.

Opposite: *Medical Campaign against Nuclear Weapons Sussex*.

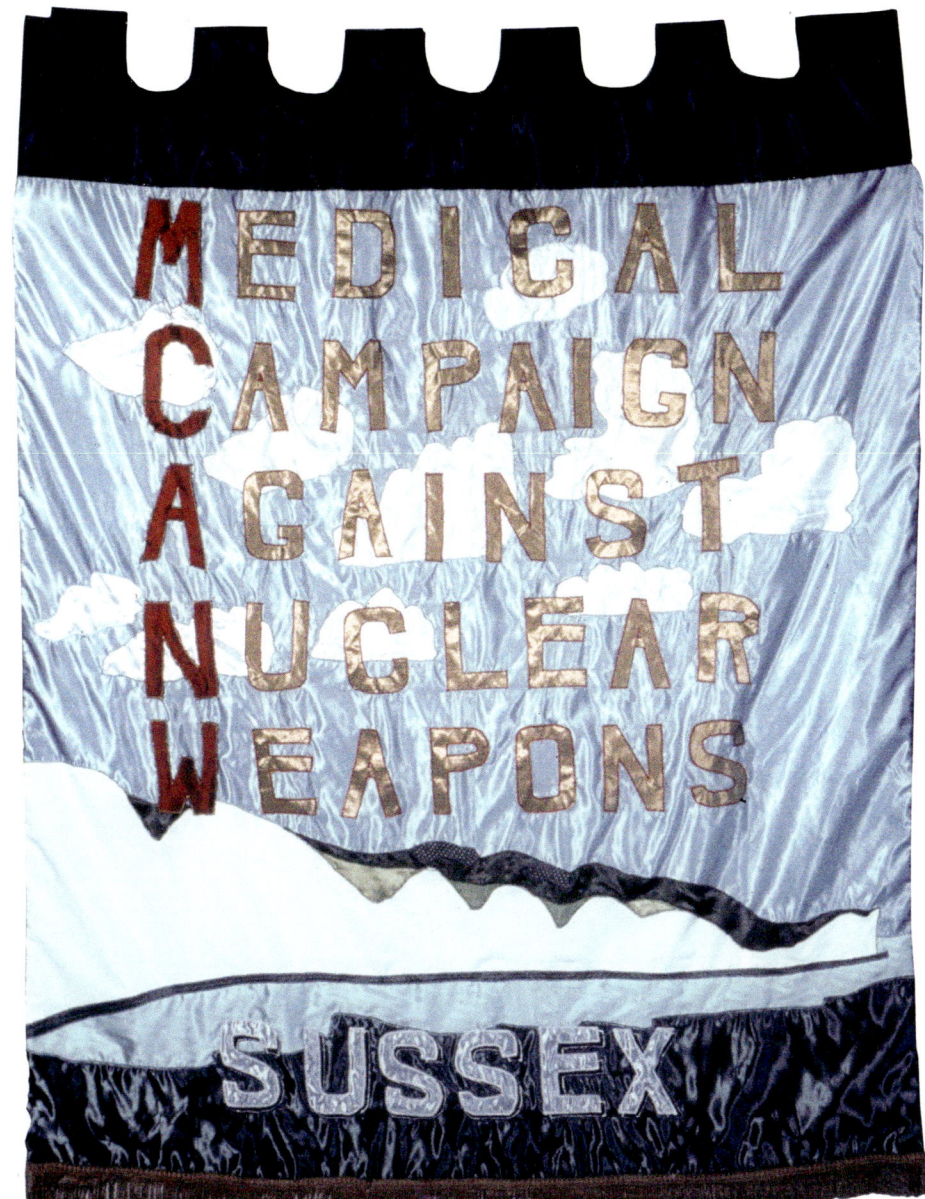

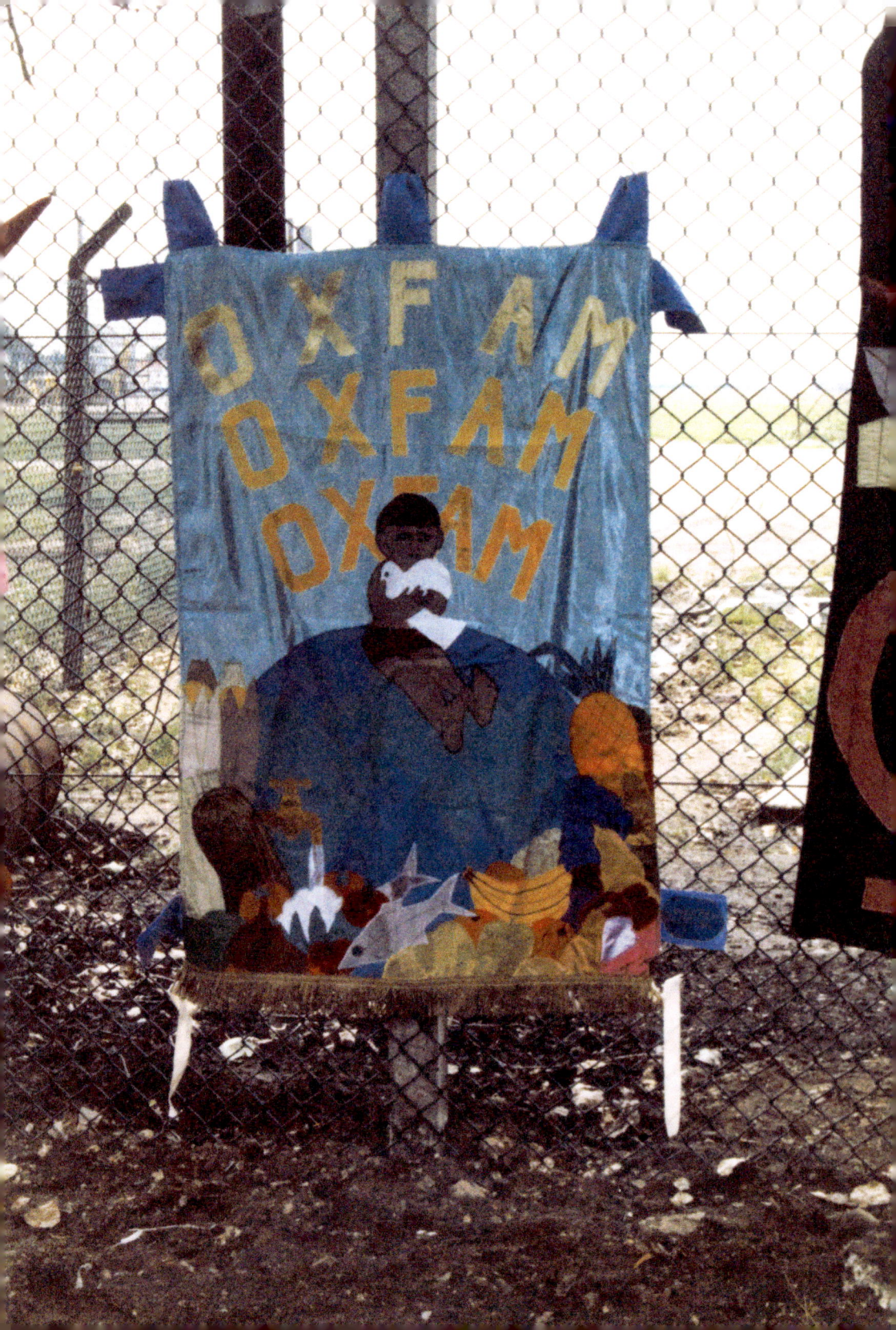

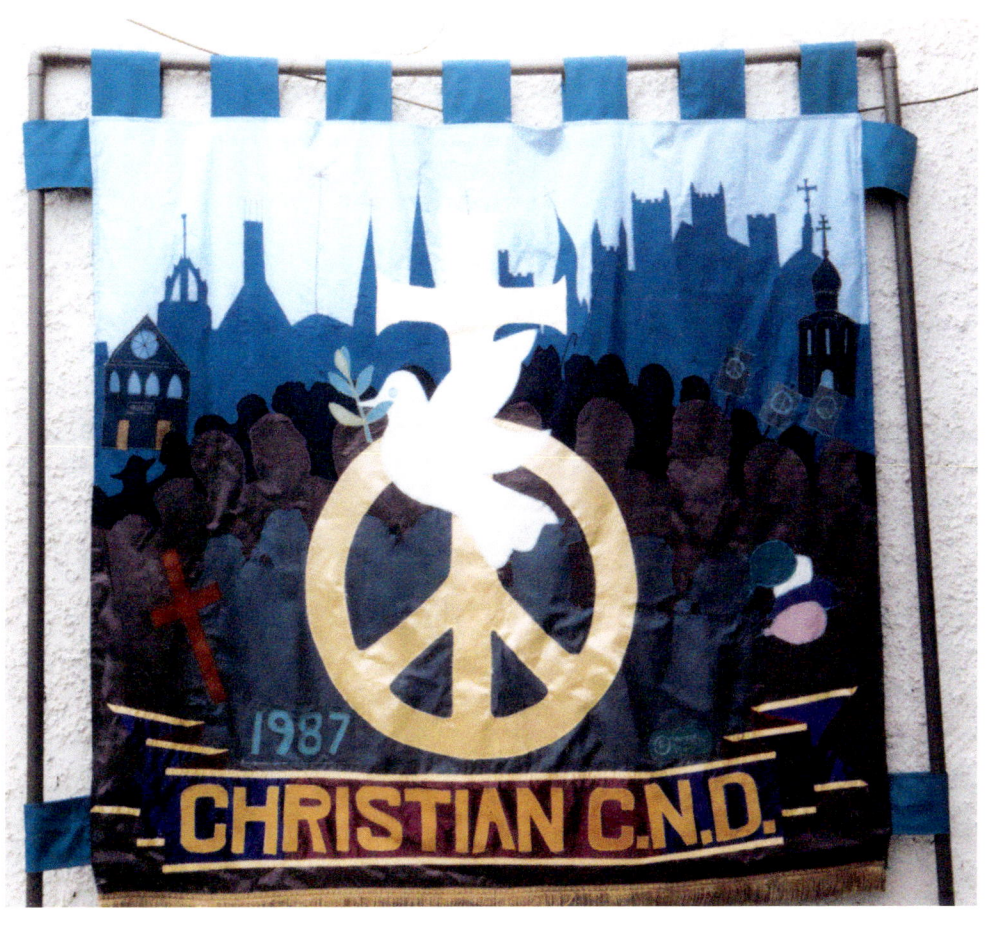

Banners commissioned from Thalia Campbell:

Opposite: *Oxfam*.

Above: *Christian* CND.

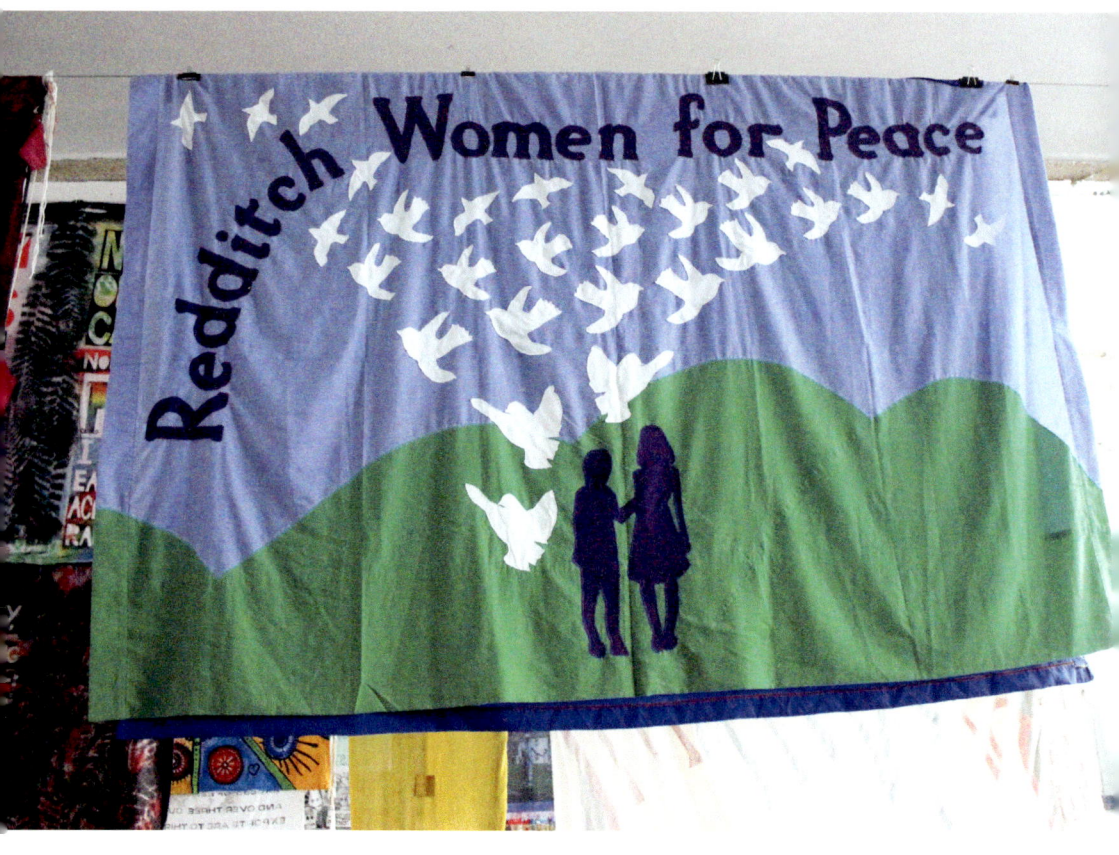

Above: *Redditch Women for Peace*. Photograph by Melanie Diggle, taken at *Banner Culture*, an exhibition by Mid Pennine Arts at Brierfield, Lancashire, in 2019.

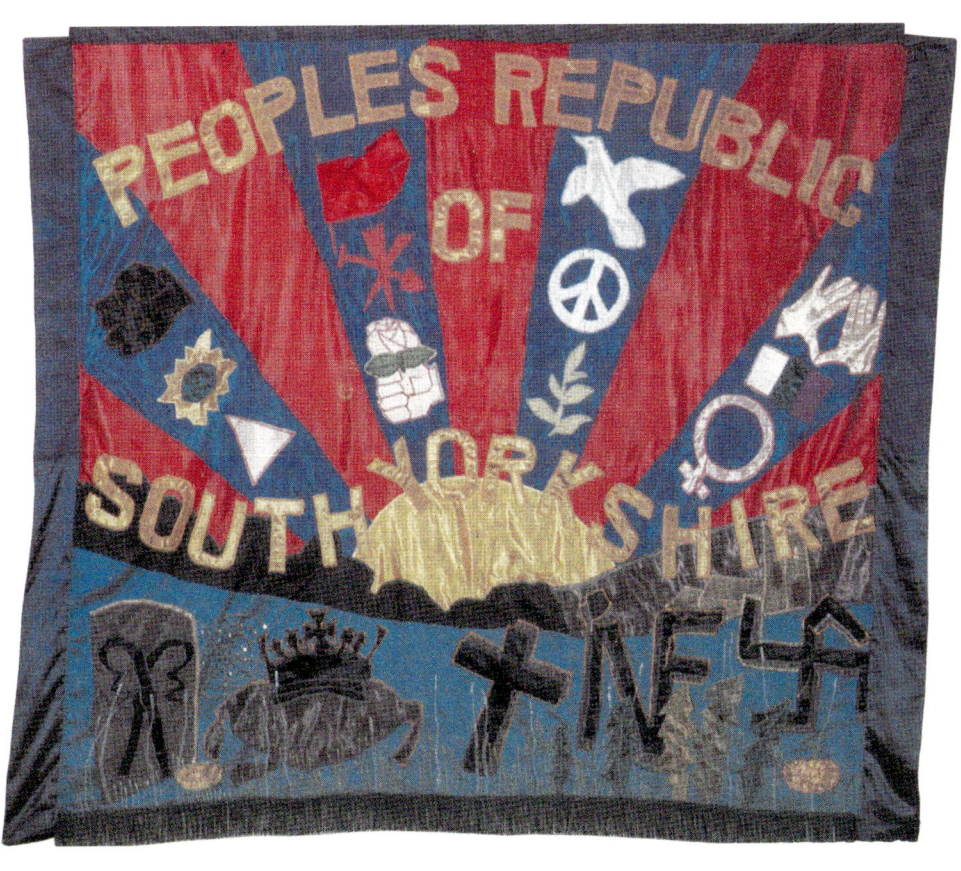

Above: *People's Republic of South Yorkshire*. Designed by Thalia Campbell in 1978 and made in 1984 for Lois and Colette Cameron-Miller who lived in Sheffield.

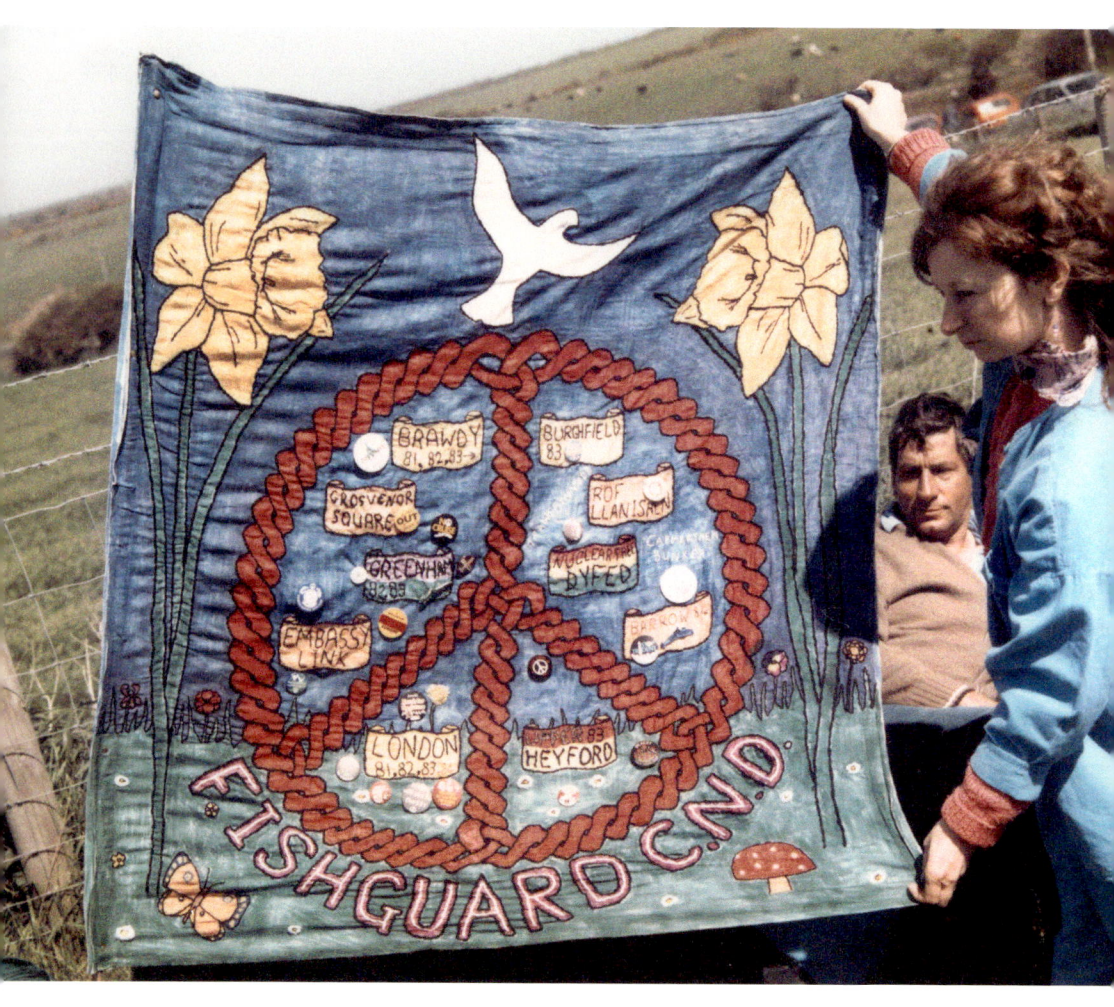

Above: *Fishguard* CND.

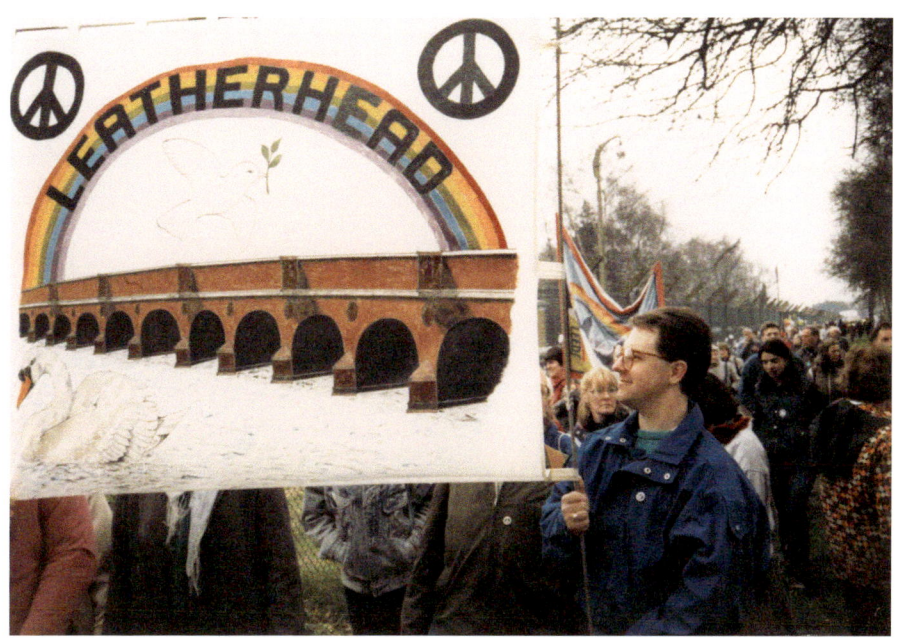

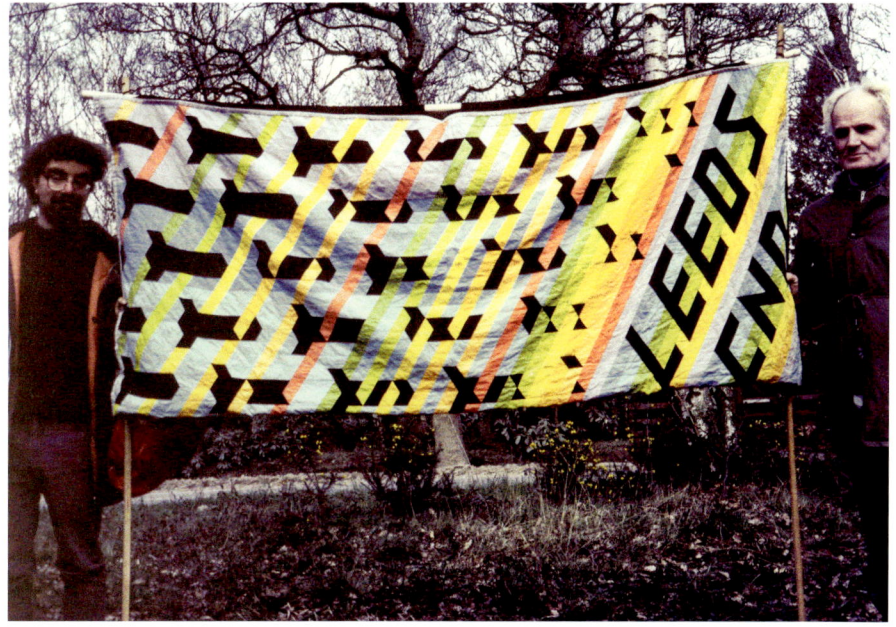

Top: *Leatherhead* CND.
Bottom: *Leeds* CND.

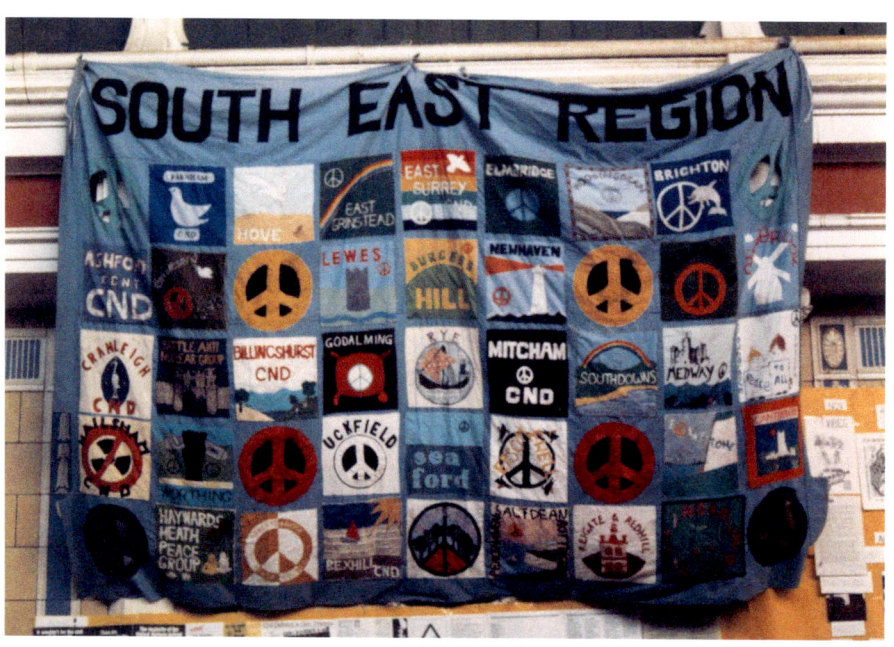

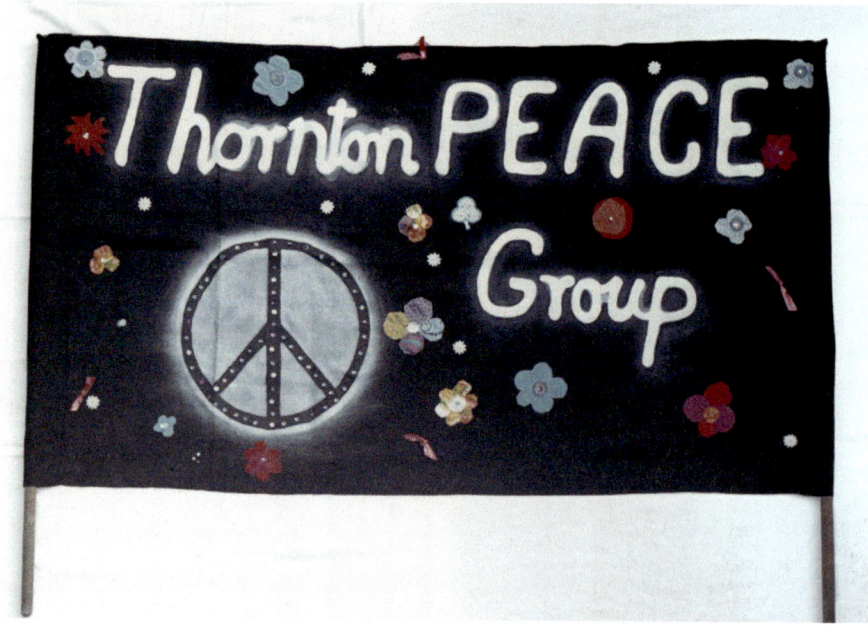

Top: *South East Region*, showing local CND groups.
Bottom: *Thornton Peace Group.*

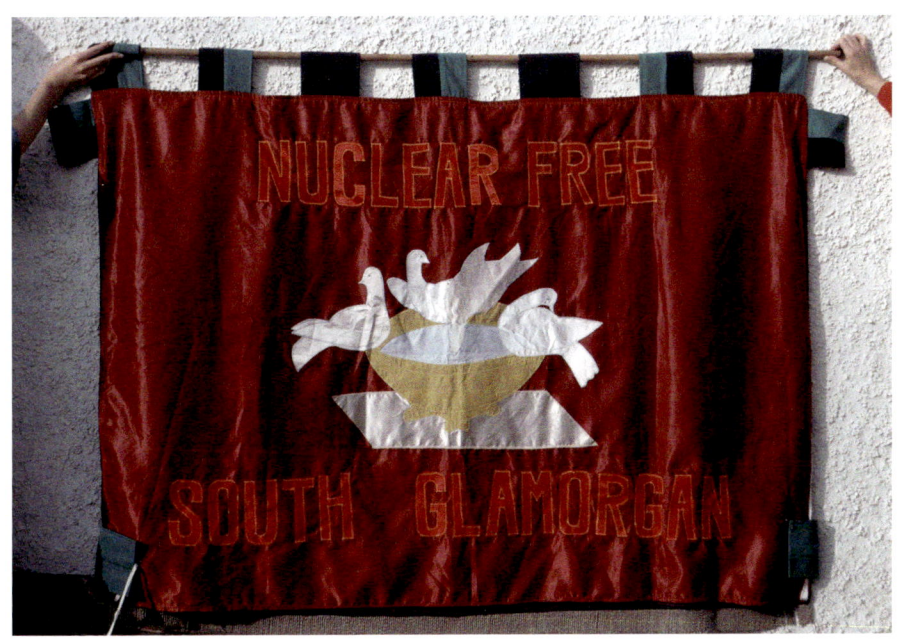
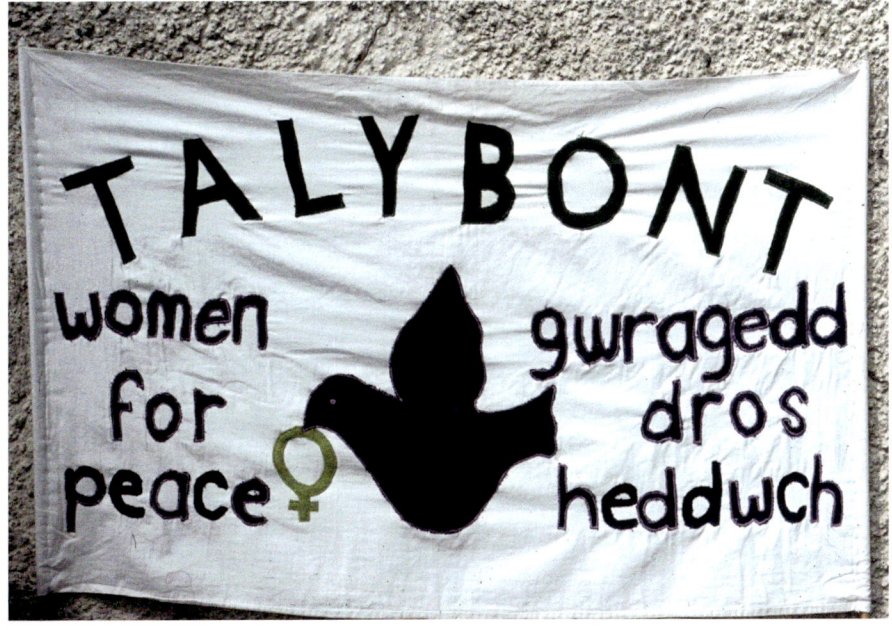

Top: *Nuclear Free South Glamorgan.*

Bottom: *Talybont Women for Peace / Talybont Gwragedd dros Heddwch.*

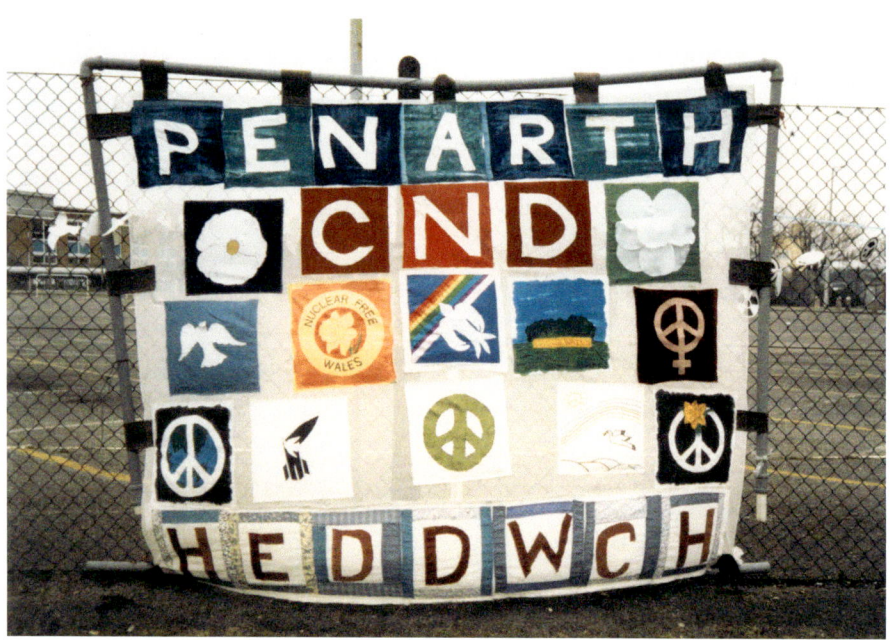

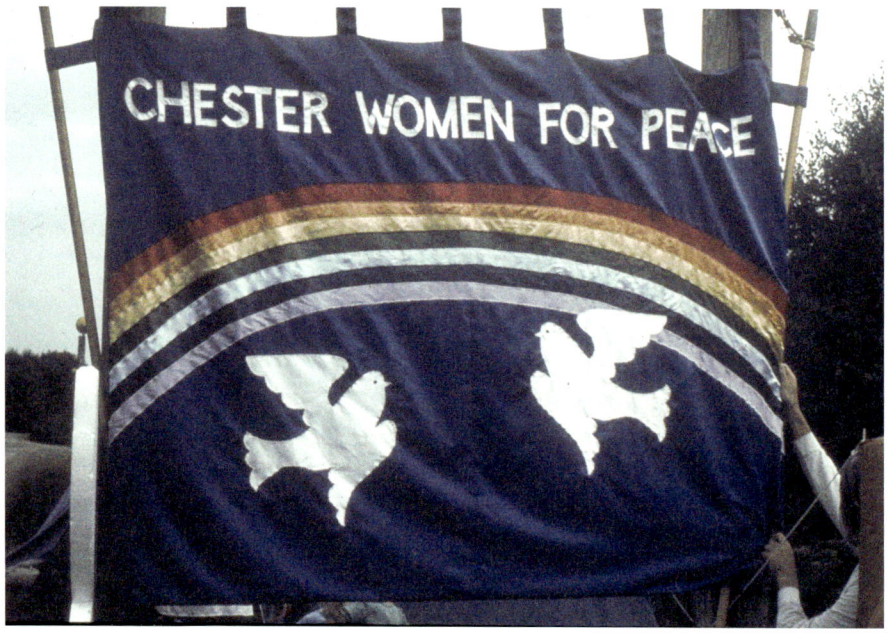

Top: *Penarth CND.*
Bottom: *Chester Women for Peace.*

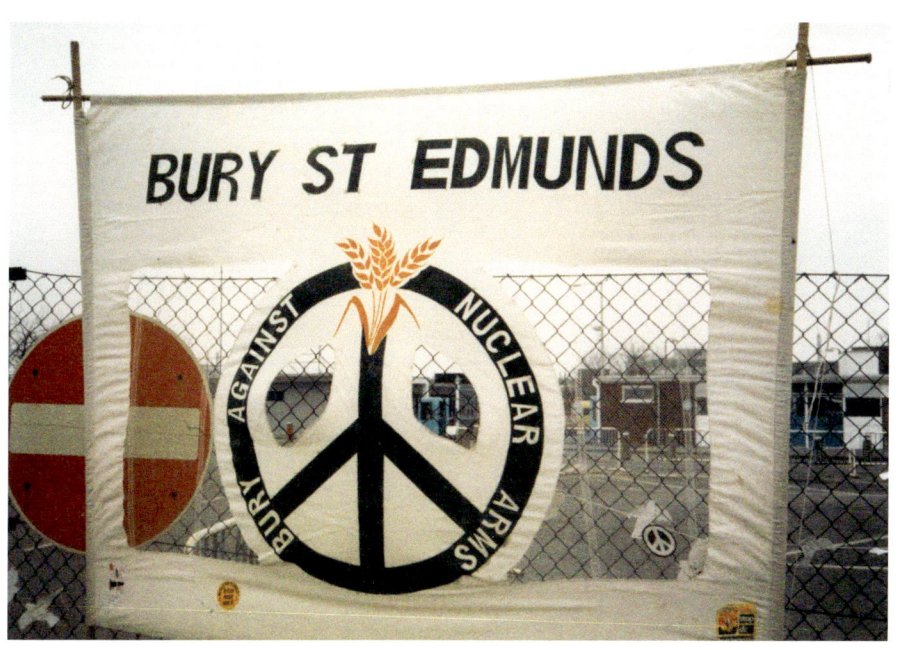

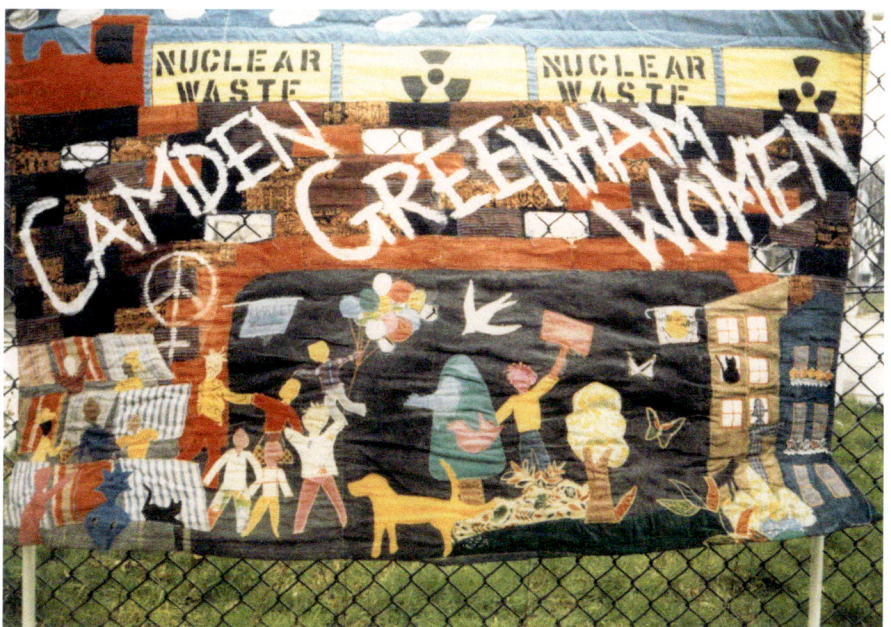

Top: *Bury St Edmunds* CND.

Bottom: *Camden Greenham Women.*

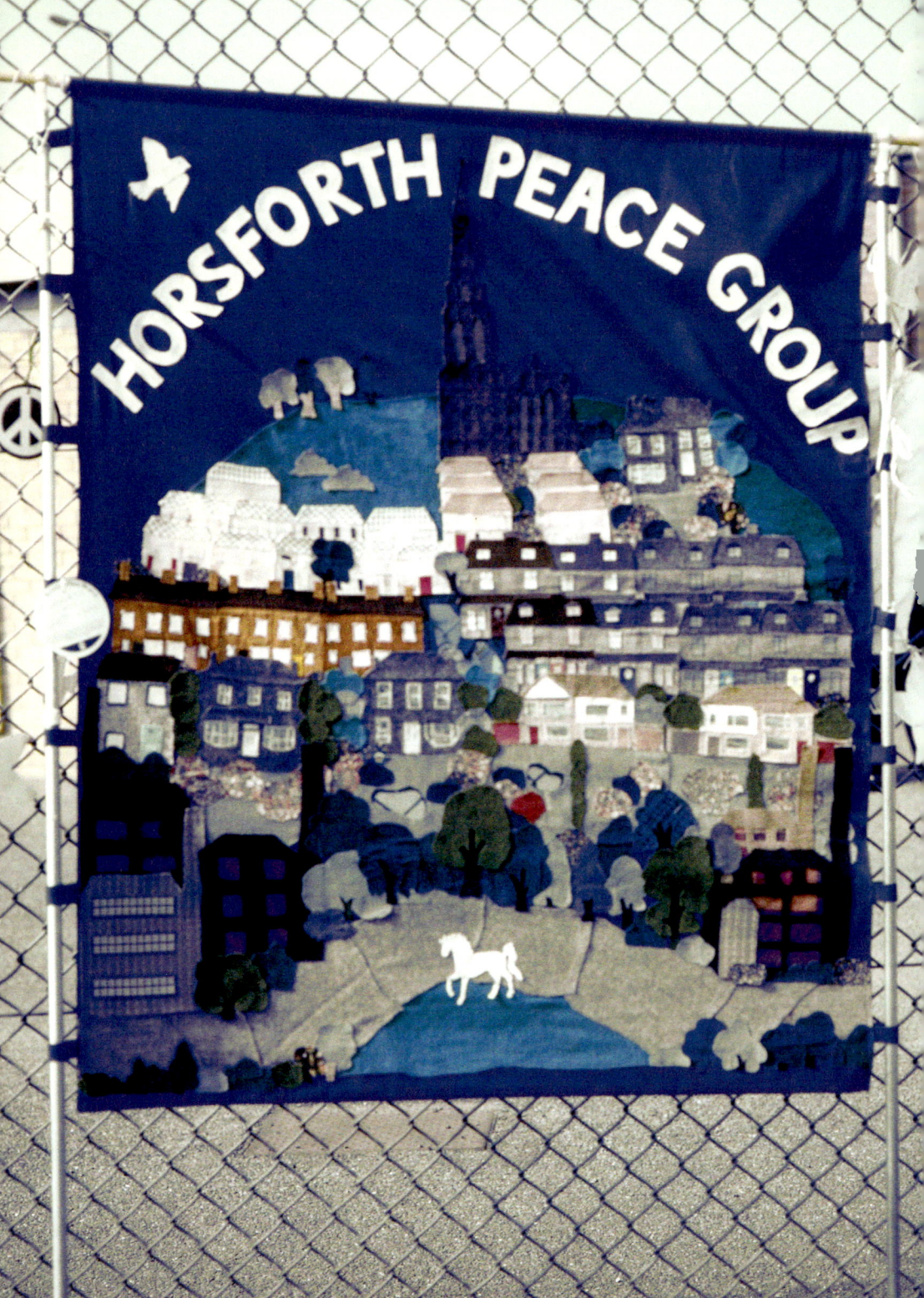

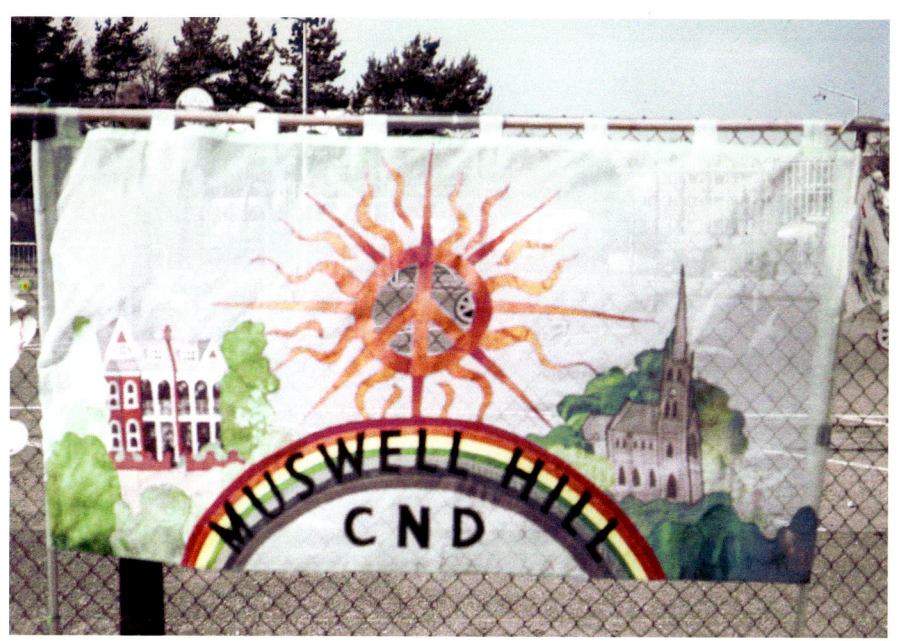

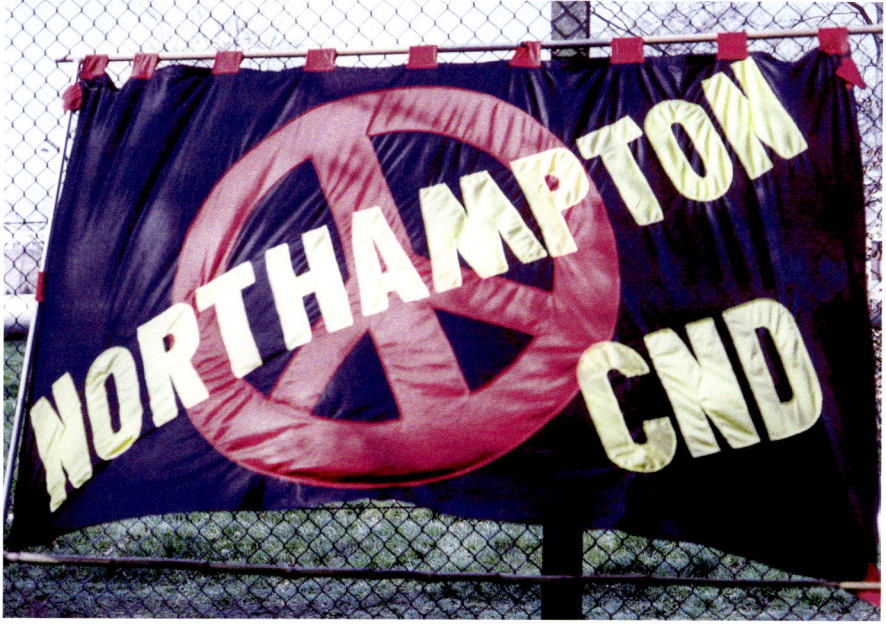

Opposite: *Horsforth Peace Group.*
Top: *Muswell Hill* CND.
Bottom: *Northampton* CND.

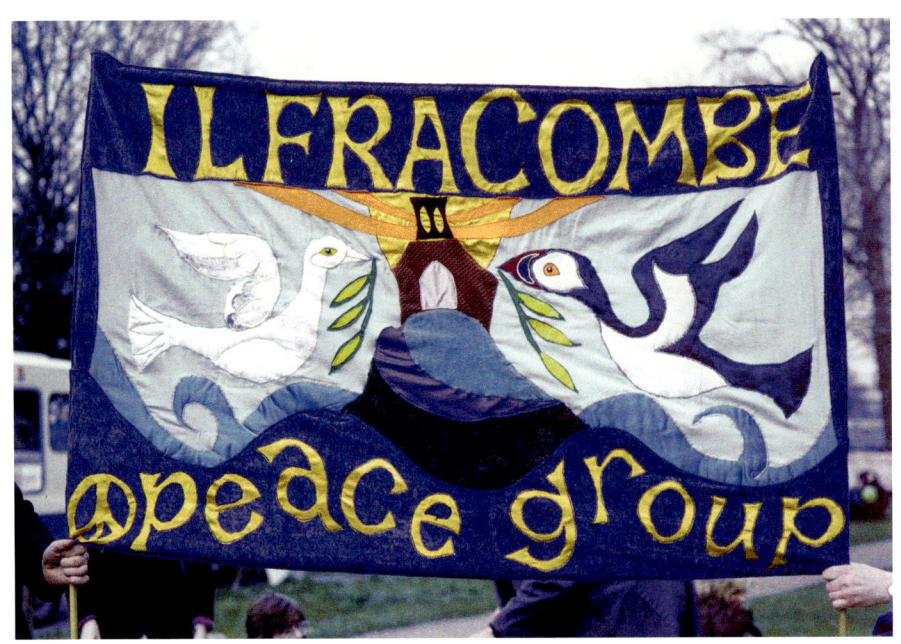
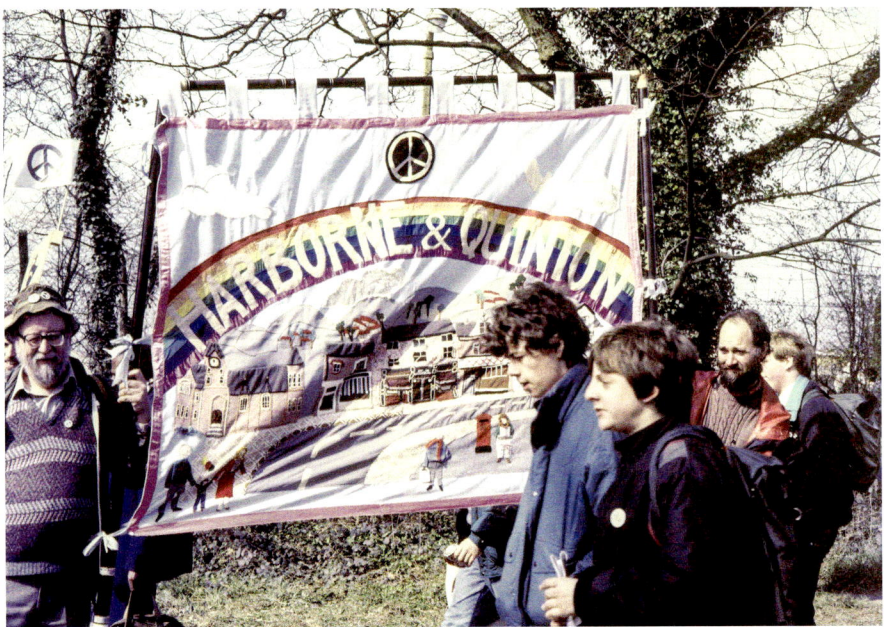

Top: *Ilfracombe Peace Group.*
Bottom: *Harborne & Quinton* CND.

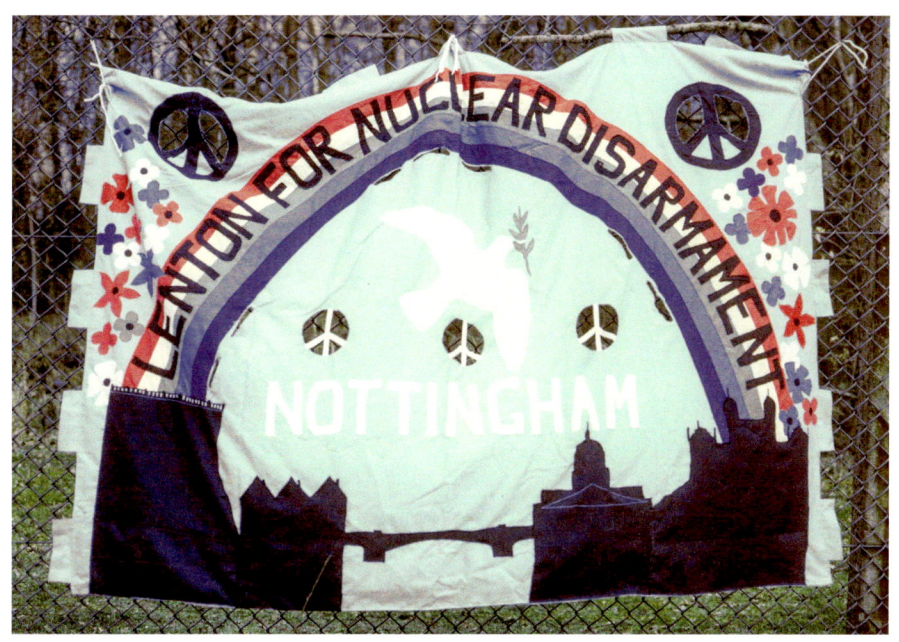

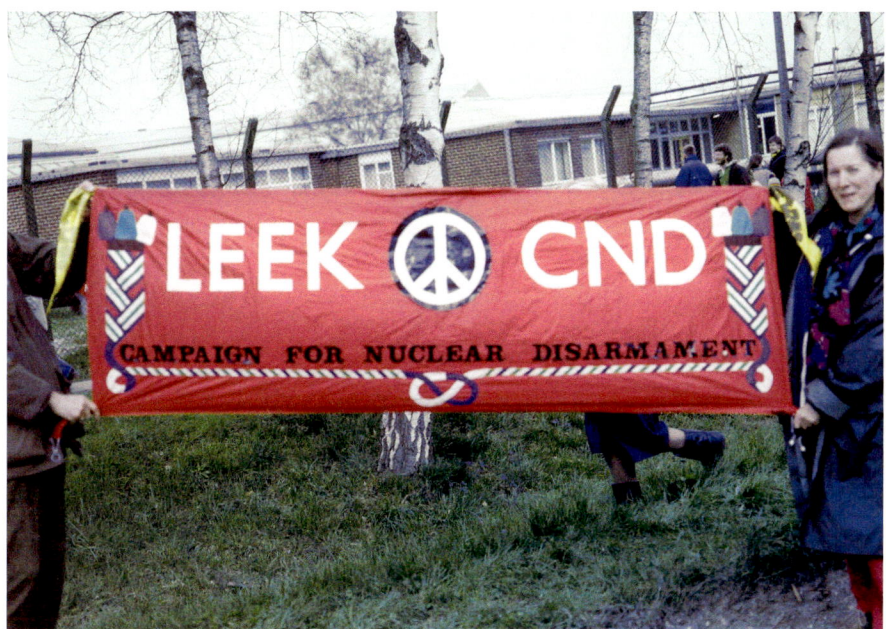

Top: *Lenton For Nuclear Disarmament, Nottingham.*
Bottom: *Leek CND.*

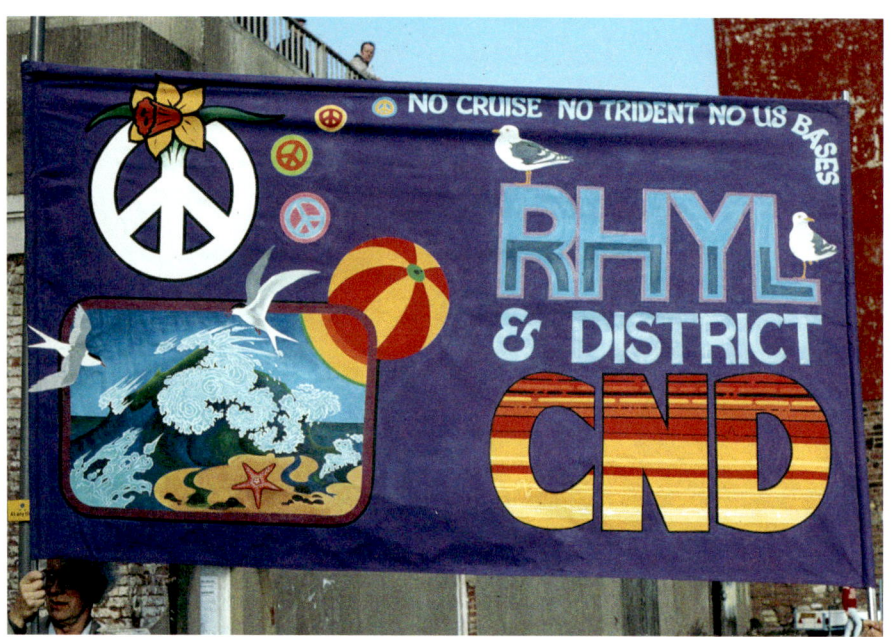

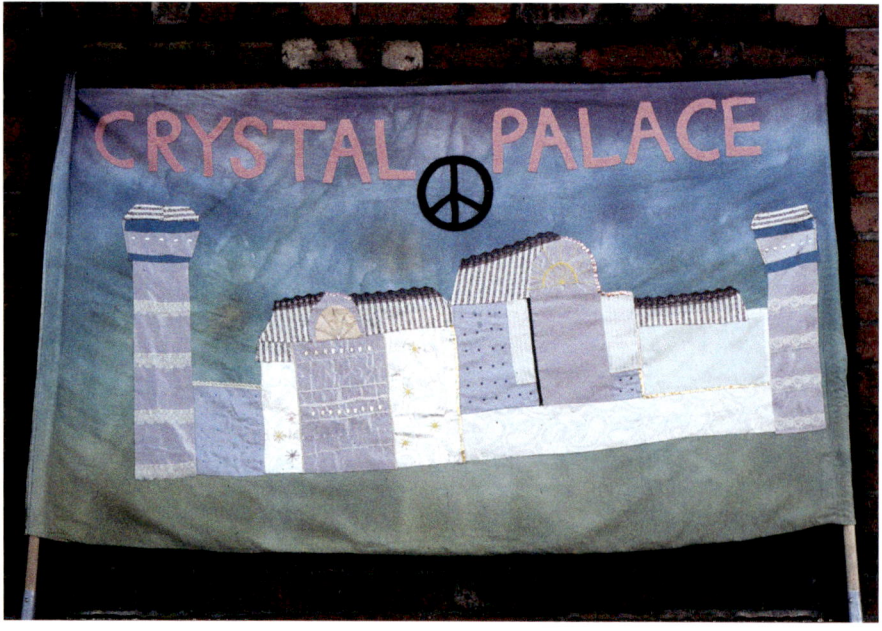

Top: *Rhyl & District* CND.

Bottom: *Crystal Palace* CND.

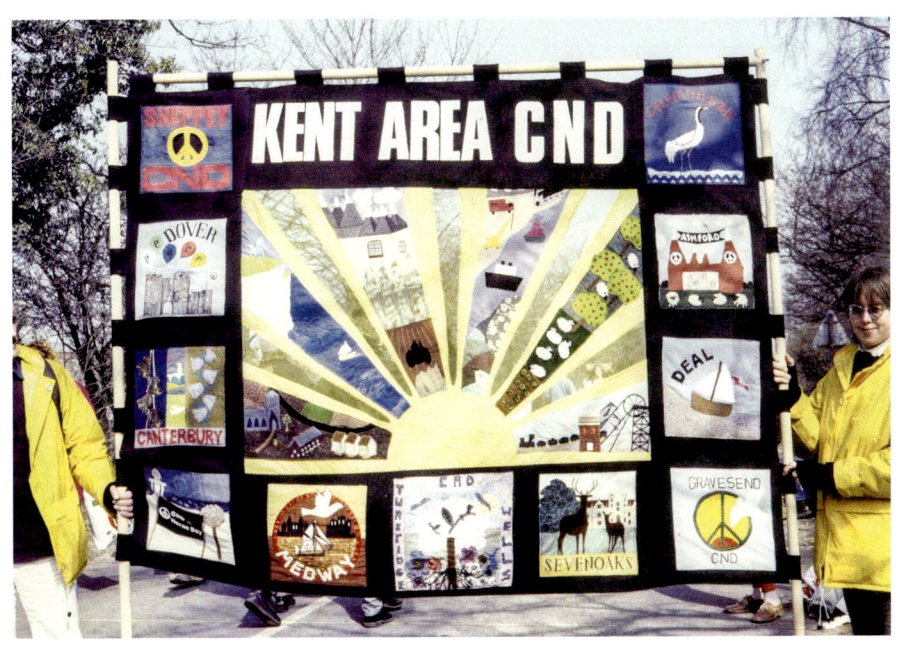

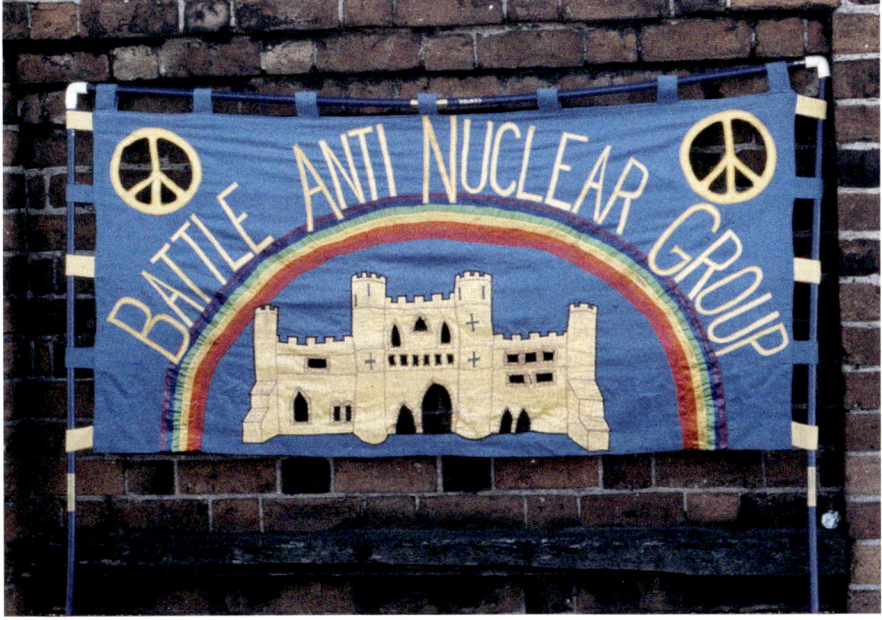

Top: *Kent Area* CND.

Bottom: *Battle Anti Nuclear Group.*

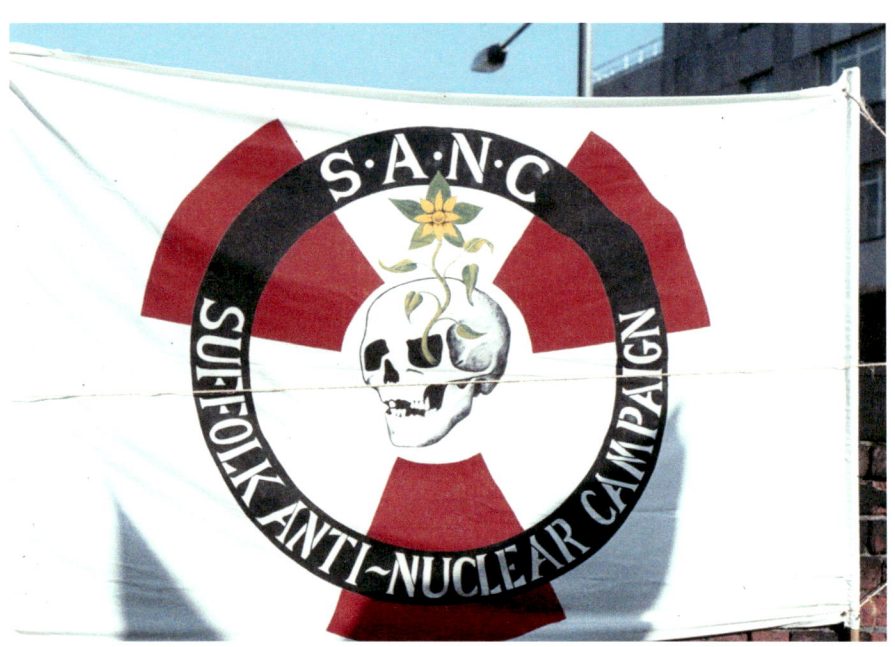

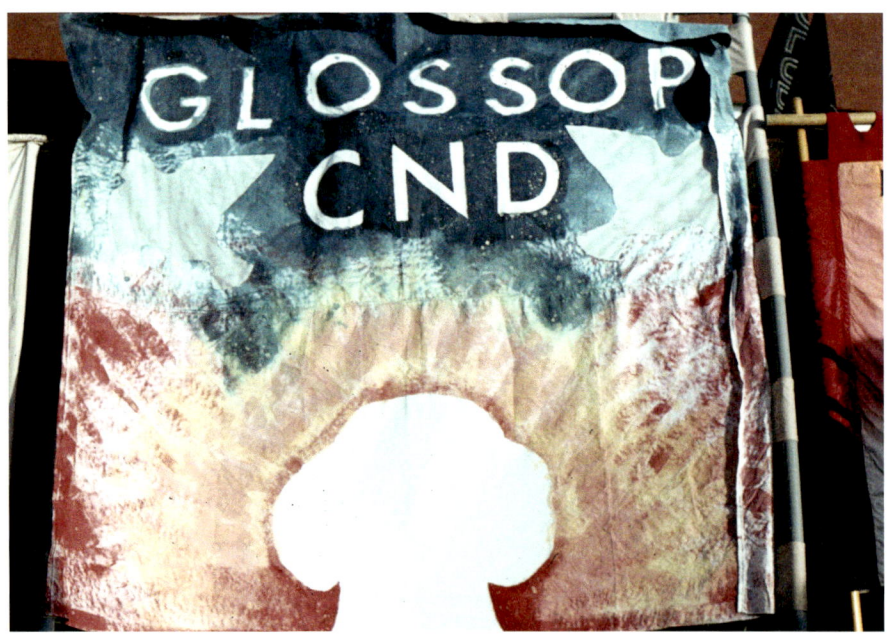

Top: *Suffolk Anti-Nuclear Campaign.*

Bottom: *Glossop* CND.

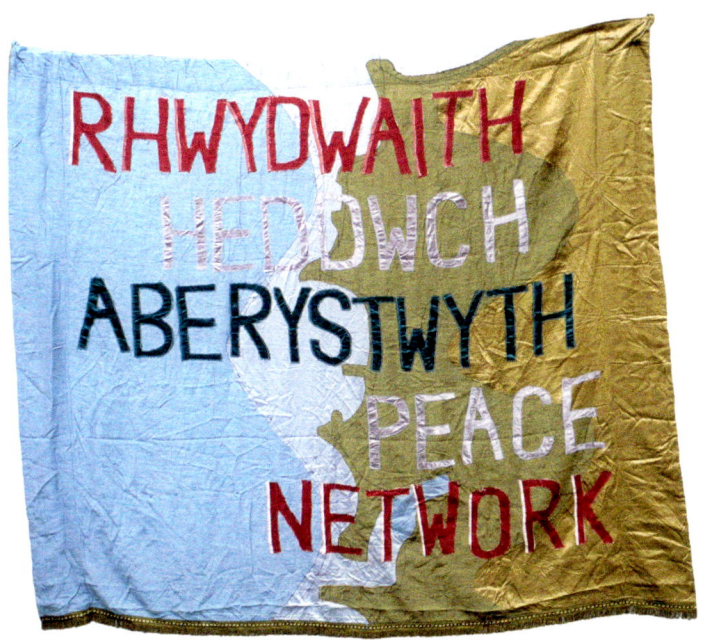
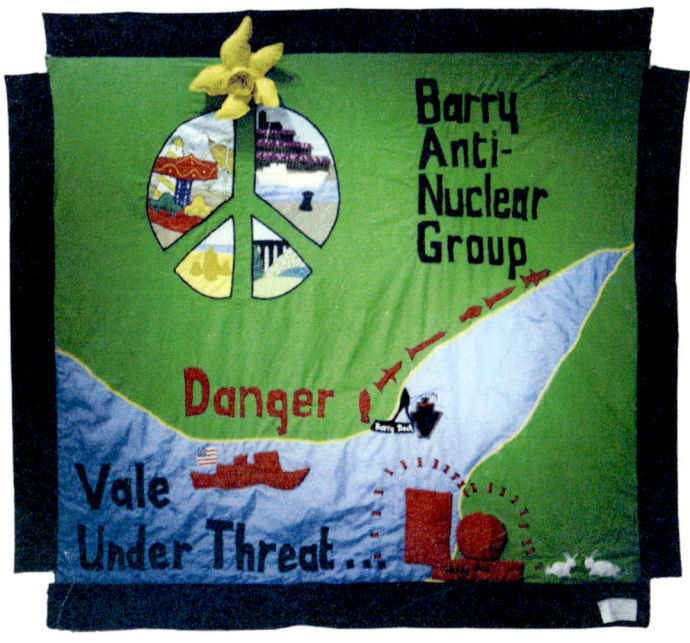

Top: *Aberystwyth Peace Network.*

Bottom: *Barry Anti-Nuclear Group.*

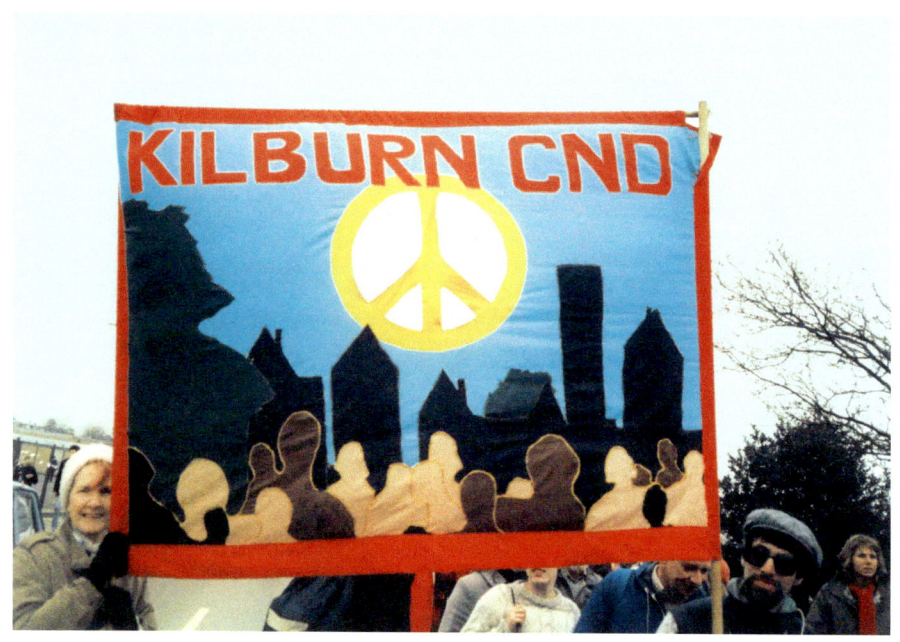
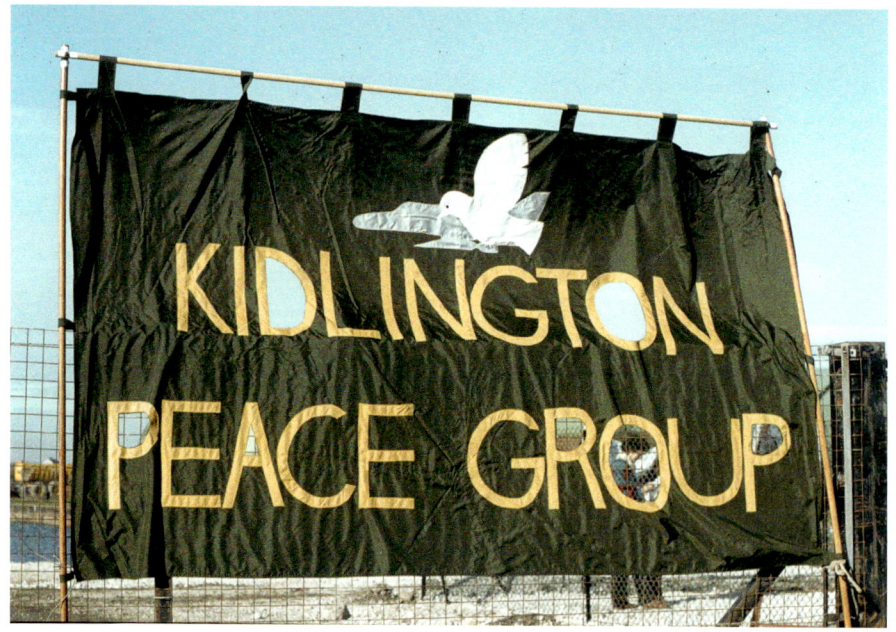

Top: *Kilburn* CND.

Bottom: *Kidlington Peace Group.*

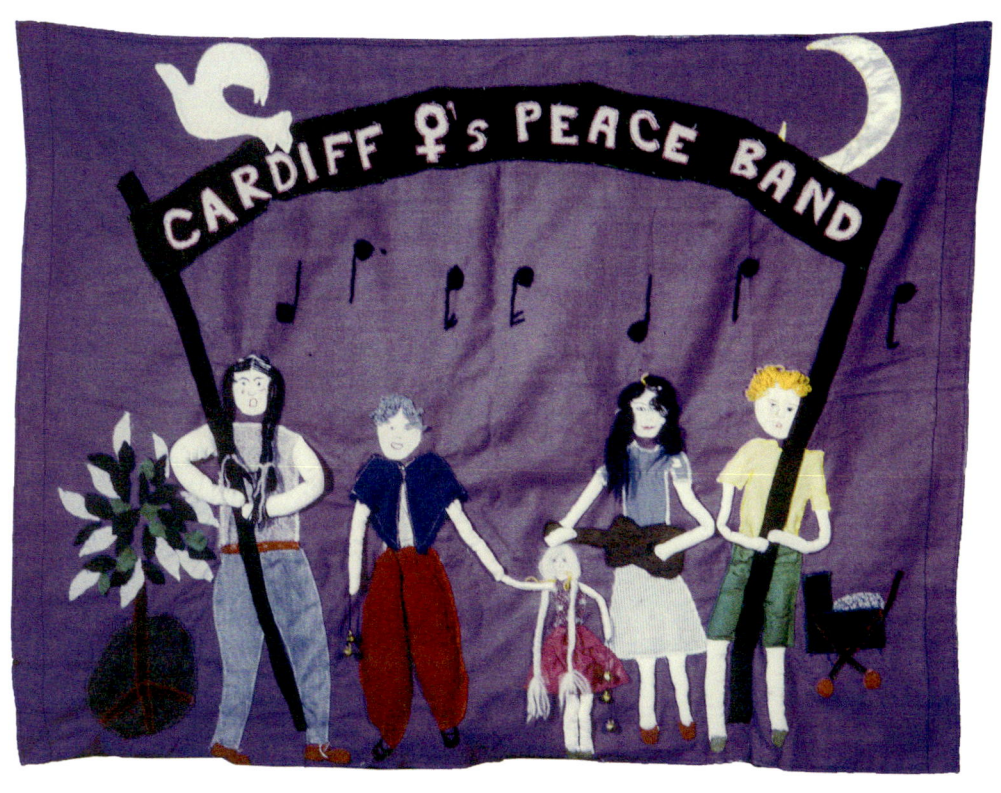

Above: *Cardiff Women's Peace Band.* Made by Linda Evans and Jane Mansfield, based on a design by Dee Beddoe.

Next pages: *Ilkeston CND.* Designed and made by Dave Brooks and Carol Wooller, October 1983.

Ilkes CND

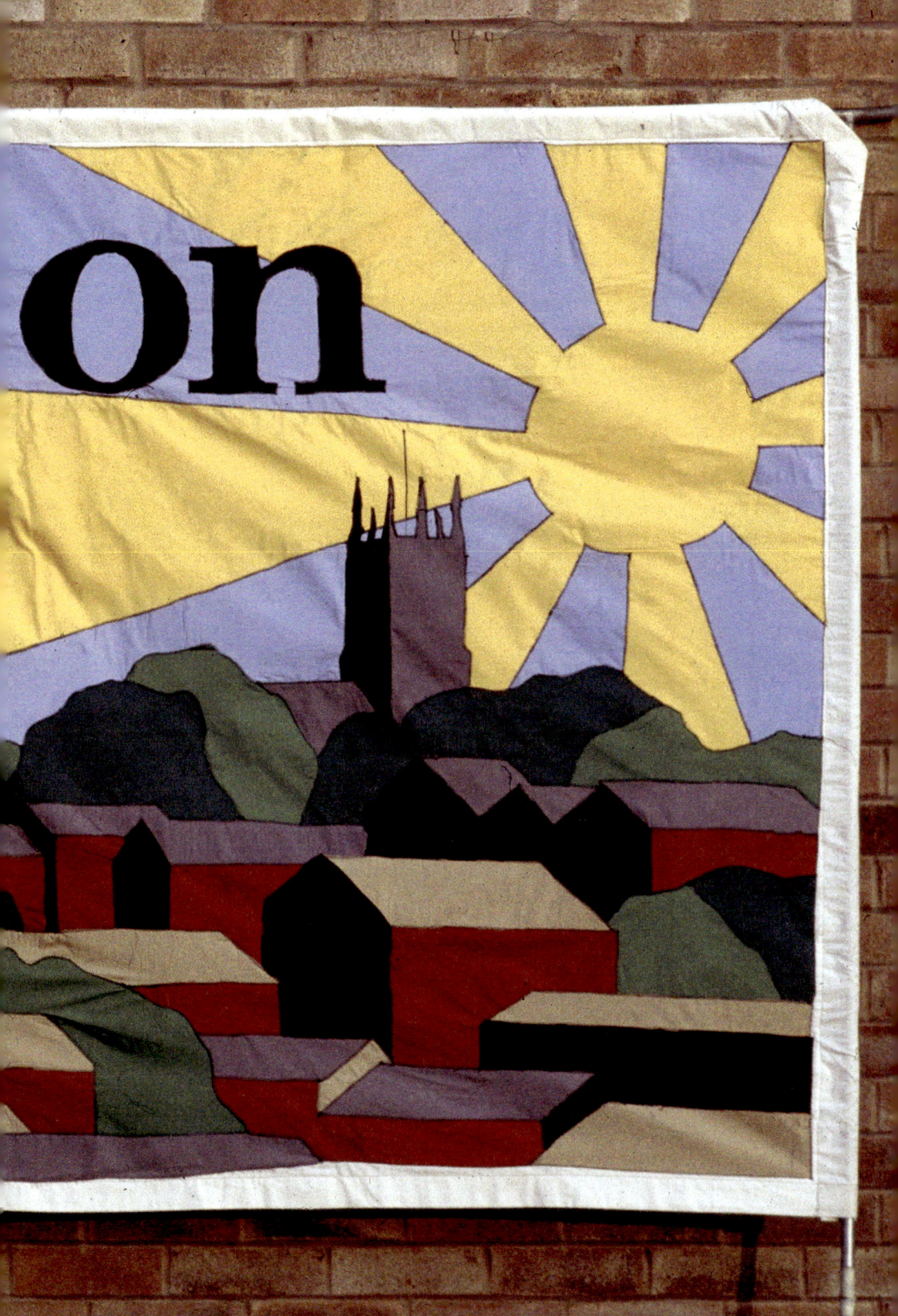

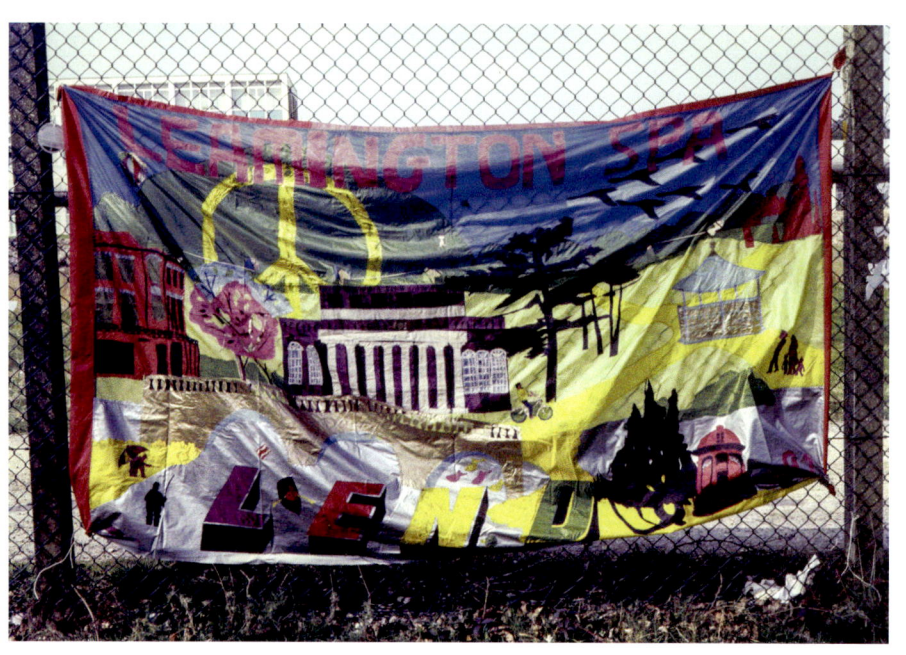

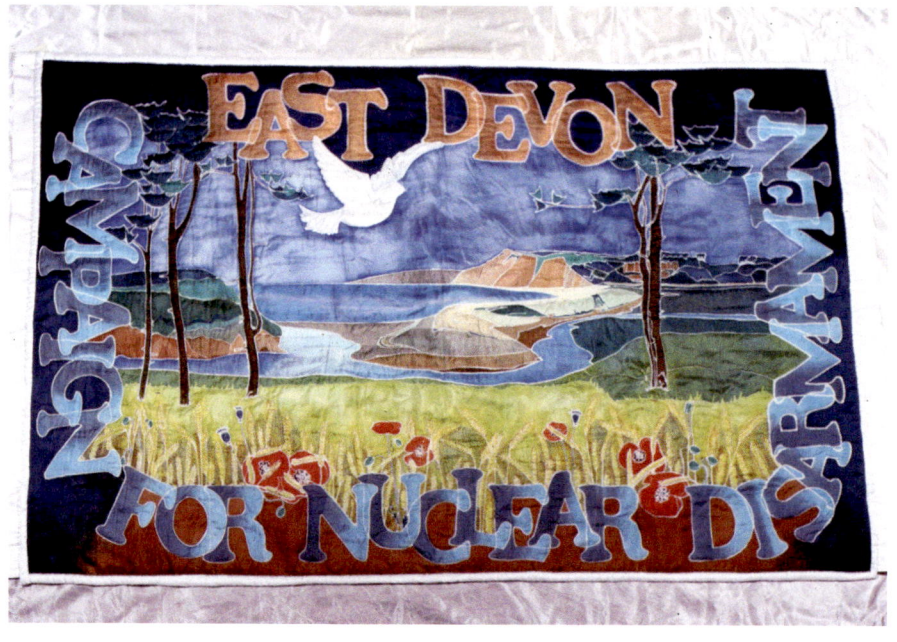

Top: *Leamington Spa* CND.

Bottom: *East Devon* CND.

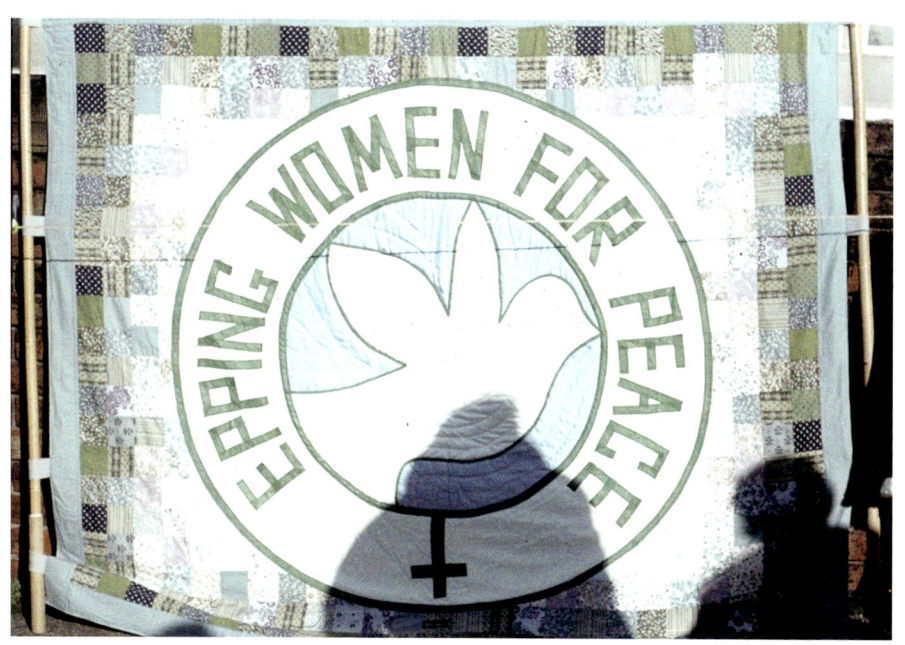

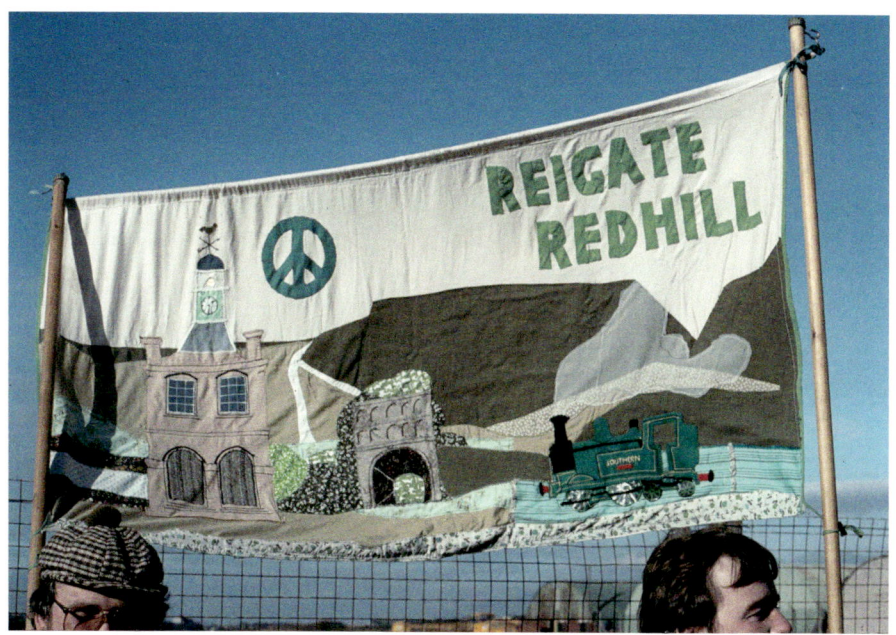

Top: *Epping Women for Peace.*
Bottom: *Reigate Redhill* CND.

Making

In an early account of the camp, Barbara Doris described the creative activities that took place at Greenham, including banner making: 'Visitors brought banners and we made our own to line the edge of the highway and the entrance to the main gate. An enormous structure of polythene, tarpaulin and branches was built as a communal area... along the wall was a large table with leaflets, badges, posters and donated flowers... In one corner was a stack of material, old sheets, and paint for making banners... and wool for weaving webs.'[50]

Such behaviours are a recognised characteristic of protest camps: '... [they] are often "laboratories of insurrection imagination", spaces in which experimental, collaborative and richly creative actions are dreamed up and deployed... infused with art, protest camps often include designated areas for creative productions and performances of music, art, theatre. When creativity is used not only as an escape or accoutrement but as central to strategies of action, colourful and effective forms of resistance take shape'.[51]

Just as Greenham banners can be divided into the carefully made and spontaneous creative acts, often for an immediate purpose, they can also be categorised by their place of making – at or away from the camp – and their maker; a collective or individual; an artist or amateur.

The origins of many banners have gone unrecorded. The maker is most usually recognised if they define themselves as an artist or if the banner is kept as part of a personal or organisational collection, so linking it to their activity.

Least is known about banner makers who do not define as artists, who are more likely, although not exclusively, responsible for impulsively made designs. The haste of making usually causes such banners to be valued less (they may only last a single event or protest), and so the likelihood that they are kept or linked to an individual is reduced. Photographs of Greenham tell us that there were many more banners than have survived and many more makers than those who are recognised.[52]

Opposite: Thalia Campbell sewing in her workshop in Borth, Wales.

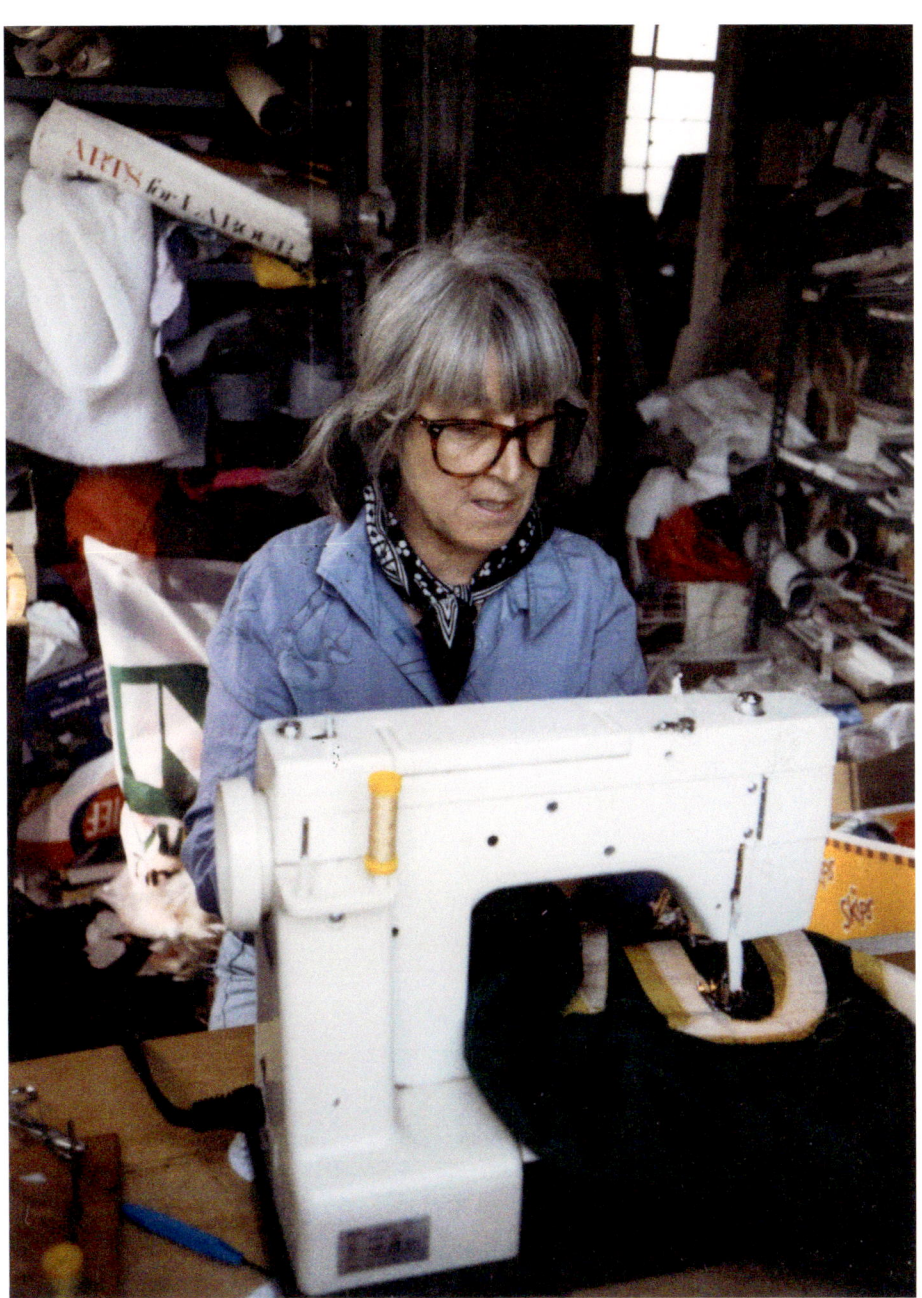

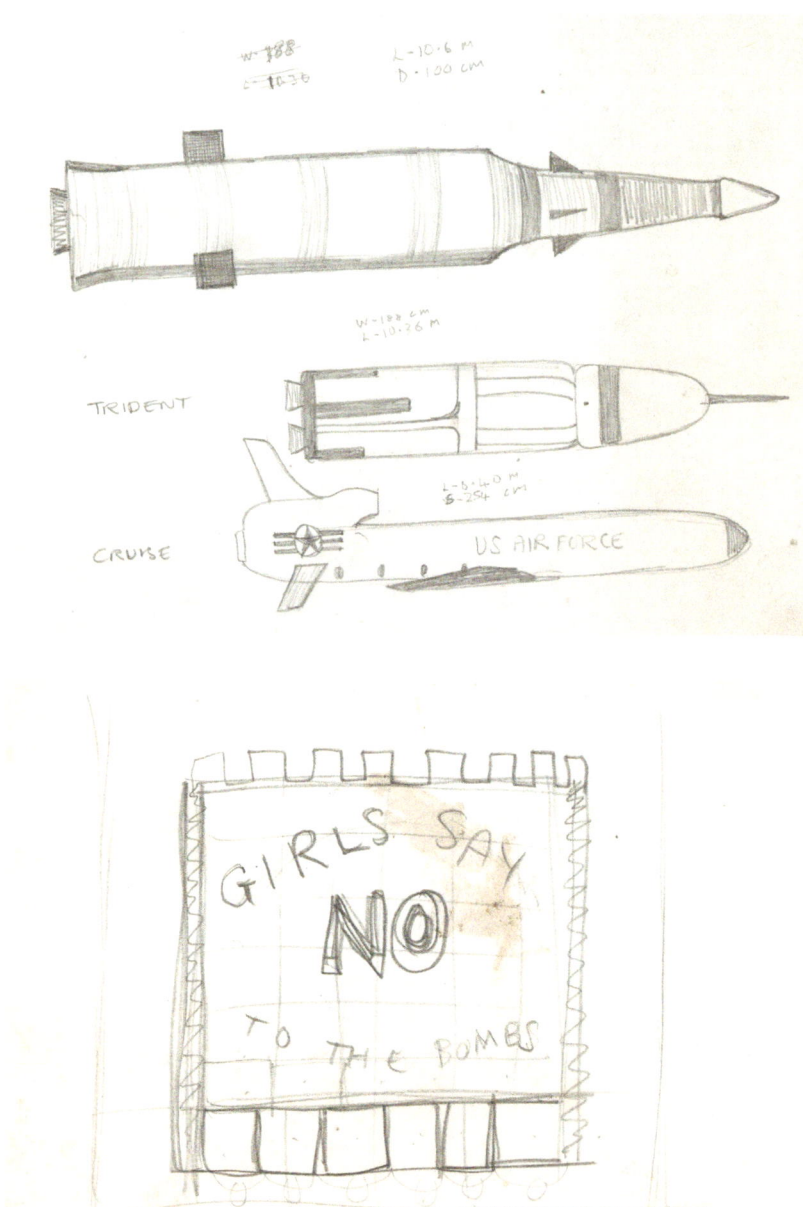

Top: Sketches by Ian Campbell of missiles.

Above and opposite: preliminary sketches by Thalia Campbell
for *Girls Say No to the Bombs* (page 74–75), *It's Us or Them* (page 78–79),
Greenham Common Womens Peace Camp (page 10–11 and 120–121).

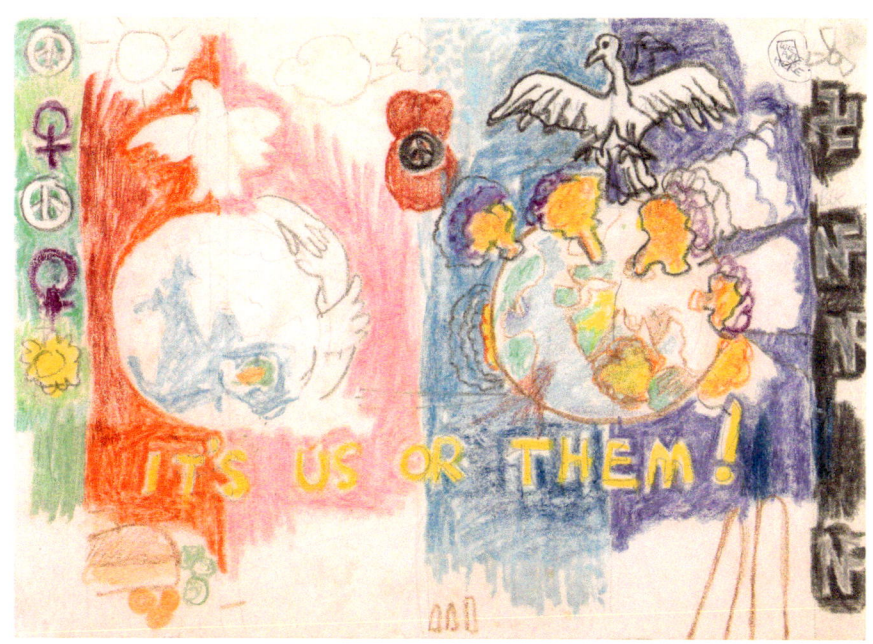

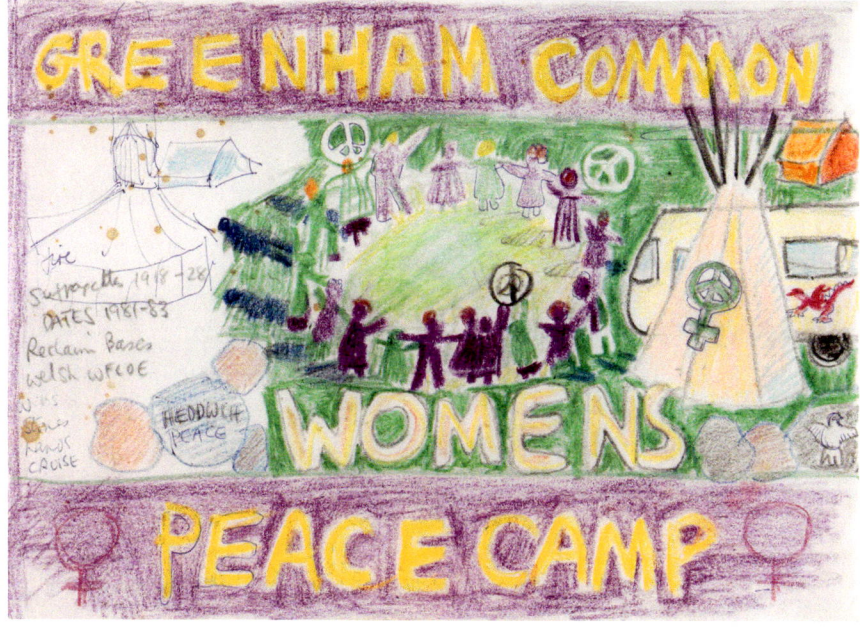

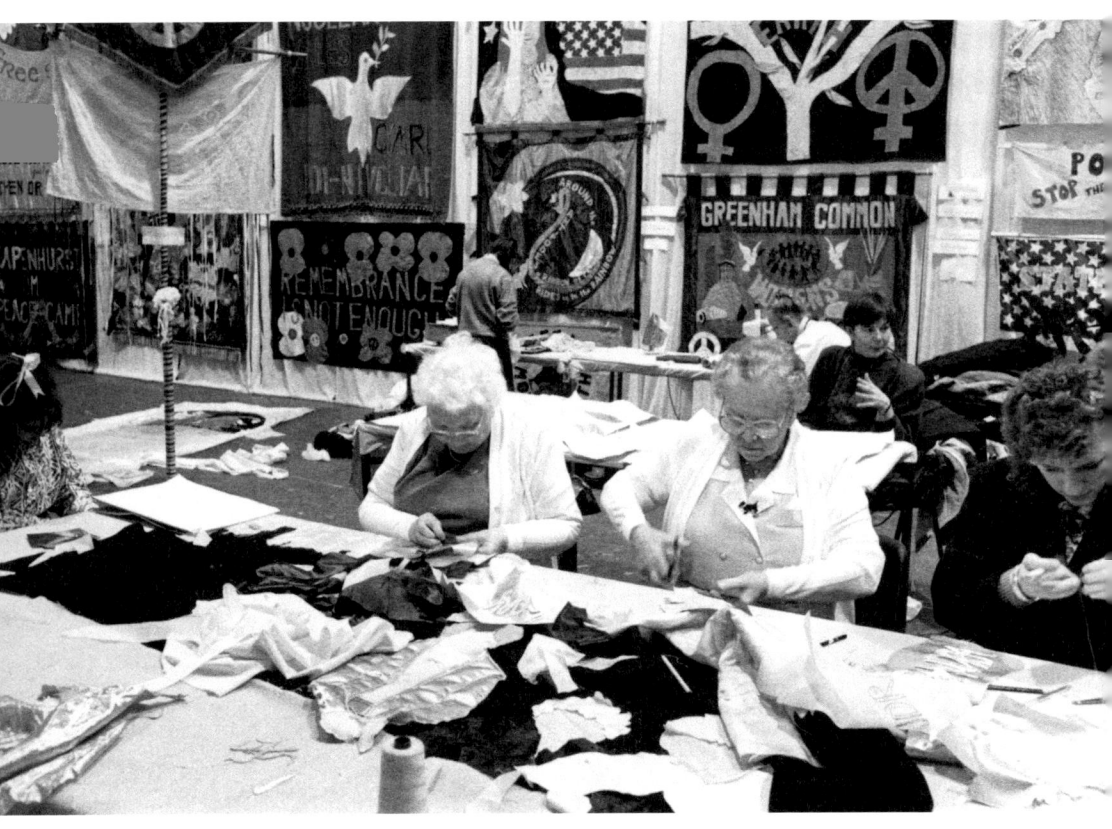

Above and opposite: Making banners at banner workshops, mid 1980s.

Next pages: *Women for Life on Earth*. This was one of three banners using this design made in different banner workshops, with groups, run by Campbell. This version incorporated a reused curtain and was designed and made by the WFLOE (Llandrindod Wells) group, in remembrance of Hiroshima.

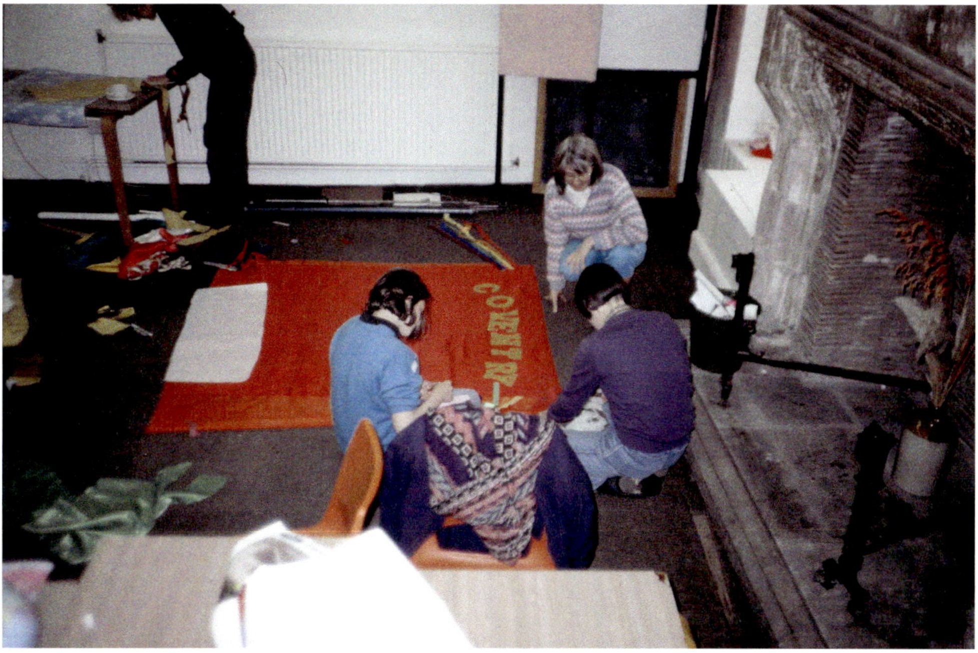

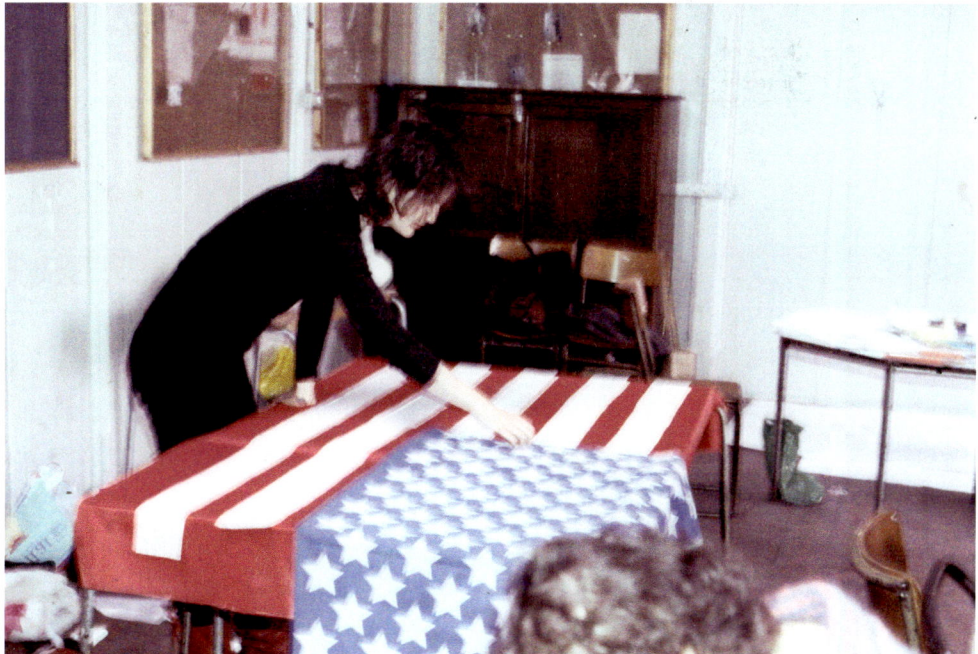

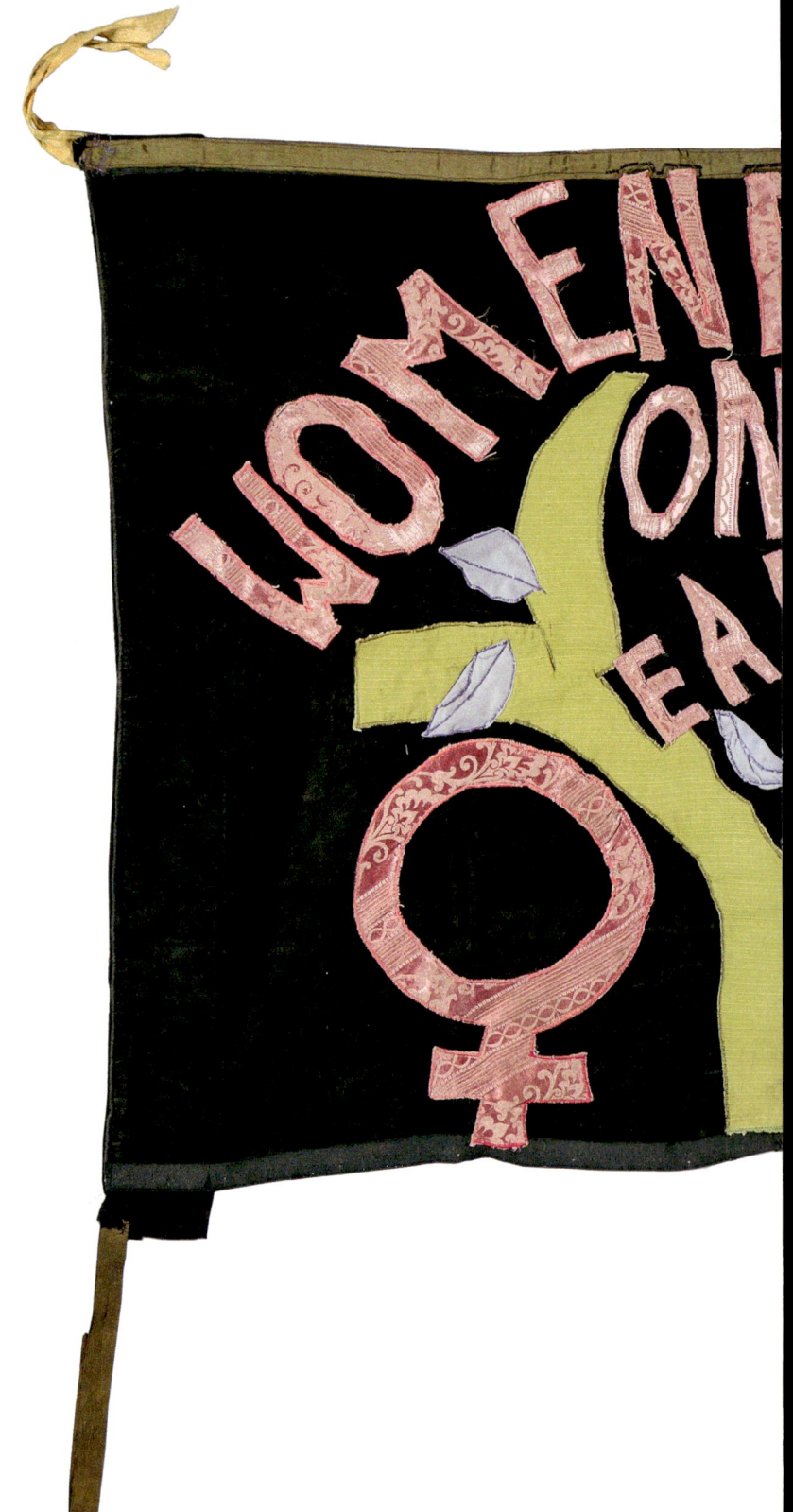

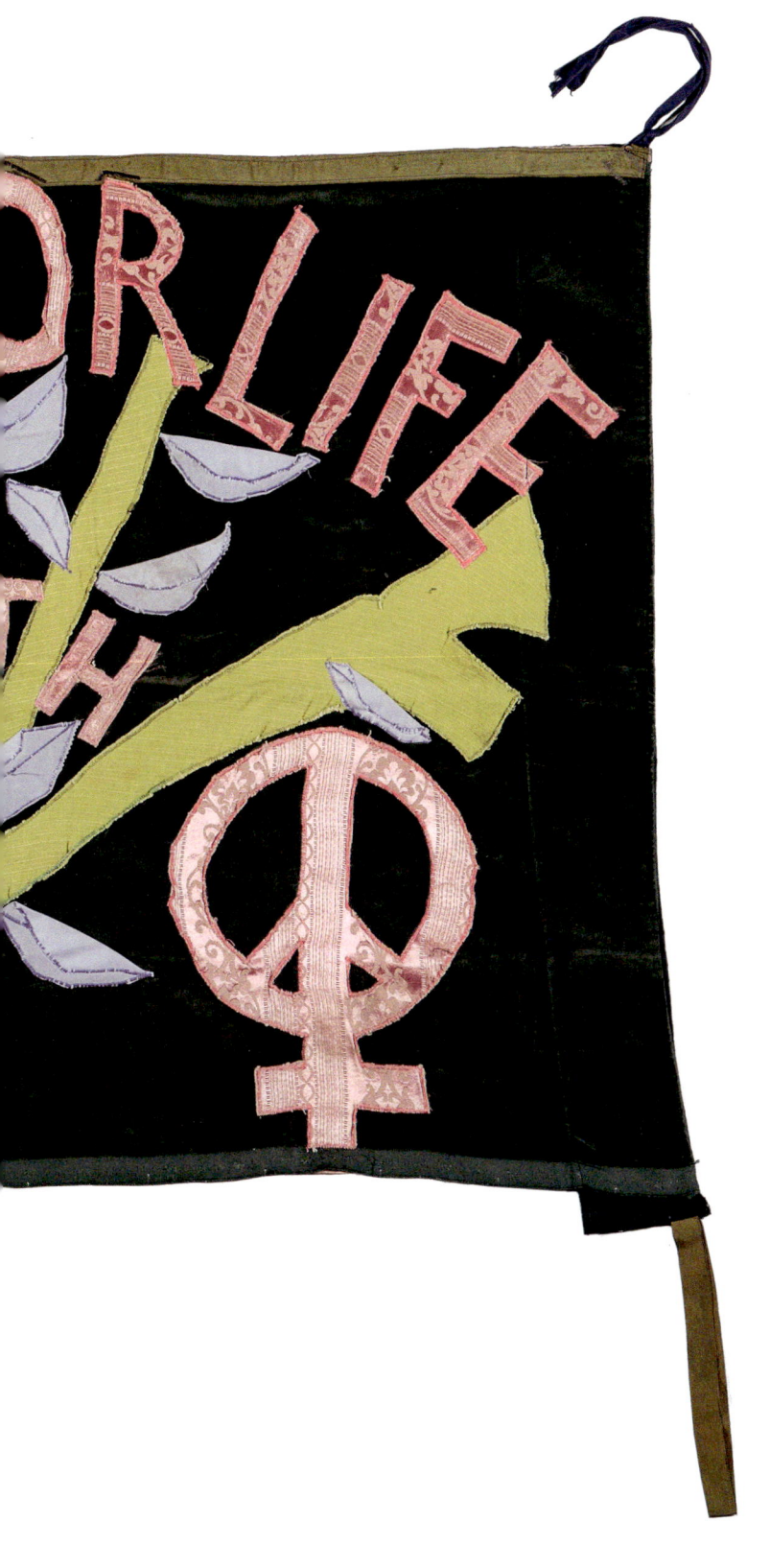

Creativity at the Camp

Testimonial such as Barbara Doris' (page 178) provides evidence that banner making was undertaken onsite at Greenham. To this can be added the remembrances of Barbara Harford and Sarah Hopkins, who recall the making of a sign naming the camp: 'The encampment at the main gate wasn't really called anything at first, it was just referred to as the Peace Camp. But one weekend, a woman who was visiting painted the immortal words "Women's Peace Camp" on big pieces of board in green, white and violet colours (the suffragette colours representing the first letters of their demand: Give Women Votes!). It was done in a flurry of creativity and energy. The boards were decorated with rich purple fruit and a white dove of peace. Everyone helped put them up on display to the passing traffic.'[53] A banner made by Jamima Latimer at Blue Gate employed the materials she had to hand. The female symbol, with poppies growing in the centre, is filled with small, appliquéd fabric patches, cut from her clothes. The slogan 'Peace?' is sewn on in white letters. The design is attached to fraying sack cloth. The result is impactful, though improvised. Latimer moved to Greenham aged 17, and lived at the camp from 1989 to 1990.

Creative activity undertaken at Greenham was often applied to the surrounding environment, as well as the creation of objects. For example, the decoration of boulders delivered to Yellow Gate to prevent the women camping there: '29 September [1983] – After the shock of seeing these great boulders dumped... we decided to do a bit of landscaping ourselves... Jayne pulled a ball of red wool out of her bottomless bag and began weaving angry webs across the gorse bushes. 30 September [1983] – ...Today we got up to a bit of bother to put it lightly. We've been painting the rocks with beautiful things; we've made signs and written words with them, but it has to be seen to be believed.'[54]

Paint was used to apply slogans to the Base runways, and surrounding roads: 'women were painting signs and symbols all over the road in a variety of colours. It was a good paint-drying day, and although we all got pretty well splattered, the paint was not too smudged by people walking over it.'[55]

Opposite: Peace banner by Jamima Latimer.

Next pages: At the fence, Greenham, 1983. Photograph by Janine Wiedel.

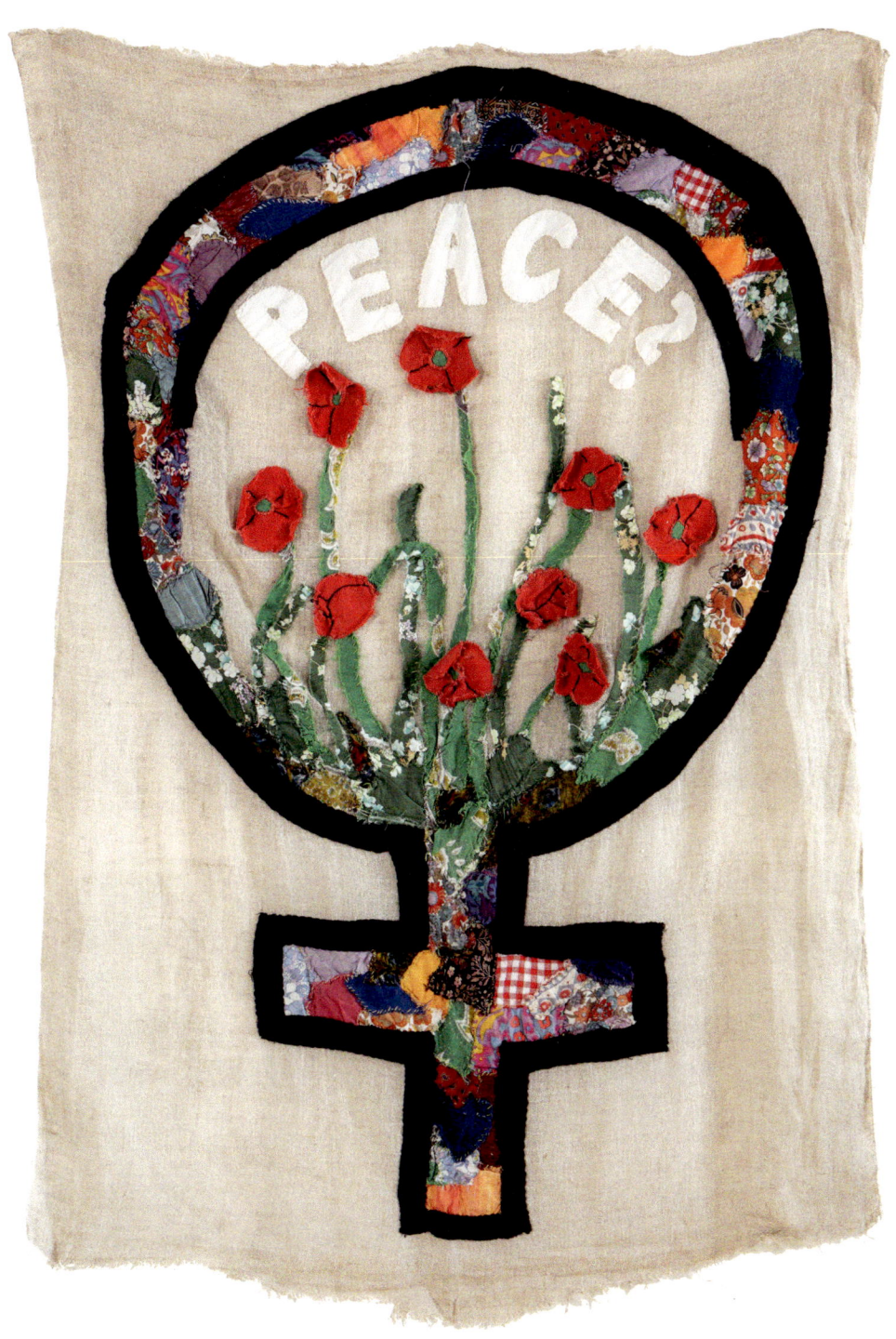

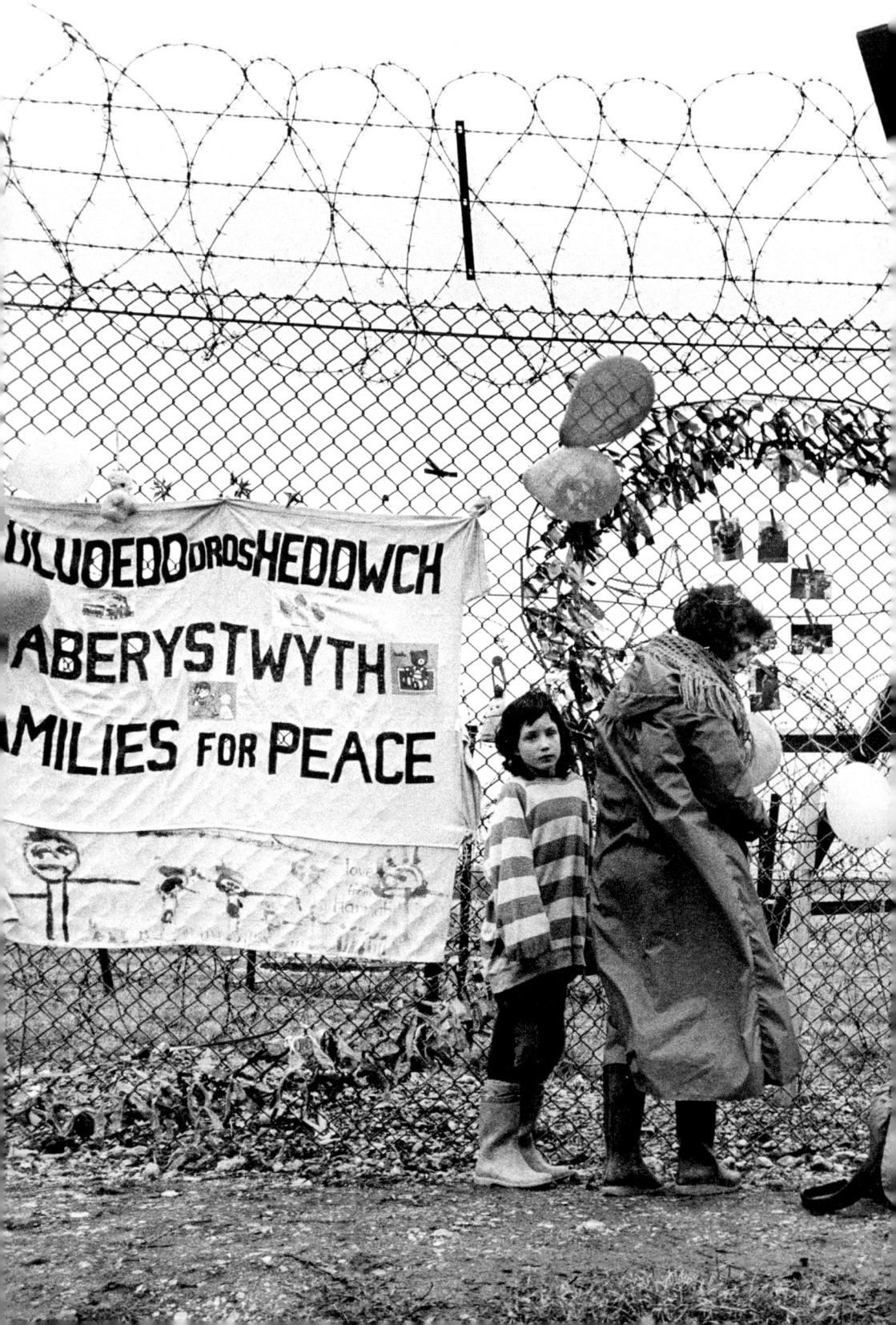

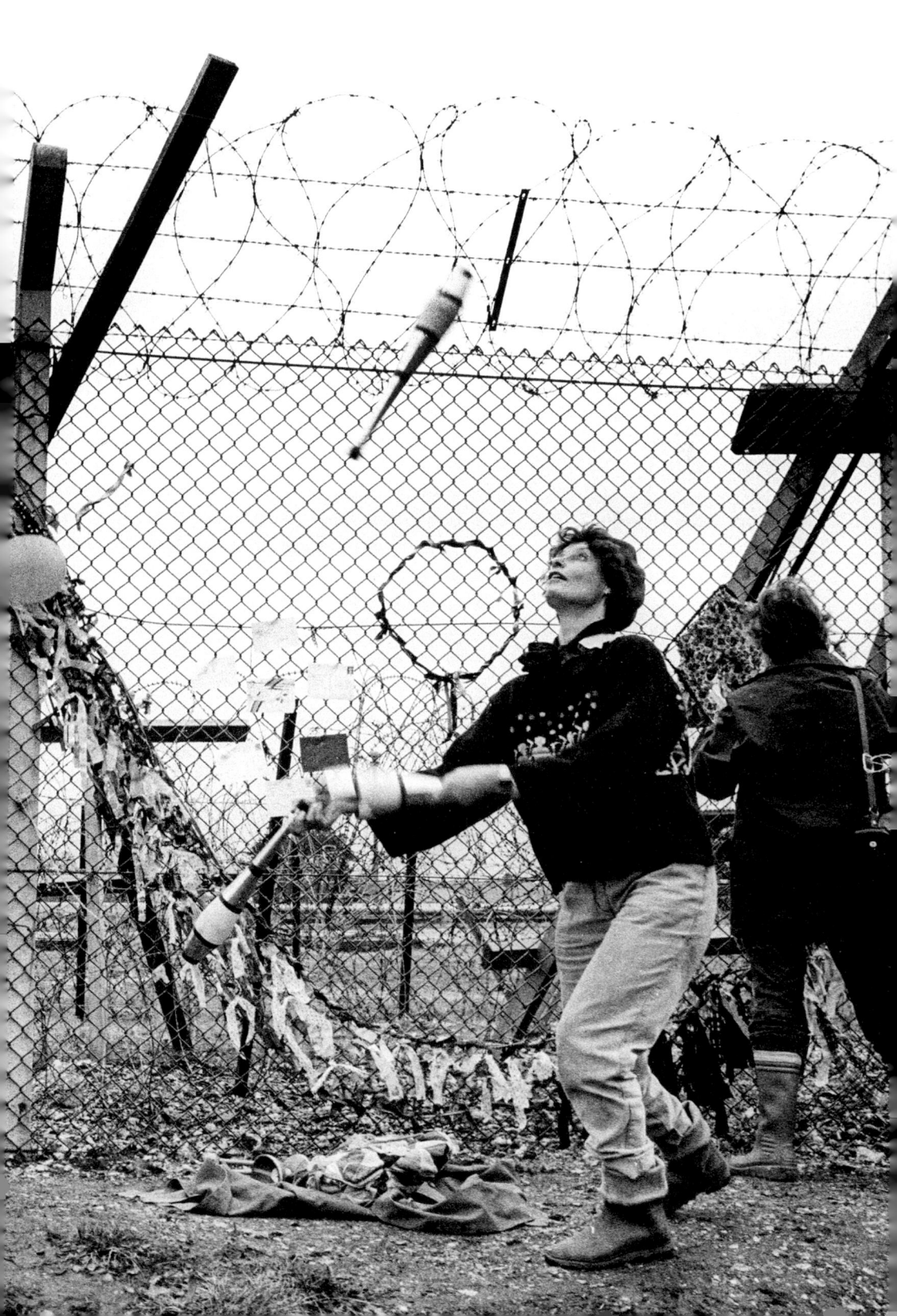

Special events were a stimulus for making. For example, the collaborative artwork created for the Full Moon festival in 1983, coordinated by Howse, with others at Yellow Gate. The invitation to participate in the festival read: 'At USAF Greenham Common, Newbury, Berkshire on the 25th June, a Rainbow Dragon will be born by joining the creative work of thousands of women… Women are making pieces of patchwork, banners, cloth paintings to join into the Rainbow Dragon for the future.' A papier-mâché dragon head was created, with a body formed from decorated textiles, sent from all over the world. The joined pieces of cloth made a body miles long, to surround the base.

At the camp creativity took three forms; activity undertaken to disrupt the operation of the base and encourage recognition, debate and publicity for the cause, including preparations for large events such as Embrace the Base; homemaking and embellishment of the site, which also often declared the nature of the cause; and personal creative acts, undertaken by individual women to process and record their experiences and those of their fellow campaigners. The Greenham women wrote poetry, diaries, books, leaflets, newsletters, and chain letters, composed, and sang songs, made badges and created art, including banners.

The Greenham Song Book, published by a Manchester-based group of Greenham supporters, contains the lyrics and music for eighty-four tunes. Many compositions set new words to a known melody, such as 'There's a hole in your fence dear Major, dear Major', based on 'There's a hole in your bucket'. The book includes 'You Can't Kill the Spirit', which was released as a 7-inch single. Other songs share the sentiment and words that appear on banners:

> Hey you Gen 'rals in the Military
> What d'you need more atom bombs for?
> You got enough bombs to kill us ten times
> Yet still you keep on asking for more
> Take the toys away from the boys
> Take the toys away from the boys

The centrality of creativity to the women's campaigning is illustrated in a poem called *A Memo for Peace* by Viv Wynant 'dedicated [in 1982] to the women at the Greenham Peace Camp; and to all those who live their lives in the struggle for peace and freedom.'

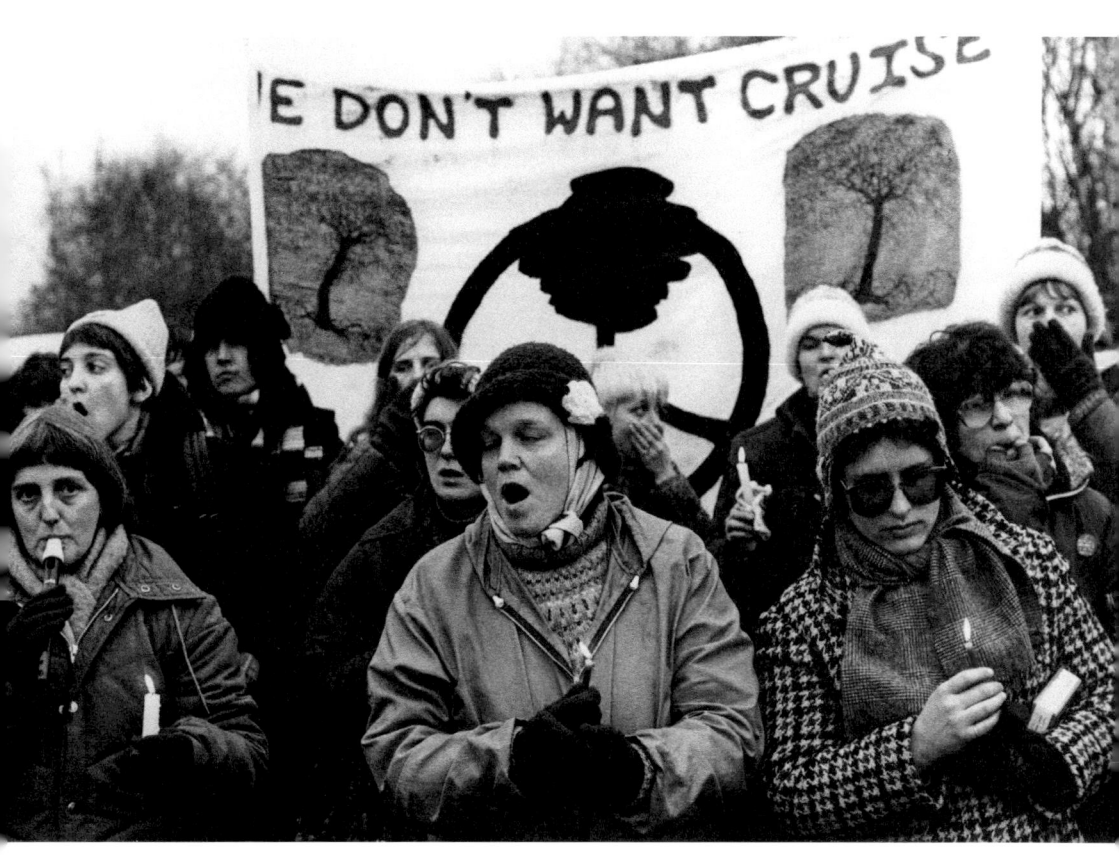

Singing at Greenham Common, 1983. Photograph by Janine Wiedel.

'...and let us remind ourselves
that we are many
who struggle
who cry out
who suffer in silence
even those who burned
to remind us
who march on marches
picket embassies
campaign and demonstrate
sign the petitions
hand out leaflets
write to newspapers
lobby MPs

who often go unheard

who join hands
who sing songs
who write the words
who play the music
who surround the barricades
with clowns with children
who weave coloured ribbons
between the barbed wire
who offer flowers
to the guards
who light the candles
singing softly into night...'[56]

Greenham women daily came together to make and sing, to share ideas and contribute to the cause. These activities were a focus for their energies during the nineteen years spent camping at Greenham, some uncomfortably cold or disrupted by the eviction of a camp, others warm around the campfire or energised by evading arrest after cutting their way into the base.

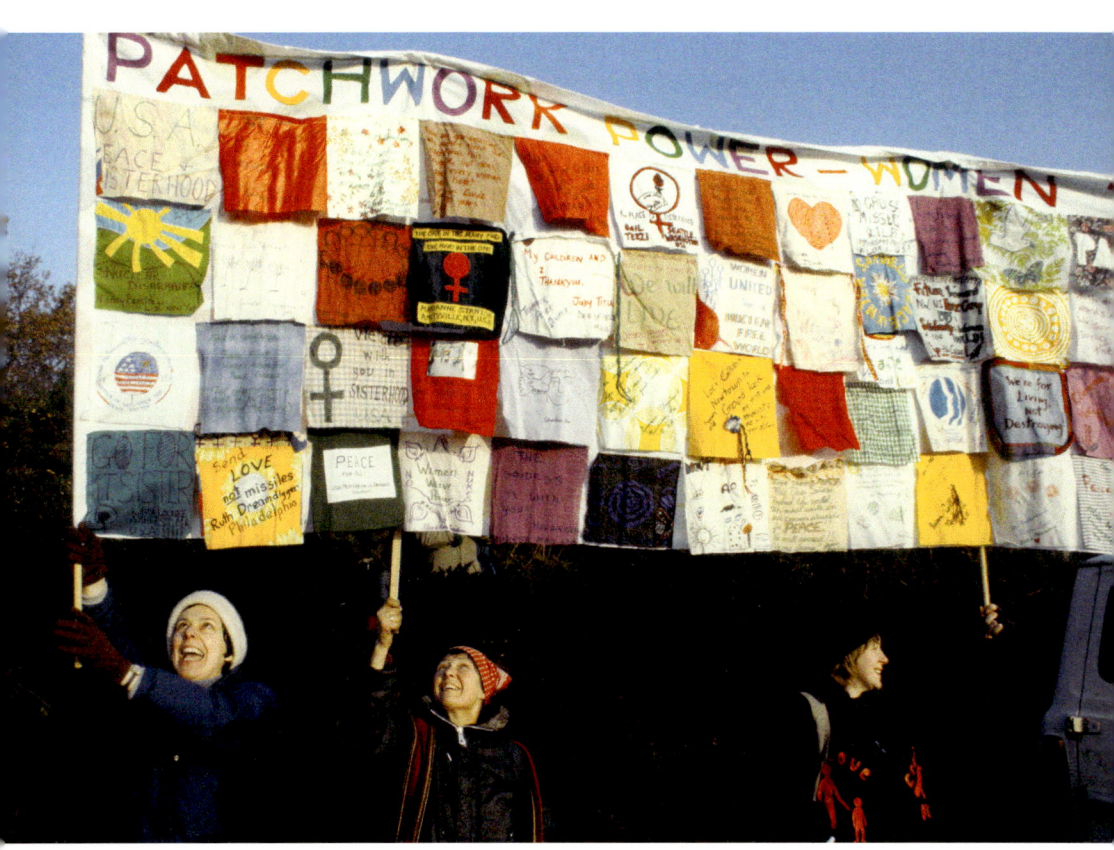

Above: Greenham Common patchwork, made in 1982. Photograph by Mike Goldwater.

Next pages: The patchwork (now in the collection of the Peace Museum, Bradford) on display in *Banner Culture*, an exhibition by Mid Pennine Arts at Brierfield, Lancashire, in 2019. Photograph by Melanie Diggle.

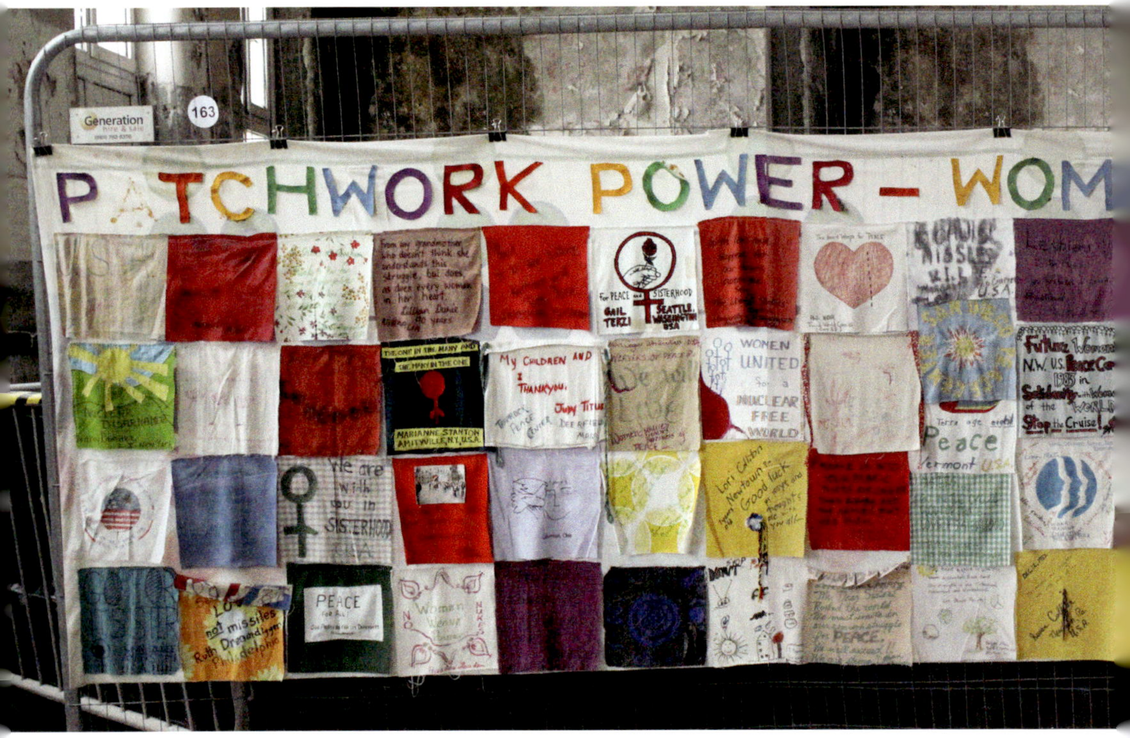

PATCHWORK POWER – WOMEN FORMING THE WORLD

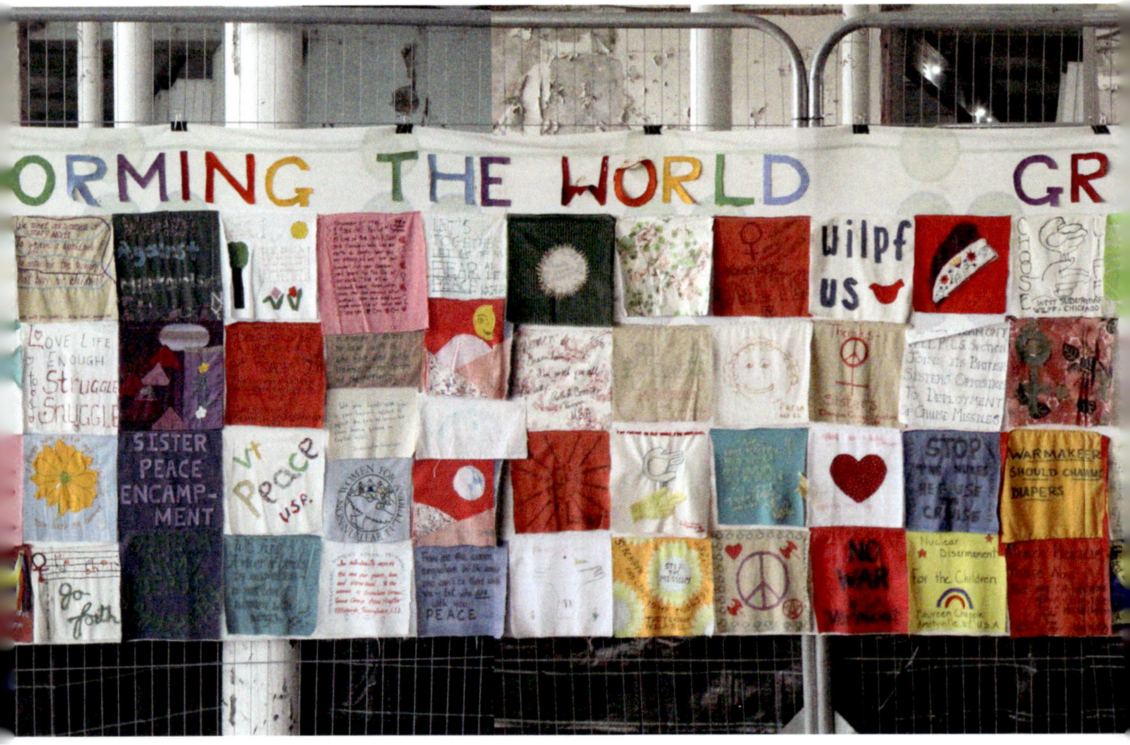

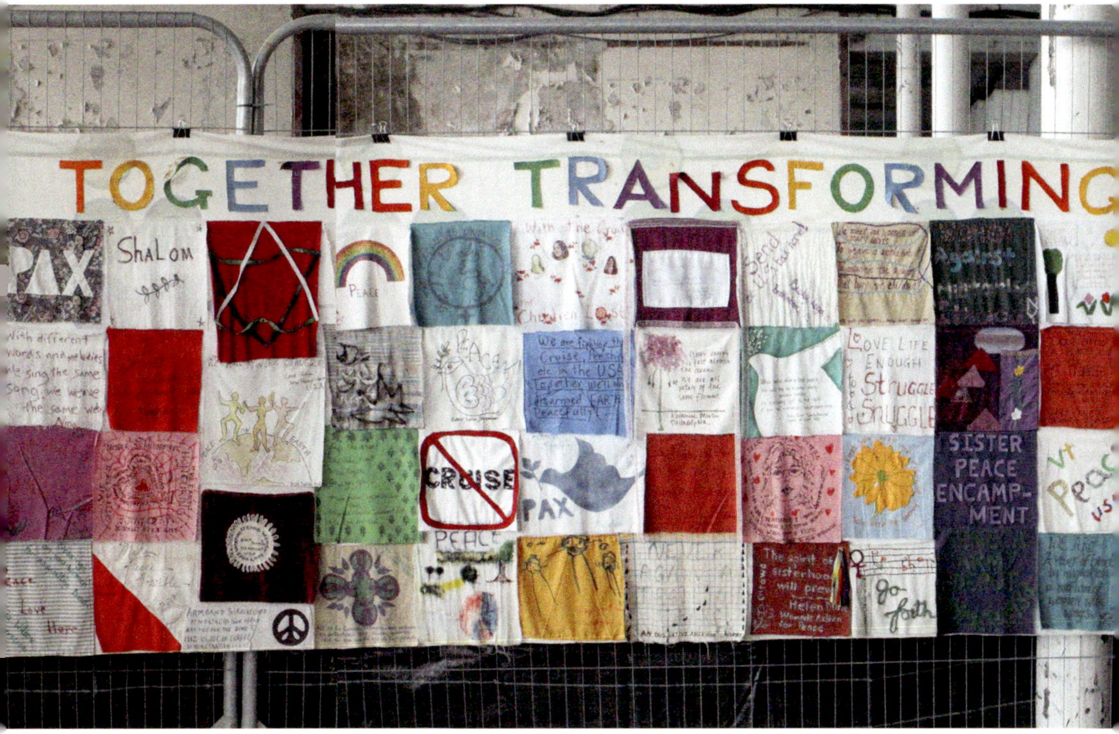

TOGETHER TRANSFORMING ...NHAM COMMON 1982

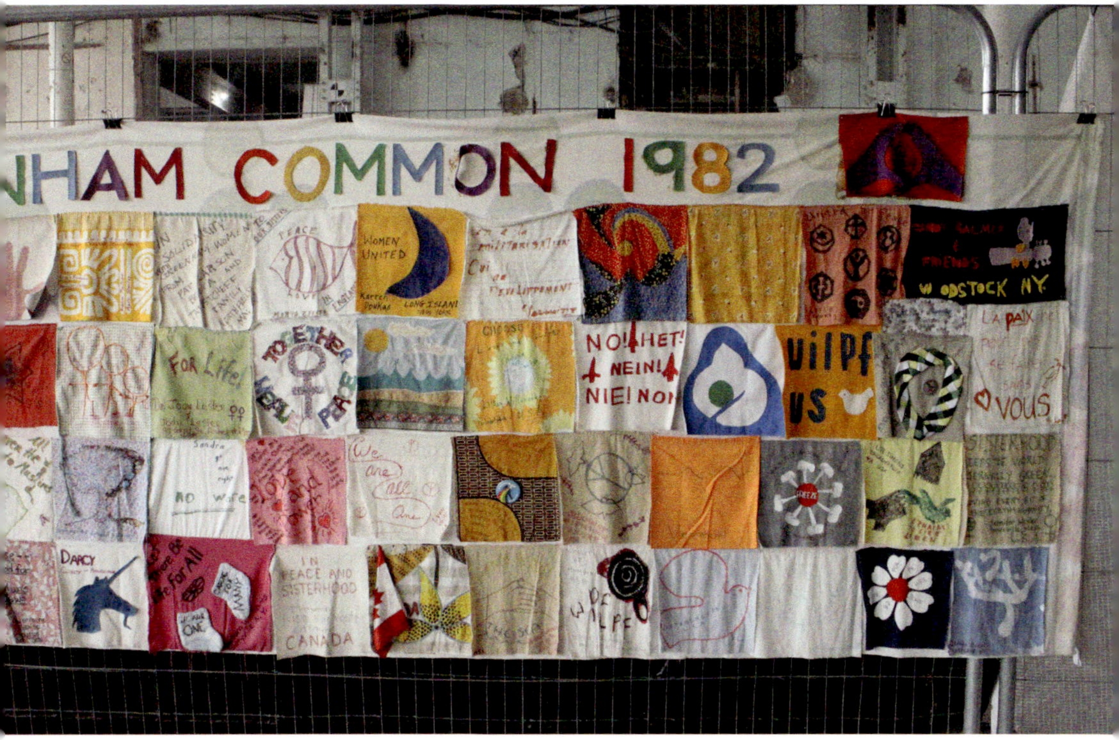

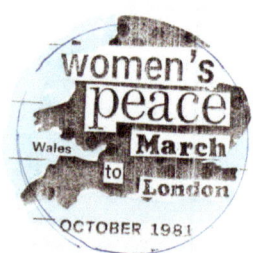
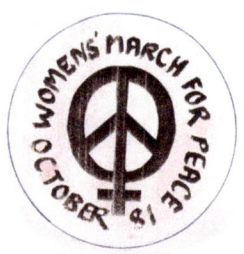
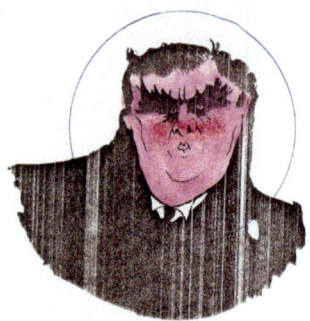

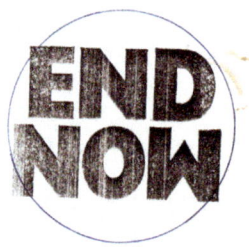
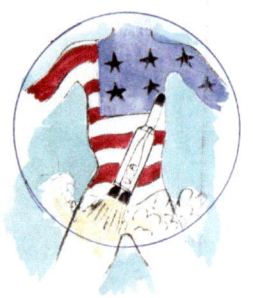

Above: Photocopied and hand-coloured sheets to cut out for badges.
Part of the Ian & Thalia Campbell collection at the National Library Of Wales.

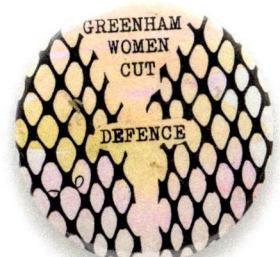
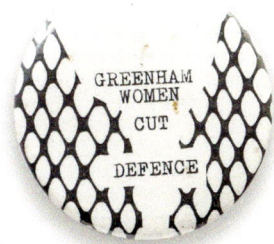
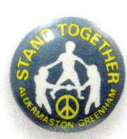
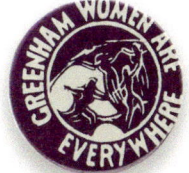
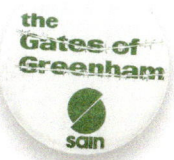
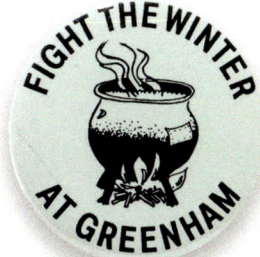
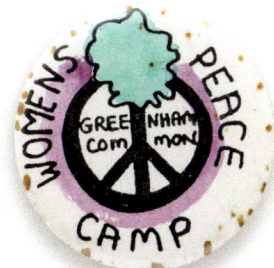
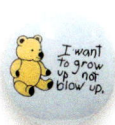
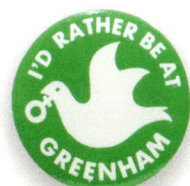
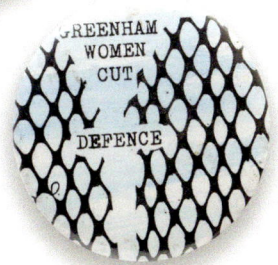

Above: Greenham badges, mostly hand-made.
From the collection of the Peace Museum, Bradford.

Artist Banner Makers

More complex banner designs, including those by named artists and visiting campaigning groups, were most often made away from the camp, and brought to site for display and use.

Artist Katrina Howse recalls that her ability to make banners and other artwork on site was limited by the relentless camp evictions, sometimes multiple times in one day, which resulted in the destruction of property in the 'muncher' (a rubbish truck). She describes that it was 'necessary to be able to keep everything of value in a rucksack'.[57] Her chosen medium for banners – paint – particularly necessitated a space where they could be made and dried safely. For this reason, prior to 1987, her work at Greenham took the form of small scale drawings, and when larger was made away from the camp, as was the case for her banner series in protest at the 1986 bombing of Libya.

This changed for Howse in 1987, when a small plot of land adjacent to the Common was purchased with Greenham women's funds, enabling the creation of 'The Sanctuary'. Ownership of the land meant it was free of the threat of eviction. Women could relax and recuperate when they were there, rather than being on constant alert. Two tepees were erected: one for sleeping, the other for creative activity. Here Howse had a space to draw, paint and make banners. She recalls that a range of activities took place in the tepee; Janet Tavner would dye and spin wool, Beth Junor wrote, and Aniko Jones grew marigolds to extract the oil.

Artist banner-maker Thalia Campbell is arguably the most recognised maker of Greenham banners – due to the quantity of her designs and the circulation of postcards depicting her banners, that resulted in orders for replicas and bespoke commissions. Most Greenham designs were made in a workshop at her then home, in Borth, Wales. Campbell often collaborated with her husband, Ian Campbell, also an artist. Other makers joined them, including Mary J Coughlin, Jan Higgs, Liz Forder, Jo Pate and Giles Bradley, to learn and make. Their banner making skills were also shared at workshops, delivered to groups across Wales and beyond.

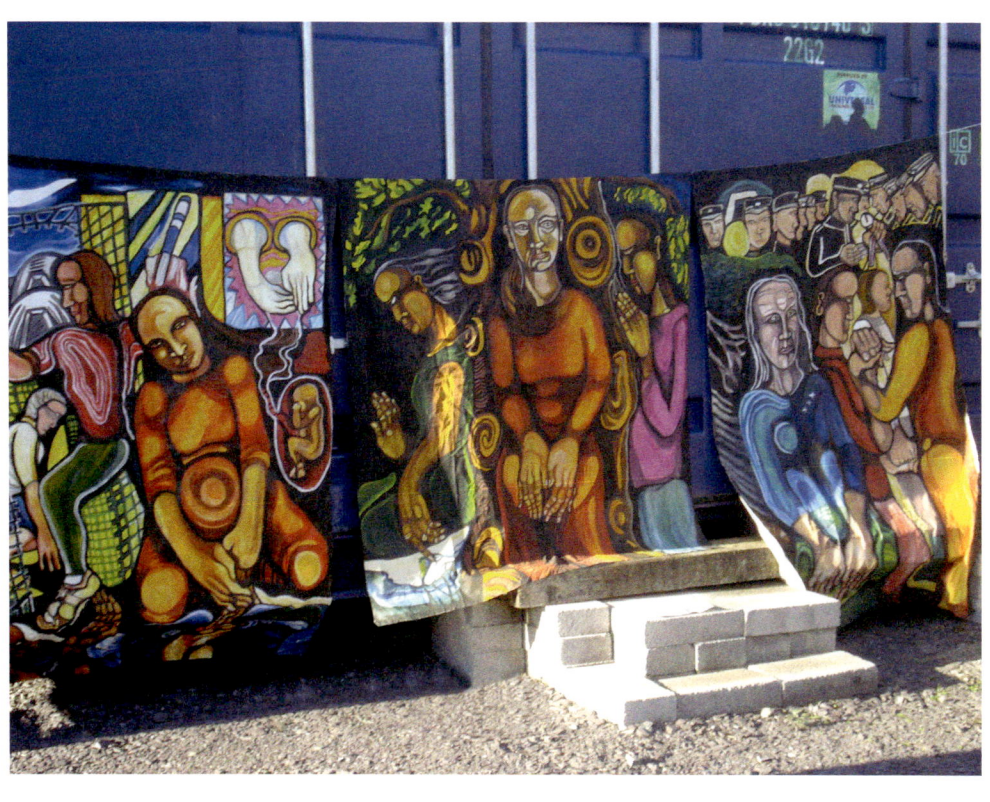

Banner triptych by Katrina Howse, panels from left to right:
*Reflected in the Water, Atomic Weapons Establishment (AWE), Aldermaston;
Underneath the Oaks at Aldermaston; Taking Non Violent Action against Trident
Warheads at AWE Burghfield*, 1992–3.

Campbell made paintings before banners, and her bold, graphic language in paint hints at the designs in textile that followed. Both Howse and Campbell used their artistic experience and talent for the purposes of protest. Campbell describes thinking: 'I could be another woman around the fire [at Greenham] or could use my art and political skills and knowledge.'[58] She cites the reaction of the 'gutter press', when they interviewed her and other women on the first march to Greenham, as the stimulus for starting to make protest banners. Recounting that reporters were more interested in photographing the women in their short skirts than writing about the focus and demands of their protest.

The composition and messaging of each of Campbell's appliqué banners is carefully designed, including the text. A new alphabet was drawn from scratch, for each banner. The alphabet is necessary to ensure the flow of letters, suitable to the scale and layout. Campbell believes that a banner's impact is strengthened by contrasting colours, and the design should include a 'shout and a whisper'.[59] The 'shout' gets your attention, and the 'whisper' is a more subtle continuance of the message. This is illustrated by her *State Terrorism No, No, No* (page 66) banner. The accusation that the USA are state terrorists is bold; the 'whisper' takes the form of net patches, visible when you look more closely, each naming a different American war.

For Campbell, the first stage in designing a banner is a drawn or ink sketch, to which colours are added, before the drawing is taken to the fabric shop. As well as using new materials, off-cuts may be sourced. Campbell recalls purchasing pieces of coat lining fabric from the Laura Ashley factory in Wales. She describes practical considerations in selecting fabrics for a banner; the ground must be heavier than the material applied to it and the whole banner should be kept as light as possible, to avoid sagging. To ensure the fabric would hold-up to being carried and hung, Campbell adds tape into the seams and double sews them for strength.

This banner making process differs little from that employed by the Artists Suffrage League, encapsulated in the pamphlet *Banners and Banner Making*, written by Artists Suffrage League Chair Mary Lowndes in 1908. The pamphlet advises a would-be maker on colour, design and form: 'A banner is a thing to float in the wind, to flicker in the breeze, to flirt its colours for your pleasure, to half show and half conceal a device you long to unravel; you do not want to read it, you want to worship it. Choose purple and gold for ambition, red for courage, green for long-cherished

Letters cut from cereal packets and cardboard, used as a guide to cut fabric for banner texts. Now in the Ian & Thalia Campbell collection at the National Library Of Wales.

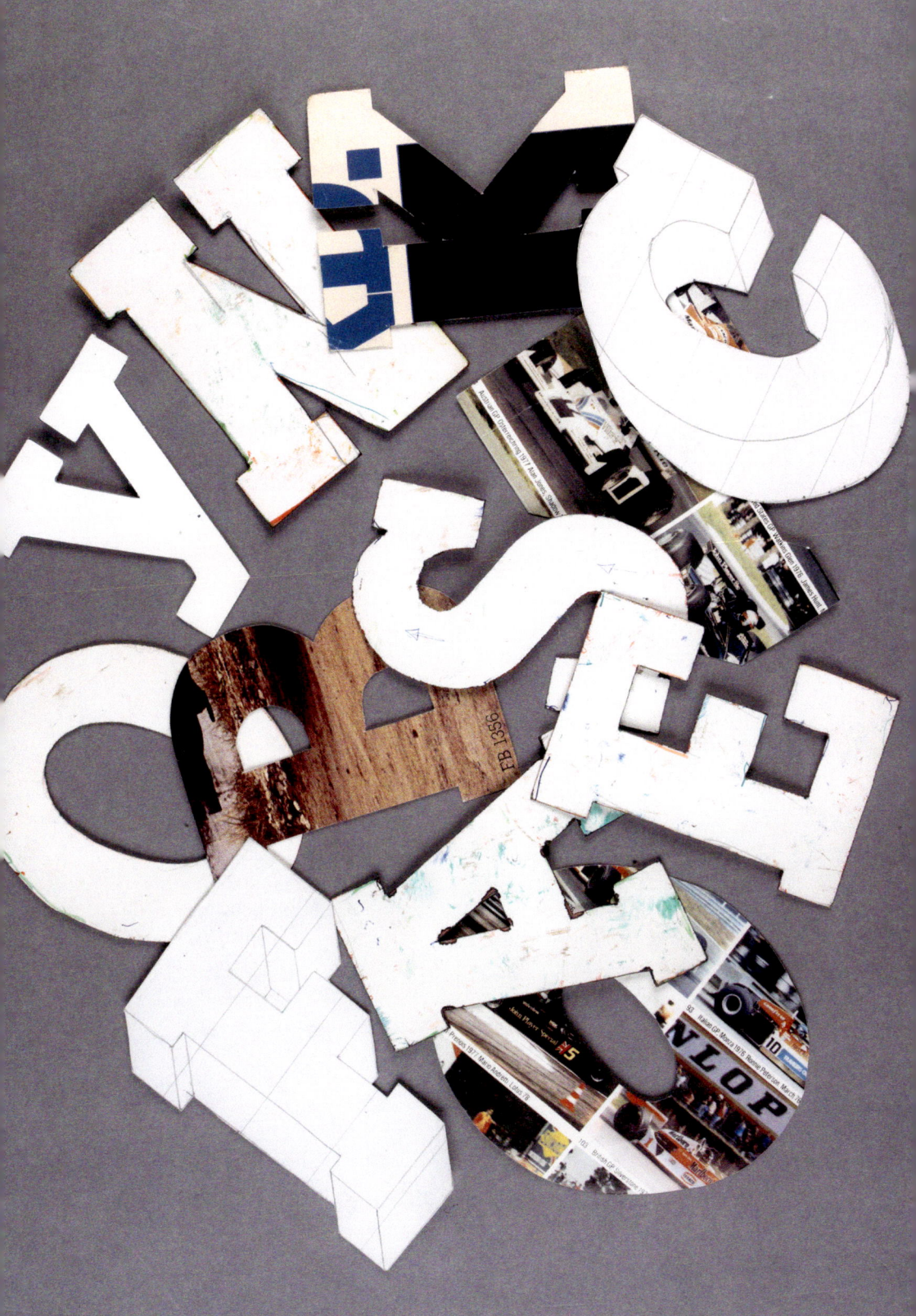

hopes... The upper edge must be devised for the attachment to the bar... in cutting the lower edge exhibit your fancy, and give the breeze a chance.' Lowndes pencil, ink and watercolour designs are captured in an album in The Women's Library Collection at the London School of Economics; one of Campbell's sources of inspiration. Howse's designs are painted in a distinctive bold and colour-rich style. They evoke the visceral experience of living at the Greenham camp, incarceration and campaigning. Prior to living at Greenham, she worked as a community mural artist in Sheffield and became involved in the peace and women's movements whilst at Sheffield University, participating in the active CND and counterculture movements in the city. There were other artists connected to the camp besides Campbell and Howse. Ginette Leach, who lived at Orange Gate, recalls one: 'we met up with Rose who was photographing and sketching as she went. She is a painter and told us she had hitchhiked down from Sheffield.'[60] Yet as Greenham banner makers Howse and Campbell's work stands out.

Opposite: *Holding Our Ground, Yellow Gate*.
Ink on paper drawing by Katrina Howse.

Next pages: Women at the fence at Greenham, 1983.
Photograph by Homer Sykes.

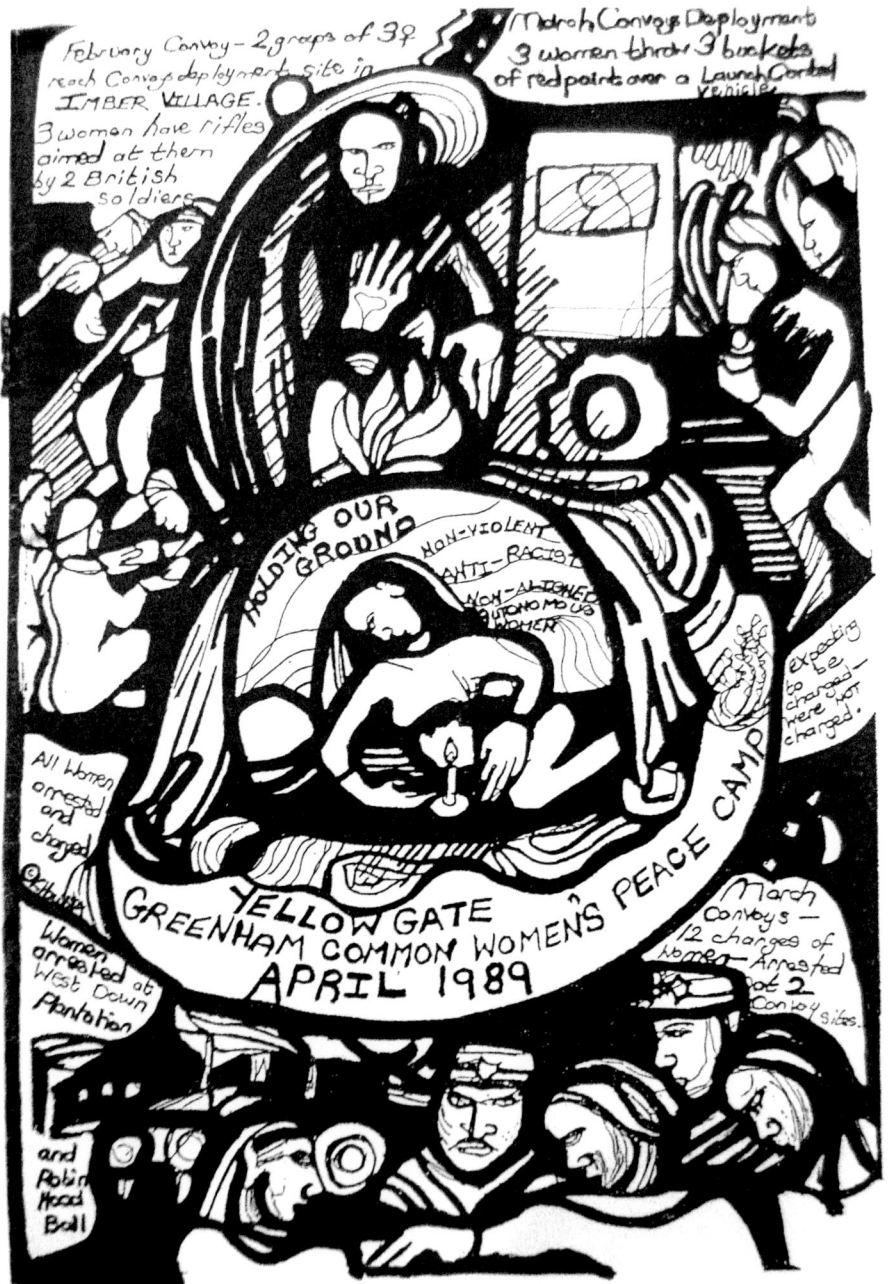

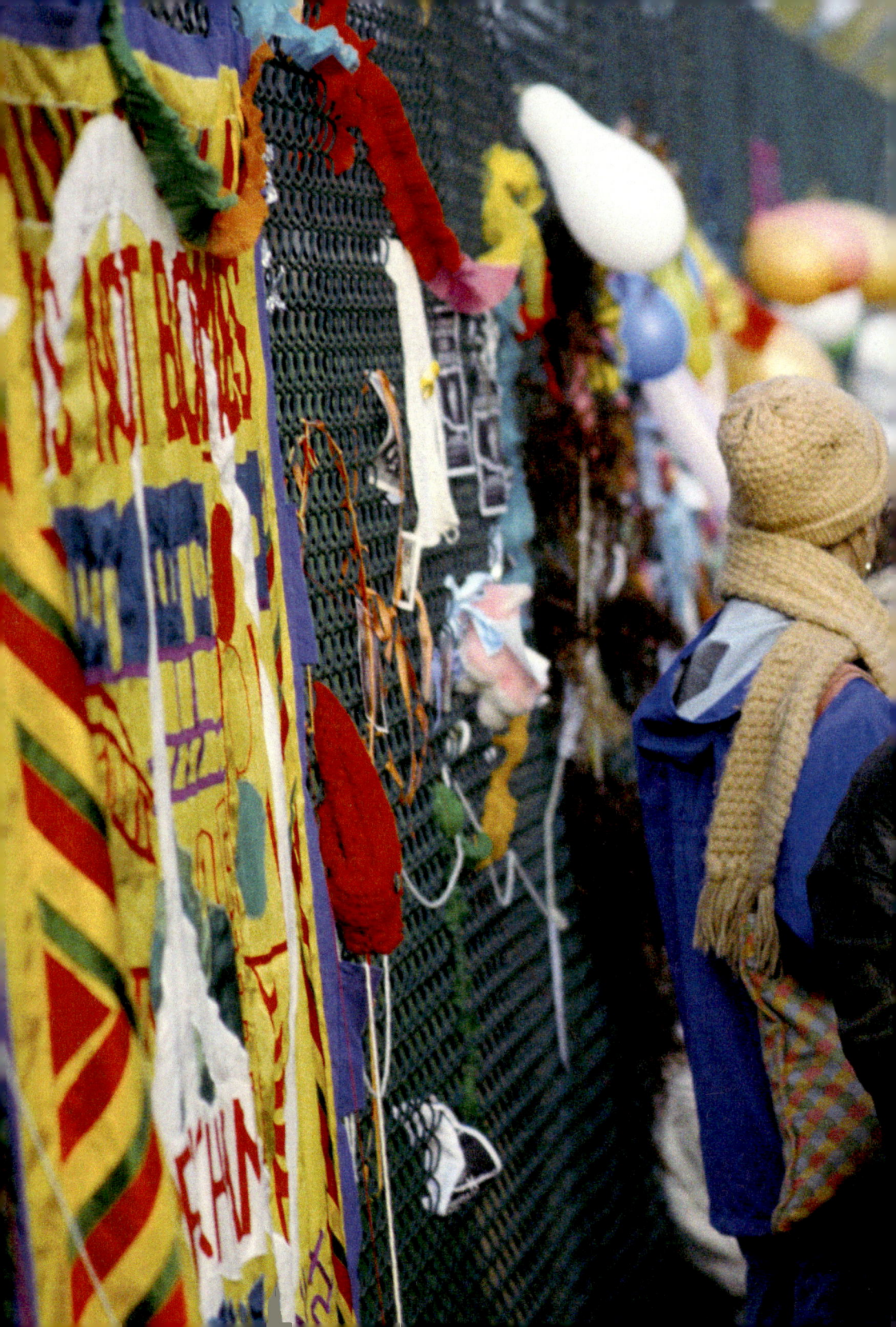

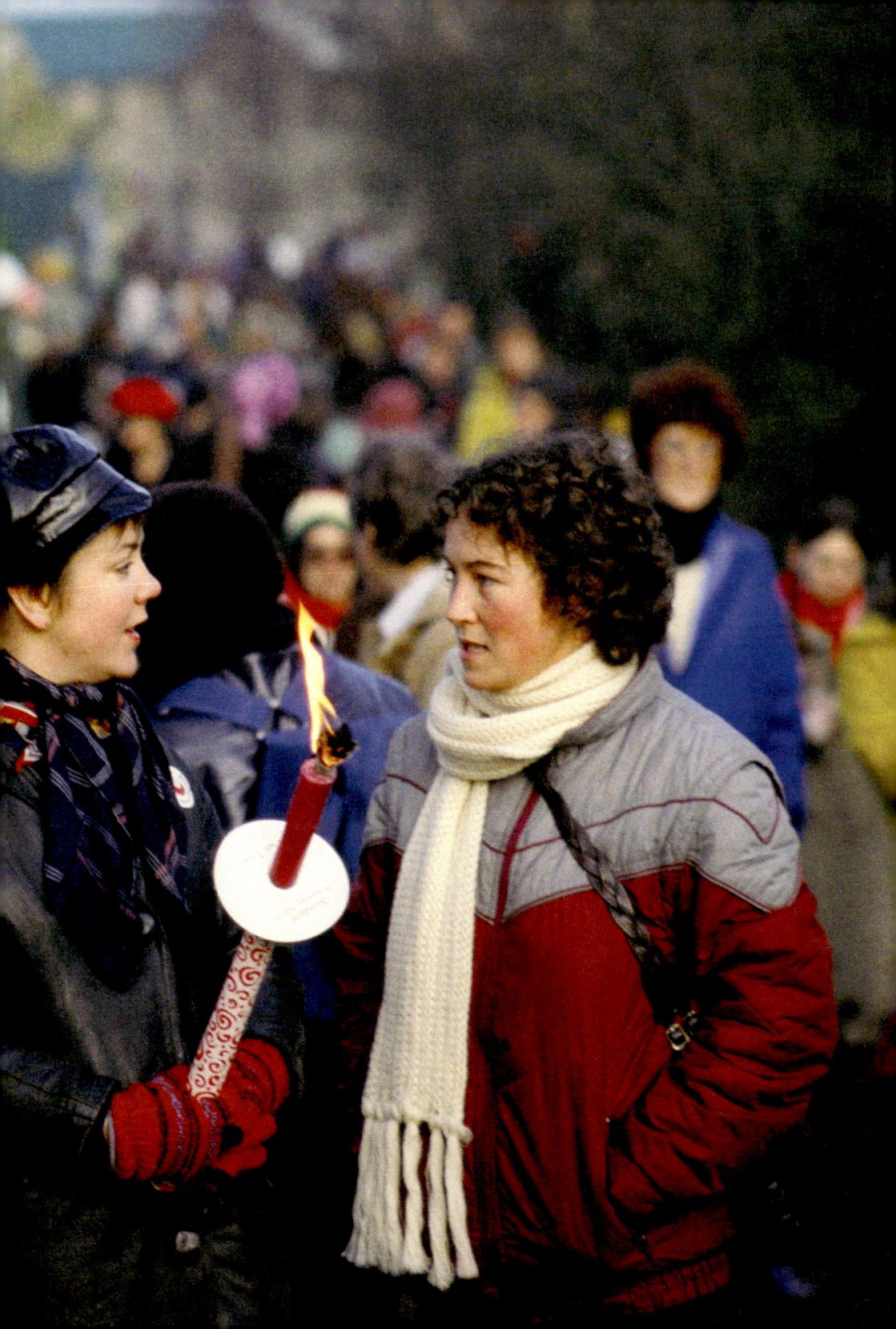

At Greenham Common: Ginette Leach

Ginette Leach joined the protests at Greenham and wrote about her experiences in *Orange Gate Journal. A Personal View of the Greenham Common Women's Peace Camp*, from which this account of the Embrace the Base event in 1983 is taken.

9–13 December 1983

Hilary and I had a long, dark, wet and windy drive to Greenham on Friday evening, not getting to the Orange Gate until 11.30. There was only one woman still wandering around, so we had a drink and went to bed in the car. It was still blowing like mad and we felt it would be noisy in a bender – and anyway it's hard to knock on bender 'doors' and ask if there is any room inside, although I did try.

The next morning, we met old friends and new ones, and all day women were arriving. There were 270 Americans from Minnesota over for nine days to meet Greenham women and give general support. They also support their own Peace Camps in the USA and had been sponsored by women's groups from back home, who paid the airfares. They came, I think, because they were so ashamed of Reagan. One of the permanent residents at the Orange Gate is Sally and on Saturday morning, a car drew up with Americans in it asking for her. It was her mother Barbara, who had arrived before her letter to say that she was coming. We found Sally. She and her mother had a fantastic time talking, and Barbara moved into Sally's bender, and was still there when I left.

Preparations were being made all around us for the following day's demo. There were plenty of troops inside the fence, and far more police than I had seen last time I was there. On the outside, marquee tents and loose shelters were being erected. Hilary and I were quite surprised that the demo was not just going to be with mirrors, musical instruments, etc., but we were going to try to get the fence down again. There was quite a lot of discussion about where this should take place, and of course, we said that we would do what we could to help. I was not sure what the reaction of some of the Deal people [visitors from Kent] would be to this, but they did not have to join in. They were coming up in a mini bus and the Peace Van just for the day on Sunday, and there were children with them, including Esther.

In the afternoon, Hilary and I drove round to the Green Gate, which neither of us had seen before. It is very lovely, quiet, and peaceful in the woods, with lots of tents there, but the silos are very close, which makes the reality inside the fence very real and overpowering. There was meant to be a mixed demo at that gate on the afternoon we were there, but apart from the fact there were quite a lot of men with the women wandering round the fence, nothing much seemed to happen and there was a strong Christian element around. The Buddhist nuns were chanting and when a couple of them recognised us, they carried on beating their instruments and just bowed to us. We bowed back: what else does one do under such circumstances?

We went back to the Orange Gate, where we were given instructions as to how to use the 'baby'. This is a ratchet-and-lever thing that is hooked to the fence on one side, and round a sturdy tree on the other with a length of rope: the idea is to pull down the fence (hopefully). There were obviously going to be problems with it, so that night when it was dark, about six of us went on to the Common where the runway feed-in lights are, and tried it out on two of the posts. We certainly got them to bend, but I think we felt it was going to be a slow operation. But with the cutting with 'knitting needles' [bolt cutters], the 'tea party' [a protest involving entering the camp] could probably take place. Also, we hoped that there would be so many women around that our activities would not be spotted too soon.

We had some supper and a bit of a party, a sing-song and a dance with Marion playing her accordion and giving barn dance instructions, which on frozen ground and in a rather alcoholic haze were not all that easy to follow. Eventually we went off to the car to sleep, and were glad of all the sleeping bags and blankets we had, as it was freezing hard by this time, and trips to the shit pit were decidedly chilly. I had left some orange juice in the car door pocket. In the morning, this was frozen hard, as were all the windows on the car on the inside. Cleaning teeth in ice crystals that will not pour out of the container takes some doing, but personally I would much rather have cold, still air rather than wind, which cuts right through you.

We had breakfast, and all morning women arrived, most of them bearing gifts of some sort: clothes, blankets, food, drink, money – £300 to the

Orange Gate alone. There were piles of plastic bags everywhere. The place looked a hell of a mess, but we just piled it all into the washing tent and the kitchen bender and left it there for the time being. Much to our surprise, the police were letting vehicles come to all the gates, so we kept an eye out for the Peace Van, and Hilary and I walked down to the road to see if it had arrived. First, I saw Melanie and Robert who had brought a vine to plant, then I met Jill Tweedie, Alan Briers, Jane and a friend, and I took them back to the camp and introduced Hil to various residents. Diana showed her the bender that I had helped to make. Then I saw Sian and Cleise wandering off round the fence and I joined them as we decided to find a good place to use the 'baby'. We were told that some London women had brought 100 'knitting needles' with them so we dispersed some of these round the place, and then walked towards the Main Gate, and decided that the area around the swamp was the best area for fence pulling and cutting, as it would be hard to get police reinforcements there. Mind you, by this time, more and more police were moving into position, but also more and more women were stationing themselves round the fence and we were obviously going to have a fantastic turnout. We knew some of them were prepared to be active, but we had no idea how many.

We went back to the Orange Gate, having fixed our spot, and there I met Elizabeth and Kirstie with the children. By this time it was one o'clock and suddenly the whole place erupted with noise. Shouting, banging, musical instruments being played, (I hooted the car horn, and others copied me) and for about five minutes, there was this amazing noise everywhere. The papers estimated about 30,000 women, but as usual, it is impossible to tell. All I know is that there were one-hell-of-a-lot around where I was.

By two o'clock, those prepared for action – Sian, Zoe, Cleise, Charlie, Rebekah, Annie, Margaret, Sally, Ruth, Hilary, Penny, Jean, Miranda, Diana, Nikki, Gerry, Marion, Shirley, Leslie, me, etc., etc., etc. – collected our 'knitting needles', and went off down the fence. We decided our action should take place at three. We found a really muddy, mucky spot, and stood around and some sat down where the 'baby' was going to be fixed on to a tree, and just as the yelling and shouting started, we made for the fence. I cut like hell, and just as a policeman was about to grab the cutters, I chucked them behind me to someone else. An Inspector was going up and down the line of women with his men trying to stop us, but we went on cutting, but then got the idea of pulling the fence, just by womanpower. My God, it worked! I think we all thought that those posts were sunk ten feet into the ground. They are not! The fence shook and wobbled, and swayed.

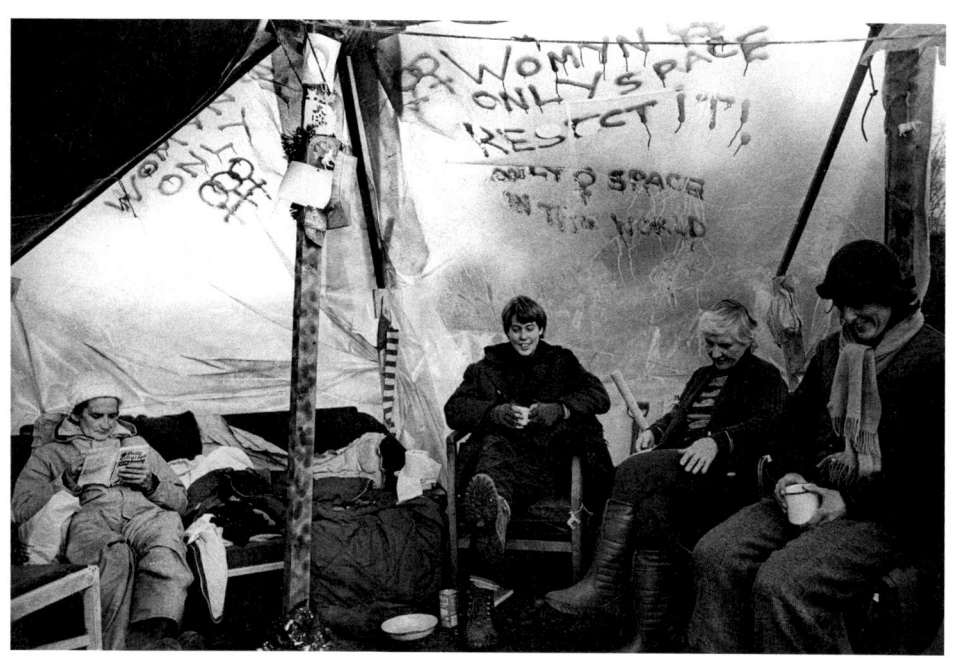

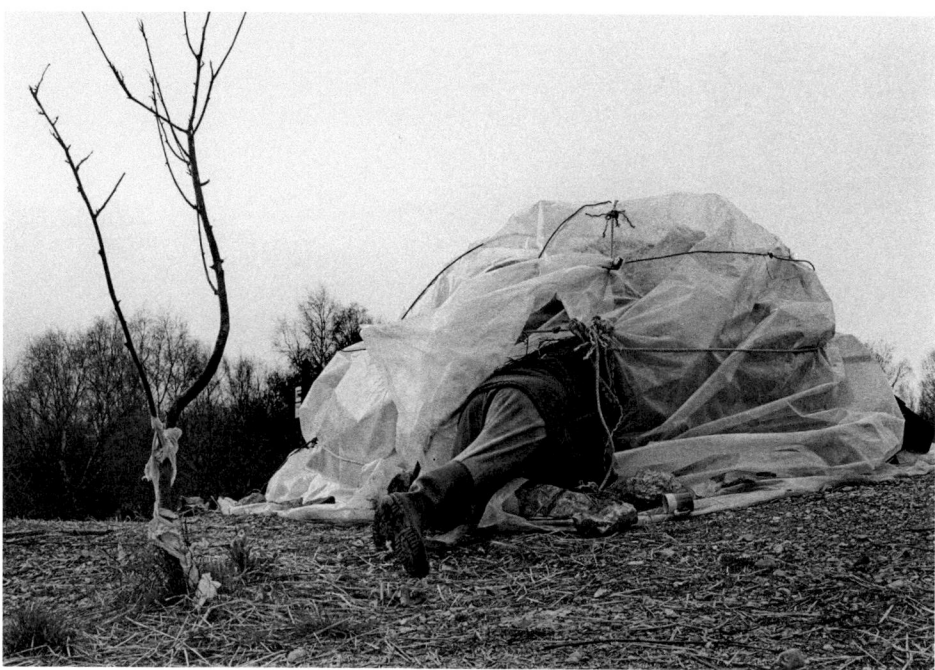

Above: 'Benders': wood and plastic shelters at Greenham.
Photographs by Janine Wiedel.

The 'baby' was captured and hurled inside, but it didn't matter. We just heaved in unison, and while we heaved, the cops pulled us off, but we went back, again and again. A burly policeman sat on top of me, but I still had my fingers inside the fence, pulling all the time. Then a section with a post came down, and I saw Sian, Charlie and others chuck some carpet over the barbed and razor wire, and climb in for their 'tea party' and stand on top of the hill waving their arms. Some soldiers grabbed them, but instead of making arrests, shoved them back outside to us, over the wire again. The police were getting rough, so we moved a few yards away, and went on pulling and more fence gave. At one point, I was being pulled by a policeman from outside and a soldier was thumping my knuckles from the inside, but I hardly felt it. Most times when I was hurled off, the women standing and encouraging us caught me, but once I went with a crash on my back. By this time, we were all covered with mud, which was almost knee-high in places. The police linked arms and tried to lean against the fence to stop it coming down, so for a few minutes, I put my arms each side of a helmet and unravelled the wire round his head. When I was exhausted and realised I could not do much more, I went and found Hilary and we squelched our way back to the Orange Gate. Diana came with us, and although large sections of the fence had not been touched, back at the Orange Gate we met up with more of the Deal party. When I saw the fence swaying there, Diana and I went up to it and started all over again until once more we were worn out. I felt as though my arms had been pulled out and the knuckles on my right hand were swelling fast. By this time, it was quite dark apart from the arc lights, and most of the activity was dying down.

 I did not want to go. This always happens to me. To hell with the cold, muck, discomfort etc., etc., it's people who count, and once I get to Greenham, I forget everything and just want to stay on. The people back in the real world say it's like a drug, I suppose they're right. Anyway, I found Hilary and the others, and they said I should stay. But Hilary had to get back so she joined the others in the Peace Van, fourteen by this time, as some had walked from the Main Gate. So, she took her things and went off with them. I was sorry to see her go, but she has commitments and now I have shed mine. It's taken a hell of a long time, but I think at last I've done it.

 I did not want to sleep in the car on my own, so Zoe said I could share her bender and Anne Marie was there as well. Luckily, I had the sense to put my things in 'Bender 13' quite early on in the evening, as I can't remember what happened later on. I do remember we had supper, and a lot to drink, and Miranda took me for a walk on the Common in the

Opposite: Thalia Campbell's banners at Blue Gate on the day of a summer blockade.

freezing cold to try and straighten me out, but I can't remember what she said or why. The next thing I can clearly remember is being shoved more to one side in the bender as I was taking up too much room, and that I had a hot water bottle in my sleeping bag. It appears that Rebekah had put me to bed, then worried that I might be cold, so made me a hot water bottle. I do have vague sort of memories about this, but nothing is at all clear. Mind you, I do not think I was the only woman in this state. My only (weak) excuse is that it was a reaction to the day's activities.

During the night I was aware of a sprinkling noise on the bender, and when Anne Marie decided to get up, she pulled aside the polythene door and there was the world white with snow. It looked beautiful, but cold. Zoe and I stayed in bed and Anne Marie brought us coffee, so we sat and smoked and talked for an hour or so. She told me a bit about her life as a single parent, and her problems of bringing up her daughter on her own. Her daughter is now fourteen and a half and had been there the day before, but had gone back home and to school. It has not been an easy life for Zoe, but she, like me, gains enormous strength from Greenham.

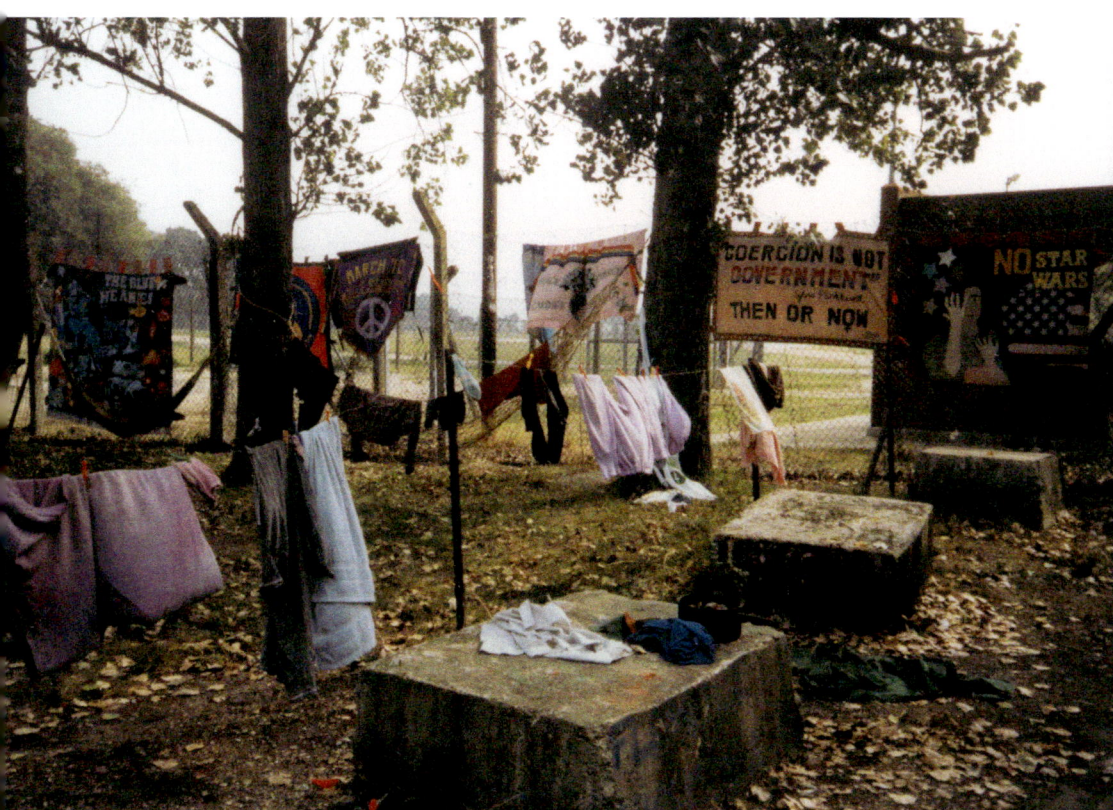

At Greenham Common: Juliet Nelson

Juliet Nelson wrote this account of Greenham in May 1983, and it was originally published in *Greenham Women Everywhere*. See also the photograph on pages 12–13.

As soon as we arrived at the camp a woman came down the path towards us and asked us if we'd heard the plan – to go on to the base at dawn and on to the silos, using ladders and carpets for the barbed wire! We were all amazed; it was such an incredible plan! I immediately felt really strongly that I wanted to do it. I had to try hard to hold back, to think about it rationally. We were worried about being charged under the Official Secrets Act.

But I knew my feelings about it would win over and that I'd end up going over the fence. It was because it was all centred around those missile silos. I think they're a focal point of all the negative things that are going on in the world – paranoia, greed, misuse of power, violence, a lack of imagination for alternatives. In my mind I saw them as revolting man-made boils on the earth's surface, full of evil. I wanted to let out all the feelings I have about the threat of nuclear war – the fear and the dread. And I wanted to concentrate on the future, to feel optimistic and get strength and hope that we can stop it. I kept thinking about celebrating life. What actually happened was that I did that. When we got on to the silos, even though we were so excited, I stood quietly for a few moments, with my eyes closed, and let it all drain out of me. After that I just kept thinking about being alive!

There were about 60 of us at the last planning meeting, all quite calm, but there was a nervousness in the air. The next morning it was very still and dark outside as we crept into the back of the van. The journey to the base seemed endless. I was leaning forward looking out of the window, so I could see when we arrived. The only thing I could make out in the back of the van were the white women-signs painted on the tabards we were wearing so that we wouldn't be mistaken for terrorists, to make it obvious who we were.

The atmosphere was electric when we got to the base. We got out of the van as quietly and quickly as we could and immediately made our way to the perimeter fence. By the time we got there the first lot of women were going over, and half of them were already waiting on the other side.

Ahead of us we saw the aluminium ladders. I remember seeing three on each side, leaning against the fence. It seemed ridiculously easy – there were streams of women going over the fence, over the carpet, making it so ineffectual. There was a queue to get over. Just then we saw vehicle headlamps in the distance coming towards us. My heart sank. We knew we'd been seen, and wondered whether we'd manage to get over in time. It turned out to be a small vehicle with only two police inside.

I was on the ladder, about to go over, I was on the carpet... They whipped the ladders away and I was left stranded on the top wondering how I was going to get down. I scrambled over the wire at the top, jumped down, and then I put the ladder back up. The two police were running from side to side with their arms out, backwards and forwards, saying 'Stop, go back' – as if we'd all stop and go back. I remember deliberately running wide in a curve to avoid them, and running like hell. I remember getting there and scrambling up the slope. It was covered in mud and very slippery. At the top there was a big ledge of concrete we had to climb on to. A woman leaned down to offer me a hand up. I said, 'Hang on a minute, I can't manage just yet.' I had to get my breath back, I was really puffing. I climbed up that last bit of concrete and felt really pleased – I'd got there!

Every now and again we'd link arms in a big circle and dance around the top of the silo. We were all ecstatic, overtaken by the brilliance of the feeling that we'd actually done it! We took off our tabards and hung them on wooden posts to leave some trace and remind the workmen that we'd been there, to make them think about it, and we planted a lovely colourful 'Peace 83' banner on the sloping side. The top of the silo was covered in bits of concrete rubble and wooden planks which we arranged into women's peace signs. When we began to explore the top of the silo we could see that we were only on one half of it. In between the two halves there was a deep rectangular pit with lots of steel reinforcing bars running across it like a grid. I suppose they were going to concrete it over. We went over to the far end and we could see the enormous airstrip. It looked really desolate. You could see for miles. There was nothing – just the watery sun coming up.

We were on top of the silos for about one hour and 20 minutes. A police car or two arrived first, then quite a bit later the buses arrived. I don't think they could believe how many of us there were. There we were on the top, celebrating New Year! The police walked around the bottom of the silo for quite a while, looking puzzled. Then some MoD police arrived and some military personnel.

When we saw the MoD police climbing up the side of the silo we all sat down around the edge of the big wooden peace sign, linked arms and just waited. They broke the circle and started lifting women down one by one. The police on the top picked up the women and passed them to the ones further down who dragged the women down the slope. One of the ones on the top was really nasty, much bigger than the rest, and he looked really threatening. I hoped he wouldn't be the one to get me. When they took a woman from the circle we all linked arms again and moved inwards, so the circle got smaller and smaller. The atmosphere changed but all the time we were friendly to the police.

One came to get me, and I went limp. He dragged me to the ledge and passed me over to two others, placing me on the ground on my front. I had my head facing down the slope…it was quite steep… They picked me up by the wrists and somehow my arms were pulled backwards as they dragged me. I thought they'd dislocate my shoulders. It was really painful. They said 'Get up and walk, you silly bitch. Are you going to get up and walk?' I was carried like that for about 20 yards or so. It was so painful I just said 'Please, put me down. I'll walk.' So they put me down and I walked. For the rest of the weekend I was extremely stiff and under my arms felt very bruised.

I had a conversation with one of the police near the bus. The other one had gone off again to get someone else. I said, 'Why don't you think about what you're doing? Don't you ever think about what you're protecting here?' I was just met with stony-faced silence. I gave up and sighed and said, 'How will we ever get through to you?' He said, 'You don't realise, you already have, but this time you've overstepped the mark.'

We were all whisked off to Newbury nick, singing all the way. When we arrived, we were taken down to the cells in the basement and put into a small room, which was the biggest cell they'd got. The noise of our singing was deafening. The police seemed to be affected in the same way as the base personnel – completely awestruck that we'd done it and that we were so jubilant about it.

We'd asked on the bus what we were being charged with and they said breach of the peace which was a big relief! They spent the whole day processing us. We were taken to a little room at the end where there were two police. One read out the charge sheet and took down particulars – names and addresses. Afterwards we were put into different cells, smaller, like pens. There were little bits of paper stuck to the walls outside with our surnames listed – the kind of thing that if we hadn't been feeling so good we'd probably have felt really angry about. We kept asking where we'd be taken to. They either didn't know or they wouldn't tell us.

Our cell door was opened. I was called out and put into another cell down the corridor. It was a different kind of cell, with no bench, just a loo with no chain. The chain was on the outside, I suppose so they can check what goes down the loo. It felt horrible in that cell by myself.

We heard the cell doors being unlocked. We were let out and led outside. There was a riot van waiting, with cages like tiny cupboards with a grid, all painted white. We were told that we were going to Oxford. Two of the women had to sit in a tiny space in the middle between the cages, and they had their wrists handcuffed together behind their backs. I felt very frightened, and horrified that we were going to travel all that distance in such a confined space, locked in, with our hands handcuffed like that.

All of a sudden, I realised how barbaric it was and that I didn't have to do it. They got one handcuff on my left arm and they kept trying to grab my right arm to get the other handcuff on it, while I waved my right arm about so that they couldn't grab it. I was determined not to be handcuffed. I said that we weren't going to get away, that I'd deliberately put myself in this position and that we weren't going to escape with the police van and the doors locked. The more I went on the more determined I became and the more frightened. I said 'What if there's an accident? How on earth are we going to protect ourselves?' They kept telling me not to argue. I thought that sooner or later I'd have to give in to their authority, but then I thought, just because they're police in uniforms I don't have to do it. They were shouting by this stage and I was shouting back, 'You don't have to do this. It's not necessary. It's just spite and humiliation.' Finally they gave in. They let the other women out and took their handcuffs off and handcuffed us to each other in a line. I was on the end so I had a free hand. I remember feeling so relieved.

Greenham Banners Beyond the Campaign

Campbell and Howse's designs and other Greenham banners have been displayed and contextualised in exhibitions of art, as well as exhibits concerned with peace and campaigning, women's art, and protest art, during the Greenham campaign and since. Campbell was commissioned to make two Greenham banners to include in the British Council international touring exhibition '"A Woman's Place" 50 Years of Photographs of Women'. The show, curated by Diana Souhami, opened at the South Bank Centre in London in 1984 and toured to thirty countries. One of the banners Campbell contributed to this exhibition was a version of her *Greenham Womens Peace Camp* design. She made four versions of this, over several years, adding new motifs describing the activities of the camp each time.

In 1983 Campbell curated and toured her own exhibition titled '100 Years of Women's Banners', which travelled to regional UK galleries, halls and churches until 1991. It included examples of historic banners, her own designs and some borrowed from individuals and groups. As the project went on for several years, and some banners could not be borrowed for the duration, Campbell remade some designs she admired. For example, a version of the *Take A Risk For Peace Now* banner, which had originally been created by a women's group in Totnes, Devon. She recalls that people frequently offered banners to be added to the exhibition, and it became necessary to devise a definition of a women's banner to justify those she could and could not accept. Each exhibited banner had to be either made by a woman, for any cause, or made by a man or woman for a woman's cause.

A detail of a Howse banner was used on the cover of the 1995 book *Greenham Common Women's Peace Camp: A History of Non-Violent Resistance 1984–1995*, by Beth Junor, which is also illustrated with Howse's drawings.

Greenham banners were exhibited in the Victoria and Albert Museum exhibition 'Disobedient Objects' (26 July 2014 – 1 February 2015), and the Imperial War Museum's 'Peace Power: Fighting for Peace' (23 March – 28 August 2017). Greenham ephemera, including postcards of banners, was shown by Nottingham Contemporary in 'Still I Rise: Feminisms, Gender,

Resistance, Act 1' (27 October 2018 – 27 January 2019). The increasingly plural definition of the materials with which fine art can be made, and some redressing of the male art historical bias in the twenty-first century, makes these broader readings of Greenham banners ever more likely.

As time has passed following the closure of the Greenham Women's Peace Camp in 2000, the banners have become part of the evidence of women's and peace campaigning through history. Where they survive, with their diversity of demands, they evoke the spirit and determination of the women who believed in nuclear disarmament.

The Greenham banners have been followed by banner designs that protest against wars waged by the western world, and the continued production and sale of nuclear and other arms, as well as women's banners continuing to demand equal rights and proclaiming 'Me Too'. In a quest to understand the diversity of voices in the past, banners are a vital source.

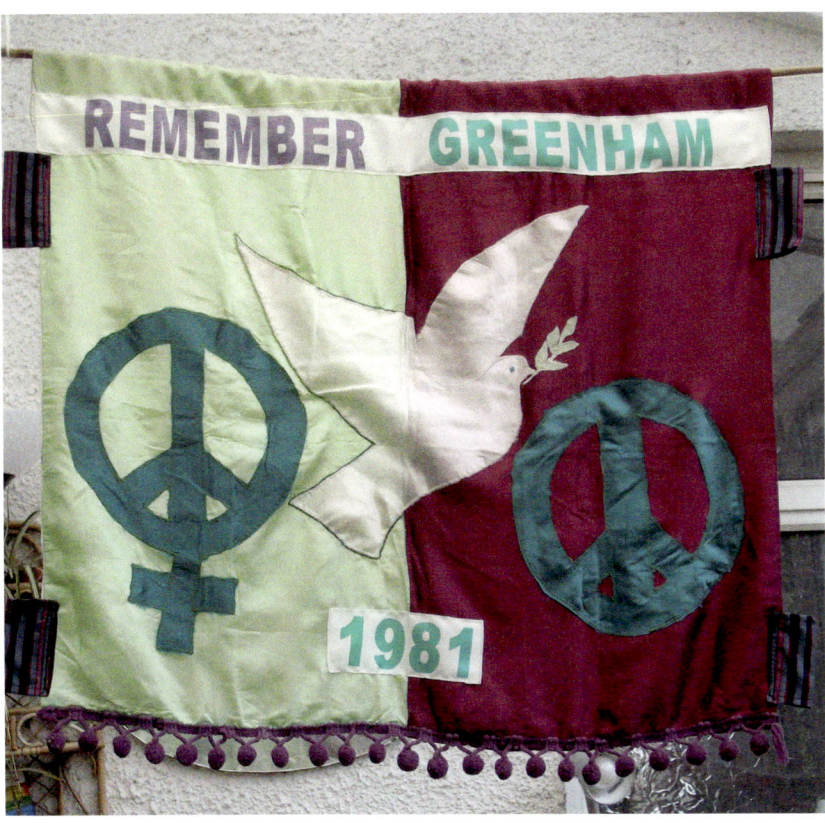

Above: *Remember Greenham 1981*, by Thalia Campbell.

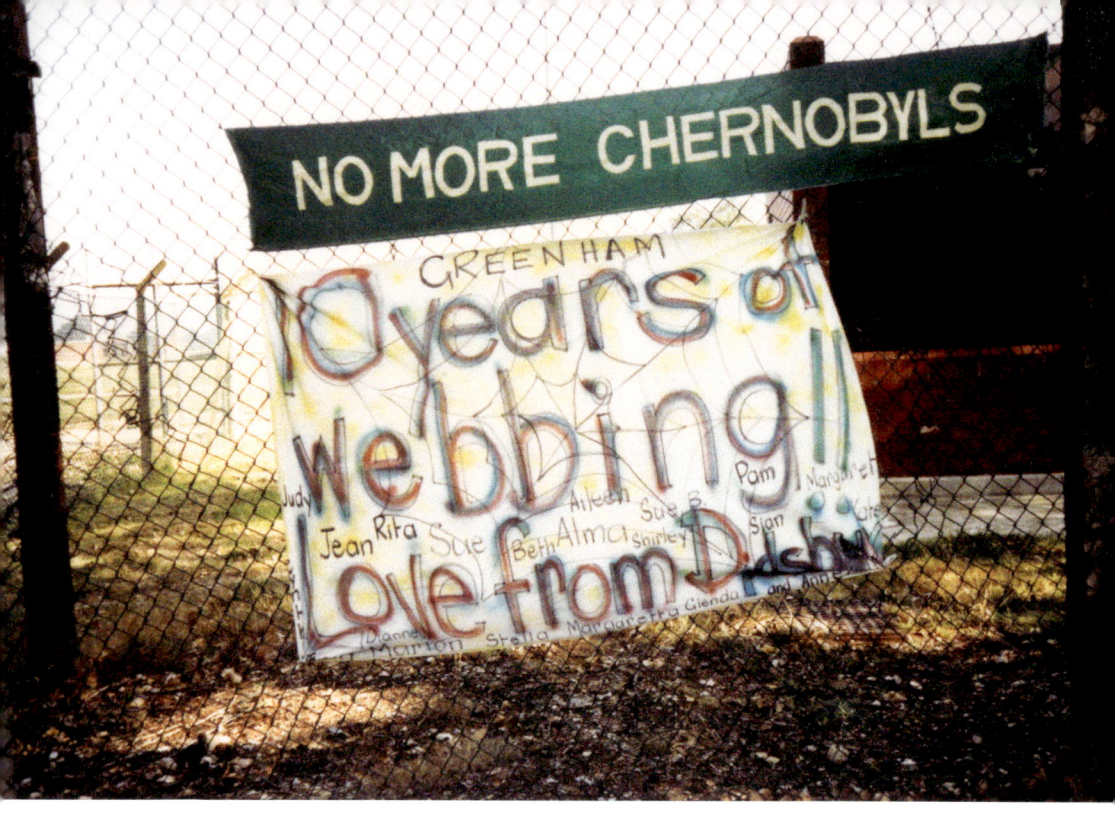

Above: *No More Chernobyls* and *10 Years of Webbing!! Love from Didsbury* on the fence at Greenham.

Author's Note

This book explores the role that banners played at the Greenham Common Women's Peace Camp and in the campaign at large. It does not present a comprehensive assessment of the politics or diversity of women's experiences at Greenham, or a definitive account of the banners, such are the quantity of women who participated in the protest. It is hoped that its publication and the 40th anniversary of the founding of the camp may bring to light more extant banners, to enrich our understanding of the extraordinary creativity and passion they stand for.

The only record of many of the banners are photographs taken at Greenham or related protests, and many of the images in this book reflects that. For this reason, it has not always been possible to attribute these banners to a particular maker or group, or to include their dates or measurements.

Author's Acknowledgements

Special thanks go to Greenham women Thalia Campbell and Katrina Howse, and Thalia's husband Ian Campbell, for generously sharing their remembrances and photographs, as well as Richard Embray and Elinor Jansz of Four Corners Books for the opportunity to explore the Greenham banners in depth. I would also like to thank Charlotte Hall at The Peace Museum, Bradford, staff at Glasgow Women's Library and Elen Phillips at National Museums Wales for their time and assistance, as well as Moira Vincentelli for her past research and writing on this subject. I first encountered the women of Greenham Common as assistant curator at The Women's Library (then part of London Metropolitan University and formerly the Fawcett Library) from 2002–2008, where I was privileged to catalogue the museum collections. I would like to acknowledge all my colleagues at the Library, in particular the then curator Gail Cameron and archivist Maxine Willett, as well as archivist Gillian Murphy, who continues to work with the collection at the London School of Economics.

Finally, I would like to thank the many people who have been instrumental in encouraging me in my career, and supporting my interest in history and textiles, and writing about them: Kate Arnold-Forster, Antonia Byatt, Mary Brooks, Susan and Philip Dew, Edward and Faye Dew, Birgit Dohrendorf, Dinah Eastop, Richard Gamester, Midge Gillies, Sally Johnson, Isabel Keim, Karine Lepeuple, Shaun Levin, Fiona Moorhead, Zoe Roberts, Cat Rowe, Jane Ruddell, Mairead Smith, Janet Stoneman, Clare Summons, Brandon Taylor, Peter Taylor, Sarah Turner, Helen Walsh, Mathew Weir, Nigel and Maureen Weir, Claire West, and Charles and Teddy White.

Publisher's Acknowledgements

The publishers would like to thank: Cath Barnes, Yorkshire CND; Tom Campbell, Iwan ap Dafydd, Llyfrgell Genedlaethol Cymru / The National Library of Wales; Stefan Dickers, Bishopsgate Institute; Melanie Diggle at Mid Pennine Arts; Charlotte Hall, Peace Museum; Eva Herzog; Danielle Inga; Lauren Iredale, The Artworks, Halifax; Kay Kays, National Museum Wales; Gwyn Kirk and Alice Cook; Ginette Leach and Mark Leach; Katrina Legg, Assistant Archivist at the Richard Burton Archives, Swansea University; Dr. Gillian Murphy, LSE Library; Laura Russell and Heather Mountjoy, Archivists and Melanie Taylor, Records Assistant, at Glamorgan Archives.

Banner Makers

In addition to those designers and makers credited in the captions, the following are known to have helped make banners displayed at Greenham: Giles Bradley, Angus Campbell, Dulcie Campbell, Hamish Campbell, Ian Campbell, Lucy Campbell, Tom Campbell, Mary Coughlin, Ellen Diederich, Caroline Goodbend, Jan Higgs, Greta Kathleen, Linda Norris, Leslie Owen, Jo Pate, Bettina Vogelman as well as participants in banner making workshops in the UK and abroad.

Bibliography

Anon, *Greenham Song Book*. Manchester Women's Press, n.d. (circa 1983/4).

Philip Attwood, *Badges*. The British Museum Press, 2004.

Ed Barber (photographs), Zoe Fairbairns and James Cameron (text), *Peace Moves Nuclear Protest in the 1980s*. Photographs by Ed Barber. Chatto and Windus. The Hogarth Press, 1984.

Caroline Blackwood, *On the Perimeter. Caroline Blackwood at Greenham Common*. Fontana Paperbacks, 1984.

Wilmette Brown, *Black Women and the Peace Movement*. Falling Wall Press, 1983.

Cambridge Women's Peace Collective (eds.), *My Country is the Whole World. An Anthology of Women's Work on Peace and War*. Pandora Press, 1984.

Thalia Campbell (ed.), *100 Years of Women's Banners*. Thalia Campbell, 1990.

Thalia Campbell and Mervyn Wilson (eds.), *Each for All and All for Each. A Celebration of Co-operative Banners*. National Co-operative Education Association, 1994.

Alice Cook and Gwyn Kirk, *Greenham Women Everywhere. Dreams, Ideas and Actions from the Women's Peace Movement*. Pluto Press, 1983.

Nicky Edwards, *Mud*. The Women's Press Limited, 1986.

David Fairhall, *Common Ground. The Story of Greenham*. I.B. Tauris &Co. Ltd, 2006.

Maryam Fanni, Matilda Flodmark and Sara Kaaman (eds.), *Natural Enemies of Books. A Messy History of Women in Printing and Typography*. Occasional Papers, 2020.

Anna Feigenbaum, Fabian Frenzel and Patrick McCurdy (eds.), *Protest Camps*. Zed Books Ltd., 2013.

Jean Gaffin and David Thoms, *Caring and Sharing. The Centenary History of the Co-operative Women's Guild*. Holyoake Books, 1993.

John Gormon, *Banner Bright*. Penguin Books Ltd., 1976.

Barbara Harford and Sarah Hopkins (eds.), *Greenham Common: Women at the Wire*. The Women's Press Limited, 1984.

Beth Junor, *Greenham Common Women's Peace Camp: A History of Non-Violent Resisteance 1984–1995*. Working Press, 1995.

John Kippin, *Cold War Pastoral Greenham Common*. Black Dog Publishing Limited, 2001.

Ginette Leach, Orange Gate Journal. *A Personal View of the Greenham Common Women's Peace Camp*. Meta-Synthesis, 2014.

Jill Liddington, *The Long Road to Greenham. Feminism and Anti-Militarism in Britain since 1820*. Virago Press, 1989.

Sharon MacDonald, Pat Holden and Shirley Ardener (eds.), *Images of Women in Peace and War. Cross-Cultural and Historical Perspectives*. Macmillan Education Ltd, 1987.

Ra Page (ed.), *Protest. Stories of Resistance*. Comma Press, 2017.

Rozsika Parker, *The Subversive Stitch. Embroidery and the making of the feminine*. The Women's Press Limited, 1984.

Ann Pettitt, *Walking to Greenham. How the Peace-camp began and the Cold War ended*. Honno, 2006.

Polly Russell and Margaretta Jolly (eds.), *Unfinished Business. The Fight for Women's Rights*. British Library, 2020.

Lyn Smith, *People Power. Fighting for Peace from the First World War to the Present*. Thames and Hudson, 2017

Penny Strange, *I'll Make a Man of You... A Feminist View of the Arms Race*. Five Leaves Publications, 1983.

Dorothy Thompson (ed.), *Over Our Dead Bodies. Women against the Bomb*. Virago Press Limited, 1983.

Lisa Tickner, *The Spectacle of Women: Imagery for the Suffrage Campaign 1907–14*. Chatto & Windus, 1987.

Anna Vinegrad (ed.), *Women Making History. Processions the Banners*. Profile Books Ltd., 2020.

Brenda Whisker, Jacky Bishop, Lilian Mohin and Trish Longdon (eds.), *Breaching the Peace. A collection of radical feminist papers*. Onlywomen Press Ltd., 1983.

Archives and Collections

Bishopsgate Institute, London
Archive of Format Photographers Agency.
London School of Economics.
  The Women's Library
  Photographs, documents, papers of participants, books, postcards, badges, posters related to Greenham, and other protests.
National Library of Wales / Llyfrgell Genedlaethol Cymru: Ian and Thalia Campbell Papers
  Photographs and papers relating to banner making, Greenham, and other protests.
Peace Museum, Bradford
  Photographs, badges and documents from Greenham and other protests, as well as appliqués by Daphne Morgan. Many banners including: Borchester CND; The British People are Prepared...; Coercion is Not Government; Girls Say No to the Bombs; Greenham Common Women's Peace Camp; Remembrance is Not Enough; State Terrorism No, No, No; Take a Risk for Peace Now; Women's Struggle Won the Vote...
People's History Museum: National Banner Survey
St. Fagans National Museum of History, National Museum Wales / Sain Ffagan Amgueddfa Werin Cymru, Amgueddfa Cymru
  Postcards, flyers, and banners, including: Greenham Common Women's Peace Camp; No; Women for Life on Earth.
Swansea University: Richard Burton Archives / Prifysgol Abertawe: Archifau Richard Burton
  Archive of photographer Raissa Page.
Women's Archive Wales, the Glamorgan Archives / Archif Menywod Cymru, Archifau Morgannwg
  Documents and photographs from the peace group 'Women for Life on Earth'.
Women's Library Glasgow
  Badges, music, leaflets and other materials relating to Greenham Common and the women's peace movement.

Notes

1 Anna Feigenbaum, Fabian Frenzel and Patrick McCurdy (eds.), *Protest Camps* (Zed Books, 2013), p. 21
2 Alice Cook and Gwyn Kirk, *Greenham Women Everywhere* (Pluto Press, 1983), p. 45
3 Ann Pettitt, *Walking to Greenham* (Honno, 2006), p. 42
4 Ibid, p. 43
5 Ibid, p. 43
6 Moira Vincentelli, 'Women For Peace' in *Women's Banners* (Thalia Campbell, undated), p. 22; Thalia Campbell, interviewed by the author, 2020
7 Thalia Campbell, interviewed by the author, 2020
8 Jill Liddington, *The Long Road to Greenham. Feminism and Anti-Militarism in Britain since 1820* (Virago Press, 1989), p. 23
9 Barbara Harford and Sarah Hopkins (eds.), *Greenham Common: Women at the Wire* (The Women's Press Limited, 1984), p. 15
10 Ibid, p. 16
11 *The Guardian*, 13 November 2013
12 Sarah Hipperson, in John Kippin, *Cold War Pastoral, Greenham Common* (Black Dog Publishing, 2001), p. 20
13 Wilmette Brown, *Black Women and the Peace Movement* (Falling Wall Press, 1983)
14 *The Observer Magazine*, 12 December 1982, p. 10
15 Vincentelli, 'Women For Peace', p. 22
16 Campbell, interview
17 Liddington, *The Long Road to Greenham*, p. 145
18 *People Power* exhibition caption, Imperial War Museum, London, 2017
19 Hipperson, *Cold War Pastoral*, p. 135-144
20 Cook and Kirk, *Greenham Women Everywhere*, p. 45
21 Ibid, p. 65
22 Campbell, interview
23 *The Guardian*, 2 Sep 2013

24 Barbara Harford and Sarah Hopkins (eds.), *Greenham Common: Women at the Wire*, p. 126
25 Campbell, interview
26 Harford and Hopkins, *Greenham Common: Women at the Wire*, p. 100
27 Nigel Noble (director), *The Ribbon Starts Here*, documentary video (Noble Enterprises, 1988)
28 Campbell, interview
29 Campbell, interview
30 Sarah Hipperson, Greenham Common Women'ws Peace Camp website, greenhamwpc.org.uk
31 Harford and Hopkins, *Greenham Common: Women at the Wire*, p. 10
32 Pettitt, *Walking to Greenham*, pp. 24–26
33 Cook & Kirk, *Greenham Women Everywhere*, p. 80
34 Linda Bellos, Carolle Berry Joyce Cunningham, Margaret Jackson, Sheila Jeffreys, Carol Jones, 'Is Greenham feminist?' in *Breaching The Peace* (Onlywomen Press, 1983), p. 20
35 Brown, *Black Women and the Peace Movement*, p. 20
36 Ibid, p. 34
37 Liddington, *The Long Road to Greenham*, p. 6
38 Ibid, p. 187
39 Ibid, pp. 7–8
40 Campbell, interview
41 Hipperson, *Cold War Pastoral*, p. 21
42 Liddington, *The Long Road to Greenham*, pp. 240–241
43 Sharon MacDonald, Pat Holden and Shirley Ardener (eds.), *Images of Women in Peace and War. Cross-Cultural and Historical Perspectives* (Macmillan Education Ltd, 1987), p. 195
44 Rozsika Parker, *The Subversive Stitch. Embroidery and the making of the feminine* (The Women's Press Limited, 1984), p. 211
45 Vincentelli, 'Women For Peace', p. 22
46 Campbell, interview
47 MacDonald, Holden and Ardener, *Images of Women in Peace and War*, p. 196
48 Cook & Kirk, *Greenham Women Everywhere*, p. 72
49 Parker, *The Subversive Stitch*, p. 200
50 Harford and Hopkins, *Greenham Common: Women at the Wire*, p. 22
51 Feigenbaum, Frenzel and McCurdy, *Protest Camps*, p. 116
52 This is also true of banners historically. It is estimated that 10,000 banners 'were made from the time of the first reform bill in 1832 until the beginning of the Second World War', of which only a very small fraction survive in museums and other collections. John Gorman, *Banner Bright – An Illustrated History of Trade Union Banners* (Penguin Books, 1976), p. 22
53 Harford and Hopkins, *Greenham Common: Women at the Wire*, p. 19
54 Ibid, p. 67–68
55 Ginette Leach, *Orange Gate Journal. A Personal View of the Greenham Common Women's Peace Camp* (Meta-Synthesis, 2014), p. 99
56 Cook & Kirk, *Greenham Women Everywhere*, p. 78
57 Katrina Howse, interviewed by the author, 2020
58 Campbell, interview
59 Campbell, interview
60 Leach, *Orange Gate Journal*, p. 43

Image credits

Pages 2, 4, 6–8, 10–11, 28, 34–35, 39, 43–47, 52–56, 60, 61 (top), 65, 66 (bottom), 69–71, 74–81, 87, 92–94, 96–97, 106–107, 114, 116–118, 122–123, 125, 129, 132, 135, 137–139, 142–145, 147, 149–155, 158–177, 179–183, 196, 201, 211, 217–218 Ian and Thalia Campbell Papers, © The National Library of Wales / Llyfrgell Genedlaethol Cymru

Pages 12–13, 83, 84–85 photographs by Raissa Page. © Adrianne Jones, courtesy of the Richard Burton Archives, Swansea University

Pages 14, 16–23, 26–27, 40–41, 62–63, 88–89, 109, 111–113, 115, 197 from the Peace Museum, Bradford, photographs by Eva Herzog

Pages 25, 29 and 30 photographers unknown, held at the Glamorgan Archives. Courtesy of Women's Archive Wales / trwy garedigrwydd Archif Menywod Cymru.

Page 33 Women's Library, LSE

Pages 50–51, 58–59, 120–121, 157, 184–185 St. Fagans National Museum of History © National Museum Wales / Sain Ffagan Amgueddfa Werin Cymru © Amgueddfa Cymru

Page 66 (top), 140 from the collection of the Peace Museum, Bradford

Page 67 Jacob Sutton / Gamma-Rapho via Getty Images

Page 73 Brenda Prince, courtesy Bishopsgate Institute

Pages 82, 146, 156, 194–195 photographs by Melanie Diggle, Mid Pennine Arts, from the exhibition Banner Culture (2019)

Pages 99, 100–101, 204–205 photographs by Homer Sykes © Homer Sykes

Pages 105, 130, 131, 199, 203 © Kathrine Jones (formerly Katrina Howse)

Pages 126–127 photograph by Edward Barber © Edward Barber Archive

Page 141 Phil Crean / Alamy Stock Photo

Page 187 courtesy Jamima Latimer, photograph by Eva Herzog

Page 193 photograph by Mike Goldwater / Alamy Stock Photo

Four Corners Irregulars
A series of books presenting a visual history of modern British culture. This is book 8.

Titles include:
1. Eyeball Cards, The Art Of British CB Radio Culture
2. UFO Drawings From The National Archives
3. Poster Workshop 1968–1971
4. Leeds Postcards
5. Face In The Crowd
6. Wobbly Sounds, A Collection Of British Flexidiscs
7. Nuclear War In The UK

…with further volumes in preparation.

Set in Starling and printed on Garda Matt Art Ultra.

Published in 2021 by Four Corners Books
56 Artillery Lane, London E1 7LS

Designed by John Morgan studio
morganstudio.co.uk

Print production by Martin Lee
Reprography by Martin Chapman
Printed in Italy by Printer Trento
Second printing, 2024

Distributed in the UK by Art Data
artdata.co.uk

ISBN 978-1-909829-18-3

More webbing at
www.fourcornersbooks.co.uk

Image credits are listed on page 223.

Text © Charlotte Dew

Page 192, 'Memo for Peace'
© 1982 Viv Fogel (formerly Viv Wynant)

Pages 206–211 by Ginette Leach, from *A Personal View of the Greenham Common Women's Peace Camp* (Meta-Synthesis, 2014).

Pages 212–215 by Juliet Nelson, from *Greenham Women Are Everywhere*, edited by Alice Cook and Gwyn Kirk (Pluto Books, 1987).

This volume © Four Corners Books 2021

Every effort has been made to secure copyright approval and ensure accuracy but if there are omissions please contact us at hello@fourcornersbooks.co.uk and the corrections will be included in any future editions of this book.